D1338179

What the experts say about some of Marc Dawson's previous books

ABC Cricket Quiz (1986) – "This book is probably one of the best of its kind, and unless history repeats itself in my lifetime I may never get another opportunity to witness such an all-round masterpiece on sporting questions."
– former West Indies opening batsman Gordon Greenidge

Cricket in Question (1989) – "An intriguing book full of facts, figures and events about the history of world cricket. It allows you to relive some of the magical moments of the game."
– former New Zealand all-rounder Richard Hadlee

Cricket Extras 2 (1994) – "Marc Dawson once again exposes cricket's universal appeal."
– former Australian wicketkeeper Ian Healy

Through the Covers (2005) – "Marc Dawson's fine book gives a lot of food for thought. I heartily recommend this book to all number crunchers."
– former Zimbabwe fast bowler Henry Olonga

The Cricket Tragic's Book of Cricket Extras Volume 2 (2010) – "Another in the long line of remarkably researched products from Marc Dawson. The high quality of the work is deserving of success."
– Indian cricket statistician Rajesh Kumar

Outside Edge (2013) – "A wonderfully entertaining book that will amuse and entertain in equal measure."
– Steve Dolman, Derbyshire County Cricket Club

INSIDE EDGE

INSIDE EDGE

ANOTHER ECLECTIC COLLECTION OF CRICKETING FACTS, FEATS & FIGURES

Marc Dawson

Pitch Publishing
A2 Yeoman Gate
Yeoman Way
Durrington
BN13 3QZ
www.pitchpublishing.co.uk

Also available *Outside Edge* by Marc Dawson
ISBN 978-1-90917-855-7

A CIP catalogue record is available for this book
from the British Library

ISBN 978 178531-028-7

Typesetting and origination by Pitch Publishing
Printed in Great Britain by Bell and Bain Ltd, Glasgow

Contents

Foreword

THE fascination with our great game continues to grow. We now have three forms of cricket that are thriving at all levels. This has created a broader base of interest in the community. Test cricket in my view is still the flagship of all formats, and it's the game all players want to master. Cricket's followers have developed through the growth of the various media platforms and of the recent success of Twenty20 cricket around the world. There was a time when our fathers and grandfathers introduced the game to us through Test matches over the summer, now we have our grandchildren and children introducing the new brand of the game, Twenty20. It's contagious either way. The wheel has turned and turned for the better from a participation point of

view, whether one plays, umpires, watches, scores, studies or just chats about the game, it's all a healthy pastime.

Marc Dawson has once again produced an absorbing book on our game which covers all areas imaginable with an intriguing approach. You will have a chance to see the game through others and reflect on their view and lose yourself in your own opinion; it's like that healthy discussion that is carried out in the members' bar during tea or after play.

We have for ever been lost in the real facts and history in almost everything we do, cricket is no different, and statistics have always been the measure of a player or team over time. With *Inside Edge* you will be taken on an extraordinary journey of facts that gravitate around our game. Some will shock you and others will captivate you like a classical mystery. I am sure you will be lost in partnership with it for a number of sessions. Enjoy ...

Tom Moody
former Australian Test cricketer

Hit and Run

- While no batsman had ever scored a double-century in the first ten World Cups, two did so in the 2015 edition. West Indies opener Chris Gayle was first cab off the rank with 215 against Zimbabwe in Canberra only to have his record usurped a month later by New Zealand opener Martin Guptill who made an unbeaten 237.

After going 19 months without a three-figure score in one-day internationals, Gayle let loose with a World Cup-record 16 sixes becoming the first batsman to score 175 or more in an innings in first-class, List A and Twenty20 cricket and the first to attain the feat of a century in a Twenty20 international, a double-century in a ODI and a triple-century in a Test match.  Along the way, Gayle and Marlon Samuels (133*) staged a second-wicket 372-run stand, the highest partnership for any wicket in List A cricket.

The West Indies opener marked the 1,000th international match to be staged in Australia by hitting the first World Cup 200 on the same day – 24 February – that Sachin Tendulkar had made the first 200 in a one-day international, in 2010.

Gayle then watched his record taken in a quarter-final in Wellington as New Zealand compiled a match-winning 393/6 against the West Indies with Guptill scoring his country's first double-century in one-day international cricket.

11

- Within a single of scoring his maiden double-century in the County Championship, Kent batsman Brendan Nash pulled the plug on his innings in the match against Gloucestershire at Cheltenham in 2013. Battling exhaustion on what was the hottest day of the summer at the time, the Australian-born former West Indies Test batsman retired on 199.

- On his way to a century in a second XI match in 2013, Lancashire batsman Jordan Clark hit six sixes in over. Clark, who made his List A debut for the club in 2010, took to the bowling of Yorkshire spinner Gurman Randhawada for the full house of sixes during the match at Scarborough. On the same day, in a first-class match at Cambridge, Middlesex wicketkeeper Adam Rossington (103*) also hit the jackpot with six consecutive sixes. Facing Cambridge MCCU's Akbar Ansari, Rossington hit a six off the last five balls of an over, then struck another off the first ball of his next.

- After Charlie Bull had carried his bat in a first-class match in 1935, his opening partner repeated the feat in the second innings. Bull scored 57 not out in Worcestershire's first innings of 150 against Lancashire at Kidderminster while Harold Gibbons carried his bat for 83 in their second-innings follow-on total of 148. The match provides the only instance of different openers carrying their bats for the same team in each innings of a first-class match.

- Simon Katich celebrated his 50th first-class match for New South Wales with a fifty, becoming the fifth batsman to score 500 runs in Sheffield Shield finals. Batting against Tasmania in Hobart in 2010/11, the Blues skipper hit 96 and joined Martin Love, Tom Moody, Stuart Law and Geoff Marsh in reaching the 500-run milestone in Shield finals. Love was the first batsman to achieve 1,000 runs, posting 1,107 with five centuries and a further three fifties.

- With an innings of 107 against the West Indies at Kingston in 2014, Jimmy Neesham became the first player to score centuries in his first two Tests but against different opponents. The eighth batsman overall to score a ton in each of his first two Tests from debut, the New Zealand medium-pacer had made an unbeaten 137 in his first Test, against India at Wellington, earlier in the year.

- Soon after making a move from New Zealand to Australia in 2011, former Test all-rounder Chris Cairns hit a scorching century for his new club in the national capital. Playing for North Canberra Gungahlin (319/5), the 41-year-old smashed 141 off 66 balls in a one-day match against the Australian National University (124). His last 90 runs came off just 27 deliveries.

- Will Williams marked his first-class debut in 2013/14 by being dismissed handled the ball. Batting at No. 10 for Canterbury against Otago at Dunedin, Williams became the first player to be out in such fashion in his first match.

- Madhya Pradesh batsman Aditya Shrivastava began his first-class career in 2014/15 in record-breaking style becoming the first batsman to score a ninety and a century on debut. Opening the batting against Karnataka at Indore, Shrivastava scored 91 in the first innings and an unbeaten 108 in the second for a match-total of 199.

- Appearing in his first Test against Australia in nearly a decade, Younis Khan marked the occasion with a match-winning pair of centuries. With 106 at Dubai in 2014/15, Younis became the first Pakistani to make a Test hundred against all nine other countries and with an unbeaten 103 in the second innings became the first Pakistani to pass the milestone of 25 Test centuries.

    Younis continued his sumptuous form in the second Test at Abu Dhabi, becoming only the second batsman to score three centuries on the trot against Australia after England's Herbert Sutcliffe (155, 176, 127) in 1924/25. On the same day in 1976/77 that Pakistan's 19-year-old Javed Miandad had become Test cricket's youngest double-centurion, Younis – already Pakistan's oldest to score a 200 – struck 213 aged 36 years and 336 days. He took part in two stands worth 150, including one of 181 for the fourth wicket with a 40-year-old Misbah-ul-Haq, who became the oldest batsman to score two centuries in the same Test, beating a 39-year-old Don Bradman.

    After making 101 in the first innings, Misbah matched it in the second, equalling Viv Richards's Test record of a ton off 56 balls. On fire from ball one, the skipper jetted his way to fifty off just 21 balls in 24 minutes – both Test records. From the ball that followed Misbah's historic century, Azhar Ali got to a hundred as well, with the pair providing just the second instance of two batsmen from the same team scoring a century in each innings of the same Test. For the first time, three batsmen from the same side scored two tons in a Test in the same series, while the trio also provided the first instance of three batsmen from one team aggregating 200 runs in the same Test.

TWO BATSMEN FROM SAME SIDE WITH A PAIR OF CENTURIES IN SAME TEST

Batsmen	Scores	Test	Venue	Season
Ian Chappell	(145 and 121)			
Greg Chappell	(247* and 133)	Australia v New Zealand	Wellington	1973/74
Azhar Ali	(109 and 100*)			
Misbah-ul-Haq	(101 and 101*)	Pakistan v Australia	Abu Dhabi	2014/15

- Australia's Michael Bevan made history with the bat during the 2000 County Championship when he scored a pair of 150s in a match and shared in two partnerships in excess of 250. Representing Sussex, Bevan struck 166 and 174 in the match against Nottinghamshire at Hove, and, with Richard Montgomerie, put on second-wicket stands of 292 and 265, the first time two batsmen had shared two partnerships of 250-plus in the same first-class match.

TWO DOUBLE-CENTURY PARTNERSHIPS BY SAME PAIR IN A FIRST-CLASS MATCH

Stands	Wkt	Batsmen	Match	Venue	Season
220 and 286	1st	Bert Sutcliffe and Don Taylor	Auckland v Canterbury	Auckland	1948/49
222 and 282	1st	Paul Pollard and Tim Robinson	Notts v Kent	Trent Bridge	1989
227 and 220	1st	Graham Gooch and John Stephenson	Essex v Northants	Northampton	1990
292 and 265	2nd	Richard Montgomerie and Michael Bevan	Sussex v Notts	Hove	2000
257 and 228*	1st	Marcus Trescothick and Arul Suppiah	Somerset v Yorkshire	Taunton	2011

- After making his one-day international debut in a series against a World XI in 2005/06, Australia's Cameron White didn't get a bat until his fifth match when he made a duck. Batting at No. 8 against New Zealand at Christchurch, White copped a first-baller from Chris Martin, and didn't score his first run until his seventh match, when he made 45 against the New Zealanders at Hobart in 2006/07.

- The day after Australia had been snubbed in the ICC's 2008 One-Day International Team of the Year, Ricky Ponting and Shane Watson recorded the country's first 250-run partnership in the 50-over game. Despite being rated the No. 1 side in one-day internationals at the time, no Australian made the cut for the best composite side of 2008. The following day, Australia slaughtered England in a Champions Trophy match at Centurion, with Watson (136*) and Ponting (111*) putting on an unbeaten 252-run stand for the second wicket off just 242 balls. One of Watson's seven sixes struck a spectator in the head, while Ponting traversed the 12,000-run milestone in one-day internationals, the first Australian to do so.

  After beginning the tournament with two ducks, Watson ended it with two unbeaten centuries. He followed his 136 with a match-winning 105 against New Zealand in the final at Centurion, bringing up his hundred with two consecutive sixes.

- After scoring 16 in his first one-day international innings, Afghanistan batsman Mohammad Shahzad hit centuries in his next two. He made

110 against the Netherlands at Amstelveen in 2009 and 118 against Canada at Sharjah in 2009/10.

- Jason Gillespie marked his 31st birthday in 2006 by becoming the first Australian to score a double-century in his final Test match, an innings of 201 not out against Bangladesh. The following year, the fast bowler celebrated his 32nd birthday with another history-making century, this time in his first match for Yorkshire. With an unbeaten 123, Gillespie made the highest score by a Yorkshire No. 10 and with Tim Bresnan (116) added 246 for the ninth wicket against Surrey at The Oval, erasing the county record of 192 set by George Hirst and Schofield Haigh in 1898.

- When India and Sri Lanka played at Rajkot in 2009/10, the match provided the first instance of both sets of openers achieving a first-wicket stand of 150 in the same one-day international. India's Virender Sehwag (146) and Sachin Tendulkar (69) put on 153, while the Sri Lankan pair of Upul Tharanga (67) and Tillakaratne Dilshan (160) added 188.

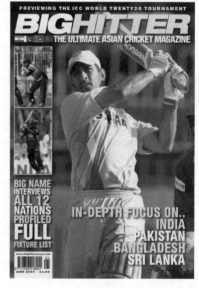

The wicketkeeping captains – Mahendra Singh Dhoni (72) and Kumar Sangakkara (90) – both scored fifties batting at No. 3, with three 150-plus and four 100-plus partnerships in the match, both firsts in one-day internationals.

Both centurions got to the 100-mark in fewer than 75 balls – Sehwag scored his century off 66 deliveries, while Dilshan needed 73. A total of 825 runs was scored in the match, with Sri Lanka failing by just three runs in its quest for victory. Batting first, India made 414/7 with the visitors reaching 411/8 after its 50 overs.

> **"I was actually supporting Sri Lanka. My superstition is that whenever I support India, they lose. So I was supporting Sri Lanka."**
>
> Virender Sehwag

- Thirteen years after making his one-day international debut, Bangladesh's Minhajul Abedin scored his maiden half-century, making two within four days. Appearing in his last one-day international tournament, Minhajul – who played in his country's first ODI, against Pakistan at Moratuwa in 1985/86 – hit an unbeaten 68 against Scotland at Edinburgh and 53 not out against Australia at Chester-le-Street in the 1999 World Cup.

- New Zealand batsman Richard Jones was dismissed in his first Test and one-day international innings for the same score, in the same fashion, and by the same bowler. In the first innings of his only Test – at Wellington in 2003/04 – he was bowled for 16 by Pakistan's Abdul Razzaq. He went exactly the same way on his ODI debut – bowled for 16 by Razzaq – in Lahore a month before.

- On his way to an unprecedented fourth instance of twin tons in a Test, Ricky Ponting became the first batsman to fail by the narrowest of margins in chasing down the milestone. Having scored 101 in the first innings against South Africa at the MCG in 2008/09, Ponting missed out on his second hundred when he was caught off the bowling of Morne Morkel for 99. The only other batsman to score 99 and a century in a Test is England's Geoff Boycott, who followed up a first-innings 99 against the West Indies at Port-of-Spain in 1973/74 with 112.

- In his first Test match against Bangladesh, New Zealand's Martin Guptill scored a century and a record-breaking half-century. In the first innings of the match, at Hamilton in 2009/10, Guptill hit 189 in 444 minutes, with 18 fours and a six, sharing a triple-century stand with Brendon McCullum. In the second innings, Guptill slammed an unbeaten 56, becoming the first, and to date only, batsman to score a Test match fifty that contained sixes (three) but no fours.

- The New Zealand A team began its 2014 tour of England and Scotland with a 50-over win against Northamptonshire after two of its Africa-born batsmen with the same christian name both struck identical centuries. The South African-born Colin Munro, batting at No. 5, and the Zimbabwe-born Colin de Grandhomme, at six, shared a 199-run partnership with both scoring 151, the highest identical score by two batsmen in the same List A match.

- While it took 18 matches for the first century to be scored in Australian first-class cricket, it took just one more to see the second. Victoria's Dick Wardill is credited with the country's first first-class hundred, an innings of 110 against New South Wales at Melbourne in 1867/68. In the next match considered first-class, Wardill's team-mate Joseph Phillips scored Australia's second first-class ton with 115 against Tasmania at the MCG in 1868/69.

• After 24 runs batting at number six in his first three innings of 2013, Derbyshire's Chesney Hughes carried his bat for a double-century in his next. With a duck in his previous innings, Hughes asked to open the batting against Yorkshire at Leeds and scored a maiden first-class double-century. With an unbeaten 270, he came close to the club's all-time record of 274 by George Davidson in 1895. Despite his efforts, Hughes ended up on the losing side, with Derbyshire going down by an innings.

HIGHEST FIRST-CLASS SCORES BY A BATSMAN FOR TEAM THAT LOST BY AN INNINGS

Score	Batsman	Match	Venue	Season
309	Vijay Hazare	The Rest v Hindus	Mumbai	1943/44
270*	Chesney Hughes	Derbyshire v Yorkshire	Leeds	2013
231	John Jameson	Warwickshire v Indians	Birmingham	1971
224	Paul Prichard	Essex v Kent	Canterbury	1997
219	Cyril Poole	Nottinghamshire v Derbyshire	Ilkeston	1952

HIGHEST FIRST-CLASS SCORES BY A BATSMAN CARRYING HIS BAT

Score	Batsman	Match	Venue	Season
357*	Bobby Abel	Surrey (811) v Somerset	The Oval	1899
318*	W.G. Grace	Gloucestershire (528) v Yorkshire	Cheltenham	1876
305*	Bill Ashdown	Kent (560) v Derbyshire	Dover	1935
272*	Robert Relf	Sussex (433) v Worcestershire	Eastbourne	1909
270*	Chesney Hughes	Derbyshire (475) v Yorkshire	Leeds	2013

• The Sri Lankan opening pair of Tillakaratne Dilshan and Upul Tharanga dominated the 2011 World Cup with two double-century stands, one of which was a record-breaker for the tournament. A 282-run partnership against Zimbabwe at Pallekele beat the previous best in the World Cup of 194 between Pakistan's Saeed Anwar and Wajahatullah Wasti in a 1999 semi-final. Dilshan made 144 and Tharanga 133, the first time that both openers had scored centuries in the same World Cup innings, a feat they would repeat later in the tournament. Dilshan – with bowling figures of 4-4 – became just the second player after the Netherlands' Feiko Kloppenburg to score a century and take four wickets in the same World Cup match.

The Zimbabweans also posted a century opening stand with Brendan Taylor (80) and Regis Chakabva (35) reaching 116. The 398 runs aggregated by both opening pairs became the highest in a one-day international, surpassing the 368 runs scored in the match between Sri Lanka and England at Leeds in 2006.

Two matches later, the Sri Lankans put on another double-ton stand, humiliating England in a quarter-final match in Colombo. Chasing a target of 230 for a semi-final berth, Dilshan (108*) and

Tharanga (102*) powered Sri Lanka to a ten-wicket victory over the Poms and another bunch of records. Dilshan and Tharanga became the first pair to record two 200-run stands in a single World Cup tournament and the first pair to twice score centuries in the same innings of a World Cup match.

Dilshan ended the tournament as its most productive batsman with exactly 500 runs, and in partnership with Tharanga fashioned 800 at an average of 100.00. Dilshan hit 61 fours, the most by any batsman, while Tharanga and Sachin Tendulkar came second, hitting 52 each.

- South Africa's Alviro Petersen made history against India at Kolkata in 2009/10 by becoming the first batsman to score exactly 100 in his debut Test innings. Four batsmen had previously made 100 not out in their first Test, while West Indies opener Basil Williams made ten and 100 on his Test debut, against Australia at Georgetown in 1977/78. After taking part in a double-century stand with Hashim Amla, Petersen's dismissal triggered a remarkable collapse, which saw South Africa – at 218/1 – lose their last nine wickets for 78. Amla held his head high, becoming just the ninth batsman to score a pair of centuries in a Test despite ending up on the losing side, and finished the two-match series with a healthy 490 runs at an average of 490.00.

- Of the nine centuries scored by Australian batsman Graeme Wood, three came to an end on 100. His second such score, against Pakistan at Melbourne in 1981/82, contained just three boundaries, a set of numbers matched by Allan Border two summers later. In the second Test against the West Indies at Port-of-Spain in 1983/84, Border followed 98 not out in the first innings with an unbeaten 100 in the second, which also contained just three fours. The world record for most Test scores of 100 is four by England's Len Hutton.

- New Zealand's Matt Poore made it into the 40s a record four times in Test match cricket without ever reaching a half-century. His highest score of 45 came on his Test debut in 1952/53 against South Africa at Auckland. Naimur Rahman – Bangladesh's first captain – possesses a similar record in one-day internationals with four scores in the 40s and a highest innings of 47, while his best in eight Tests was 48.

- During a one-day international against Zimbabwe at Bulawayo in 2011/12, New Zealand's Kane Williamson faced the final ball of the match on 93 not out and managed to bring up a century. Facing debutant Njabulo Ncube, Williamson received a no-ball head-high beamer which he hit to the boundary. With another ball to be delivered, and with Ncube banned from bowling, the Kiwi No. 6 then struck three off Elton Chigumbura to reach 100 not out. New Zealand ended up losing the match, after Malcolm Waller smashed an unbeaten 99.

- In a low-scoring first-class match at Trent Bridge in 1879, Thomas Foster top-scored for Derbyshire with an aggregate of just 26. In an innings-and-99-run defeat to Nottinghamshire, Foster was the only batsman to score more than five in his side's first-innings 16 with seven, and was the only one to reach double figures in their second-innings 44, scoring 19.

- Francis Noyes made 21 appearances in first-class cricket, making history in one match by batting twice in each innings. His team-mate Thomas Barker had been unable to take his place in the Nottinghamshire XI against Hampshire at Southampton in 1843 after breaking his leg on the opening morning. Noyes was then permitted to bat four times in the match, scoring 31 and eight in the first innings, and five and nine in the second.

SCOREBOARD
HAMPSHIRE v NOTTINGHAMSHIRE – SOUTHAMPTON 1843

NOTTINGHAMSHIRE	1st innings		2nd innings	
H. Maltby	c Dorrinton b Hervey-Bathurst	2	b Hervey-Bathurst	0
S. Redgate	c Martin b Hervey-Bathurst	41	b Hervey-Bathurst	0
F. Noyes	c Bodie b Day	31	c Weir b Day	5
J. Guy †	c & b Day	46	c Dorrinton b Day	14
W. Clarke	c Martin b Day	12	c Day b Hervey-Bathurst	30
A. Bass	run out	0	b Day	8
C. Creswell	c & b Day	43	c Barfoot b Hervey-Bathurst	2
F. Noyes	c Barfoot b Hervey-Bathurst	8	b Hervey-Bathurst	9
H.J. Porter	not out	6	b Hervey-Bathurst	1
J. Chapman	run out	8	c Weir b Hervey-Bathurst	0
E. Patchitt	b Hervey-Bathurst	0	not out	0
Extras	(8 b, 4 w)	12	(8 b, 1 w)	9
Total	(all out)	**209**	(all out)	**78**

- During the West Indies' 269 in the first Test against New Zealand at Bridgetown in 2002, two of their batsmen hit identical half-centuries off the same number of balls. The only two fifties in the innings, Chris Gayle and Brian Lara both hit 73 off 131 deliveries.

- Upon reaching 69 against England at the SCG in 2002/03, Steve Waugh became only the second Australian after Allan Border to reach the milestone of 10,000 Test runs. Coincidentally, Waugh got there on the same day, ten years later, and on the same ground as his former captain. Border achieved the feat in his 136th Test, against the West Indies in 1992/93, the second batsman to pass the barrier after India's Sunil Gavaskar did so in 1986/87.

- Sri Lanka's Naveed Nawaz scored 99 runs on his Test debut in 2002, but was never selected again. With scores of 21 and 78 not out, against Bangladesh at Colombo, the No. 3 batsman savoured a victory in his only appearance and left the scene with a Bradmanesque Test average of 99.00.

- Batting against Ireland at Aberdeen in 2008, New Zealand's Brendon McCullum and James Marshall became the first set of openers to both score 150 in the same one-day international innings. Appearing in his 134th match, McCullum made 166, while Marshall came up with 161, both achieving their maiden ODI centuries. McCullum reached his hundred off 107 deliveries, while his next 50 runs required just 20. In all, he belted 11 fours and ten sixes.

    In unison, the two ploughed on to a record NZ opening stand of 274 and a total of 402/2, which also included an unbeaten 59 off 24 balls from the No. 3, Ross Taylor. The Irish (112) were never in the hunt, consigned to a record 290-run drubbing. The top score for the hosts came off the bat of the New Zealand-born Peter Connell, who contributed 22 down the order at No. 10.

> **"The Irish attack had all the impact of a gnat's nibble on the posterior of a desensitised elephant."**
>
> BBC correspondent Mark Woods

- After being 3/3 and 17/5 in a 50-over match against Argentina in 2010, the United States were saved by a pair of centuries from numbers seven and eight. Batting first in the ICC World Cricket League match, the USA reached 306/6, with unbeaten centuries from Aditya Thyagarajan (102*) and Rashard Marshall (122*).

    Earlier in the year, Thyagarajan had taken part in another rescue mission with an undefeated 72 on his Twenty20 debut, coming in at 25/6 against Ireland at Abu Dhabi. He was involved in a world-record seventh-wicket Twenty20 stand of 99, unbeaten, with Orlando Baker (28*).

- At the age of 41, Warwick Armstrong led Victoria to victory over South Australia at the MCG in 1920/21, becoming the first batsman to score 400 runs in a first-class match in Australia. With a double of 157 not out and 245, he remains the only batsman to achieve a double-century and a century in the same Sheffield Shield match.

- Marcus North, who was dropped after 21 Tests, scored a century on his debut against three different countries. After a century (117) on his Test debut, against South Africa at Johannesburg in 2008/09, he scored an unbeaten 125 in his third Test – his first against England – at Cardiff in the 2009 Ashes. North also marked his first Test against New Zealand with a three-figure score – 112 not out at Wellington in 2009/10. He made a half-century (79) on debut against the West Indies, at Adelaide in 2009/10 and hit 128 in his second Test against India, at Bangalore in 2010/11.

  Sri Lanka's Kumar Sangakkara went one better than North, scoring a hundred on his Test debut against four countries with a double-century against Pakistan. He also scored half-centuries on debut against three other opponents.

- South African import Johannes Myburgh scored a neat 300 runs in a match for New Zealand side Canterbury in 2008/09, but ended up on the losing side. Out for 199 in the first innings against Central Districts at New Plymouth, he made 101 not out in the second.

- One of the youngest South African batsmen to score 1,000 first-class runs in a season, Rilee Rossouw thumped the country's fastest triple-century in 2009/10. The Eagles' No. 3 hit 319 off 291 balls on the opening day of the first-class match against Titans at Centurion, bringing up 47 fours and eight sixes. The 20-year-old's knock formed part of a gargantuan second-wicket stand of 480 with Dean Elgar (156*), a South African record for any wicket, beating a 441-run effort between Carl Bradfield and James Bryant, also for the second wicket, for Eastern Province against North West in 2002/03. The Rossouw-Elgar partnership also became the highest first-class stand by a pair who finished up on the losing side, passing 470 by Warwickshire's Alvin Kallicharran and Geoff Humpage against Lancashire at Southport in 1982.

  Rossouw's 319 was the second-highest number of runs scored by a South African in a day's play, six behind Barry Richards's 325 for South Australia versus Western Australia in 1970/71, but the most in South African domestic first-class cricket. With 64 in the second innings, Rossouw scored 383 runs in the match, a world-record number for a batsman on the losing side.

- At stumps on the third day of the West Indies-England Test at Port-of-Spain in 1973/74, both of the batsmen were unbeaten in the 90s. A first in Test match cricket, Geoff Boycott was on 91, but fell for 93 the next morning, while Dennis Amiss progressed from 92 to 174.

- Bermuda's Irving Romaine matched the deeds of some of the world's best in 2006 by scoring a century in his first one-day international innings as captain. Players such as Sanath Jayasuriya, Sachin Tendulkar and Glenn Turner had all begun their ODI captaincy days with a hundred, with Romaine becoming the first to do so from a non-Test playing country. Batting at No. 4 against Canada in Toronto, Romaine had the distinction of scoring Bermuda's first one-day international ton, a 111-ball 101, that included 13 fours and five sixes.

  Scotland's Gavin Hamilton was the second Associate country captain to launch his ODI captaincy with a century, hitting 119, also against Canada, at Aberdeen in 2008. He took part in a double-century opening stand of 203 with Fraser Watts (101), but ended up on the losing side.

- When Taufeeq Umar scored a second-innings 135 against the West Indies at Basseterre in 2011, it represented the Pakistan opener's first Test century in eight years. The longest gap between Test match hundreds belongs to Warren Bardsley, whose career was interrupted by the First World War. The Australian opener had to wait 14 years between a score of 164 against South Africa at Lord's in 1912 and 193 not out against England, again at Lord's, in 1926.

  After beginning his Test career with a century on debut – 104 against Bangladesh at Multan in 2001 – Taufeeq's next four centuries were 111, 135, 111 and 135. In 2002/03, Taufeeq scored a pair of 39s against South Africa at Durban – his opening partner Saleem Elahi also scored 39 in the first innings.

- During the 1896 Ashes, each of the four batsmen who were visiting England for the first time all passed the milestone of 1,000 first-class runs on tour. Joe Darling made 1,555, Frank Iredale 1,328, Clem Hill 1,196 and Harry Donnan 1,009. Seven batsmen completed the tour with a thousand runs, matching the feat of the 1893 Australians.

• Victoria's Brad Hodge celebrated a new version of the limited-over game in 2010/11 by scoring the competition's first two centuries. Batting against Western Australia in Perth, Hodge hit 134 not out in the short-lived Ryobi One-Day Cup split-innings format, and followed it a week later with an unbeaten 140 against Queensland in Brisbane. In the first game, Hodge reached 58 after the first 20 overs, and after spending some time in the field resumed his innings progressing to 135 in the next 25 overs. He repeated the feat at the Gabba, making 54 by the break and going on to 140, to win his second consecutive man-of-the-match award.

• A Victorian club cricketer scored a century batting right-handed in 2007/08, having made his previous hundred batting left-handed. The ambidextrous Laurie Tyquin's ton as a southpaw – for the Ashford club against Sunbury – came five years after his previous century: **"For some reason I'm a better defensive batsman batting left-handed and a better attacking batsman batting right-handed. Don't ask me why. We've got a few blokes in the team who can defend pretty well, but they are a bit slow, so I decided to swap."**

• When South Africa suffered consecutive identical margins of defeat in 1924, Jack Hobbs and Herbert Sutcliffe established England's highest opening partnership at Lord's. Coming in to the second day of the match, both openers began the morning at 12 not out and both went on to centuries with a first-wicket stand of 268. Hobbs (211) scored 199 runs in the day, Sutcliffe (122) made 110, while Frank Woolley joined in with an unbeaten 134. It was the first time that as many as three England batsmen had scored 100 runs on the same day in a Test. After going down by an innings and 18 runs in the first Test at Edgbaston South Africa lost by an innings and 18 at Lord's.

THREE BATSMEN SCORING 100 RUNS IN A DAY DURING A TEST

Day	Batsmen	Match	Venue	Season
1	Percy McDonnell 103, Billy Murdoch 145* (211), Tup Scott 101* (102)			
		Australia v England	The Oval	1884
2	Jack Hobbs 199 (12*-211), Herbert Sutcliffe 110 (12*-122), Frank Woolley (134*)			
		England v South Africa	Lord's	1924
2	Walter Hammond 127 (54*-181), Les Ames (115), Bryan Valentine (112)			
		England v South Africa	Cape Town	1938/39
3	Mike Hussey 103, Michael Clarke 135, Adam Gilchrist 102*			
		Australia v England	Perth	2006/07

• In 1997, two Sri Lankan batsmen struck over 750 runs in international matches in a month. In April, Aravinda de Silva hit a record 842 runs, while the month of August saw 781 runs off the bat of team-mate

Sanath Jayasuriya. The next instance of 750 runs in a calendar month did not occur again until 2005 when the West Indies' Chris Gayle scored 760 in May.

- A few days after scoring a half-century in a match against the West Indians in Canberra in 2012/13, Jono Dean became only the second batsman to hit a triple-century in ACT first-grade cricket. After opening the batting for the Prime Minister's XI at Manuka Oval and belting 51 off 40 balls, Dean hit a history-making unbeaten 300 in a day for Queanbeyan against Ginninderra. He then starred with the ball, taking 3-9 off five overs with two maidens.

- In 1958, Worcestershire's Dick Richardson topped 1,000 first-class runs for the summer but with a top score of just 60. In 1965, Lancashire opener David Green scored a record 2,000 runs in the season without the aid of a century. In 63 innings, Green scored 2,034 first-class runs, passing 50 on 14 occasions with a best of 85 against Warwickshire at Blackpool.

- When Inzamam-ul-Haq scored a Test-best 329 at Lahore in 2002, he managed to beat his opposition's first-innings total by a record 256 runs on his own. In reply to Pakistan's 643 in the first Test at Gaddafi Stadium, New Zealand made just 73. In 2011/12, Michael Clarke also posted a Test-best 329, unbeaten, at Sydney, and outscored India's first-innings total of 191, beating it by 138.

- Sri Lanka's Tillakaratne Dilshan celebrated his 50th Test match with a pair of centuries. The first batsman to achieve such a feat, he peeled off 162 and 143 against Bangladesh at Chittagong in 2009/10. The previous instance of a batsman marking his 50th Test with a hundred was in 2004/05 when Chris Gayle made the record books by scoring a triple-century (317) against South Africa at St John's.

- After making a duck in his first Test innings, West Indies fast bowler Cameron Cuffy improved his best score in his next five innings. From his debut in 1994/95, Cuffy's first six scores were 0, 0 not out, one, two, three not out and four.

- Captaining Scotland on his debut in 2006, Ryan Watson top-scored with an innings of 80 against Pakistan at Edinburgh. He also took part in a fifth-wicket stand of 118 with Neil McCallum (68), the first instance of a century partnership between debutants in a one-day international.

- Australian one-day international specialist Ian Harvey joined a select band in 2007 by scoring a century on his first-class debut for Derbyshire. He followed his 136 against Essex at Chelmsford with 153 in his next – and final – first-class match, against Somerset at Taunton.

- Opening the batting at Christchurch in 2013/14, Calum MacLeod became the first Scotland batsman to reach 150 in a one-day international. He struck a man-of-the-match 175 in a World Cup qualifier against Canada, hitting 14 fours and five sixes. His opening partner, Matty Cross, also made the record books, becoming the first wicketkeeper to achieve five dismissals on his ODI debut. He took six catches behind the stumps and effected two run outs in a 170-run win.

  On the same day in the same tournament, at Lincoln, the Netherlands' Wesley Barresi (137*) and Kenya's Irfan Karim (108) provided just the fourth instance in ODI history of opposing wicketkeepers scoring a century in the same match.

- During the Sri Lanka-India Test at Colombo in 2010, Kumar Sangakkara and Sachin Tendulkar became the second and third batsmen to complete a suite of 150s against all other Test-playing countries. The first batsman to achieve the feat was Steve Waugh, when he hit an unbeaten 156 against Bangladesh at Cairns in 2003.

- Pakistan's Misbah-ul-Haq made it into double figures in his first innings in first-class, one-day international and Test cricket and was dismissed for the same score each time. He made 28 on his first-class debut, for Sargodha against Karachi City CA Whites in 1998/99, 28 on his Test debut, against New Zealand at Auckland in 2000/01, and 28 on his ODI debut, against New Zealand at Lahore in 2002.

- At the age of 18 an Australia under-19 batsman etched his name in the history books in 2011/12 when he became the youngest player to score a century on his first-class debut in the Sheffield Shield. Kurtis Patterson struck an imperious 157 off 189 balls for New South Wales against Western Australia at the SCG, sharing a double-century stand with Simon Katich. Seven months earlier, Patterson had scored a century on his debut for the Australian under-19 Test side against the West Indies in Dubai.

  Patterson only got his chance to play for his state after Nic Maddinson – the previous youngest Blues player to score a debut hundred – was called up to represent Australia A. The previous summer, Maddinson, at the age of 18 years and 294 days, scored 113 opening the batting against South Australia at Adelaide. He also took part in a sizeable partnership, one of 153 for the second wicket with Usman Khawaja, who raised his maiden double-century in first-class cricket. The Islamabad-born left-hander scored 214 on the same day that Sachin Tendulkar fell for 214 during the second Test against Australia at Bangalore. Despite his glittering debut, Patterson didn't get another first-class match for a full two years.

- Daniel Warwick struck a history-making triple-century in club cricket in Victoria in 2007/08, scoring half of the runs with a broken bat. Captaining the Baxter club, Warwick hit an unbeaten 305 against Somerville, reaching the triple-hundred with a bat busted when on 150: **"I could see it was broken and getting worse as I went along, but I still seemed to be hitting them all right, so I stuck with it."** His knock included 21 sixes and 20 fours, the first 300 in the Mornington Peninsula competition in 50 years.

- Mark Ramprakash walked off the field in a match at Chesterfield in 2010 with 99 beside his name, having celebrated a century just moments before. Scoreboard operators at the Surrey-Derbyshire match had incorrectly added three runs to Ramprakash's score, which saw him wave his bat to acknowledge the century milestone, only to have his total pared back to 99 upon his dismissal.

- Andrew Strauss achieved an unusual distinction against Ireland in the 2011 World Cup by scoring 34 on his 34th birthday. The previous highest score in a one-day international by a batsman matching his number of years with number of runs was Australia's Kim Hughes, who made 28 on his 28th birthday, against the West Indies in Sydney in 1981/82.

  New Zealand's Ross Taylor celebrated his 27th birthday during the 2011 World Cup with a rousing 131 not out against Pakistan in Kandy. He became the fourth batsman to achieve a birthday hundred in a one-day international, after India's Vinod Kambli and Sachin Tendulkar and Sri Lanka's Sanath Jayasuriya, but the first to do so in the World Cup.

- After making a pair in his first Test, Sri Lankan batsman Chamara Silva responded with a century in his second. He opened his Test career with two ducks against New Zealand at Christchurch in 2006/07, and scored a match-winning 152 not out in his fourth innings against the Kiwis at Wellington a week later.

  In 2012/13, Dean Elgar became the tenth South African to cop a pair on his Test debut, but the first to go on and score a century. In his third match – against New Zealand at Port Elizabeth – Elgar scored 103 not out at No. 7 in his fourth innings for the Proteas.

TEST CENTURY HOT ON THE HEELS OF A DEBUT PAIR

Inns	Test #	Batsman	Score	Match	Venue	Season
4th	2	Chamara Silva	152*	Sri Lanka v New Zealand	Wellington	2006/07
4th	3	Dean Elgar	103*	South Africa v New Zealand	Port Elizabeth	2012/13
5th	3	Saeed Anwar	169	Pakistan v New Zealand	Wellington	1993/94

• Sri Lanka's Lahiru Thirimanne suffered the ignominy of being run out without facing a ball when he fronted up for the opening one-day international against Australia in 2012/13. His MCG diamond duck was then followed by a maiden international century in the 50-over game, a match-winning 102 not out in Adelaide.

DIAMOND DUCK AND CENTURY IN CONSECUTIVE ONE-DAY INTERNATIONALS

Batsman	Scores	Matches	Venues	Dates
Grant Flower (Z)	0	v Bangladesh	Harare	08-04-2001
	142*	v Bangladesh	Bulawayo	11-04-2001
Jesse Ryder (NZ)	0	v Pakistan	Hamilton	03-02-2011
	107	v Pakistan	Auckland	05-02-2011
Lahiru Thirimanne (SR)	0	v Australia	Melbourne	11-01-2013
	102*	v Australia	Adelaide	13-01-2013

• During a one-week period in 2013/14, South Africa wicketkeeper Quinton de Kock scored a century in three consecutive one-day internationals against India. A few days shy of his 21st birthday, the opener – with scores of 135, 106 and 101 – became the first batsman to achieve three centuries in a three-match series, and the first to score four hundreds without a fifty.

He also became the first batsman to take part in three consecutive 150-run partnerships – 152 with Hashim Amla at Johannesburg, 194 with Amla at Durban and 171 with A.B. de Villiers at Centurion.

• Appearing on his Test debut in 2013, Zimbabwe's Timycen Maruma scored ten in each innings and was dismissed in the same fashion by the same bowler. A first in Test cricket, Maruma also became just the second Test debutant to face the first ball of a match and also be involved in the first dismissal of their opposition. In the same Test – at Harare – Bangladesh captain Mushfiqur Rahim also made two identical scores (3 and 3) while his opposite number, Brendan Taylor, hit a pair of centuries (171 and 102*).

150 AND 100 BY A CAPTAIN IN A TEST MATCH

Scores	Captain	Match	Venue	Season
189 and 104*	Alan Melville	South Africa v England	Nottingham	1947
153 and 115	Bob Simpson	Australia v Pakistan	Karachi	1964/65
107 and 182*	Sunil Gavaskar	India v West Indies	Calcutta	1978/79
333 and 123	Graham Gooch	England v India	Lord's	1990
171 and 102*	Brendan Taylor	Zimbabwe v Bangladesh	Harare	2013

• When Alastair Cook lost his wicket on 190 at Kolkata in 2012/13, it represented the first time he'd been run out in a Test since making his debut in 2005/06. Cook had gone a world-record 170 innings before such a dismissal; for the record, India's Kapil Dev was *never* run out in his entire Test career of 131 matches and 184 innings.

- After scoring his maiden 150 in a Test match, India's M.S. Dhoni went on to become the first wicketkeeping captain to pass 200. Dhoni was at his dominant best against Australia at Chennai in 2012/13, scoring 224, with 24 fours and six sixes. The first captain to score 150 batting at No. 6 in a Test against Australia, his innings was the highest by an Indian skipper and the first example of a 200 by an Indian wicketkeeper. Dhoni also became the first keeper to score a double-century in a Test and not take a catch.

  Australia's Moises Henriques (68 and 81*) also sparkled with the bat, becoming the first No. 7 to score 60 or more in each innings of his Test debut. With 149 runs, he broke the record for most runs by a No. 7 debutant, previously held by England's Matt Prior, who made 147 (126* and 21) against the West Indies at Lord's in 2007. Henriques took the record on Prior's 31st birthday. In the first innings, Henriques and Michael Clarke (130) shared the 100th century stand for Australia against India in Harbhajan Singh's 100th Test.

- When Chris Gayle scored 333 against Sri Lanka in 2010/11, he matched Graham Gooch's 333 at Lord's in 1990. The highest score in Test match cricket to be scored twice is just one higher – 334 – by Don Bradman at Leeds in 1934 and equalled by Mark Taylor (334*) against Pakistan at Peshawar in 1998/99.

- Australian imports Tom Moody and David Hussey both scored centuries in their first three County Championship matches against Essex. With Desmond Haynes also achieving the feat, Moody did so for Worcestershire with innings of 181 not out at Ilford in 1991, 178 at Kidderminster in 1992 and 108 not out at Worcester in 1994. Hussey's threesome, for Nottinghamshire, comprised a 116 at Southend-on-Sea and 124 not out at Trent Bridge in 2004, and 275, also at Trent Bridge, in 2007.

- After scoring centuries in his first two first-class innings for Somerset in 2004, Ricky Ponting made the highest score by a batsman on his debut for Surrey in 2013. In his only three matches for Somerset, Ponting hit 112 against Yorkshire at Scarborough, 117 and 18 not out against

Glamorgan at Taunton and 50 against Durham at Chester-le-Street. Ponting was run out for 192 in his first innings for Surrey, and bowed out in fine style with 169 not out against Nottinghamshire at The Oval in his final first-class innings. In seven matches in the County Championship, Ponting scored 790 runs at a record-high average of 112.85 for players with at least 500 runs.

- Dropped on 99 in a one-day international in 2011/12, the West Indies' Kieron Pollard went on to his maiden century which included a record ten sixes against India. Batting at No. 6 in the match at Chennai, Pollard was last man out for 119, having reached three figures off 98 balls. Earlier, India's Manoj Tiway had also scored his maiden century, retiring hurt on 104.

  The previous occasion of two maiden centuries from opposing batsmen in the same one-day international was in 1994/95 at Centurion Park in Verwoerdburg in South Africa. Dave Callaghan scored an unbeaten 169 for the home team, while Adam Parore hit 108 for New Zealand. For both batsmen it was their only century in one-day internationals.

- In the space of just three days, Wellington opener Michael Papps hit two consecutive scores of over 150 in the New Zealand Ford Trophy 50-over series of 2012/13. He made an unbeaten 162 in a win against Otago at Wellington and backed it up with 154 in a loss against Central Districts at the same ground. In the first match, Stephen Murdoch also scored a big hundred – 136 – with the pair putting on 273 for the second wicket.

  In the same season, Northern Districts medium-pacer Anurag Verma improved upon his two previous best scores of one not out and two by hitting fifties in consecutive innings batting at No. 10. He hit an unbeaten 52 against Central Districts at Hamilton and, a few days later, cracked a speedy 58 against Canterbury at Mount Maunganui.

- New Zealand No. 11 Willie Watson made the record books in 1990/91 when he fell lbw in four consecutive Test innings to Pakistan's Waqar Younis. Watson was out lbw five times in the series, a record matched by Pakistan's Misbah-ul-Haq, against England in 2011/12. When Watson was caught behind in the second Test against Sri Lanka at Hamilton later in the season it was the first time he was dismissed other than lbw since making his debut in 1986.

- Pakistan's Umar Akmal once made a half-century in 11 balls. Opening the batting against India in the Hong Kong International Sixes tournament in 2011/12, Akmal hit 52 not out with seven sixes and two fours at a strike rate of 472.73.

- The West Indies put on a record-breaking half-century last-wicket stand at The Oval in the 2013 Champions Trophy with no runs off the bat of the No. 11. Darren Sammy (56*) and Kemar Roach (0*) shared an unbeaten 51-run partnership against India, the first half-century tenth-wicket stand in a one-day international which contained no contribution from the last man in.

- After making ducks in his first two innings in first-class cricket, Hamish Rutherford became the first New Zealand batsman to score a century on his Test debut at Dunedin. Opening the batting against England at University Oval in 2012/13, Rutherford hit 171 in his first Test innings, after his father, Ken Rutherford, had scored a pair opening the batting on his Test debut at Port-of-Spain in 1984/85. His 171 beat a Test record that had stood since the very first Test of all, overtaking Charles Bannerman's 165 (retired hurt) at Melbourne in 1876/77 as the highest-ever score by a batsman in his first Test innings against England. The 23-year-old Rutherford also had the distinction of outscoring England's first-innings total of 167 on his own.

  Rutherford and Peter Fulton scored three centuries between them in the series, signalling the first time that a pair of NZ openers had scored as many in a three-match contest. Out of Tests for four years, the 34-year-old Fulton scored a maiden Test hundred (136) at Auckland, adding 110 in the second innings. His maiden Test century came exactly a decade after his maiden first-class century – an unbeaten 301 for Canterbury against Auckland in Christchurch in 2002/03. Despite his triple-century, he ended up on the losing side, with Auckland claiming victory by four wickets.

- Following his first four Tests against Bangladesh, England's Ian Bell celebrated a world-record average of 488. After scoring 65 and 162 – both times not out – against the Bangladeshis in 2005, Bell (pictured) then made 84, 39 not out and 138 in a two-match series in 2009/10.

  Bell became the first batsman to obtain a 450-run Test average against a particular opposition, breaking Mohammad Yousuf's record of 424, also set against Bangladesh, in the early 2000s (102*, 72, 204*, 46).

- During consecutive tours of South Africa, India's Zaheer Khan joined V.V.S. Laxman at the crease in a Test at exactly the same score and proceeded to add exactly the same number of runs. At Johannesburg in 2006/07, Zaheer and Laxman came together at 148/7 in the second innings, adding 70 runs for the eighth wicket, and repeated the feat in the Durban Test of 2010/11.

- While most of the Australian top-order flopped in the 2013 Border-Gavaskar Trophy, two fast bowlers made the record books with unprecedented performances batting at number nine. At Mohali, Mitchell Starc became the first number nine to be dismissed for 99 in a Test, sharing a 97-run partnership with Steve Smith, who made 92. It was only the second instance in Test history of two players from one side scoring in the nineties and sharing a partnership in the 90s, after Mark Boucher (92) and Lance Klusener (97), who took part in a 94-run stand against Sri Lanka at Cape Town in 2001/02.
  Minus Starc for the following match at Delhi, Peter Siddle (51 and 50) top-scored for Australia in each innings, becoming the first batsman to score two half-centuries at number nine in the same Test. In his next first-class innings, Siddle brought up his maiden first-class century, scoring an unbeaten 103 for the 2013 Australia A side against Scotland at Edinburgh.

- In 2010, and appearing in his 20th match, the then-20-year-old Ireland batsman Paul Stirling became the first batsman from a non-Test playing country to score 150 in a one-day international. Opening the batting against Canada at Toronto, Stirling hit 177 in 177 minutes with 21 fours and five sixes.

- When Dwayne Smith scored 20 and an unbeaten 105 at Cape Town in 2003/04, he became only the sixth debutant to achieve a hundred in the fourth innings of a Test match. The second West Indian to achieve the feat, he copied the scores of his predecessor, Len Baichan, who also made 20 and an unbeaten 105 on his Test debut, against Pakistan at Lahore in 1974/75.

- In the calendar year of 1978, the West Indies' Norbert Phillip made four consecutive Test scores of 26. In the fifth Test against Australia at Kingston, he scored 26 and 26 not out; in his next Test series – against India – he then made 26 at Mumbai and 26 at Bangalore. Phillip was dismissed for 26 again later in the series, in the fifth Test at Delhi.

- Out for a duck at Cape Town in 1902/03, Jimmy Sinclair got another chance to bat on the same day and made amends by scoring a century. The only batsman to achieve such an unusual feat, Sinclair followed a first-ball duck with 104 on day two of the third Test against Australia.

- Back in the side after an injury break, South Africa's J.P. Duminy achieved an unbeaten 150 in a one-day international and took part in two 150-run partnerships. Batting against the Netherlands at Amstelveen in 2013, Duminy shared a 151-run stand for the third wicket with Colin Ingram (82) and an unconquered 152-run stand for the fourth with Faf du Plessis (62*).

- After scoring seven in the first innings against South Africa at Cape Town in 2014/15, Kraigg Brathwaite became the first batsman in a Test match to get off the mark with a seven. Facing his ninth ball in the second innings, the West Indies opener hit Vernon Philander for three then benefitted from four overthrows.

  Five batsmen – Patsy Hendren, Vijay Hazare, John Wright, Brian Lara and Andrew Symonds – have previously made a record eight runs off one ball in a Test, while the first-class record stands at ten. Albert "Monkey" Hornby did so for Lancashire against Surrey at The Oval in 1873, followed by Derbyshire's Samuel Wood against MCC at Lord's in 1900. The most runs scored off a single ball without the aid of overthrows is nine by Frederick Ponsonby for MCC against Cambridge University at the Parker's Piece ground in 1842.

- During the South Africa-Pakistan Test at Cape Town in 2012/13, two batsmen scored 111 in the same innings. A first in Test match cricket, Younis Khan and Asad Shafiq were both dismissed by Vernon Philander. In the second innings, Mohammad Hafeez and Nasir Jamshed became just the fifth pair of openers to be dismissed lbw for a duck.

- Two Australian-born fast bowlers made the record books with the bat in 2013 when they combined for a record-breaking last-wicket stand at Northampton in the County Championship. Batting at numbers ten and 11 against Essex, Steven Crook (88*) and Trent Copeland (70) both hit ten fours and a six in a tenth-wicket partnership of 117.

- When the England pair of George Gunn and Andy Sandham added 173 against the West Indies at Kingston in 1929/30 they did so with a combined age of 90 years and 200 days. In his final Test, Sandham produced a triple-century (325) and a century opening stand with Gunn, the oldest pair to share a 100-run partnership in Tests.

- After becoming the first batsman to score a double-century for his country in a Test, Mushfiqur Rahim then became the first Bangladesh wicketkeeper to take five catches in an innings. Captaining Bangladesh against Sri Lanka at Galle in 2012/13, Mushfiqur hit a neat 200; in the following Test in Colombo, he took five catches in Sri Lanka's first innings. The following month, he then became the first Bangladesh wicketkeeping captain to score two half-centuries in the same Test, hitting a match-winning 60 and 93 against Zimbabwe in Harare.

- During a run of six consecutive one-day internationals in 2013, Pakistan's Nasir Jamshed was dismissed each time for a score that contained a zero. After making two tens against South Africa, he then made 20, 20, 0 and 50.

- Pakistan's Imran Nazir clubbed a quickfire century in a 50-over match in 2013/14, becoming the first batsman to reach a List A 150 in fewer than 75 balls. The 31-year-old – who had last appeared in a Test a decade earlier – opened the batting for Zarai Taraqiati Bank against Sui Northern Gas Pipelines at Islamabad and made 189, reaching 150 off 65 balls.

- When Middlesex attained a ten-wicket win at Trent Bridge in the 2013 County Championship, their Sydney-born opening batsmen both scored a pair of fifties and shared in two 100-run first-wicket partnerships. Both former under-19 Australian ODI players, Chris Rogers hit 50 and 51 not out, while Sam Robson made 76 and 55 not out. For Nottinghamshire, Ed Cowan – who, like Robson, was born in the Sydney suburb of Paddington – also hit a half-century (61) at the top of the order.

  Two matches later, the Middlesex pair broke the county first-wicket record against Surrey that had stood for a century. Both scored centuries this time – Rogers 214 and Robson 129 – in a 259-run opening partnership after Middlesex had been forced to follow-on in the match at Lord's. Their stand beat the previous best of 232 by Plum Warner and James Douglas at The Oval in 1907.

  In 2014, Rogers and Robson put on a 181-run stand at Lord's, with Middlesex successfully chasing a victory target of 472 set by Yorkshire. Former England bowler Angus Fraser, the Middlesex director of cricket, rated Rogers's knock of 241 not out as one of the best he'd seen by a Middlesex batsman: **"I've seen special innings from Desmond Haynes, Mike Gatting, Mark Ramprakash and Jacques Kallis, but I don't think I've seen anything to better that. I'm numb, to be honest. It's a big statement, but I think that's one of the great Middlesex performances. It's a game supporters will be talking about in decades' time. It was special."**

- During his historic innings at Chittagong in 2005/06, Australia's Jason Gillespie became the first nightwatchman to take part in a triple-century partnership in a Test match. In what turned out be his final Test innings, Gillespie scored an unbeaten 201 at No. 3 against Bangladesh, sharing a 320-run fourth-wicket stand with Mike Hussey.

- England's Tip Foster only scored one century in Test match cricket and left the game with a record difference of 236 between his highest and his second-highest scores. His top effort was a record-breaking 287 on his Test debut, at the SCG in 1903/04, while his next best was 51, in the final of his eight matches, against South Africa at The Oval in 1907.

- Despite posting a world-record score in one-day international cricket, Charles Coventry had to be content with sharing the man-of-the-match award. After scoring 194 not out – then the equal-highest innings in a ODI – at Bulawayo in 2009, the Zimbabwe No. 3 watched on as Bangladesh opener Tamim Iqbal hit a match-winning 154: "**I congratulated him** [Coventry] **and told him that he could keep the trophy. He deserved it. You don't make world records every day. It was a truly magnificent innings.**"

- England XI openers Alastair Cook and Michael Carberry warmed up for the 2013/14 Ashes by both batting through the opening day of a tour match against Australia A at Hobart. The two finished the day unconquered with a record opening stand at Hobart of 318, with Cook scoring 154 and Carberry 153. Both batsmen ended their innings by retiring.

- In 2013, the Indian-born Sam Agarwal became the first batsman to score a first-class triple-century in a UK university match. Captaining Oxford University against Cambridge at Fenner's, Agarwal struck an unbeaten 313 off 312 balls, clubbing 41 fours and three sixes.

  Seven scores of 300-plus were scored in 2013 – all off the bats of players born in Asia – including the highest innings to date by a wicketkeeper in first-class cricket. Representing the Colts Cricket Club, Kusal Perera scored 336 off 275 balls against Saracens Sports Club in Colombo.

TRIPLE-CENTURIES BY WICKETKEEPERS IN FIRST-CLASS CRICKET

Score	Player	Match	Venue	Season
336	Kusal Perera	Colts v Saracens	Colombo	2012/13
321	Billy Murdoch	New South Wales v Victoria	Sydney	1881/82
314*	Clyde Walcott	Barbados v Trinidad	Port-of-Spain	1945/46
308	Srikar Bharat	Andhra v Goa	Ongole	2014/15
300*	Imtiaz Ahmed	PM's XI v Commonwealth XI	Mumbai	1950/51

- When Australia's Michael Bevan was run out for six in a 1996 World Cup match against India in Mumbai, it represented the first occasion he'd been dismissed in single figures in one-day internationals since his debut 26 matches earlier. While he didn't bat in his first match – against Sri Lanka at Sharjah in 1993/94 – Bevan reached double figures in his first 19 innings in ODIs, a world record.

- In a quarter-final of the 2013/14 Duleep Trophy, the South Zone pair of Baba Aparajith and Manish Pandey shared two century partnerships in the same innings. Both scored double-centuries separated by just a single run – Aparajith 212 and Pandey 213 – in the match against West Zone at Chennai, raising stands of 190 for the fourth wicket and 140 for the sixth. Pandey, who had retired hurt when on 104, scored his third first-class double-century, while Aparajith became just the fourth batsman to score 200 on his Duleep Trophy debut.

- Tariq Baig only appeared in five first-class matches, but scored three centuries. With 27 and a duck on his first-class debut for Lahore City in 1988/89, the wicketkeeping Baig made scores of 112 and four in his third match and two identical scores of 103 in his penultimate match, opening the batting against Bahawalpur at Lahore in 1989/90. He became only the third batsman in first-class history to score as many as three centuries in a career and never be dismissed between 50 and 99. The others before him were Ferozuddin, who appeared in 19 first-class matches between 1917/18 and 1934/35, and fellow Indian N.P. Madhavan, who made 11 first-class appearances in the early 1980s.

- After becoming the first batsman to complete five Test centuries in a row, Everton Weekes was dismissed in identical fashion by the same bowler at Calcutta in 1948/49. With scores of 128 at Delhi and 194 at Mumbai, Weekes peeled off twin tons (162 and 101) at Calcutta, caught and bowled by India debutant Ghulam Ahmed in each innings.

- In New Zealand's total of 174 at Leeds in 2013, as many as five batsmen made it into the 20s but no further. Their openers – Peter Fulton and Hamish Rutherford – put on a 50-run stand with scores of 28 and 27 respectively, while numbers ten and 11 also made a 50-run partnership, reached off just 24 balls. Neil Wagner hit 27 off 15 balls, while Trent Boult made an unbeaten 24, also off 15. While their stand of 52 was the fastest for the last wicket in Test history, Wagner and Boult survived 48 balls in the second innings, the longest on record that a pair had batted without scoring a run.

  Later in the year, Boult stuck around for another important last-wicket stand, adding 127 with B.J. Watling against Bangladesh at Chittagong. With an unbeaten 52, Boult became just the 15th No. 11 to score a half-century in a Test.

NUMBERS ONE AND 11 BOTH SCORING A HALF-CENTURY IN SAME TEST INNINGS

Opener	No. 11	Match	Venue	Season
Rodney Redmond (107)	Richard Collinge (68)	New Zealand v Pakistan	Auckland	1972/73
Adam Bacher (64)	Pat Symcox (54)	South Africa v Australia	Adelaide	1997/98
Peter Fulton (73)	Trent Boult (52*)	New Zealand v Bangladesh	Chittagong	2013/14

- Fresh from his dumping from the Australian ODI team in 2013, David Warner set about his return by scoring 500 domestic one-day runs in four innings at the same ground in a week. In a series of matches in the 2013/14 Ryobi One-Day Cup played at North Sydney Oval, Warner scored 139 against Queensland, 138 against Victoria, 32 against South Australia and 197 against Victoria.

  His 197, that contained 20 fours and ten sixes, overshadowed an earlier century (117) from Daniel Christian who shared an opening stand of 202 with Rob Quiney (89).

- When Ross Taylor scored 102 in a ODI against India at Wellington in 2013/14 it became the 5,000th century in international cricket. The 5,000 was made up of 3,690 in Tests, 1,300 in one-day internationals and ten in Twenty20s. Twelve months later, and appearing in his 150th one-day international, Taylor scored another 102 – 102 not out against Pakistan at Napier – the 100th century of New Zealand's ODI history.

- Appearing in the final of the World Cup Qualifier tournament in 2013/14, Swapnil Patil became the first batsman to make 99 not out on his one-day international debut. Patil struck his 99 off 99 balls for UAE against Scotland at Lincoln, becoming the first of three wicketkeepers in 2014 to miss an ODI century by one run. England's Jos Buttler was out for 99 against the West Indies at North Sound as was New Zealand's Luke Ronchi against South Africa at Mount Maunganui.

- Essex all-rounder Stan Nichols achieved an unusual six in a first-class match in 1935 when he cleared the fence against Yorkshire without a batting partner at the other end. During a clatter of wickets in the County Championship match at Colchester, no one had noticed that the next batsman in had not arrived, and Nichols – who appeared in 14 Tests for England – duly smashed a six, but was then dismissed next ball.

- Warwickshire opener Nick Knight carried his bat for a double-century against Hampshire at Edgbaston in 2002 with the No. 11 falling nine runs short of three figures. Sharing a last-wicket double-century partnership with Knight (255*), Alan Richardson scored 91 in what was his 32nd innings in first-class cricket having scored just 82 runs in his previous 31.

- In the same Test in which Sri Lanka's Kumar Sangakkara scored over 400 runs, two Bangladesh batsmen achieved their maiden centuries in the same innings. Shamsur Rahman (106) and Imrul Kayes (115) put on a stand of 232 at Chittagong in 2013/14, the second-highest in a Test where the second wicket started with the team yet to have scored. Their stand was just three runs short of the highest-such partnership between Australia's Bill Woodfull (141) and Charlie Macartney (151) at Leeds in 1926.

In Sri Lanka's first innings of 587, Sangakkara hit 319 – his maiden first-class triple-century – with the next highest score being 72 by Mahela Jayawardene. With 105 in the second innings, Sangakkara became only the second batsman, after England's Graham Gooch, to score a triple-century and a century in the same first-class match. With a score of 147 in his next innings – at Lord's in 2014 – he became the first batsman in Test history to three times hit a century in three consecutive innings, after doing so in 2013 and 2009/10.

- Australia's Michael Clarke marked his 150th first-class match by passing 150 and reaching the milestone of 11,000 first-class runs when he reached 111. His 230 against South Africa at Adelaide in 2012/13 included 40 fours and a six.

  Clarke passed 50 in his 50th first-class match – 151 on his Test debut, against India at Bangalore in 2004/05 – 100 in his 100th match – 138 versus South Africa at Sydney in 2008/09 – and 150 in his 150th.

  The only other batsman to have done so is South Africa's Neil McKenzie – 70 and 75 not out for Northerns against Griqualand West at Centurion in 2000/01, 101 for Northerns against North West at Potchefstroom in 2003/04 and 164 for Lions versus Dolphins, also at Potchefstroom, in 2007/08.

- After he was dismissed for 99 at Harare in 1994/95, Zimbabwe's Alistair Campbell had to wait a record period of time until he savoured his maiden century in Test match cricket. His first three-figure score of 102 came six years later, against India at Nagpur in 2000/01. The previous biggest wait for a maiden century by a batsman whose highest score was 99 had been almost four and a half years by South Africa's Trevor Goddard. After falling one run short at The Oval in 1960, Goddard then scored his one and only Test century (112) against England at Johannesburg in 1964/65.

- Victorian opener Julien Wiener enjoyed a rather brief, truncated international career for Australia in 1979/80, appearing in six Tests and seven one-day internationals in four months. He made his highest scores in both forms of the game in his final match – 50 against the West Indies in the World Series Cup at Sydney and 93 in the third Test against Pakistan at Lahore. Wiener became just the second batsman, after England's Clive Radley in 1978, to score a half-century in both his final Test and final one-day international.

- Sachin Tendulkar bowed out of domestic first-class and Test cricket in 2013/14 on a winning note by hitting a half-century in each of his final innings. After scoring a century (100*) on his first-class debut in 1988/89, Tendulkar struck 79 not out in a win for Mumbai against Haryana at Rohtak in the Ranji Trophy. Tendulkar's batting partner at the time, Dhawal Kulkarni, was born on the same day that Tendulkar made his first-class debut on 10 December 1988.

    Tendulkar then scored another 70-something in his final first-class innings, in his farewell Test. Becoming the first cricketer to appear in 200 Tests, Tendulkar scored a textbook 74 on the second day of the second Test against the West Indies at Mumbai, the same date – 15 November – that he made his Test debut back in 1989.

"Delivering the first ever ball he faced in first-class cricket is my richest memory. He defended the first two deliveries. I thought of tossing the next ball a bit so that he could step out and drive me. I was hopeful of a caught and bowled, but he drove me through the cover region. He defended the next two balls and pierced the next one through mid-wicket. After that, he played all the shots in the book. I don't remember him using up too many balls for his unbeaten 100."

Nisrag Patel,
the first player to bowl to Sachin Tendulkar in first-class cricket during
the Bombay-Gujarat match at Wankhede Stadium in 1988/89

SACHIN TENDULKAR'S 200 TESTS

Tests	Period	Runs	Avge	100s	50s
1-50	11-1989 to 03-1997	3438	49.82	11	16
51-100	03-1997 to 09-2002	4967	63.35	19	18
101-150	10-2002 to 08-2008	3472	46.91	9	15
151-200	08-2008 to 11-2013	4044	52.51	12	19
		15921	53.78	51	68

"Those 22 yards have given me everything in my life. Whatever I have today is because I spent time within those 22 yards. It's like a temple for me."

Sachin Tendulkar

- A few days on from the international exit of Sachin Tendulkar in 2013, a 14-year-old schoolboy struck the highest-ever individual score in Indian cricket. Prithvi Shaw hit 546 off 330 balls for Rizvi Springfield

(991) in the Harris Shield, beating an innings of 498 by 13-year-old Armaan Jaffer for the same side in 2010/11.

THE TOP SIX HIGHEST INNINGS OF ALL TIME

Score	Batsman	Match	Venue	Season
628*	A.E.J. Collins	Clark's House v North Town	Clifton	1899
566	Charles Eady	Break-o'-Day v Wellington	Hobart	1901/02
546	Prithvi Shaw	Rizvi Springfield v St Francis	Mumbai	2013/14
515	D.R. Havewalla	BB & CI Railways v St Xavier's	Mumbai	1933/34
506*	J.C. Sharp	Melbourne Gr. School v Geelong College	Melbourne	1914/15
502*	Chaman Lal	Mahandra College v Government College	Patiala	1956/57

- After Vijay Zol scored a century on his first-class debut in 2013/14, the teenager hit a double-century in his third match. On his Ranji Trophy debut, Zol made 200 not out for Maharashtra against Tripura at Gahunje at the age of 18 years and 340 days. On the same day, another 18-year-old, Sanju Samson, also reached a double-century in the Ranji Trophy, hitting 211 for Kerala against Assam at Guwahti.

  At the age of 17, Zol had already stamped his name in the record books with an unbeaten 451 in the 2011/12 Cooch Behar Trophy. Overtaking Yuvraj Singh's 11-year record of 358 for Punjab, Zol brought up his bumper score a day after his hero Virender Sehwag hit a double-ton in a one-day international. Playing for Maharashtra against Assam in Nashik, the left-handed opener's record knock spanned 645 minutes and 467 balls.

- When former Australian batsman Stuart Law brought up a century in a County Championship match against Sussex in 2007, he broke the world record for scoring the greatest number of first-class hundreds, but with none coming in a Test. His 119 for Lancashire at Hove was his 77th hundred at first-class level, with his highest innings in a Test being an unbeaten 54 in his only match, against Sri Lanka at Perth in 1995/96. Sussex batsman John Langridge – who played in the years 1928 to 1955, but never in a Test – was the previous holder of the record.

- In his last Test match for the West Indies, fast bowler Wayne Daniel struck a six off the very last ball he received. Daniel finished his ten-Test career with 46 runs, and a six off Australia's Tom Hogan in his farewell appearance, at Port-of-Spain in 1983/84.

- After a world-record haul of 29 dismissals in the 2013 Ashes, Brad Haddin excelled in front of the stumps in the follow-up series down under. Haddin celebrated his 50th Test by scoring his first-ever pair of fifties in the same match and went on to hit another four half-centuries in the series. The Australian wicketkeeper scored 94 and 53 at Brisbane, a match in which he also reached the milestone of 200 dismissals. Haddin's feat was only the fourth instance of an Australian keeper scoring two half-centuries in the same Test after Adam Gilchrist in 1999/2000, Ian Healy in 1994/95 and Jack Blackham in 1882/83.

Haddin became the first No. 7 batsman to score six half-centuries in a series, beating Australia's Greg Matthews, who hit five against Sri Lanka in 1992, and, with a total of 493 runs, took the record for most runs by an Australian wicketkeeper in a Test series.

MOST HALF-CENTURIES
BY A WICKETKEEPER IN A TEST SERIES

#	Player	Scores	Series	Season
6	Gerry Alexander	60, 72, 108, 63*, 87*, 73	West Indies v Australia	1960/61
6	Brad Haddin	94, 53, 118, 55, 65, 75	Australia v England	2013/14
5	Denis Lindsay	69, 182, 81, 137, 131	South Africa v Australia	1966/67

A HALF-CENTURY IN ALL FIRST INNINGS
OF A FIVE-MATCH TEST SERIES

Player	Scores	Series	Season
Warren Bardsley	132, 85, 54, 82, 94	Australia v South Africa	1910/11
Everton Weekes	128, 194, 162, 90, 56	West Indies v India	1948/49
Brad Haddin	94, 118, 55, 65, 75	Australia v England	2013/14

- A week after scoring a double-ton in a one-day international against Australia, India's Rohit Sharma was given his first Test cap and responded with a match-winning first-innings century. The first cricketer to appear in 100 ODIs without playing in a Test, Rohit hit 177 against the West Indies at Kolkata in 2013/14 – the highest score on debut by a No. 6 batsman, beating 155 by Doug Walters against England at Brisbane in 1965/66. He then hit 111 not out in the second Test, at Mumbai, becoming just the fifth batsman to score centuries in his first two Test innings.

  In 2014/15, Rohit became the first batsman to score two double-centuries in ODIs, pumping out a record 264 against Sri Lanka at Kolkata. He struck nine sixes, and a record 33 fours, smashing the previous best of 25 by Sachin Tendulkar and Virender Sehwag. India (404/5) beat Sri Lanka (251) by 153 runs – Rohit beat Sri Lanka by 13 runs.

- Opposing captains made the same score of 139 not out when India hosted Sri Lanka in the fifth one-day international at Ranchi in 2014/15. The highest individual score to date to be made twice in the same ODI, Angelo Mathews brought up his maiden century in his 138th match, while Virat Kohli scored his 21st in his 138th innings.

- South Africa's Faf du Plessis hit a maiden one-day international century in 2014, scoring 106 against Australia on the 106th anniversary of the birth of Don Bradman. Du Plessis shared a 206-run stand with A.B. de Villiers (126) in the match at Harare, the first double-century partnership for the third wicket against Australia in a one-day international.

  While it took him 49 innings to produce his maiden century, du Plessis then came up with two more and a ninety in his next four innings in a series that also involved Zimbabwe. He followed his breakthrough century with 126 in his next match against Australia, 121 against Zimbabwe and 96 in the final against Australia, finishing with a record total of 464 runs.

  When du Plessis got off the mark with a single on his way to 121 against Zimbabwe, he became the first batsman to appear in 100 consecutive international innings from debut without being dismissed for a duck. His first duck came later in the same year – in his 100th international match – during the first Test against the West Indies at Centurion.

- Dismissed for 99 in the Natal-Western Province Currie Cup match at Durban in 1936/37, Andrew Ralph then fell for 49 in the second innings. The WP opener became the first, and to date only, batsman to be dismissed one run shy of a century and half-century in the same first-class match.

- England's Alec Stewart celebrated his 100th Test with a century and a record hundred-run partnership. Playing against the West Indies at Manchester in 2000, Stewart, with 105, and Marcus Trescothick, with 66, shared a 179-run fourth-wicket stand, the only century partnership in a Test between a player appearing in his 100th match and a player appearing in his first.

- In a one-day international series against Afghanistan at Dubai in 2014/15, United Arab Emirates captain Khurram Khan struck a half-century in all three matches he played in. Sandwiched in between innings of 53 and 85 not out, Khurram struck a maiden ODI century (132*) at the ripe old age of 43 years and 162 days. He became the oldest batsman to score a one-day international hundred, overtaking Sri Lanka's Sanath Jayasuriya, who made 107 at the age of 39 against India at Dambulla in 2008/09.

- England's Joe Root began his one-day international career by passing 25 in his first ten innings at the crease. Not required to bat on his debut – against India at Rajkot in 2012/13 – Root then had scores of 36, 39, 57 not out and 31 against India and 56, 79 not out, 28 not out, 30, 28 and 33 against New Zealand. Out for 12 in his next match, he then scored 68, 38 and 48.

- Appearing in just his fourth Test match, Mominul Haque scored a record-high maiden century for Bangladesh, during which he became the first from his country to hit 25 fours in an innings. Batting at No. 4 against New Zealand at Chittagong in 2013/14, Mominul (181) began his innings at a rapid rate, reaching his fifty off 36 balls, and passing 100 off 98 with his team's score on 128.

  Team-mate Sohag Gazi also scored a maiden century in the same innings, reaching 101 not out. With B.J. Watling scoring 103, the match provided only the third instance of opposing number eights hitting a century in the same Test. Gazi followed his maiden Test ton with a five-wicket haul (6-77) the following day, becoming the first player to achieve the double of a hundred and a hat-trick in the same Test.

- A first-class match in the Australian winter of 2014 saw a world first with opposing batsmen scoring a double-century at number seven. In the Australia A-India A match at the Allan Border Field in Brisbane, wicketkeeper Naman Ojha celebrated his 100th first-class match with 219 not out, while Mitchell Marsh responded with 211, his maiden first-class double-century.

  The Australia A wicketkeeper was also in the runs with the Yorkshire-born Sam Whiteman (174) hitting a maiden first-class century and raising a 371-run partnership with Marsh. The stand between the two West Australians was the highest for the seventh wicket in a first-class match in Australia, beating a 335-run stand between Queensland's Cassie Andrews and Eric Bensted against New South Wales at Sydney in 1934/35.

  Ojha completed his 100th game with a pair of centuries, adding an unbeaten 101 in the second innings and sharing a 199-run partnership with Ambati Rayudu, who scored 100 not out. He then made it three in a row, with 110 in the following match of the series at the same venue. In his first first-class match back home, Ojha completed his fourth consecutive century, with 217 for Central Zone versus North Zone at Chandigarh.

- After beginning his first-class career in 2013/14 with a pair on debut, Mosaddek Hossain struck a double-century in his fifth match and another in his next. After six matches at first-class level, the 19-year-old from Bangladesh had scores of nought and nought, 13 and 11, seven and three, nought, 250 and 282.

- Fresh from making a century in his second Test match, India's K.L. Rahul became the first Karnataka batsman to score a triple-hundred in the Ranji Trophy. Opening the batting against Uttar Pradesh at

Bangalore in 2014/15, Rahul, aged 22, hit 337 with 47 fours and four sixes. On his Test debut – against Australia at the MCG a month before – the opening batsman appeared at six, scoring three, and bumped up the order to three in the second innings, made one. He then opened the batting in the following Test in Sydney and hit 110.

While no batsman had scored a triple-century for Karnataka in 81 years of first-class cricket, two did so in 2014/15 – Rahul with 337 and 328 by Karun Nair against Tamil Nadu at Mumbai.

- The opening match of the India-West Indies series in 1948/49 saw three batsmen obtain their maiden Test centuries in the same innings. A unique occurrence in Test match cricket, the first innings at Delhi saw Clyde Walcott (152), Gerry Gomez (101) and Robert Christiani (107) all reaching three figures for the first time, with Everton Weekes (128) also scoring a century in their total of 631.

- During the first Test against Australia at Perth in 2008/09, the South African pair of Jacques Kallis and A.B. de Villiers combined for identical partnerships of 124 for the fourth wicket in both innings. A record for the highest identical pair of partnerships in the same Test, the next highest – exactly half – also came in the same series. Openers Matthew Hayden and Simon Katich had stands of 62 in both innings of the third Test in Sydney.

- Rusi Surti was the 99th Indian Test cricketer and had a highest Test score of 99. The first Indian to play in the Sheffield Shield – for Queensland – the all-rounder appeared in 26 Tests, falling one run shy of a century against New Zealand at Auckland in 1967/68. He was dropped on 99 twice in consecutive overs, by Mark Burgess off Gary Bartlett and by Graham Dowling off Bruce Taylor.

- Brendon McCullum celebrated the opening of New Zealand's newest Test ground in 2014/15 by scoring the fastest Test match 150 to date. In New Zealand's first Boxing Day Test match in 11 years – at Hagley Oval in Christchurch – McCullum smashed 195 off just 134 balls against Sri Lanka, reaching 100 off 74 deliveries and 150 off 103.

During his record-breaking knock – the 1,000th first-class century of 2014 – McCullum struck 11 sixes, having hit the same number in his previous Test innings, against Pakistan at Sharjah. The first batsman to hit ten sixes in two Test innings, McCullum also became the first to pass the milestone of 30 sixes in a calendar year. With 33 sixes in nine Tests, he beat the previous best of 22 by Adam Gilchrist in 15 Tests in 2005 and 22 by Virender Sehwag in 14 matches in 2008.

- Records galore were broken in a domestic 50-over match at Bloemfontein in 2014/15 with Dolphins openers Morne van Wyk and Cameron Delport both passing 150 against the Knights. Opening the batting, they put on an unbroken partnership of 367, the highest first-wicket stand in List A cricket.

  The wicketkeeping captain van Wyk scored an unbeaten 175 off 227 balls, while Delport hit 169 not out, also off 227 deliveries, becoming just the second opening pair to bat through all 50 overs of a List A match. The Knights (342) responded with a second-wicket stand of 275 between Reeza Hendricks (181) and Rudi Second (107), signalling the first instance of three individual 150s and the first example of two 250-run partnerships in the same match.

  The following day, a Matador Cup game in Sydney saw two *opening* stands of 250 with Tasmania's Ben Dunk (229*) and Tim Paine (125) posting a record Australian first-wicket partnership of 277, only to see it broken by the Queensland pair of Usman Khawaja (166) and Chris Hartley (142) with 280. A total of exactly 800 runs – and just four wickets – was seen on the day, with the Bulls (402/3) hunting down Tasmania's 398/1 with 16 balls remaining, the highest successful run chase in a domestic one-day match in Australia. For the first time in List A cricket, four batsmen reached 125 in the same match.

  Dunk's 229 became the highest undefeated innings in List A cricket and the third-highest of all time. He also became the first batsman to score a double-century and end up on the losing side.

- On his way to a new personal best with the bat in 2014/15, Auckland batsman Colin Munro obliterated the record for the most sixes in a first-class innings. During his 281 against Central Districts at Napier, Munro hit 23 sixes, beating the previous record of 16 which had been achieved by Andrew Symonds, Graham Napier, Jesse Ryder and Mukhtar Ali.

- South Africa's Hashim Amla began 2015 in ominous form, taking part in three one-day international partnerships worth exactly 247. Amla and Rilee Rossouw shared an opening stand of 247 against the West Indies at Johannesburg in January, repeating the feat ten days later against the same opposition at Centurion with 247 for the third wicket. With an innings of 159 a month later against Ireland at Canberra in the 2015 World Cup, Amla then featured in another 247-run stand, this time for the second wicket with Faf du Plessis.

- Appearing in his farewell one-day international series, Sri Lanka's Kumar Sangakkara became the first batsman to hit four consecutive ODI centuries, doing so at the 2015 World Cup. With scores of 105 not out, 117 not out and 104, he made 326 runs before being dismissed, establishing a new record for most runs between dismissals in World Cup cricket. Sangakkara then made 124 against Scotland in Hobart and with two catches behind the stumps became the first player to achieve 500 dismissals in ODIs.

- After sitting on 250 at stumps on day two of the Queensland-Victoria Sheffield Shield match at the Gabba in 2014/15, Chris Lynn was dismissed without adding to his score the following morning. It became the highest score in all first-class cricket in which a batsman fell without building on his overnight position. The previous record-holder was Misbah-ul-Haq with 247 for Sui Northern Gas Pipelines against Sui South Gas Corporation at Sheikhupura in 2008/09.

- A 15-year-old set the cricket world abuzz in 2014/15 when he made the highest-ever score in limited-over cricket, blasting an unbeaten 486 in an under-16 schools tournament. Representing JSS International School, Sankruth Sriram and Dhanush Priyan (70*) stitched together an unbroken opening stand of 605 in the 40-over match against Hebron (42) at Ootacamund.

  Only a few months previously, a 14-year-old sporting a name synonymous with West Indies cricket had also scored a quadruple-century in a limited-over game. Kirstan Kallicharan hit 404 not out in a schools match in Trinidad, whacking 44 fours and 31 sixes.

- A week after becoming the first recognised batsman to be dismissed without facing a ball on his T20 international debut, Bangladesh's Soumya Sarkar produced an unsual feat with the bat in his first Test match. Batting at No. 7 against Pakistan at Khulna in 2015, Sarkar made 33 in each innings and was dismissed both times by the same two players. In the first innings, he was caught by Asad Shadiq off the bowling of Mohammad Hafeez. In the second innings, Sarkar was caught by Hafeez off Shadiq, who claimed his maiden wicket at Test level.

  In his debut T20 for Bangladesh, Sarkar had become the first batsman to be dismissed without facing a ball. The opener became only the second player to suffer such a fate, after Australian bowler Ashley Noffke at the hands of New Zealand at Perth in 2007/08.

- In his first first-class match, in 2015, Sussex medium-pacer Oliver Robinson became the first debutant to score a century at No. 9 in the County Championship. With a score of 110 in a losing cause against Durham at Chester-le-Street, Robinson also took part in the second-highest tenth-wicket partnership to involve a debutant in all first-class cricket. Batting with Matthew Hobden (65*), the two shared a last-wicket stand of 164, just short of the record 169 by the New South Wales pair of Roy Minnett (216*) and newcomer Cecil McKew (29) against Victoria at Sydney in 1911/12.

Lights, Camera, Action

- The first bowler to reach the milestone of 300 Test wickets later appeared in a UK Christmas TV movie. Fred Trueman played himself in *Charles Dickens' World of Christmas* that debuted in 1974. The film also features *Father, Dear Father* star Patrick Cargill, whose nephew Robin Jackman played in four Tests for England in the 1980s.

Fast bowler and occasional actor Fred Trueman on the set of the Dad's Army *episode 'The Test' that first aired on the BBC in 1970*

- In the year of his retirement from international cricket, England all-rounder Andrew Flintoff featured in a series of ads to promote the 50th anniversary of the TV soap *Coronation Street* in 2010. An unabashed fan, Flintoff declared a desire to make a guest appearance on the show: "**I could easily fit in and I'd love to have a go. I heard Snoop Dogg is also interested in making an appearance. If he's a fan, I'm in good company.**" In 2014, Flintoff had a cameo in an episode of the UK TV comedy *Trollied*.

- South African fast bowler Dale Steyn took a week off cricket in 2013 to appear on the set of an Adam Sandler film. Steyn had a bit part in *Blended* released in 2014: "**I was probably more nervous than playing in front of a packed cricket ground.**"

- Nicholas Hoult, who starred in the ground-breaking British TV series *Skins*, learnt the game of cricket from actor Hugh Grant. Hoult got his big break in 2002, appearing alongside Grant in the film *About a Boy*: "**When we weren't acting we'd all play cricket. We had a big match at the end of filming and Hugh was pretty good.**"

> "**Women do love a cricketer. It's one of those things. It's like Aston Martins. They just love it. I think they love the whites. They like the bit of red from the ball that's rubbed off in the groin area.**"
>
> British actor Hugh Grant

- Cricket plays a big part in an episode of the popular British TV comedy *The Goodies*. A 1976 episode, '2001 and a Bit', has the sons of the show's stars attempting to revive what was then a long-lost sport.

- Jimmy Ellis, who played the role of Bert Lynch in the BBC police series *Z Cars*, played cricket for the Lord's Taverners. In one game, he picked up the wicket of Denis Compton, caught behind by Jim Parks.

- British actor John Challis was once dismissed for 96 in a charity game when the ball came off his bat, hit the wicketkeeper in the head and was then caught at second slip. Best known for his 22-year role in the TV comedy *Only Fools and Horses*, Challis has also appeared in hit shows such as *One Foot in the Grave*, *Coronation Street*, *Doctor Who* and *Z Cars*.

> "**I feign serious injury at charity games, but that's what you do as an actor.**"
>
> John Challis

- British TV, film and theatre actor Damian Lewis once scored a century against a team called The Grannies. Lewis later appeared in the top-rating US TV series *Band of Brothers* and *Homeland*.

> **"A cricket ball broke my nose when I was a kid so I couldn't breathe through it. Before I had it operated on I used to stand on stage with my mouth slightly open."**
>
> Damian Lewis

- Richard Attenborough's 1969 film *Oh! What a Lovely War* includes a celebrated reference to cricket. Featuring an array of stars, including John Mills, Dirk Bogarde and John Gielgud, First World War generals are seen conducting their campaign from Brighton Pier with cricket scoreboards used as backdrops showing the number of soldiers killed in action.

The Academy Award-winning director of *Gandhi*, Attenborough once came a cropper in an exhibition match when he was felled by a cricket ball while fielding. Playing in a game featuring politicians and stars of stage and screen at East Grinstead in 1955, a ball sent down by Oscar-nominated actor Leo Genn to Walter Bromley-Davenport smashed into Attenborough's face, sustaining an injury that required two days in hospital.

- Former England spinner Phil Tufnell made two appearances on the British TV show *Family Affairs*, a soap that ran from 1997 to 2005 on Channel Five. His guest appearances in 2004 followed his participation in the hit reality show *I'm a Celebrity … Get Me Out of Here!*, which he won in 2003. Five years later, Tufnell and his wife Dawn starred as celebrity contestants on the ITV game show *All Star Mr & Mrs*, taking the top prize of £30,000 for a nominated charity. His extensive TV CV also includes appearances on *They Think It's All Over*, *Simply the Best*, *A Question of Sport*, *The One Show*, *Strictly Come Dancing*, *Would I Lie to You?*, *The Chase* and *The Flowerpot Gang*.

- The first episode of the BBC comedy classic *The Good Life* that made its debut in 1975 includes a scene of an office cricket team. One of its stars, Richard Briers, later appeared in another top-rating comedy – *Ever Decreasing Circles* – with an episode called 'The Cricket Match' first airing in 1984.

- Former Indian opener Sadagoppan Ramesh played a leading role in an Indian movie, *Potta Potti 50/50*, which debuted in 2011. Ramesh, who appeared in 19 Tests, had a bit part in a 2008 movie, *Santosh Subramaniam*: **"Making films is far tougher than playing cricket."**

- The British Hollywood actor David Niven earned the nickname "Hat-Trick" at his school in Buckingham after taking three wickets in three balls in a match for the Stowe second XI against Eton. While an actor in the United States, Niven was a playing member of former England captain C. Aubrey Smith's Hollywood Cricket Club in the 1930s: **"The septuagenarian captain Smith commanded respect both on field and stage as he was six feet four, ramrod straight, alert and vigorous. Every Sunday he ordered me to turn out for the club, I always called him 'sir', and though dreading long hot afternoons in the field, I obeyed."**
  Some of the big names to have played for the Hollywood club include Douglas Fairbanks jr, Laurence Olivier, Errol Flynn, Boris Karloff and Cary Grant.

Hollywood Cricket Club members Merle Oberon and David Niven (left), and Cary Grant posing in cricket gear

- Desmond Roberts, a British actor who appeared in 12 first-class matches in the 1920s and 30s, later became a star in Hollywood. When an Australian cricket team visited California in 1932, Roberts appeared in a match played on Don Bradman's birthday. With 67, he was the only batsman to reach double figures for the Hollywood Cricket Club, with Boris Karloff scoring five before he was caught and bowled by Stan McCabe.

The day before, the Australian cricketers had paid a visit to the famous MGM studios where they witnessed a number of films being made by Maureen O'Sullivan, Clark Gable and Jean Harlow. C. Aubrey Smith later captained a British Born Film Stars XI against the Australians, with Roberts opening both the batting and bowling. Smith top-scored with 24, while Bradman made a half-century for the tourists.

Australian cricketers with the cast of the 1932 movie The Mask of Fu Manchu, *including Boris Karloff (back row). Don Bradman is seated at far right in second row above C. Aubrey Smith, while Desmond Roberts is seated far left in front row*

A SELECT FILMOGRAPHY OF DESMOND ROBERTS

Cavalcade	Diana Wynyard, Clive Brook, Una O'Connor	1933
Christopher Strong	Katharine Hepburn, Colin Clive, Billie Burke	1933
Of Human Bondage	Bette Davis, Leslie Howard, Frances Dee	1934
Scott of the Antarctic	John Mills, Derek Bond, Diana Churchill	1948
The Man in the White Suit	Alec Guinness, Joan Greenwood, Cecil Parker	1951
Simba	Dirk Bogarde, Donald Sinden, Virginia McKenna	1955
I Was Monty's Double	John Mills, Cecil Parker, M.E. Clifton-James	1958

- During the 1930s and 40s, movie studios made much of the Hollywood Cricket Club's celebrity status by trotting out its stars at games for promotional events. Mickey Rooney and Elizabeth Taylor made one such appearance on the sidelines of a Sunday match to promote their 1944 film *National Velvet*. On another occasion, Rooney had called on players at the club to teach him the finer points of the game in preparation for a role in an upcoming film, *A Yank at Eton*.

- Australian batsman David Warner forked out over $6m in 2014 on a house in Sydney made famous by a British reality TV show. The waterfront mansion in South Coogee was used as the set for *Geordie Shore* in 2013.

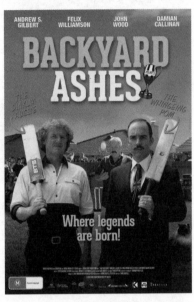

- The tale of a game of backyard cricket was turned into an Australian film in 2013 with its premiere taking place in the country town where fast bowler Geoff Lawson was born. The $300,000 budget for the film *Backyard Ashes* was raised through the selling of shares to residents and small businesses in the New South Wales city of Wagga Wagga.

> "We jokingly say this is the ultimate underdog Australian film. We thought we can't let this slide, it's too good an idea. So we said 'why don't we shoot it in Wagga?' We've got enough contacts here, we know the people, we've spent our lives working in that community. We were literally in mum and dad's backyard when we went 'why don't we shoot it here?'"
>
> director Mark Grentell

- Celebrity chef Clarissa Dickson Wright, who appeared in the *Two Fat Ladies* TV cooking programme, was an accredited cricket umpire. A player of some note at school, she regularly umpired village cricket matches in Sussex.

- An American TV series that won its first Emmy for outstanding comedy in 2010 includes a reference to cricket. In the final episode of the first season of *Modern Family*, all 11 members of the cast gather for a group portrait dressed in white, with the character of Jay, played by Ed O'Neill, mentioning cricket: **"Look at us here all in white. What are we ... a cricket team?"**

- The 22nd episode of the tenth season of the US animated comedy series *Family Guy* features a scene of cricket. The episode, which originally aired in 2012, sees the characters of Brian and Stewie responding to viewer mail, with one segment featuring a British version of *Family Guy*.

TV commentator: **Well, it's a brilliant day for a long and confusing game of cricket.**

The field is teeming with men in helmets who don't seem like they need helmets, and men not in helmets who seem like they probably should be wearing helmets.

Oh, he's batted it clear out of the stadium.

Is that good? We don't know, but it's what we do!

- During the making of a TV documentary for the BBC, *Monty Python* star Michael Palin drew the attention of the Vietnamese military while filming a cricket match in Hanoi. After tossing the coin in the match between British and Indian expatriates, Palin was ordered to turn off the cameras. Because the game was played on land owned by the air force, filming was deemed to be a security risk. The story gets a run in the fourth episode of the series *Full Circle* that made its debut in 1997.

I was born, brought up and first had cricket instilled into me in Sheffield where, if you believe William White's history of the city, the game of cricket was recorded as early as 1757 by Town Trustees – and here I quote – "attempting the abolition of brutal sports by paying 14s 6d to the cricket players on Shrove Tuesday to entertain the populace and prevent the infamous practice of throwing at cocks". Imagine the late Brian Johnston having to explain that in the tea interval.

As a boy growing up in the 1950s, without a television, let alone a mobile phone or a games console, when a social network was church on Sunday mornings – and "five of us lived in't shoe box in't middle o't road" – I used to find great solace, and here's a sad admission, in staging entire cricket matches, on my own, in our back garden. These were no ten-minute diversions. They were five-day games, played in real time.

Our kitchen was the Long Room from which I would emerge, via the back door, as whoever the current top opening batsman might be. If it was, say, 1955, I would be Hanif Mohammad of Pakistan or David Sheppard or Len Hutton for England. I would acknowledge the applause as I made my way slowly round the hedge, past the dustbins, to take up my position in front of the drainpipe beside the dining-room window. I'd take my time, checking my guard, adjusting my essential underwear, narrowing my eyes as I scanned an imaginary field, taking a deliberately long time before letting my gaze finally come to rest on the brooding black eyes and thunderous brow of an imaginary Fred Trueman, tossing the ball from hand to hand, up by the garage door.

His first ball pitches short, I swing, connect and it bounces unstoppably to the boundary. I barely need to run further than the dustbins before strolling back to the drainpipe, knowing that the fury I'd unleashed was going to make for a very exciting morning indeed.

Of course there could be frustrating moments. I might be Johnny Wardle, two runs off a whirlwind fifty, facing a rampant Fazal Mahmood, when my mother comes up the drive with her shopping and walks right across the pitch.

"What are you doing dear?"

"Nothing!"

How could I explain what it was like to be Johnny Wardle at that moment? To have taken eight for 42 in the Pakistan second innings, and to be two short of a match-winning half-century with the light fading fast?

"Have you done your maths homework?"

Looking back now I take comfort from the fact that my imaginary cricket matches did more for my later career than any maths homework ever did. In what seemed the desperately ordinary world of Sheffield, cricket fed my hungry imagination, kept me in touch with a glamorous world I knew I'd never be part of. In the same way I could read *The Old Man and The Sea*, knowing there was precious little chance of wrestling an 18 foot marlin in the River Don, or feast my eyes on Gina Lollobrigida, knowing that she would almost certainly never come north of Nottingham, I could, with the help of a stocky yellow *Almanack*, recreate Lord's in my back garden.

For me many seventh heavens meet under this roof. One of my earliest heroes – in common, I'm sure, with many of my generation – was the swashbuckling Australian all-rounder Keith Miller. And just to be in the same room through which he must have strode after hitting seven sixes in one innings for the Dominions against England in 1945, one which lodged on the roof above us, is to have some kind of dream fulfilled. To be at Lord's at all is to feel the gloved hand of history upon the shoulder.

– from an address by Michael Palin
at Lord's in 2013 marking the publication of the 150th edition of
Wisden Cricketers' Almanack

- *Monty Python*'s John Cleese, who went on to appear in a number of Hollywood blockbusters, once dismissed the great Denis Compton in a schools match against MCC. Representing Clifton College in 1957, Cleese scored 13 not out in each innings against Tonbridge at Lord's.

- In a break in play during the New Zealand-England Test match at Wellington in 2001/02, members of the crowd were given the chance to take part in a film. *Lord of the Rings* director Peter Jackson stood on the pitch armed with a microphone and urged spectators to make growling noises that could be used in a scene in *Two Towers*.

"He came into the dressing room holding a cigarette holder, wearing a dressing gown, sandals and a t-shirt with a picture of Darren Gough on it."

Lord of the Rings cast member Sean Bean
on meeting fellow actor Peter O'Toole

- During the making of *The Hobbit* in New Zealand in 2011, British actor Ian McKellen took time off to be match referee-cum-umpire in a game staged to support victims of an earthquake that had devastated Christchurch. Hollywood actor Russell Crowe was also involved in the celebrity fundraiser, coaching one of the teams that included his Test-playing cousin Martin Crowe.

Russell Crowe, the junior cricketer

"You feel so close to the game. This is my second time at Lord's. I came here in 2009. I wanted to come here earlier but my cousin, Martin, insisted that the first time I came to Lord's I had to go with him, and I didn't know why until he casually walked me through the Long Room and ... 'Oh, there's Martin's portrait.'"

Russell Crowe

- While filming *The Lion in Winter* in France in 1968, an internationally-acclaimed Hollywood actress had a lesson in cricket. Katharine Hepburn played the game with her co-star, the cricket-loving Peter O'Toole, declaring: **"I was absolutely terrible. It isn't as easy as baseball."**

Katharine Hepburn on the set of the film The Lion in Winter *in 1968 and Peter O'Toole in 1991*

- London-born actor Kunal Nayyar, who shot to fame in *The Big Bang Theory,* is a major cricket fan who co-produced and narrated the Indian cricket documentary *Beyond All Boundaries* released in 2014. Nayyar, who plays the role of Raj in the US sitcom, teamed up with filmmaker Sushrut Jain who documented three cricket-mad Indians and the frenzy that surrounded India's participation at the 2011 World Cup: **"When the director approached me to do the narration for the film, I watched a lot of the footage he had obtained shooting the film**

and saw what he was doing with it. I was blown away. Being a huge cricket fan myself and having followed Team India's every move during the 2011 World Cup to see a film like this being made that captured both the intensity of the fan stories and the World Cup cricketers was awesome. I simply had to get involved."**

"I've never played here [USA] ... there are leagues in Los Angeles, but it's so hard to find the time. On *Rules of Engagement* there's a South African-Indian actor named Adhir Kalyan, who's a phenomenal actor and good friend of mine, and he's a very good cricket player. He plays in a league and tells me about it. I'm just not good enough and I haven't played in so long. I played a lot for fun and at school. I was never really great, but I was a huge cricket fanatic. For me, getting on the field was a dream. Anytime we had a moment, we'd go into our driveway with a tennis ball and cricket bat and play."

The Big Bang Theory's Kunal Nayyar

- The American sitcom *Rules of Engagement* that debuted in 2007 includes cricket in an episode first broadcast in 2010. In the season-four episode 'Harassment', the character of Jeff, played by Patrick Warburton, and Timmy, played by Adhir Kalyan, square off with a game of cricket.

"They were so kind as to include a cricket episode in *Rules of Engagement*. I was born and raised playing cricket, and I have a great passion for it and I make sure that even here in the States I get all the games that are happening from in and around the world. I'm not one of these people who come from abroad, a foreign culture, and starts judging the culture here because it's different, and I've really taken to baseball. The two sports share a lot in terms of the strategy, and the individual battles that happen, but each is a pretty special game. Though many people find them both to be long and tedious and boring, but I find them both to be fascinating."

Adhir Kalyan

- Fast bowler Brett Lee, who took on the lead role in a major Bollywood film announced in 2014, is listed in the credits of an Australian blockbuster of the 1990s. The Oscar-winning *Babe*, a heart-warming film about a pig that starred US actor James Cromwell, sees Lee listed as one of the animal handlers: "**When you think about being out on the cricket field, I've always looked at it as some form of acting anyway. When you walk over that white line, you take on this big, tough fast bowler [persona].**"

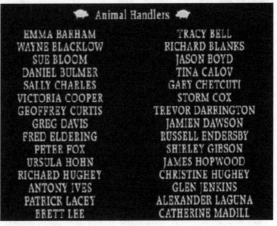

🐖 Animal Handlers 🐖

EMMA BARHAM	TRACY BELL
WAYNE BLACKLOW	RICHARD BLANKS
SUE BLOOM	JASON BOYD
DANIEL BULMER	TINA CALOV
SALLY CHARLES	GARY CHETCUTI
VICTORIA COOPER	STORM COX
GEOFFREY CURTIS	TREVOR DARRINGTON
GREG DAVIS	JAMIEN DAWSON
FRED ELDERING	RUSSELL ENDERSBY
PETER FOX	SHIRLEY GIBSON
URSULA HOHN	JAMES HOPWOOD
RICHARD HUGHEY	CHRISTINE HUGHEY
ANTONY IVES	GLEN JENKINS
PATRICK LACEY	ALEXANDER LAGUNA
BRETT LEE	CATHERINE MADILL

"I have never really followed the game of cricket, but I quite like watching Brett Lee. I have been crazy about his looks since I was a young girl. He's so yummy."

Indian actress Sonakshi Sinha

- Nigel Havers, a BAFTA-nominated British actor of stage and screen fame, is a cricket enthusiast from way back who started playing the game at school when he was six. Havers is best known for his long-running stint on *Coronation Street* and for his role in the award-winning 1981 film *Chariots of Fire*. In 2001, he took on a major TV role involving cricket, playing A.J. Raffles in the BBC production *The Gentleman Thief*.

- The chairman of an English cricket club has been nominated at the US Emmy Awards for his role in a hit British TV show. Jim Carter – whose film credits include *The Madness of King George* and *The Wind in the Willows* – plays the part of Charles Carson, a butler, in the period drama *Downton Abbey*: "**I run a cricket club, which takes up a massive amount of time. Takes up more time than *Downton*, almost.**"

British actor and cricket fan Jim Carter from the UK TV show Downton Abbey

- Cricket plays a part in a South African film, *Spud*, released in 2010. Set in a boarding school, Australian-based actor Troye Sivan takes on the role of John "Spud" Milton, while John Cleese plays the part of his teacher: "**Milton, that forward defensive was as porous as a whore's drawers.**"

- An Australian actor travelled from Hollywood to London in 1952 to seek funds for a film on the life and times of Don Bradman. Ron Randall – a former Sydney public school cricketer – was after £170,000 for his project: "**I have been trying to get this film made for years, but in America, Bradman and cricket mean nothing.**"

- Don Bradman makes an appearance in a 1936 Australian film called *The Flying Doctor*. Bradman played himself in the movie that won an award at the 1937 Venice Film Festival.

- Two of the stars of *The Amazing Spider-Man 2* film had a go at cricket in 2014 during a promotional trip to Singapore. Andrew Garfield and Jamie Foxx received tips from Bollywood actor Sameer Kochhar, the host of a TV show on the Indian Premier League.

> **"Picked up the game of cricket in Singapore, you could say I'm a natural."**
>
> US actor Jamie Foxx

- Former Indian captain Anil Kumble made his cinematic debut in 2008, with a bit part in the Bollywood film *Meerabai Not Out*. The movie also stars Mandira Bedi, who plays the role of a teacher whose great love in life is cricket and Anil Kumble: "**Anil has a tiny role with me in *Meerabai Not Out*. I am Meerabai, a cricket-crazy fan. Anil is such a charming man ... he took my wicket.**"

- Bangladesh all-rounder Shakib Al Hasan made his acting debut in 2013 when he shot a scene for the movie *Shob Kichu Pechone Fele* (*Leaving Everything Behind*). The all-rounder made a grand entrance in the film, parachuting on to a local beach where he played cricket with five friends who are the main characters in the movie.

- British actor Francis Matthews, best known for his role as Paul Temple in the BBC detective series, introduced Hollywood actress Ava Gardner to the game in 1956. In Britain for the filming of *Bhowani Junction*, she reportedly said she thought cricket was a "stupid game". Matthews, who also appeared in the hit TV shows *The Avengers* and *Heartbeat*, was a member of the Stage Cricket Club.

- The revered British television compere Magnus Magnusson is hailed as one of Iceland's most talented cricketers. Born in the capital Reykjavik, Magnusson moved to Britain becoming vice-captain of the first XI at Edinburgh Academy. One of the defining faces and voices of the BBC, he fronted the *Mastermind* TV quiz show for a quarter of a century from 1972 to 1997.

- When a British film premiered in Sydney in 1930 one of the lead actors was on hand to spruik the movie, and to inform the audience of the latest cricket score. After speaking via telephone for several minutes promoting *Rookery Nook*, Tom Walls was asked about the latest score in the Ashes Test match at Lord's. Not only did he reveal the total, "**England, six wickets for 281**," he also listed the scores of each batsman.

- UK actor Roger Lloyd Pack, who appeared in the TV shows *Only Fools and Horses* and *The Vicar of Dibley*, once broke a finger while playing for Harold Pinter's Gaieties cricket club. Lloyd Pack learnt the game at school in Hampshire managing a few matches for the first XI: "**I think the highest score I ever made was 64, followed by 39 not out, and I can remember almost every shot in those two innings.**"

- A highly respected West End theatre director played a part in the development of a young Adam Gilchrist. Hugh Goldie – who made his London acting debut in 1952 and staged his first production the following year – played cricket for Oxfordshire and was a stalwart of the Richmond club in London. As its chairman, he signed up a 17-year-old Gilchrist to play for the club in 1989.

- A 1991 episode of the top-rating US sitcom *The Cosby Show* features a scene of cricket. In the season-seven 'There's Still No Joy in Mudville', the Bill Cosby character Cliff Huxtable (pictured) plays a game of cricket with two West Indian friends in the family living room.

A SELECTION OF TV SHOWS THAT CONTAIN CRICKET REFERENCES

The Adventures of Lano and Woodley (Australia)
All Creatures Great and Small (UK)
The Big Bang Theory (US)
Bergerac (UK)
Blackadder Goes Forth (UK)
Bored to Death (US)
Brideshead Revisited (UK)
Brittas Empire (UK)
The Buddha of Suburbia (UK)
Buffy the Vampire Slayer (US)
Californication (US)
Charters and Caldicott (UK)
The Comic Strip Presents (UK)
Coronation Street (UK)
The Cosby Show (US)
Dad's Army (UK)
Desperate Housewives (US)
Downton Abbey (UK)
Doctor Who (UK)
Ever Decreasing Circles (UK)
Family Guy (US)
Fawlty Towers (UK)
Frasier (US)
The Good Life (UK)
The Goodies (UK)
Hancock's Half Hour (UK)
Heat of the Sun (UK)
Home and Away (Australia)
House (US)
Housos (Australia)
Howzat! (Australia)
The Inbetweeners (UK)
The Inspector Lynley Mysteries (UK)

Inspector Morse (UK)
In Treatment (US)
The IT Crowd (UK)
Keeping Up Appearances (UK)
Kingdom (UK)
Killing Time (Australia)
The League of Gentlemen (UK)
Life's Too Short (UK)
A Little Bit of Fry and Laurie (UK)
Little Britain (UK)
Love Thy Neighbour (UK)
Lowdown (Australia)
The Magicians (UK)
Modern Family (US)
The Moodys (Australia)
Monty Python's Flying Circus (UK)
Neighbours (Australia)
The Office (UK)
Outrageous Fortune (NZ)
Outside Edge (UK)
Packed to the Rafters (Australia)
Play for Tomorrow (UK)
The Prisoner (UK)
Rake (Australia)
Rules of Engagement (US)
Sherlock Holmes (UK)
Shooting Stars (UK)
The Slap (Australia)
The Straits (Australia)
Studio 60 on the Sunset Strip (US)
Summer Heights High (Australia)
The Two Ronnies (UK)
Underbelly (Australia)
West Wing (US)
The Young Ones (UK)

• When actress Catherine Zeta-Jones resided in the Welsh village of Mumbles, a cricket club devised a plan to take advantage of their local celebrity. In 2003, the president of the Mumbles Cricket Club, Mark Portsmouth, announced that any player who could land a six in their yard would receive £100: "**It would have to be a massive six, but it would be fun if someone did it. Can you imagine them** [Zeta-Jones and husband Michael Douglas] **returning the ball?**"

- Former England batsman Jim Troughton, whose grandfather Patrick was the second Doctor Who, made his acting debut in 2014 in a BBC radio show. Jim played the part of cricketer Colin Blythe in the radio drama *Home Front*: "**I am surrounded by actors in my family ... I'm not much of an actor, but this was more like reading**

British actor Patrick Troughton, the second Doctor Who, and grandfather of Jim Troughton, who appeared in six one-day internationals for England in 2003

than acting as it's for radio and I had my lines in front of me. It was good fun."

  Jim's father David Troughton also appeared in the *Doctor Who* series, while the cricketer's uncle Michael Troughton has a long list of TV appearances to his credit, including *Minder, The Bill* and *The New Statesman*. Jim's younger brother is Sam Troughton, who starred alongside Billie Piper in the 2005 horror film *Spirt Trap*, while his cousin is Harry Melling from the *Harry Potter* series.

- Within the space of a few weeks in 2013, two big names of film became cricket entrepreneurs. Hollywood star Mark Wahlberg, of *Boogie Nights* and *Ted* fame, was the first, taking an equity interest in the Caribbean Premier League franchise the Barbados Tridents: "**I am a huge cricket fan now.**" The Scotland-born Gerard Butler – whose film credits include *Law Abiding Citizen* and *RocknRolla* – then purchased a stake in the Jamaica Tallawahs: "**It is obvious that this tournament is the home of the greatest party in sport.**"

> "**He** [Mark Wahlberg] **was congratulating his team the other day for being unbeaten. But after playing my team, they were not unbeaten, let me just say that.**"
>
> Gerard Butler,
> whose Jamaica Tallawahs team took out the inaugural
> Caribbean Premier League in 2013

- In the same week that George Bailey made his Test debut for Australia in the 2013/14 Ashes, Hollywood announced a sequel to the 1946 Christmas classic *It's a Wonderful Life*. The Frank Capra-produced original starred James Stewart as George Bailey.

- Glenn Robbins, an Australian comedian of *Kath and Kim* fame, padded up for a celebrity cricket match at the MCG in 2007. Opening the batting with former Test star David Boon, Robbins faced three balls before losing his wicket for a duck to New Zealand fast bowler Danny Morrison.

- On the eve of the 2010/11 Ashes series, Shane Warne made his debut as a TV talk show host on Australia's Channel Nine network. The one-hour variety show *Warnie* opened with viewing figures of 854,000 around the nation, but numbers dropped to below 500,000 by the second episode. The series was dumped with one show to go. In polls conducted by the *Weekend Australian* and *Daily Telegraph* newspapers, *Warnie* was voted the worst TV show of 2010.

- Albert Finney, who appeared in films such as *Tom Jones*, *Murder on the Orient Express* and *Erin Brockovich*, played cricket at school. Finney was a wicketkeeper in the first XI at Salford Grammar in Manchester.

Albert Finney (third from left, back row) with his school cricket team in 1953

- The esteemed British actress Peggy Ashcroft, who appeared in dozens of films and TV shows between the 1930s and 80s, once played in a ladies team against a male XI that included fellow actors Harry Andrews and Robert Shaw. Dame Peggy captained her side, with the men bowling underarm and batting left-handed.

- A former champion sprinter who was hired as a fitness trainer for the New Zealand cricket team in 2011 is the son of an international film director. Chris Donaldson is the son of the Australian-born Roger Donaldson, whose film credits include *The Bank Job*, *The Recruit* and *The World's Fastest Indian*.

- Hampshire's Hesketh Hesketh-Prichard appeared in 86 first-class matches in the early 1900s and wrote a novel with his mother that was later turned into a film. *Don Q, Son of Zorro* was rated by the *New York Times* as one of the top ten films of 1925.

- Among the throng to pay tribute to Sachin Tendulkar after he scored his 100th international hundred in 2012 was a leading Bollywood actress from Pakistan. An effusive Veena Malik declared she was an unabashed fan of the Indian batting maestro: **"I'm a Pakistani, but I have prayed for a long time for this moment. Sachin Tendulkar doesn't belong to one nation, caste or creed. His game is adored by cricket lovers all across the world and I am a super-duper fan of Tendulkar."**

Tendulkar's historic milestone coincided with another momentous moment in Indian cricket. The retirement of long-time team-mate Rahul Dravid drew plaudits from Bollywood superstar Shahrukh Khan: **"They say sport serves society by providing vivid examples of excellence. To me the most vivid and dependable has to be Rahul Dravid."**

Indian actor Shahrukh Khan, as a youngster, playing cricket

- The makers of a popular US film used cricket in 2013 to promote the comedy *Anchorman 2: The Legend Continues*. The 50-second clip featured Will Ferrell as the hapless TV newsreader Ron Burgundy talking about the 2013/14 Ashes series which coincided with the premiere of the film in Australia.

> "At this moment Australia and England are locked in a mighty battle of sport. A battle that has raged for 100 years. The pride of each nation is at stake. The spoils, an all-mighty trophy cut from the bone of the gods. He who holds this trophy holds the key to the heart of his nation. Behold the majesty of the prize ... What is this thing? That can't be the trophy. Looks like a shot glass-sized urn. Is this a joke? This is what they're fighting for? I give up!"

- Nasser Hussain, the Indian-born former England Test captain, scored an acting gig in a major Bollywood film released in 2011. A number of other big-name cricketers make an appearance in *Patiala House*, including Andrew Symonds, Kieron Pollard, Herschelle Gibbs and Shaun Tait.

Actor Akshay Kumar (pictured), who played the lead character, took his role so seriously he hired a former Test match bowler to improve his technique: "**I think I am a good enough bowler now to play on a national level.**"

- When the British comedian and actor Terry-Thomas moved to the United States in the 1960s to further his career, he found time to play the occasional game of cricket. Appearing in Hollywood films such as *It's a Mad, Mad, Mad, Mad World* and *How to Murder Your Wife*, Thomas once played in a charity match alongside fellow actors Joan Collins, Milton Berle and Carroll Baker.

Terry-Thomas (far right) with fellow actors Peter Sellers (second from left) and Eric Sykes (front), during a charity cricket match in 1957

Stephen Fry ©
@stephenfry

David Warner is the Dick Dastardly or possibly Terry-Thomas of cricket. Stylish, wicked but impossible not to admire. #TMS

21/11/2013 12:28 pm

- A British comedy from 1934 that revolves around a cricket match has been listed as one of the "most wanted films of all time". *Badger's Green* (pictured), starring Valerie Hobson and Bruce Lester, is included on the British Film Institute's register of movies missing from its collection.

The story is set in the quiet and secluded district of Badger's Green, just at the time of the opening of the cricket season. But the peace is a very short-lived one, for along comes a Mr Butler with a huge development scheme – a scheme to provide rows upon rows of bungalows, places of entertainment, a sanitary laundry and all that goes to making a modern village. The bigwigs are immediately up in arms at the proposal, the doctor, the major and the third citizen resolutely agreeing to stand together to prevent this outrage. It is left, however, for a cricket match to decide the issue – and, although the Badgers are defeated, Mr Butler withdraws his scheme as a token of respect to the doctor, who risked his life for the village.

Daily Film Renter, 1934

- Oliver Gordon, who reportedly took over 6,000 wickets in club cricket in England, was an actor of some note appearing in a number of films in the 1930s. His cricketing career spanned half a century, playing for Harrow, MCC and Buckinghamshire.

• Venkatesh Prasad and Javagal Srinath opened the bowling for India in a number of Tests in the 1990s and early 2000s later appearing alongside each other in a film. The two fast bowlers had parts in the 2014 movie *Sachin! Tendulkar Alla* (*Sachin, not Tendulkar*), with Prasad taking on the role of a coach to an autistic cricket-loving boy named Sachin: "**At first, I told him** [the director] **that I would not be interested, but as I listened to the story and my character narration, I was intrigued. Add to that the fact that Suhasini** [Maniratnam] **was in the film, and I was hooked. Suhasini is a dear friend of the family, and, as an actress who has done hundreds of films, we have sort of grown up on her work. I took up the film only for her.**"

A SELECTION OF MODERN-DAY MOVIES THAT CONTAIN CRICKET REFERENCES

Animal Kingdom (Australia 2010)
Backyard Ashes (Australia 2013)
Becoming Jane (UK 2007)
The Big Lebowski (US 1998)
Cemetery Junction (UK 2010)
The Darjeeling Limited (US 2007)
The Deal (US 2008)
Dean Spanley (UK 2008)
Fool's Gold (US 2008)
Frost/Nixon (US 2008)
Hansie (South Africa 2008)
Hat Trick (India 2007)
Heavenly Creatures (NZ 1994)
Hit for Six! (Barbados 2007)
I Know How Many Runs You Scored Last Summer (Australia 2009)
I Love You Too (Australia 2010)
The Inbetweeners 2 (UK 2014)
Iqbal (India 2005)
Jerry Maguire (US 1996)
Lagaan (India 2001)
Look Both Ways (Australia 2005)
Meerabai Not Out (India 2008)
Mrs Caldicot's Cabbage War (UK 2000)
Main Hood Shahid Afridi (Pakistan 2013)
Nanny McPhee (UK 2005)
Notes on a Scandal (UK 2006)

Oblivion (UK 2003)
Outsourced (US 2006)
Patiala House (India 2011)
Potta Potti 50/50 (India 2011)
Run Fatboy Run (UK 2007)
Sachin! Tendulkar Alla (India 2014)
Safe House (US 2012)
Save Your Legs! (*Knocked for Six*) (Australia 2012)
Seducing Doctor Lewis (Canada 2003)
Shaun of the Dead (UK 2004)
Sinhawalokanaya (*The Cricket Film*) (Sri Lanka 2011)
Slumdog Millionaire (UK 2008)
Snowtown (Australia 2011)
Something Borrowed (US 2011)
Spud (South Africa 2010)
The Square (Australia 2008)
Stumped (India 2003)
Tangiwai – A Love Story (NZ 2011)
Teenage Mutant Ninja Turtles (US 1990)
Texas Killing Fields (US 2011)
Tom Brown's Schooldays (UK 2005)
Victory (India 2008)
Wolf Creek 2 (Australia 2014)
Wondrous Oblivion (UK 2003)
Zero Dark Thirty (US 2012)

- A famous face from 1980s American TV was spotted during the fifth Test of the 2010/11 Ashes in Sydney with David Hasselhoff soaking up proceedings on day two. In Australia to promote a brand of ice cream, the star of *Knight Rider* and *Baywatch* (pictured) turned up with Mark Holden, a former judge on the TV show *Australian Idol*.

- A cult American TV series and a cult Australian cricketer were credited in 2013 as the main contributors to a steep rise in the sales of a brand of whisky. Former Australian batsman and well-known beer drinker David Boon switched sides in 2011 by taking part in an advertising campaign for Canadian Club pre-mixed drinks. At the same time, the *Mad Men* TV series featured the character Don Draper – a Manhattan advertising executive – drinking Canadian Club. Two years later, Canadian Club became the first new brand in a decade to break into the Australian top ten ready-to-drink list.

- Sussex wicketkeeper Rupert Webb later became an actor, scoring a role in the 1994 romantic comedy *Four Weddings and a Funeral*. Webb, who kept for Sussex throughout the 1950s, married actress Barbara Whatley, who had reportedly turned down a marriage proposal from Elvis Presley during the making of a film in the United States.

- While England were taking on Australia in 2010/11, a former Ashes-winning captain and an Aussie TV star did battle in a match organised by London's Metropolitan Police. Mike Gatting and Gold Logie award-winning actor Ray Meagher, of *Home and Away* fame, led two teams of schoolchildren with Gatting's side winning by two runs.

Mike Gatting and Australian actor Ray Meagher in London in 2010 promoting children's participation in sport

- An Oscar-winning American film star was guest of honour at a Twenty20 cricket match staged in Los Angeles in 2008. Billed as the "Hollywood Ashes", *Braveheart* star Mel Gibson tossed the coin for the inaugural game that featured a former Australian captain. In his first match since his retirement in 2004, Steve Waugh scored 40 off 26 balls, including a six that came close to cleaning up Gibson in the VIP tent.

  Australian actor Cameron Daddo played in the 2009 edition, scoring 23 off 17 balls, while former Queensland fast bowler Michael Kasprowicz captained the side and top-scored with an unbeaten 29.

British actor Julian Sands bowling in a Hollywood Twenty20 match

THOMAS PLANT'S DREAM TEAM

David Gower (E)
Alec Stewart † (E)
Viv Richards * (WI)
Ian Botham (E)
Andrew Flintoff (E)
Imran Khan (P)
Vic Marks (E)
Shane Warne (A)
Merv Hughes (A)
Brett Lee (A)
Phil Tufnell (E)

British auctioneer Thomas Plant, from the TV shows Bargain Hunt, Antiques Roadshow *and* Flog It!

DAVID HARPER'S DREAM TEAM

Ricky Ponting (A)
Steve Waugh * (A)
Brian Lara (WI)
Sachin Tendulkar (I)
Ian Botham (E)
Jacques Kallis (SA)
Richard Hadlee (NZ)
Adam Gilchrist † (A)
Shane Warne (A)
Glenn McGrath (A)
Fred Trueman (E)

BBC TV antiques expert David Harper

- Sarah Potter, the daughter of British screenwriter Dennis Potter, scored a Test century for England. Appearing in the fourth of her seven Tests, Potter hit 102 against India at Worcester in 1986. An opening fast bowler, Potter took eight wickets in Tests and ten in one-day internationals.

> "I was lucky that I worked for my father. He was often understandably short-tempered about my typing errors or sloppy filing, but even when we were full-on, say, trying to get out the scripts for *The Singing Detective*, he never once stopped me from running off towards the river, where our local sports centre and the cricket nets were, bat tucked under my arm."
>
> Sarah Potter

- British comedian Tony Hancock was a highly-regarded cricketer at school, achieving a record haul of 70 wickets in 1937. In 1958, Hancock was playing in a charity match and trapped Australian captain Ian Craig in front with his second ball. But the umpire turned down his appeal, saying the crowd had turned up to watch the Australians bat.

- One of America's leading child actors of the 1930s later went on to play for the United States national cricket team. Cliff Severn (pictured), whose film credits include *A Christmas Carol* and *How Green Was My Valley*, was a pioneer of the game in California playing for the Hollywood Cricket Club alongside fellow thespian C. Aubrey Smith. At the age of 39, Severn made his debut for the United States against Canada in Calgary in 1965, scoring 26 and four batting at No. 6.

- In an appearance on the US TV show *Late Night with Jimmy Fallon* in 2012, *Harry Potter*'s Daniel Radcliffe played cricket on stage with the host. In the same year, Fallon also played cricket on the set with UK actor Hugh Laurie, star of the *Blackadder* comedy series and the US medical drama *House*.

  In 1995, Laurie opened the bowling in a celebrity cricket match against a team of England women players at Roehampton. After being run out for ten, Laurie opened the bowling attack with *EastEnders* star Leslie Grantham (1-23), finishing up on the losing side with figures of 0-23.

Jimmy Fallon: **One point two billion people watched the 2011 cricket World Cup this week. Unfortunately, reaction to the cricket World Cup over here in America was … [crickets chirping].**

– from the US chat show *Late Night with Jimmy Fallon*, 2011

- Popular US actor Matthew McConaughey became a big fan of cricket when he travelled around Australia in the late 1980s. The star of blockbusters such as *The Lincoln Lawyer* and *The Wolf of Wall Street,* McConaughey cottoned on to the game while working at a farm in regional New South Wales: **"We'd come in for a 'smoko', and put the cricket on. And I'm talking the full-on, five-day matches, back when Curtly Ambrose and Desmond Haynes were rollin' for the West Indies. I also went to two West Indies-Australia matches and I remember my days at the Tests – you eat a hot dog, you take a nap, you wake up, then maybe you catch the first wicket. Then you drink some beer and then take another nap. It was cool man."**

- Lou Ferrigno, who found fame on television screens as The Incredible Hulk, once appeared in a testimonial cricket match for a former England Test cricketer. The internationally-renowned bodybuilder and actor was a guest at the match in Los Angeles in 1981 for Norman Gifford, who later captained England at the age of 44 in a one-day international series at Sharjah in 1984/85.

- A 2015 World Cup moment was picked up a major TV network in the United States with Pakistan's Haris Sohail named the "World's Worst Person in Sports". Sohail was reportedly spooked by what he claimed was a ghost in his hotel room in Christchurch, with Keith Olbermann (pictured) handing the Pakistan batsman the unwanted award on his top-rating ESPN sports show.

A Family Affair

- A pair of brothers once combined for a triple-century partnership in the final of a major first-class tournament after their team had been asked to follow-on. In The Rest's all-out total of 387 in the 1943/44 Bombay Pentangular Tournament Final against Hindus, the Hazare brothers added exactly 300 in partnership, with Vijay taking control: **"I tried to play from both ends. The result was I scored 309 and Vivek only 21."** The total of 387 remains the smallest in first-class cricket to contain a triple-century.

    The Wells brothers of Sussex engaged in a similar rescue act in a match during the 1987 County Championship. Following-on against Kent at Hove, Alan hit an unbeaten 161, while his elder brother Colin made an unbeaten 140 in a fourth-wicket stand of 303.

- The father and a brother of the former Madras-born England Test captain Nasser Hussain also played first-class cricket. Joe Hussain appeared in a single first-class match, for Madras in 1964/65, as did Nasser's older brother Mel, for Worcestershire in 1985.

- South African fast bowler Morne Morkel shone with the bat on his first-class debut, securing a ninth-wicket partnership of 141 with his brother Albie against the touring West Indians in 2003/04. After the pair had opened the bowling for Easterns at Benoni, Albie then hit 132 and Morne an unbeaten 44 in a first-innings total of 313.

- In 1989/90, Azhar Hossain struck Bangladesh's first half-century in a one-day international, opening the batting with a score of 54 against New Zealand at Sharjah. In 1998/99, his nephew Mehrab Hossain hit Bangladesh's first one-day international century (101), against Zimbabwe at Dhaka.

- In the same week that England's Joe Root scored 200 off 298 balls in a Test match, his younger brother Billy scored 200 off the same number of balls for the Nottinghamshire club. Joe's maiden Test match double-century – unbeaten – came in the first Test against Sri Lanka at Lord's in 2014, while Billy scored his 200 for the Notts second XI, against Derbyshire at Nottingham. Joe became the first batsman to make two scores of 175 or more in consecutive Test innings at the home of cricket, after 180 against Australia in 2013.

  The same month of June saw another set of brothers scoring near-identical centuries – both against international sides touring the UK. In his second Test match for England – the second against Sri Lanka at Leeds – Sam Robson scored a maiden Test century of 127, while his younger brother Angus scored 126 (retired out) for Leicestershire in a three-day match against the Indians at Grace Road.

- During 2008, two brothers made their international debuts – but for different countries. James Pattinson took out man-of-the-match honours in his first match for Australia in the Under-19 World Cup, while his older brother Darren made his Test debut for England, against South Africa at Headingley. James's debut match – against Nepal in Malaysia – was captained by Michael Hill, whose mother Sharyn Fitzsimmons appeared in three Tests for Australia in 1978/79.

  In 2009/10, the fast-bowling Pattinsons became the first siblings to appear together in a first-class match for Victoria for nearly 50 years when they played against South Australia at Melbourne. Darren and James opened the bowling in the match – in which neither took a wicket nor scored a run – becoming the first brothers to represent Victoria since Bob and David Cowper in the 1960s. When James made his Test debut in 2011/12, he and Darren became the first set of brothers to play Test cricket solely for a different country. James appeared in his first Test for Australia, against New Zealand at Brisbane, after Darren's single Test for England.

- Three sets of brothers played in the South Australia-New South Wales Sheffield Shield match in 1909/10. Roy and Leslie Minnett and Edgar and Mick Waddy lined up for the visitors, while Les, Clem and Stanley Hill played for South Australia. Edgar scored 118 in his side's first-innings total of 184, while Clem scored the other century in the match, with 205 in South Australia's first innings.

- In the same match that his brother became the first wicketkeeper to achieve seven dismissals in a first-class innings in Australia, Bill Tallon posted career-best bowling figures. Don Tallon picked up nine dismissals against Victoria at Brisbane in 1938/39, while Bill took 2-87 and 5-77, with Don achieving a stumping off his brother in each innings.

- Kate and Alex Blackwell, the first set of identical twins – male or female – to play cricket for Australia, combined for a match-winning 100-run stand in a one-day international against England at the MCG in 2007/08. Opening the batting, Alex scored a maiden century (101) in Australian colours, while Kate hit an unbeaten 57.

- When Kyshona Knight made her debut for the West Indies in 2012/13, she joined her identical twin sister Kycia in the team. The first twins to play for the West Indies, Kycia made her debut in 2011.

  The first match in which they played together – a one-day international against Sri Lanka in Dominica – featured a team-mate who also had a cricket-playing twin. Anisa Mohammed's twin Alisa made her debut for Trinidad and Tobago in 2007/08.

> "We get them mixed up at times but I think it's all about understanding them and getting to know them as time goes on. Even though they are twins they are two different characters. They're identical, but if you look at them carefully you can see the difference. It's not a problem for me because I've known them for a long time."
>
> West Indies women's captain Merissa Aguillera

Kyshona and Kycia Knight during the 2013 Women's World Cup

- A set of twins made their debuts for Australia in 2008/09, with one later appearing in an Ashes Test match. Adam Coyte made his debut for the Australian under-19s in a one-day international at Hobart, while his twin sister Sarah debuted for the Australian Women's under-21s in Sydney. In 2010/11, Scott, the older brother of the Coyte twins took a hat-trick for New South Wales in the Sheffield Shield, while Sarah made her Test debut for Australia, against England at Blacktown in Sydney.

- Brothers Thomas and William Eden made their first-class debuts in the same match for New Zealand side Nelson in 1874/75. In their next appearance together, at Nelson in 1876/77, they bowled unchanged with Wellington all out for just 37, Thomas taking 3-17 and his brother 5-17. They returned remarkably similar figures in the second innings as Wellington fell for a total of 60 – 14-2-28-3 for Thomas and 14-4-24-4 for William.

- Former Pakistan Test batsman Mohammad Ilyas staged a hunger strike in 2007 in protest against a ban forbidding him entry to Lahore's Gaddafi Stadium. His exclusion followed a stoush with the Pakistan Cricket Board and national selectors over their decision not to pick his son-in-law Imran Farhat for a one-day international series against Sri Lanka: **"If Imran performs and he is not selected again then I will also stage a protest. The war is on with PCB and I will fight it for the sake of dignity and self-esteem of a former Test cricketer."**

- When South Africa toured Australia in 1963/64, they played in a match that included the father of a future Test cricket superstar. Stan Gilchrist, the father of Adam, represented Australian Universities in a two-day match in the Queensland town of Toowoomba. Although he made a duck with the bat, he picked up 2-59 with the ball, accounting for big names Colin Bland and Graeme Pollock.

- Sri Lanka's Malinda Warnapura followed in the footsteps of his uncle Bandula by opening the batting on his Test debut. Bandula captained Sri Lanka in their inaugural Test, against England at Colombo in 1981/82, while his nephew Malinda opened his Test account with a duck, against Bangladesh at Colombo in 2007.

- Stuart MacGill's grandfather once dismissed the great Don Bradman in a first-class match at the WACA. Charlie MacGill, an opening batsman, appeared in six first-class matches for Western Australia, taking 19 wickets, dismissing Bradman for 42 at Perth in 1939/40. Stuart played in 184 first-class matches – for Western Australia, New South Wales, Somerset and Nottinghamshire – taking 774 wickets at 30.49. His father Terry also played first-class cricket, securing 23 wickets in 12 games for WA at an average of 40.04.

- When the South African-born Ollie Hutton made his debut in 2004, he joined both of his grandfathers who had also played first-class cricket. Yorkshire's Len Hutton was one, who appeared in 79 Test matches for England between 1937 and 1955; Ben Brocklehurst was the other – he played in 64 first-class matches for Somerset, making his debut against Hutton and Yorkshire at Taunton in 1954.

- In a one-day international against Australia at Port-of-Spain in 1994/95, West Indies openers Phil Simmons and Stuart Williams were both dismissed for a score of six. The next time both West Indies openers went for six in a ODI came in 2014 against Bangladesh at St Kitts, with Simmons's nephew Lendl and Chris Gayle dismissed on the same score.

- Brothers Andy and Pete Blomerus shared all ten wickets in a club match in England in 2008, becoming the first twins to perform the feat in the Hampshire League. Andy took 6-28 and Pete 4-34 for Gosport Borough in their 150-run victory over IBM South Hampshire.

- The father-and-son combination of Lisle and Lisle McNamara both played for the South African province of Griqualand West and both played the same number of first-class matches. The father appeared in 35 matches between 1936/37 and 1950/51 with a top score of 119, while his son had a ten-year career of 35 games starting in 1962/63, acquiring a best score of 78.

- During 2010, Pakistan made history when three brothers from the same family kept wicket in international matches. Replacing Zulqarnain Haider, Adnan Akmal – the 200th Pakistani to appear in a Test – donned the gloves for Pakistan against South Africa, in the same year as his brother Kamran. Umar, a middle-order batsman, also stood behind the stumps for the first time in 2010 – in place of Haider – during a one-day international against the South Africans in Dubai.

- On the same day that James Marshall scored a first-class century for the touring New Zealanders at Chelmsford in 2008, his twin brother Hamish scored one for Gloucestershire. James hit 128 in the NZ win over Essex, while Hamish made 105 against Glamorgan in the County Championship at Bristol.

- The father of South African legend Mike Procter also played first-class cricket, making his debut against the touring England side in 1938/39. After horrible figures of 2-114 off 13 overs for Eastern Province against MCC at Port Elizabeth, Woodrow Procter took 3-28 and 2-22 against Border in his second, and final, first-class appearance, in 1939/40. Mike Procter's brother Anthony also played first-class cricket, as did their cousin Andrew.

- A pair of brothers starred in Papua New Guinea's first-ever one-day international, played in Australia in 2014/15. Chris Amini captained the side to a memorable first-up four-wicket win over Hong Kong in the match at Townsville, while his brother Charles top-scored, steering his side home with an unbeaten 61 batting at seven.

On a historic day for Papua New Guinea, and the Amini family, Chris emulated his father, Charles, who, in 1996/97, had also captained PNG against Hong Kong in the ICC Trophy in Kuala Lumpur. The brothers' grandfather, Brian, also skippered PNG in the late 1970s, as had their mother, Kune, who led their country in the 2007/08 World Cup Qualifying Series in South Africa. In 2006, Kune and her sister-in-law Cheryl batted PNG to a win over Japan in a 50-over match in Port Moresby, scoring 41 not out and 29 not out respectively.

In the same season that his mother led PNG in South Africa, Colin Amini was captain in the under-19 World Cup in Malaysia.

BROTHERS MAKING ONE-DAY INTERNATIONAL DEBUTS IN SAME MATCH

Brothers	Match	Venue	Season
Ian and Greg Chappell (A)			
Dayle and Richard Hadlee (NZ)	Australia v England	Melbourne	1970/71
Sadiq and Mushtaq Mohammad (P)	New Zealand v Pakistan	Christchurch	1972/73
Minhajul and Nurul Abedin (B)			
Maurice and Tito Odumbe (K)	Bangladesh v Pakistan	Moratuwa	1985/86
Steve and David Tikolo (K)	India v Kenya	Cuttack	1995/96
David and Collins Obuya (K)	Kenya v West Indies	Nairobi	2001
Bjorn and Deon Kotze (N)	Zimbabwe v Namibia	Harare	2002/03
Paul and John Mooney (I)			
Dom (I) and Ed Joyce (E)	Ireland v England	Belfast	2006
Charles and Chris Amini (PNG)	PNG v Hong Kong	Townsville	2014/15

- South Africa's Dale Benkenstein, who made his one-day international debut in 1998/99, is the son of Martin Benkenstein who played first-class cricket for Rhodesia. Dale's twin brothers – Brett and Boyd – also appeared in first-class cricket.

- A pair of brothers made their domestic debuts in the West Indies in 2007/08, with one doing so at the age of 50. Slow bowler Carlton Saunders and his younger brother Henry appeared in their only match – a Twenty20 – for Turks & Caicos against Montserrat in Coolidge.

- A half-brother of South African-born England batsman Jonathan Trott made his debut for another country in 1999, scoring the only unbeaten 50 in the match. Kenny Jackson, who made his first-class debut in 1988/89, struck an undefeated 88 for the Netherlands against Cambridgeshire in the NatWest Trophy.

- Free State batsman Justin Orchard only appeared in a single first-class match, as did his uncle Eric Orchard. Justin, who marked his first of two innings at the crease with a duck in 1995/96, is the son of umpire Dave Orchard – who played in 43 first-class games for Natal – and grandson of Kenneth Orchard, who turned out in four matches for Natal in the late 1940s.

- Victoria's Richard Philpott only made one first-class appearance, in Australia's inaugural first-class match at Launceston in 1850/51, under the captaincy of his brother William. Richard's grandson also played first-class cricket, appearing in 19 matches for Somerset between 1904 and 1911.

- A cricket club closed down by the onset of the Second World War was resuscitated 67 years later in 2006. The first delivery for the new Etchingham and Fontridge club was bowled by Matt Neve, whose grandfather had sent down the final ball for the club before it shut down in 1939. Neve's great-grandfather also played for the club in the 1930s.

- Following the Border-Gavaskar Trophy in 2011/12, Australia played a different set of brothers in consecutive internationals against India. For a Twenty20 match at the MCG, Shaun and Mitchell Marsh were included in the XI, while for a one-day international that followed – also at the MCG two days later – Mike and David Hussey played.

- In 2012/13, a son of a former Indian Test player made his first-class debut in a domestic tournament in Sri Lanka. Digvijay Amarnath became a third-generation first-class cricketer with his father Surinder appearing in ten Tests and his grandfather Lala, 24. Two of Digvijay's uncles – Mohinder and Rajinder – also played first-class cricket, with the former appearing in 69 Tests.

  A few weeks later, Fabian Cowdrey made his first-class debut, for Cardiff MCCU against Glamorgan at Sophia Gardens. Fabian's father Chris, grandfather Colin, and great-grandfather Ernest had all played first-class cricket. Fabian's uncle, Graham Cowdrey, also appeared in first-class cricket.

- When Tamil Nadu's Baba Indrajith and Baba Aparajith played against Saurashtra in 2013/14 it represented the first time a set of twins had played first-class cricket in India. The then-19-year-olds were both dismissed by the same wicketkeeper-bowler combination in their first outing together in the match at Chennai.

- Jenny Wostrack, a niece of the legendary West Indies batsman Frank Worrell, played for Surrey. In six major limited-over matches for Surrey Women in 1989, she scored 135 runs with a top score of 59 not out and an average of 45.00.

- In 2010, an uncle and nephew opened the bowling in a one-day international. Kenya's Thomas Odoyo took 2-25, and his nephew Nelson Odhiambo 1-32, against the Netherlands at Voorburg.

- The final of the UK Village Cup played at Lord's in 2012 featured six pairs of brothers, with three on each side. The Heslam brothers, William and James, opened the batting for Reed, with their No. 3 Tom Greaves dismissing Woodhouse Grange's Chris Bilton with his first ball, and getting his brother Andrew Bilton soon after.

- During a first-class match against the touring New Zealand team of 1972/73, the three Chappell brothers all lined up for South Australia with each passing 50. One of only three occasions that the brothers had played for the same side in first-class cricket, Ian scored an unbeaten 101 and Trevor 63 in the second innings, while Greg made 59 in the first. The Chappells had appeared in two Sheffield Shield matches earlier in the season, against Queensland at Brisbane and against Western Australia in Adelaide.

  They also played together in two matches the following summer, with Ian and Trevor representing South Australia, while Greg played for Queensland. In a Sheffield Shield match at Brisbane, Ian captained South Australia scoring a pair of half-centuries (70 and 126), while Greg captained Queensland with a half-century (56) in his only innings. In the return match between the two sides two months later at Adelaide, Greg scored two fifties (158* and 72), while Ian scored one (54). Trevor failed to reach 20 in the two matches, with scores of 16, one, ten and six.

THE CHAPPELL BROTHERS
IN THE SAME FIRST-CLASS SIDE

	Runs	Bowling	Catches	Match	Venue	Season
Ian	27	1-1	3			
Greg	77	0-6 and 0-2	1			
Trevor	67	-	1	SA v Qld	Brisbane	1972/73
Ian	44 and 50	0-1	2			
Greg	13 and 53	0-23 and 3-5	0			
Trevor	70 and 41*	-	0	SA v WA	Adelaide	1972/73
Ian	0 and 101*	2-16	1			
Greg	59	1-45	0			
Trevor	4 and 63	-	1	SA v New Zealanders	Adelaide	1972/73

- On his first-grade debut, for the Campbelltown-Camden club in 1993/94, Brett Lee took 4-58, while his brother Shane took 5-86. Shane caught Brett's first victim in the match, against University of New South Wales. The Waugh twins also combined to take nine wickets in an innings, with Steve taking 6-53 and Mark 3-31 for Bankstown-Canterbury against Sydney in 1984/85.

- Appearing in his second first-grade cricket match in Sydney, a 16-year-old Richie Benaud scored 98 against Marrickville in 1949/50, with his father Lou taking 4-22. Richie also achieved a four-wicket haul, with Cumberland coasting to victory and the pair claiming the best father-son performance in the history of Sydney grade cricket.

- Mike Hussey and his younger brother David were both dismissed for a duck by the same bowler in a one-day international in 2011. On his debut for Sri Lanka, spinner Seekkuge Prasanna took the wickets of both brothers within the space of three deliveries in the fourth ODI at Colombo. In the second final of the 2011/12 CB Series in Adelaide, Sri Lanka's Lasith Malinga bowled the two brothers, Mike for six, and David for seven.

- On his one-day international debut, against Zimbabwe, at Harare in 2001/02, England's Jeremy Snape dismissed the Flower brothers in the same over. Andy and Grant were both stumped by James Foster, who was also making his debut.

- Pakistan's Saqlain Mushtaq once took four wickets in five balls, including a hat-trick, in a one-day international with all of his victims related to another player in the team. In the third ODI against Zimbabwe at Peshawar in 1996/97, Saqlain dismissed Grant Flower, John Rennie and Andy Whitall with consecutive deliveries and added Gavin Rennie with the first ball of his next over. Andy Flower and Guy Whittall – a cousin of Andy – were also playing in the match.

  In the second Test against Australia at Sharjah in 2002/03, Saqlain accounted for the Waugh twins – Mark and Steve – with consecutive deliveries. In the first Test of the series – played at the neutral venue of Colombo – Shoaib Akhtar had dismissed both of the Waughs for a duck within the space of three balls.

- Arjun Tendulkar, the son of Sachin, hit a maiden century in 2012 during the Mumbai Cricket Association under-14s trials. Aged 12 at the time, Arjun scored 124 in an innings victory for Khar Gymkhana against Goregaon Centre.

> **"First cricket has to be in your heart, then it gets to your brain. They key is to be madly in love with cricket, which he [Arjun] is."**
>
> Sachin Tendulkar

- England batsman Nick Compton followed in his grandfather's footsteps in 2013 when he was named one of *Wisden*'s Five Cricketers of the Year. The first instance of a grandfather and grandson achieving the distinction, Denis Compton was a winner in 1939.

- Cricket in the Victorian town of Ballarat made history in 2013 when a father and his three daughters turned out for the Combine club. Mark Sculley and daughters Rebecca, Samantha and Emily counted among five members of the family in the team, with Jason, Mark's brother, also playing.

- During the calendar year of 2008, a brother and sister both opened the bowling for Queensland in Twenty20 matches. Nathan Rimmington took 2-28 against New South Wales at Brisbane in the 2008/09 Twenty20 Big Bash, while his sister Rikki-Lee Rimmington had figures of 0-24 against Western Australia in Brisbane in the 2007/08 Women's Interstate Twenty20 tournament.

- When Kuwait took on Bangladesh at the 2014/15 Asian Games Men's Competition, its captain was a 58-year-old Bastaki Mahmoud, while their vice-captain was his son, Bastaki Fahad. In a quarter-final match of the Twenty20 series in the South Korean city of Incheon, the father and son combined to dismiss Test batsman Tamim Iqbal for 28, who scored seven more runs than the entire Kuwaiti XI (21).

> **"Though it was a bad delivery, it gave me a lot of pleasure, especially because my father took the catch. As I'm also a wicketkeeper, I have taken many catches off my father's bowling, but it was the first time that the reverse happened. I will remember this moment for the rest of my life."**
>
> Bastaki Fahad

- Sewnarine Chattergoon celebrated his 27th birthday by making his Test debut for the West Indies in 2008 and joining his brother on the international stage. When Sewnarine received his first Test cap for the match against Sri Lanka at Port-of-Spain, he went one better than his brother Hemnarine Chattergoon, who had debuted for Canada in a first-class match against the United Arab Emirates in Toronto the year before.

- When Auckland dismissed Wellington for 199 in a Plunket Shield match at the Basin Reserve in 2014/15, three brothers shared nine catches. Apart from opener Brady Barnett who was trapped leg before wicket, all other nine wickets fell after catches from the Cachopa brothers – Brad (5), Craig (3) and Carl (1).

- A six-year-old boy put his father to shame in 2013 when he outscored him in a village cricket tournament in Wales. Harrison Parsons was drafted into the local cricket team by his dad Jeremy as a joke but the youngster prevailed, scoring 24 in a match in which his father made 15.

- In the English summer of 1978, brothers David and John Steele both scored the same number of first-class runs and at the same average. In 31 completed innings each, both made 1,182 runs at 38.12.

- On his first-class debut for South Australia in 1937/38, Phil Ridings did so under the watchful eye of his father, one of the umpires. He scored 20 in his maiden first-class innings, in the match against Western Australia at Adelaide, after his dad had rejected an lbw appeal when he was on three.

  In 2006, a one-day international saw the unique instance of a father umpiring and his son playing. During the Kenya-Bangladesh match at Nairobi, Subhash Modi put up his finger in declaring his son Hitesh Modi – in his last ODI – out lbw for a score of one.

- When the touring West Indians took on Warwickshire at Edgbaston in 1923, the match provided the only instance in first-class cricket of the two umpires being the fathers of two of the players. Sydney Santall and Thomas Smart presided over the game, in which Reg Santall and John Smart played for Warwickshire.

- During the MCC tour of India in 1933/34, one of their first-class matches was umpired by a father and son. Frank Tarrant, who played in 329 first-class matches, and his son, Louis, who appeared in one, were put in charge of the Southern Punjab-MCC game at Amritsar.

  A MCC tour of the West Indies in 1947/48 also included a match overseen by a father-son combination, with Sam and Perry Burke umpiring the game against Jamaica at Kingston.

INSTANCES OF FATHER AND SON
UMPIRING A FIRST-CLASS MATCH

Umpires	Match	Venue	Season
Thomas and Thomas Sherwell	Gentlemen v Players	The Oval	1863
Frank and Louis Tarrant	Southern Punjab v MCC	Amritsar	1933/34
Sam and Perry Burke	Jamaica v MCC	Kingston	1947/48
Mysore Vijaysarathi and M.V. Nagendra	Andhra v Mysore	Bangalore	1960/61

- When New Zealand powered its way to 487/7 declared against Zimbabwe in 2000/01, a set of brothers-in-law posted their country's highest-ever fifth-wicket partnership. Nathan Astle scored 141 at No. 5, while Craig McMillan went one better, with 142 at No. 6. The big-hitting Kiwis, who married a pair of sisters, put on 222 in the one-off

Test at Wellington, beating the previous best of 183 against Pakistan in 1976/77.

During the 2004 Champions Trophy ODI tournament, Astle (145*) and McMillan (64*) forged another electrifying stand for the fifth wicket, one of 136 in 7.4 overs against the USA at The Oval, with McMillan bringing up his 50 off just 21 balls.

- South Africa's Albie Morkel got his first chance at the highest level in 2008/09, making his debut at the expense of his brother Morne who was dropped for the third Test against Australia at Cape Town. Albie went on to score a half-century (58), copying Mark Waugh, who made a half-century, and then a century, in his debut Test innings, having replaced his brother Steve in 1990/91.

- A club match in Western Australia in 2014/15 saw a father and son rewrite the local record books with a tenth-wicket partnership of 168. With Halls Head struggling at 61/9 in the match against Warnbro Swans in Mandurah, Joe Lovell came to the crease to join his father David, who went on to score 123 not out, hitting 12 fours and six sixes. Joe scored 36 having earlier taken 3-41.

- With his niece Alyssa already a member of the Australian women's Test team, Ian Healy's son Tom gained his first national call-up in 2014/15. A wicketkeeper like his dad and Alyssa, he made his debut for Australia in a youth one-day international against Sri Lanka in Colombo.

- When Craig McDermott's son Ben made his first-class debut for Queensland in 2014/15 he joined his older brother Alister in the 12, becoming the first set of siblings to play first-class cricket for the Bulls since Ian and Ken Healy in the 1980s. Batting at No. 3 in the match against South Australia at Adelaide, Ben fell for a first-ball duck, part of a hat-trick by Chadd Sayers on the first morning of the Sheffield Shield season. Sayers's father Dean appeared in three first-class matches for SA in the early 1980s, while his brother Aaron played for the state's second XI in 2007/08.

- A father and son both took five wickets in the same innings in a 30-over match in the small New South Wales town of Bexhill in 2012. Playing for Goonellabah Workers Sports against Southern Cross University, Michael Mansfield, 56, took the first five wickets to fall while his 17-year-old son Kody claimed the remaining five.

- A three-day match at Nagpur in 1963/64 saw the unique occurrence of a father taking the wicket of his son in first-class cricket. Ashok Mankad – representing the Maharashtra Chief Minister's XI – was dismissed for 24 by Vinoo Mankad, who was playing for the Maharashtra Governor's XI.

- Former opener Geoff Marsh made history in 2014 when his son Mitchell made his Test debut. Geoff became the first Australian, and just the third cricketer overall, to have produced two Test-playing sons after India's Lala Amarnath and New Zealand's Walter Hadlee (pictured).

Already the only father-and-son combination with centuries in one-day international cricket, Geoff and Shaun became the first father and son to score Test centuries for Australia when Shaun made 141 in his first match, against Sri Lanka at Pallekele in 2011.

> "I spent most of my years in the backyard bowling to him. I didn't get much sympathy from Shaun. I usually had to pretty much beg him to play and then I'd just bowl and once he'd had enough he'd hit the ball into the bushes and that was it. I'm not sure how I became some sort of batsman."
>
> Mitchell Marsh
> on the eve of the two brothers playing together for the first time
> in a Test, against India at Brisbane, in 2014/15

FATHER AND TWO SONS TO PLAY TEST CRICKET

Father and Sons	Test Debuts	Venue	Season
Lala Amarnath	India v England	Mumbai	1933/34
Mohinder Amarnath	India v Australia	Chennai	1969/70
Surinder Amarnath	India v New Zealand	Auckland	1975/76
Walter Hadlee †	New Zealand v England	Lord's	1937
Dayle Hadlee	New Zealand v England	Lord's	1969
Richard Hadlee	New Zealand v Pakistan	Wellington	1972/73
Geoff Marsh	Australia v India	Adelaide	1985/86
Shaun Marsh	Australia v Sri Lanka	Pallekele	2011
Mitchell Marsh	Australia v Pakistan	Dubai	2014/15

† *Walter Hadlee's son Barry also appeared in two one-day internationals*

- Hanif and Shoaib Mohammad are the only father and son to both pass 200 in Test match cricket. Hanif made 337 against the West Indies in 1957/58 and 203 not out, against New Zealand at Lahore in 1964/65. Shoaib matched his father in 1989/90 by also scoring an unbeaten 203, against India at Lahore, and made another 203 not out the following season, against New Zealand at Karachi.

- Although Pakistan succumbed to Australia in a semi-final of the 2010 World Twenty20 tournament, they provided the first example of brothers scoring a half-century in the same match. Kamran Akmal made 50 at the top of the innings, while his younger brother Umar scored an unbeaten 56 at No. 3. In the same match – at Gros Islet – Mike Hussey (60*) produced a 22-ball fifty, the fastest by an Australian in the competition's history, beating his brother David, who had reached 50 off 27 balls in the previous match, also against Pakistan, two weeks earlier at the same venue.

- Jahangir Khan and his son Majid Khan both achieved the all-round double of a century and five wickets in an innings on their first-class debuts. Jahangir scored 108 and took 7-42 in his first match, for Muslims against Hindus at Lahore in 1928/29, while his son produced a double of 111 not out and 6-67 for Khaipur against Lahore B in the same city in 1961/62. The only other player to achieve the double on first-class debut is Imran Bucha (120 and 5-40) for Servis Industries against Lahore B, again in Lahore, in 1976/77.

- Australia's Joe Burns followed a great-uncle into the ranks of first-class cricket in 2010/11, marking his debut for Queensland with a century. The youngster struck an unbeaten 140 and 41 against South Australia in Adelaide. Harold Burns, a wicketkeeper, appeared in five matches for Queensland in the early 1930s.

- With an innings of 107 in a Quaid-e-Azam Trophy match at Hyderabad in 2014/15, Shehzar Mohammad joined his grandfather and father in having scored a century in first-class cricket. Shehzar's grandfather Hanif made 55 first-class centuries, while his father Shoaib scored 38.

    Other families to have achieved the same feat previously are the Townsends (England) – Frank (2), Charlie (21) and David (4), the Khans (Pakistan) – Jahangir (4), Majid (73) and Bazid (15), the Huttons (England) – Len (177), Richard (5), Ben (18) and the Meulemans (Australia) – Ken (22), Robert (1) and Scott (2).

    Shehzar's maiden three-figure score – for PIA against the Hyderabad Hawks – made him the tenth member of the Mohammad family to have scored a first-class century.

- Kenya's Lameck Onyango, who made his debut for Kenya in 1996, was the first of six members of his family to play for the national team. Three of his brothers – Shem Ngoche, James Ngoche and Nehemiah Odhiambo – have also played one-day international cricket, while two sisters – Margaret Banja and Mary Bele – appeared for the Kenyan women's team.

- Shane Warne's son took a hat-trick for his school cricket side in 2014/15. Appearing in his first season for the Year 10 XI at Brighton Grammar School in Melbourne, Jackson, a pace bowler, captured four wickets in five balls finishing with figures of 5/4.

- A cousin of former Australian fast bowler Andy Bichel made his debut in the Big Bash League in 2012/13 but didn't bat or bowl in his three appearances. Chris Sabburg, whose uncle, Dirk Tazelaar, appeared in 83 first-class matches for Queensland, was part of the winning Brisbane Heat team.

Twenty20 Teasers

- After Rahul Dewan made a duck in a domestic Twenty20 game in India in 2010/11, his opening partner went on to score 99. Playing for Haryana against Punjab at Delhi, Mukul Dagar became the first batsman to score 99 not out on his Twenty20 debut.

- Upon losing Parthiv Patel to the first ball of a match at Cuttack in the 2012 IPL, the Deccan Chargers pair of Cameron White and Kumar Sangakkara put on a record third-wicket partnership of 157 against Pune Warriors. Manish Pandey was also dismissed first ball, the first time in the IPL that both teams had lost a wicket off the first ball of their innings.

- An IPL match at Uppal in 2014 saw three batsman top-scoring with 68. Hyderabad opener Aaron Finch and Mumbai's Lendl Simmons and Ambati Rayudu were each dismissed for 68, the highest score in the match.

- In 2010/11, New Zealand's Tim Southee became the first bowler to take five wickets and a hat-trick in the same Twenty20 international. Southee struck five times in nine deliveries during the first Twenty20 against Pakistan at Auckland, finishing with 5-18, with his hat-trick the second by a New Zealander, and the third overall, in international Twenty20 cricket.

- Deccan Chargers fast bowler Ishant Sharma dismissed four batsmen for a duck in a fiery spell in the 2011 IPL, taking five wickets against Kochi Tuskers. After four overs of the match, the Tuskers were reeling with individual scores of 0, 4, 0, 0, 0 and 0 emblazoned on the scoreboard. Sharma took 5-12 in three overs in the match, in which seven Kochi batsmen failed to get off the mark.

- During the running of the third Twenty20 international, two debutants returned the identical bowling figures of 3-20. In the match against South Africa at Johannesburg in 2005/06, New Zealand spinner Jeetan Patel and his team-mate Nathan Astle both posted figures of 4-0-20-3.

    Two debutants also claimed three wickets in the very first Twenty20 international, played between New Zealand and Australia at Auckland in 2004/05. Michael Kasprowicz took 4-29, after Kyle Mills had picked up 3-44 opening the bowling for the hosts.

- To mark the 20th Twenty20 international, South Africa and the West Indies provided the first instance of rival teams recording a 100-run partnership in the same match. Played at Johannesburg in 2007/08, Chris Gayle (117) and Devon Smith (35) began proceedings with a 145-run opening stand, while Herschelle Gibbs (90*) and Justin Kemp (46*) responded with an ultimately match-winning third-wicket partnership of 120.

- When Australia beat Pakistan by 34 runs at the 2010 World Twenty20 competition, the match provided the first instance of all 20 wickets falling in the shortest form of the game. Australia's last over was also record-breaking with as many as five wickets tumbling, another first in international cricket.

- Western Australia sprung a big surprise in the opening match of the 2010/11 Big Bash tournament by picking a 36-year-old Victorian fast bowler who hadn't played state cricket for three years. Mick Lewis – famous for conceding a record 113 runs in his final one-day international – opened the bowling for the Warriors against the Tasmanian Tigers at Perth, taking two wickets in his opening over, and three in the match, the first wicket coming off his very first ball. So left-of-field was Lewis's resurrection, the Cricinfo website had initially listed another player – Oxford University batsman Mark Lewis – on its scorecard.

    Another debutant also picked up a wicket with his first delivery in the match. Tasmania import Ryan ten Doeschate, from the Netherlands, dismissed big guns Luke Pomersbach and Chris Gayle in his only over, while their other overseas player, Pakistani Naved-ul-Hasan, took 3-19.

- Despite losing a Twenty20 match in 2012 by 20 runs, the Wayamba United team made history with a 120-run partnership. Chasing 172 to beat Uva Next in the Sri Lanka Premier League, Wayamba crashed to 27/7 before the first instance in Twenty20 of a 100-run stand for the eighth wicket. Azhar Mahmood led the charge with an unbeaten 75, with Isuru Udana hitting 42.

- David Warner was a stand-out performer during the 2011 Champions League becoming the first batsman to score two consecutive Twenty20 centuries. The New South Wales batsman cracked a blinder against the Chennai Super Kings, his unbeaten 135 off 69 balls becoming the highest score to date in the tournament's history. Batting left- *and* right-handed, Warner smacked 11 fours and eight sixes, with his 92 runs in boundaries establishing a new benchmark in the competition. One of his sixes off Blues team-mate Doug Bollinger was sent sailing 108 metres out of the stadium. In his next innings – against Bangalore – Warner was just as brutal, thrashing six fours and 11 sixes in an unbeaten knock of 123, in vain, against Bangalore. Chris Gayle – who would later partner Warner at the top for the Sydney Thunder in the Australian Big Bash League – was even more ferocious, scoring 92 off 41 balls, with eight fours and eight sixes, and a strike rate of 224.39.

  Warner was the leading run-scorer in the competition and the only one to top 300. He made 328 runs in five matches at an average of 109.33 and also scored the most runs in boundaries (228), followed by Gayle (204). His elation at scoring back-to-back hundreds was short-lived, suffering back-to-back ducks in his next two Twenty20 innings. Facing South Africa in a two-match series, the Australian opener was run out off his first ball at Cape Town and then copped a nine-ball duck at Johannesburg.

- When Dirk Nannes picked up his maiden five-wicket haul in Twenty20 cricket, he did so at the home of cricket. Playing for Surrey against Middlesex at Lord's in 2011, the Victorian took a match-winning 5-40, which he later described as "absolute rubbish": "**I was bowling terrible all day, but batsmen kept finding the fielders. It was more a case of their bad day turning good for me.**"

- En route to the first below-50 total in British Twenty20 cricket, Paul Collingwood claimed a hat-trick and a match-winning haul of 5-6. Representing Durham in the Friends Life Twenty20 tournament in 2011, Collingwood presided over a Northamptonshire collapse that saw them all out for just 47 in 12.5 overs.

- Appearing in his only Twenty20 international, South Africa's Alfonso Thomas took a wicket with his first delivery. The opening fast bowler took 3-25 in the match against Pakistan at Johannesburg in 2006/07, becoming just the second bowler to take a wicket first-up on his Twenty20 international debut. The first to do so was Australia's Michael Kasprowicz (4-29), who took wickets with his first two deliveries, in the very first Twenty20 international, against New Zealand at Auckland in 2004/05.

- Barbados slow bowler Ashley Nurse had two five-wicket hauls to his credit in his first ten Twenty20 matches. In his fourth match – the final of the 2010 Caribbean Twenty20 – Nurse took 5-35 against Guyana at Port-of-Spain, although he ended up on the losing side. He then took 5-26, six matches later, against Trinidad and Tobago at Bridgetown in 2010/11. Nurse had a hand in all seven of T&T's dismissals, with a catch, a run out and five wickets, but again failed to be on the winning side.

  Nurse had taken 16 wickets at 16 after his first ten Twenty20 matches, earning a call-up for the West Indies. With no experience in first-class cricket, and just one List A match in 2007, Nurse made his West Indies debut in a Twenty20 international against Pakistan at Gros Islet in St Lucia in 2011.

- On his debut in English domestic Twenty20 cricket, West Indies all-rounder Kieron Pollard sparkled with a match double of a half-century and three wickets. In his first match for Somerset – at Lord's in 2010 – Pollard took 3-26 against Middlesex and then slammed an unbeaten 89 off 45 balls with seven fours and seven sixes. Passing the milestone of 1,000 runs in Twenty20 cricket, one of his sixes came close to clearing the Lord's Pavilion.

- The Perth Scorchers pulled off a tight win over the Melbourne Stars at the MCG in the 2011/12 Big Bash after losing its last five wickets in the last over. The final-over mayhem saw three wickets fall on 135 with three run outs.

- Following scores of nine, eight and nought, opener Craig Simmons struck a scorching ton for Perth in the 2013/14 BBL, reaching three figures off just 39 balls. The fastest century to date in the competition, Simmons hit 102 with eight sixes and eight fours against the Adelaide Strikers at the WACA.

  Two matches later, Simmons became the first batsman to score two centuries in the competition's history, bringing up 112 against the Sydney Sixers at the SCG, an innings that contained 11 sixes and four fours.

- Appearing in his first big-time Twenty20 match, an Australian under-19s player took a wicket with his first delivery in the 2011/12 Big Bash League. On his debut for the Adelaide Strikers, 18-year-old spinner James Muirhead took 2-17 against the Brisbane Heat at the Gabba. In his second match, Muirhead impressed again with another two-wicket haul, this time against the Perth Scorchers at the WACA. With 2-37, he dismissed their two imports, South African Herschelle Gibbs for 65 and former England Twenty20 captain Paul Collingwood for 18.

- The Netherlands went from hero to zero at the 2014 World Twenty20 tournament with a record-busting high score in one match and a record low in their next. In a Group B match against Ireland at Sylhet, the men in orange needed to reach a victory target of 190 in 14.2 overs to advance to the next round of the competition, doing so with 37 balls to spare. Stephan Myburgh (63) struck a 17-ball fifty, while South Australia's Tom Cooper hit a 15-ball 45. As many as 30 sixes were seen for the first time in a Twenty20 international, with Ireland responsible for 11 off 20 overs and the Dutch 19 off 13.5.

  But cheers turned to tears three days later with the Dutch all out for 39 at Chittagong, the first total under 50 in Twenty20 internationals. Sri Lanka ripped through the line-up – which contained four Australians – with both openers out for a duck and just one batsman passing ten.

  The tournament final – between India and Sri Lanka – saw all 22 players either batting or bowling, but no participant doing both, a world first in any international match.

- On its way to a total of 70 in a Twenty20 international at Belfast in 2008, Bermuda's innings contained just a single boundary. Opener Chris Foggo hit the only four of the innings off the fourth ball of the match against Canada.

- Tom Huggins took five wickets in five balls in a Twenty20 match for English club side Bury St Edmunds in 2010. Huggins appeared in 11 first-class matches and six Twenty20s for Northamptonshire in the early 2000s but never bowled a ball.

- To mark the 200th match in the IPL, both teams made 200 with David Warner and Virender Sehwag both scoring fifties. One of the most explosive opening pairs possible on the world stage, the dynamic duo put on a 146-run stand in 11.4 overs for the Delhi Daredevils against Kings XI Punjab in the 2011 edition of the IPL.

  Both openers were dismissed for 77, with Warner getting to his fifty off 29 balls, and Sehwag 28. Sehwag was a little unkind on Australia's David Hussey, who was appearing in his first match of the tournament. Sehwag swatted the Kings XI Punjab's most expensive signing for three consecutive sixes, before Hussey picked him up going for a fourth.

- Appearing in his third Twenty20 match, a 20-year-old spinner took a stunning hat-trick off the first three balls of the innings against Barbados in the 2012/13 Caribbean Twenty20 tournament. Opening the bowling, Derone Davis took 4-5 for Combined Campuses and Colleges in a 12-run victory at Port-of-Spain.

- During the 2013 IPL, Australia's James Faulkner became the first bowler to pick up two five-wicket hauls in the competition. Both hauls – 5-20 and 5-16 – for the Rajasthan Royals came against the same opposition – Sunrisers Hyderabad – and in the same season.

- Zimbabwe pulled off a humdinger of a win over the West Indies at Port-of-Spain in 2009/10 after the match began with a record 20 dot balls and three wickets. With a wicket to the first ball of the match from spinner Sulieman Benn (4-6) and a five-wicket haul to Darren Sammy (5-26), Zimbabwe's 105 was too good for the West Indies, which fell for 79, incurring a 26-run loss.

- When South Australia hosted Tasmania in the Twenty20 Big Bash in 2009/10, eight wickets fell in the space of just 13 balls. In an action-packed match at the Adelaide Oval, the Redbacks (131) lost their last six wickets for four runs – with four batsmen dismissed in an over – while Tasmania (108/9) lost its first two wickets for none.

- Despite a century and a five-wicket haul in a 2011 Champions League match, South Australia was pipped at the post by a six off the final ball. The Redbacks began the game against the Royal Challengers in Bangalore with a century from opener Daniel Harris (108*), just the third hundred ever struck in the tournament, and the second in consecutive days by an Australian, after New South Wales' David Warner (135*) against Chennai. With a victory target of 215, Shaun Tait took a maiden five-wicket haul (5-32), and with six runs needed off the final ball, Bangalore's wicketkeeper Arun Karthik lifted Daniel Christian high into the crowd to seal his side's dramatic progression into the semi-finals.

- Fourteen years after his last appearance for Australia, Michael Di Venuto made his debut for another country. In 2012, the then-38-year-old lined up for Italy in the World Twenty20 qualifiers in the United Arab Emirates, top-scoring with an unbeaten 42 in his first match, against Oman. Di Venuto shared a match-winning stand of 84 with the Melbourne-born Peter Petricola (39*), while another Australian starred with the ball. Carl Sandri – also born in Melbourne and a former Victorian second-XI player – took 4-9 in his first Twenty20 appearance.
  The 2012 tournament featured another to switch sides. Geraint Jones – a wicketkeeper who appeared in 34 Tests for England – played for Papua New Guinea, the country of his birth, making a duck on his debut in the match against Afghanistan.

- After taking 1-25 in a 2009 Twenty20 Cup match at Cardiff, Gloucestershire's Steve Kirby scored 25 in 25 minutes. He became the first batsman in all Twenty20 cricket to reach 25 batting at No. 11.

- On his way to a maiden five-wicket haul in Twenty20 cricket, Worcestershire's Daryl Mitchell caught and bowled three of his opponents. Mitchell, who opened the batting and captained the side, took a match-winning 5-28 against Northamptonshire in 2014; team-mate Shaaiq Choudhry also claimed a caught-and-bowled dismissal.

- After picking up a handy 1-15 against Leicestershire in 2006, Mark Ealham starred with the bat, thrashing an unbeaten 31 off just seven balls batting at No. 7. The Nottinghamshire all-rounder pulverised his attack with four sixes and a further boundary for a record strike rate of 442.85.

- Bowling to a state team-mate at Mumbai in the 2013 IPL, Mitchell Johnson had three catches dropped off successive deliveries. Mike Hussey, opening for the Chennai Super Kings, hit three balls in a row to the same fielding position, occupied by Kieron Pollard who dropped all three chances.

- New Zealand fast bowler Tim Southee opened the batting for Essex in a Twenty20 match in 2011 and proceeded to bring up his maiden 50 in the shortest form of the game. Southee reached the milestone in just 19 balls on his way to a swashbuckling 74 off 34 in the match against Hampshire at Chelmsford. He struck six fours and five sixes with an imposing strike rate of 217.65.

  Later in the same tournament – the Friends Life Twenty20 – Southee achieved his first six-wicket haul, taking 6-16 against Glamorgan at the same venue.

- Opening the bowling in a domestic match against the Lahore Lions in Pakistan in 2011, Sarmad Anwar went wicketless while becoming the first bowler to concede 80 runs in Twenty20 cricket. The Sialkot paceman went for 81 off his four allotted overs and then failed to score a run in the match, at Faisalabad.

- A tied Twenty20 match in South Africa in 2013/14 featured a world-record five catches taken by a fast bowler. In the Lions' innings of 156 against the Warriors at East London, Ayabulela Gqamane held on to his five as a substitute fielder.

- Two months on from making his Test debut for Bangladesh, medium-pacer Al-Amin Hossain took a hat-trick and five wickets in an over in a Twenty20 innings. After three overs for UCB-BCB in the Victory Day Twenty20 Cup match against Abahani Limited in Sylhet in 2013/14, Al-Amin was brought back for the last and took a wicket with his first delivery. After a dot ball, he then removed the next four batsmen with consecutive deliveries to finish with figures of 5-17.

- A Bangladesh Premier League match in 2012/13 saw the Khulna Royal Bengals thrash Duronto Rajshahi after their openers had put on an unbeaten 197. The first time a side batting first had completed its innings without the loss of a wicket, New Zealand's Lou Vincent scored 89 and Shahriar Nafees 102.

  In another BPL match played on the same day, Brad Hodge, playing for Barisal Burners, became the first batsman to pass the milestone of 5,000 runs in Twenty20 cricket: **"I am just very happy. I have made 10,000 plus runs in the Sheffield Shield and 5,000 in Twenty20s. It means that I have performed well over the course of my lifetime."**

- A Twenty20 match at Bridgetown in 2013 saw two bowlers claim a maiden five-wicket haul with no batsman reaching 15. Representing Barbados in the Caribbean Premier League, Bangladesh import Shakib Al Hasan took 6-6 against Trinidad and Tobago which was dismissed for 52 in 12.5 overs. Fidel Edwards then picked up 5-22, with Barbados claiming victory with 72 balls to spare.

- A Sri Lankan batsman went the tonk in 2013 hitting 277 in a Twenty20 innings in Lancashire. The 30-year-old Dhanuka Pathirana, who made his first-class debut in 2001/02, belted 29 sixes and 18 fours in a 72-ball knock for Austerlands against Droylsden in the Saddleworth League: **"Everything seemed to hit the middle. I was seeing it like a football. It was like a dream ... I think I did some serious damage to some of the vehicles in the car park."**

- In his only big-time match in any format, Llewellyn Armstrong captained the Bahamas in the 2006 Stanford 20/20 series at the age of 43 and top-scored for his side with an unbeaten 40. Another player aged over 40 top-scored for the opposition on his debut, with Pearson Best hitting a match-winning 74 for Cayman Islands.

- On its way to a Twenty20 total of 96 and a ten-wicket drubbing in 2013/14, Pakistan Television lost its first five wickets without a run on the board. Playing against Pakistan International Airways at Lahore, five of their top six batsmen made ducks in the worst-ever start by any team in Twenty20 cricket.

- After falling for a duck in a 2013/14 Big Bash League match against Perth at the SCG, Sydney Sixers all-rounder Moises Henriques came back to the crease and copped another. With the scores locked at 153 after 40 overs, the Sixers faced a one-over decider, the first in the competition's history. Pakistan import Yasir Arafat took 4-24 for the Scorchers and a match-winning 2-1 in the eliminator, dismissing Henriques for a duck, who bagged the BBL's first unofficial pair.

- Sent in to bat in the first Twenty20 match at Auckland in 2012/13, the top six in England's batting order all hit a six, a first in Twenty20 international cricket. Michael Lumb struck two sixes, Alex Hales one, Luke Wright four, Eoin Morgan three, Jonny Bairstow two and Jos Buttler three. In a high-scoring encounter at the postage stamp-sized Eden Park ground, New Zealand and England hit 27 fours and 23 sixes.

  The following match between the two sides, in Hamilton, saw the first instance of opposing wicketkeepers – Brendon McCullum (74) and Buttler (54) – scoring a half-century in the same match.

- Middlesex got off to a rollicking start to win a Twenty20 match at Hove in 2013, taking 26 runs off the first over. Chasing a total of 149 for victory against Sussex, the innings began with four leg-byes, then five consecutive boundaries (4, 4, 4, 6, 4) by Paul Stirling off Lewis Hatchett, who finished with figures of 0-22 off his only over.

- The first player to achieve two Twenty20 hat-tricks later became one of the victims in the first instance of four wickets in four balls in Twenty20 cricket. Representing West Indies A against India A at Bangalore in 2013/14, Andre Russell removed four batsmen in a row, including Yuvraj Singh who collected two hat-tricks in 2009.

- In the 58th match, and in Mumbai's 13th, of the 2013 IPL, their million-dollar signing Glenn Maxwell finally made his debut. The biggest signing of the season, Maxwell made his first appearance – against the lowly-rated Pune Warriors – dropping a catch, bowling a single over and scoring an unbeaten 13.

- A domestic Twenty20 match at Rawalpindi in 2011/12 saw as many as nine ducks, with the Lahore Lions contributing six. The Lions (113) lost their first three wickets for ducks and their final three for nought, with the Peshawar Panthers contributing three in a losing total of 79.

- After making a duck batting at seven against Rajasthan at Abu Dhabi in the 2014 IPL, Kolkata wicketkeeper Robin Uthappa was promoted to the top of the order and proceeded to string together a record ten consecutive scores of 40 or above. All came in the merry month of May in matches on Indian soil – 47, 65, 47, 46, 80, 40, 67, 83 not out, 41 and 42.

- A Twenty20 competition played on the Greek island of Corfu in 2012 featured a Pakistani batsman hitting two centuries in a day. Representing Spain in the second division of the European Championship Twenty20 tournament, 38-year-old Tariq Ali Awan hit 150 not out off 66 balls against Estonia, then padded up later in the day for an innings of 148, off 55 balls, against Portugal.

- Chris Gayle was in the groove at Bangalore in 2013, smashing the fastest century and the highest innings to date in Twenty20 cricket. Opening the batting for the Royal Challengers against the Pune Warriors in the IPL, Gayle raced to the three-figure mark off 30 balls and left the field unconquered on 175 after 66. With a strike rate of 265.15, Gayle's knock was peppered with 13 fours and a world-record 17 sixes, becoming the first player to pass the tally of 100 Twenty20 sixes at a particular venue. Next on the list at the time was David Hussey, with 50 at Trent Bridge.

  Aaron Finch, who made his Twenty20 international debut for Australia in 2010/11, was the most harshly treated of the seven bowlers who had to face Gayle on his day of days. Finch sent down five balls and was done for 28 runs, conceding four of Gayle's 17 sixes: **"That was simply the best innings I've ever seen. It was just a guy on fire."**

  With a new record-high team score of 263/5 in Twenty20 cricket, Gayle then starred with the ball, taking 2-5. Later in the competition, Gayle became the first player to attain 1,000 Twenty20 runs in three different calendar years, doing so consecutively between 2011 and 2013. He also became the first batsman to reach the milestone of 400 sixes in Twenty20 cricket – number two at the time was fellow West Indian Kieron Pollard with 263. In 2015, Gayle then became the first to hit 500 T20 sixes.

> **"I understand the kind of shock and awe that Chris [Gayle] generates through his batting exploits. One match I'll never forget is a Twenty20 trial for the Jamaica team back in 2006, where he smashed 196 off 68 deliveries and got out in the 15th over. It was on a first-class ground, Chedwin Park in St Catherine, Spanish Town and against an attack that consisted of Jerome Taylor, Marlon Samuels and Nikita Miller, all of whom had already played for West Indies. I was thankfully in Chris's team. And man, did he smash the leather off the cricket ball that day."**
>
> former West Indies batsman Wavell Hinds

- Despite reaching a total of 50 in a Twenty20 match in England in 2009, all 11 members of the Newbury under-11s failed to score a run. Nine batsmen were bowled, while the other was run out, in the match against Mortimer West End. Newbury's 50-run total came from 19 wides and six no-balls, with each worth two in the junior competition.

- A 41-year-old Brian Lara made a comeback to competitive cricket in 2010/11, making his debut for the Zimbabwean domestic team Southern Rocks. In his first-ever Twenty20 match, Lara scored 65 off 47 balls with eight fours and a six against Mashonaland Eagles at Harare.

- With as many as four debutants, Australia crushed Pakistan in a Twenty20 international at Dubai in 2014/15 in Aaron Finch's first match as captain. Three bowlers – Cameron Boyce (2-10), Kane Richardson (1-13) and Sean Abbott (1-17) – made their debuts and each claimed a wicket in their first over.

- During a run of five consecutive Twenty20 internationals in 2009 and 2010, West Indies opener Andre Fletcher managed just eight runs with four ducks. Three of the ducks came in consecutive matches in four days in London, with one at Lord's and two at The Oval.

- When the Kolkata Knight Riders beat the Hobart Hurricanes at Hyderabad in the 2014/15 Champions League, three of their bowlers returned identical bowling figures. The first three bowlers employed by Kolkata – Yusuf Pathan, Andre Russell and Sunil Narine – each took 4-0-24-1.

- Shahid Afridi played an explosive innings in an unofficial Twenty20 match at Nairobi in 2007/08, smashing a 15-ball 57 against Uganda. Pakistan crushed the African nation by 148 runs in the Twenty20 Quadrangular tournament with Afridi the standout, smashing seven sixes in his unbeaten knock. In the 17th over, Afridi hit five sixes and a four off Emmanuel Isaneez, collecting another two sixes and a four off the following over.

- A world first took place in a first-round Group A match at Chittagong in the 2013/14 World Twenty20 when two debutant bowlers claimed a wicket with their first delivery. Hong Kong's Pakistan-born Nadeem Ahmed became just the seventh bowler to achieve the feat in Twenty20 internationals, with Nepal's Paras Khadka becoming the eighth.

- Australian import Daniel Christian was on fire during a Twenty20 match at Canterbury in 2014 claiming an all-round double of 129 and 2-29 for Middlesex against Kent. He reached his fifty off 27 balls and his hundred off 46, posting a new high for a batsman at No. 5 in Twenty20 cricket.

- On his debut in Twenty20 cricket, Upul Jayasena hit one of the fastest fifties on record. Playing for the Sinhalese Sports Club against Badureliya in Colombo in 2014/15, Bandara struck a match-winning 54 not out off 14 balls, smacking three fours and six sixes.

- Following a series of three single-digit scores, Aaron Finch came alive in 2013 with the first innings of 150 in a Twenty20 international. Opening the batting against England at Southampton, Finch muscled his way to a match-winning 156 off 63 balls, the first century by an Australian in a Twenty20 international and the first by any batsman in England. After smashing a six off the first ball of the match, he went on to collect another 13, establishing a new record for the most sixes in an innings, reaching his 50, 100 and 150 with shots that cleared the fence. The Victorian batsman also took part in two century partnerships – 114 for the second wicket with Shaun Marsh and 101 for the third with Shane Watson – a first in Twenty20 internationals.

  Australia maintained a cracking pace throughout the 20 overs reaching 248/6, the highest total to date in a Twenty20 international against a Test nation. With 209/6 in reply, England then produced the highest total to date by a team batting second and losing.

  Batting for the first time in a Twenty20 international, England's Joe Root hit an unbeaten 90 after bowling one over to Finch and Marsh which cost him 27 runs, while, for the first time, seven bowlers conceded more than 40. As many as 450 runs were scored for the first time in a Twenty20 international – the 457 beating 428 in a tied match fought out by New Zealand (214/6) and Australia (214/4) at Christchurch in 2009/10.

  Without a single wicket in Twenty20 cricket, Australia gave a debut cap to an asylum seeker, Fawad Ahmed. The Pakistan-born spinner had appeared in just one 20-over match previously, for the Melbourne Renegades, and in his second Twenty20 international two days later at Chester-le-Street took 3-25.

- In a low-scoring Twenty20 international in Colombo in 2014/15, Nepal medium-pacer Sompal Kami pumped out the highest score by a No. 10 batsman in Twenty20 cricket. Playing against Hong Kong, Kami came in with eight of his team-mates having been dismissed for single-figure scores and struck 40, including six fours and two sixes. The previous best at ten in a Twenty20 international had been 22 by Afghanistan's Hamid Hassan against South Africa at Bridgetown in 2010.

  Chasing 73 for victory, HK recovered from 21/5 to get home with eight wickets down and one ball remaining. Hong Kong's Aizaz Khan was named man of the match after returning the record-breaking economical figures of 4-1-4-2 and top-scoring with 21 not out.

- When South Africa hosted the West Indies for a round of Twenty20 matches in 2014/15, two batsmen hit centuries, the first time this had happened in a bilateral series. With Faf du Plessis hitting 119 at Johannesburg and wicketkeeper Morne van Wyk 114 not out at Durban, South Africa became the first team to record centuries in consecutive Twenty20 internationals.

- A couple of near-40-year-olds got the Sydney Thunder franchise off to a record-breaking start in the 2014/15 Big Bash League, setting up just their second win in 22 matches. On his BBL debut – against Brisbane Heat in Sydney – former South African all-rounder Jacques Kallis put together an unbeaten 97 in a 160-run opening stand with Mike Hussey, who made 96. Former England all-rounder Andrew Flintoff made a duck and failed to take a wicket on his debut for Brisbane.

- Brett Lee bowed out of cricket in spectacular fashion, ending his career on a hat-trick. With three balls remaining in the final of the Big Bash League in Canberra in 2014/15, Lee took two consecutive wickets for the Sydney Sixers in front of a packed crowd at Manuka Oval. With the scores tied on 147, the Perth Scorchers avoided the hat-trick by taking the prize off the last ball of the match: **"It would have been awesome to win, but that's Twenty20 cricket. When it comes down to the last over, the last ball, you wouldn't have written a better script. It wasn't to be."**

Brett Lee (centre) with his Sydney Sixers team-mates in his final cricket match – the 2014/15 BBL final

Mohandas Menon @mohanstatsman
The most exciting last three balls of any cricket match! #BBL04

56   43

Political Intrigue

- Australia's first Prime Minister, Edmund Barton, was a cricketer of some note, later becoming a first-class umpire. America's first President also played cricket, with historical records indicating that George Washington took part in a game referred to as "wickets" in 1778.

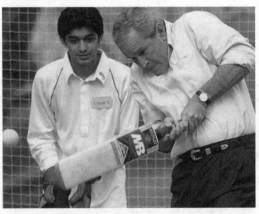

US President George W. Bush tries out cricket in Pakistan in 2006

Australia's first Prime Minister Edmund Barton (1901–1903) in cricket gear in 1870

"He is the Obama of cricket."

Indian fast bowler Praveen Kumar
on Mahendra Singh Dhoni

- V.V.S. Laxman is the great-grand-nephew of a former Indian President. Sarvepalli Radhakrishnan became India's first vice-president in 1952 and its second President, holding the position between 1962 and 1967.

- Elected to the Queensland parliament in 1983, Brian Littleproud had twice played for the state's country XI against international teams. A member of the National Party, and a minister for education and the environment, Littleproud scored a duck against the touring South Africans in 1963/64 and 17 against the Pakistanis in 1972/73.

- George Robert Canning Harris, better known as Lord Harris, was a towering figure in both cricket and politics captaining England and serving as Under-secretary of State for War. Governor of Bombay during the 1890s, Lord Harris appeared in the last of his four Tests in 1884, but kept playing first-class cricket until 1911.

- A British government minister admitted in 2007 that he would fail the so-called "Tebbit Test" by supporting India over England at cricket. Of Indian origin, Parmjit Dhanda – elected to the seat of Gloucester in the 2001 general election – said he unashamedly barracked for India: **"I'm a supporter of Liverpool Football Club and I fail Norman Tebbit's cricket test by supporting India against England at cricket."** A minister in the government of Margaret Thatcher, Norman Tebbit had once suggested that immigrants moving to Britain should be required to back the England team over those of their country of origin.

    Representing the Lords and Commons cricket team in 1994, Mr Tebbit's son dismissed the two openers who had chalked up 1,000 first-class matches between them. Opposing the Sir J.P. Getty's XI, William Tebbit dismissed John Edrich and Roy Virgin, finishing with figures of 2-93.

LETTER TO THE EDITOR
The Times – 26 September 1977
Mr Nicholas Scott is one of the leading batsmen for Lords and Commons cricket. It is therefore unthinkable that he should be dislodged by his constituency.

- In celebration of becoming the West Indies' most capped Test cricketer, Shivnarine Chanderpaul became an honorary citizen of Dominica in 2011 courtesy of the island's Prime Minister, Roosevelt Skerritt. The middle-order batsman marked Dominica's debut Test by appearing in a record 133rd Test for the West Indies and scoring his 23rd century, a match-saving 116 against India at the Windsor Park ground in Roseau.

- When the son of a Sri Lankan government minister was called up for his country's Twenty20 squad in 2013, the selection was defended by another politician. Sanath Jayasuriya – a member of Sri Lanka's national parliament and the chairman of selectors – went in to bat for the Media and Information Minister's son Ramith Rambukwella, who, at the time, had just ten domestic Twenty20 matches to his credit: "**Ramith is a left-hand batsman who bowls right arm off-spin, who can clear the boundaries and can hit hard. We don't just bring in players who perform, we also bring in players with talent.**"

Later in the year, Jayasuriya scored his first ministerial gig as a politician, becoming Deputy Minister of Postal Services.

- A former British Prime Minister resigned from the MCC committee in 2011 following a disagreement over redevelopment plans for the Lord's cricket ground. John Major (pictured), PM between 1990 and 1997, tendered his resignation after design plans for the ground had been watered down: "**For me cricket has been a lifelong and enduring passion and it will remain so. The solace the game has given me in good times and bad, the friendships I have made, and the sheer joy of the game will never fade. My decision to resign from the committee of the world's pre-eminent cricket club has been reached with very great sadness.**"

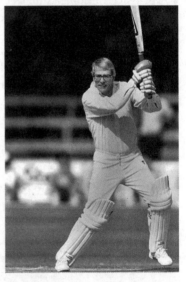

"**In Harare, Robert Mugabe told me that he thought cricket civilised people and he wanted Zimbabwe to be a nation of cricket lovers. I tried explaining the game to George Bush senior, but when I told him that it could last for five days and there might not be a positive result, I could see his eyes glaze over.**"

John Major

- Former Indian captain Mohammad Azharuddin scored a century for the Indian Parliamentarians XI in 2012. The MP got his ton against the visiting Lords and Commons cricket team in a match played at Dharmasala.

A future Australian Prime Minister top scored in a limited-over match in Sydney in 1975 batting against a team that included Test stars Jeff Thomson, Max Walker, Gary Gilmour and Kerry O'Keeffe. Playing for an invitational XI against a side billed as Australia, Bob Hawke hit 39 in 48 minutes batting at No. 8, and sent down a single over that cost five runs. Australia won the match by two wickets.

Australian Prime Minister Bob Hawke with Don Bradman at the launch of The Bradman Albums *in 1987*

SCOREBOARD
AUSTRALIA v INVITATION XI – DRUMMOYNE 1975/76

INVITATION XI		R
R.B. Simpson	c Chappell b Thomson	1
M.F. Rosen	c Robinson b Walker	15
I.R. Redpath	c Mallett b Walker	5
J. Benaud	c Thomson b Walker	9
A.W. Greig *	b Mallett	10
D.J. Colley	c McCosker b Mallett	2
T.J. Jenner	b O'Keeffe	1
R.J.L. Hawke	b Walker	39
S.J. Rixon †	st Robinson b Chappell	31
D. Lord	b Walker	22
R.J. Crippin	not out	0
Extras		7
Total	(all out – 27 overs)	**142**

"Something happened. I felt as if I were out of my body. I was hitting the ball and I suddenly knew I couldn't miss it. Every ball was coming straight to the bat. They changed bowlers and went through contortions to try to get me out but I just them and hit them, fours and sixes, until I was 78 not out. There was a New South Wales spotter there and he rushed over and talked about selection trials for me. Next game I was out for a duck."

Bob Hawke
on an innings for the ACT against a Newcastle XI

- An Australian politician who rose to the rank of Deputy Prime Minister lost a family member after a mishap with a cricket ball. The younger sister of National Party MP John Anderson died after he hit a ball into her neck while playing cricket with his father.

- In 1938, Stanley Baldwin became the first British Prime Minister to take on the presidency of the Marylebone Cricket Club. A Conservative PM on three occasions, Earl Baldwin's son-in-law George Kemp-Welch played first-class cricket for Warwickshire and Cambridge University in the 1920s and 30s.

- Arthur Jeffreys, a London-born batsman who played first-class cricket for MCC, Hampshire and New South Wales, was a Conservative Party politician elected to the seat of Basingstoke in 1887. His father, Arthur Jeffreys, was a member of the New South Wales parliament in the 1850s. A grazier, he purchased a large property in the south of the state which he named Acton, now an inner suburb of Canberra in the ACT.

- Four members of parliament played in the Prime Minister's XI match instituted by Robert Menzies in the Australian summer of 1951/52. Tasmanian Liberal MPs Athol Townley and Bill Falkinder appeared in the first match at Manuka Oval in Canberra; the Country Party's Mac Holten, a vice-captain of the Melbourne cricket club, played in 1960/61, while Don Chipp, a future leader of the Australian Democrats, appeared in the 1962/63 match, playing alongside Don Bradman.

    Harold Holt – who became Prime Minister in 1966 – was selected for the inaugural match but withdrew due to illness.

"It is occasionally left to people like me to carry with them through life a love and growing understanding of the great game – a feeling in the heart and mind and eye which neither time nor chance can utterly destroy."

Australian Prime Minister
Robert Menzies

Australian Prime Minister Robert Menzies with the opposing captains – the MCC's Ted Dexter and Don Bradman – for the 1962/63 PM's XI match in Canberra

• British Prime Minister David Cameron revealed that his biggest thrill of 2013 was receiving batting tips from former England opener Geoff Boycott. The two bumped into each other during the second Ashes Test at Lord's: "**Boycott told me, 'You've got to do it like this lad, you've got to do it like this.' He wouldn't stop until he'd got my elbow sticking out properly. It was quite extraordinary.**"

In the run-up to the 2015 general election, Labour's then-leader Ed Miliband vowed to give Boycott a knighthood if he won power. The cricket-loving Miliband cites the former England batsman as one of the people he most admires, saying he was attracted by "the charisma of imperfection". Theresa May, who became Home Secretary upon the election of Mr Cameron in 2010, is another big Boycott fan: "**He kind of solidly got on with what he was doing.**"

British Prime Minister David Cameron has a bat with youngsters in Mumbai during an official visit to India in 2013

"He [David Cameron] **was an expansive middle-order batsman who possessed all the strokes necessary to assemble a decent score. The majority of the runs scored by the future Prime Minister accrued on the leg-side of the wicket, and herein lay a fatal flaw. This tendency to strike across the line, allied perhaps to a lack of basic concentration, too often brought about a premature return to the pavilion. As a bowler, Cameron was not without merit. There was a longish run-up, carefully marked out, and he was able to bowl an accurate, probing delivery. I think that even the Prime Minister would acknowledge that he was, however, hampered by a lack of control of line and length.**"

UK *Daily Telegraph* political correspondent Peter Osborne

- An apology was sought from a British Labour Party MP in 2004 after claiming in parliament that there was "deep-rooted embedded racism in Yorkshire county cricket". The speech was delivered by Bradford North MP Terry Rooney in the House of Commons: **"Virtually every Test player from Yorkshire started in the Bradford League. About 60 per cent of cricketers in the Bradford League are from the Indian subcontinent. Not one of them, despite their skills and abilities, has ever been adopted by the Yorkshire County Cricket Club … even at trainee level."**

The club responded defiantly with chairman Robin Smith highlighting that Ajmal Shahzad had become the first British-born Asian to play for the county, a landmark achieved earlier in the year: **"To say that I am livid about Mr Rooney's comments is an understatement. The thing that annoys me most about his remarks is that they are factually incorrect. Had Rooney made the comments outside parliament, we would have been able to consider the option of suing him."**

LETTER TO THE EDITOR
The Times – 02 September 1968

Mr Richard Wainwright, my MP, is concerned about the omission of Mr D'Oliveira from the MCC South African party. I have asked him to take up with the Race Relations Board about the omission of Messrs Binks, Hutton and Sharpe, which appears to be a clear case of discrimination against the Yorkshire race.

- John George Davies, who appeared in seven first-class matches for Tasmania, later became a member of the state's House of Assembly. On his first-class debut in 1870/71, Davies was captain, wicketkeeper and opening batsman in the match against Victoria at the MCG.

Sir George held the seats of Fingal and Denison for the Liberal Party and was parliamentary speaker from 1903 until his death in 1913.

- In 2013, Australia's then-deputy Prime Minister and Treasurer used the Bodyline Test series to reignite debate about Australia becoming a republic. In an opinion piece published on the eve of Australia Day, Wayne Swan referenced the Bodyline series of 1932/33 suggesting it helped promote a greater sense of national pride that he said was still being felt 80 years on.

BODYLINE'S FINAL LEGACY MAY BE AN AUSTRALIAN REPUBLIC

Wayne Swan

There's no one source of our national character. It comes from our indigenous heritage, the struggles of the early settlers, the Federation period, and, of course, our nation's experiences at war.

And perhaps for Australians more than any other, it comes from sport.

This summer marks the 80th anniversary of arguably the most significant and defining event in Australia's sporting history: the Bodyline cricket series. Countless books have been devoted to retelling the torrid saga, but it is worth recounting because of the role it played in our national story.

At its core, Bodyline amounted to a calculated attempt by the English cricketing establishment to attack the Australians – specifically the wunderkind Don Bradman – with brutal, intimidatory, even life-threatening tactics.

Hostilities reached their zenith during the Adelaide Test match, when Australian captain Bill Woodfull was struck with a barrage of balls to the torso, including one blow just below his heart. Such was the level of animosity that a pitch invasion by the crowd was feared, with police standing guard along the boundary ready to repel the furious onlookers. At the end of this distasteful day, Woodfull uttered words that are quoted and mythologised to this very day: that while there were two teams on the field, only one was playing cricket.

This accusation of English unsportsmanlike conduct propelled a bitter stoush, elevated to forceful diplomatic cables from the respective cabinet rooms. The Australian Board of Control for Cricket's cable went as far to say that: "Unless stopped at once it [Bodyline] is likely to upset the friendly relations existing between Australia and England." In the world of diplomacy, words rarely come stronger.

The enduring impact of Bodyline is deeply rooted in Australian sporting folklore, but it was about a lot more than cricket. As esteemed historians Ric Sissons and Brian Stoddart concluded in their chronicle *Cricket and Empire*, from a British perspective, Bodyline was principally about teaching Australia "a lesson in imperial superiority".

An obvious question is how Bodyline defined the way Australians of the time viewed our place in the world, and our relationship with Britain. I think the answer throws up some surprising insights into the national character – surprising because it contradicts some of the clichéd myths that surround Australian sporting and national behaviour.

The most interesting fact about this episode is we Australians found ourselves the defenders of the supposedly English ideal of "fair play". Interesting because the accepted wisdom is that when it comes to cricket especially, we are the ruthless, the English the polite. Yes, we unleashed Lillee and Thomson. And, yes, Mitch Johnson is still breaking hands today. We play hard, but we play within both the letter and the spirit of the rules.

What the Bodyline series showed was that while we refuse to put on airs and graces, Aussies are not a ruthless, "whatever it takes" people. Rather, we are a plain-speaking lot, who play hard but fair, and expect no less. Ours is not a gentleman's code; it is a democratic code.

Douglas Jardine had no interest in honouring any such code. By directing his bowlers consistently to target the body, and placing fielders to prevent strokes to defend themselves, not only were life and limb threatened, the spirit of the game was deeply contravened. Obviously what was at stake was a sporting trophy; this was not war.

But Bodyline left a mark on our national consciousness because it symbolised wider issues of the period that actually did in the long run involve our sovereignty.

To understand that we have to put ourselves back in that summer. Australians were in the middle of the Great Depression, with the mass unemployment, homelessness and betrayal of hope that it brought. Australians did not cause that Depression and to a great extent we were powerless to tackle it because we lacked full economic sovereignty.

At home, our adherence to the gold standard and low foreign exchange reserves made it impossible to increase public spending to raise demand. Even worse, austerity was strongly recommended to us from on-high overseas – largely by English gentlemen whose gentlemanly rules had little interest in the welfare of ordinary Australians. Honouring deals between bankers was more important to them than equal sacrifice from all and fair play for working people.

The result? Catastrophic unemployment and hardship. Australians were mad as hell. So when Jardine bent the moral code to win at all costs, people joined the dots. It was only cricket, but it was typical. It symbolised the need for a new assertion of national sovereignty underpinned by the democratic rather than the gentlemanly values – to play hard, within the rules, to look after each other.

I believe Bodyline caused many Australians to wake up to the urgent need of making Australia's interests our No. 1 priority and to do so in a typically Australian egalitarian manner. Bodyline played a big role in embedding a sense of independence and a desire for true sovereignty in Australia's international outlook. It did not invent these ideas that had surfaced at various points in Australia's past – but it amplified them and took them in new directions. Wartime Labor Prime Ministers John Curtin and Ben Chifley were heavily influenced by the awakening of egalitarian national sentiment that followed the Depression, and it informed their determination to stand up for the country's defence interests.

Today Australia stands almost alone in having stayed out of recession during the most significant global downturn since that Great Depression. This in part speaks to an enduring determination for our country never again to be at the whim of anyone who claims an inherent right to make and break the rules at our expense.

The democratic and egalitarian assertion of our national sovereignty provoked during Bodyline and the Great Depression continues to serve us well on Australia Day 2013. I believe that reflecting on those events will eventually hasten the approach of an Australian republic, even if it has fallen from the national agenda over the past decade. While England will always be our most respected cricketing foe, and among our very closest allies, I think our national conversation is sold short when it does not include a debate about our relationship with the Crown.

So let's use the day to reflect on, and recommit to, the great things Australia stands for: playing hard, playing by the rules, looking after every citizen, and always defending our national interest with courage and with conviction.

- Essex and Cambridge batsman Hubert Ashton scored over 4,000 runs in first-class cricket, later becoming Parliamentary Private Secretary to the Chancellor of the Exchequer. Conservative MP for the seat of Chelmsford between 1950 and 1964, he was named a *Wisden* Cricketer of the Year in 1922 and married the sister of the Labour Party leader Hugh Gaitskell in 1927.

- British Conservative MP Chris Grayling, who became Leader of the House of Commons in 2015, claims to be the only member of the UK Parliament to have hit Dennis Lillee for four. His big moment came in a charity match for Phil Edmonds.

CHRIS GRAYLING'S DREAM TEAM

Geoff Boycott (E) *British*
Sunil Gavaskar (I) *Conservative*
Brian Lara (WI) *Party MP*
Viv Richards * (WI) *Chris*
Sachin Tendulkar (I) *Grayling*
Ian Botham (E)
Allan Knott † (E)
Shane Warne (A)
Dennis Lillee (A)
Joel Garner (WI)
James Anderson (E)

- While he was Australia's Prime Minister, Joseph Lyons played in a cricket match in Hobart in 1933 in which he batted and bowled for both sides. In his first effort, the PM scored six and with the ball took 2-3. He then top-scored with 22 (retired) and took 1-1.

- When former Australian batsman Sam Loxton switched from sport to politics he became the youngest MP to sit in the Victorian parliament. Aged 34, Loxton wrestled Prahran from the Labor Party by the slender margin of 14 votes in the 1955 state election and held on to the seat under Premier Henry Bolte for 24 years.

> **"In 1948, I served under that genius Bradman, and then in 1955, I served under that other genius, Bolte."**
>
> Sam Loxton

- The two big guns who went head to head in Pakistan's general election in 2013 were both former first-class cricketers. Running for the prime ministership were the PML's Nawaz Sharif – who had one first-class match in 1973/74 – and the PTI's Imran Khan, who appeared in 382 first-class games between 1969 and 1992.

  On the eve of the election, Imran ended up in hospital after an accident at a rally, with Mr Sharif going on to claim victory, becoming Pakistan's Prime Minister for the third time.

> **"Politics is cut-throat. I find myself far better equipped than my colleagues because I learnt to compete and take knocks from sport. There is no better preparation for politics ... it is the ultimate in character-building."**
>
> Imran Khan

Imran Khan, the politician, at a rally in Islamabad in 2008

- Bangladesh pace bowler Ziaur Rahman, who made his Test debut in 2013, shares the same name as his country's seventh President. Three years previously, Nelson Mandela Odhiambo – a medium-pacer named after South African President Nelson Mandela – made his Twenty20 debut for Kenya.

  N.A.M. McLean, who appeared in 19 Tests for the West Indies, sports the names Nixon (Richard Nixon – 37th US President) Alexei (Alexei Kosygin – Soviet Union Premier) McNamara (Robert McNamara – 8th US Defence Secretary). His cousin Reynold McLean, who played in ten first-class matches, possesses the middle names Julius and Jefferson. Fellow West Indian Nikita Miller, who made his Test debut in 2009, was named in honour of former Soviet leader Nikita Khrushchev.

> **"We named him after Mandela because he was born when the South African leader was touring Kenya after his release from prison."**
>
> Nelson Mandela Odhiambo's uncle Thomas Odoyo

> "When I met Mr Mandela it was one of the most memorable days of my life. A truly inspirational human being. He will live on in my heart forever."
>
> former Indian batsman Sachin Tendulkar on the death of Nelson Mandela in 2013

South Africa's first black President Nelson Mandela with two future members of parliament – Mohammad Azharuddin (left) and Sachin Tendulkar – during the South Africa-India Test match at Cape Town in 1996/97

- When Australia took to the field for the opening Test against Pakistan in Dubai in 2014/15, players wore black armbands to mark the death of an Australian Prime Minister. Gough Whitlam – who has a cricket oval named in his honour in Sydney – was Australia's 21st Prime Minister between 1972 and 1975 when his government was brought down by the Liberal Party's Malcolm Fraser. On the day Mr Fraser died in 2015, the Australians wore black armbands in the World Cup quarter-final match against Pakistan in Adelaide.

Australian Labor Party legend Gough Whitlam wields the willow, with party comrades Bob Hawke and Clyde Holding behind the stumps

- A leading Ireland all-rounder incurred the wrath of officialdom in 2013 when he took to social media upon the passing of former British Prime Minister Margaret Thatcher. After the news of her death had trickled through, John Mooney, who made his one-day international debut against England in Belfast in 2006, tweeted: "**I hope it was slow and painful.**"

> Journalist: **Mr Howard, it's a cause for reflection, I guess for all of us, when somebody passes like this. Have you reflected on how … what sort of funeral you might like?**
>
> John Howard: **Good heavens, no! Gee whiz, gee … Lord, no. Right** [looking to other journalists]**, ask me about the Ashes … please! No connection** [laughter]**.**
>
> former Australian Prime Minister John Howard
> facing journalists prior to the funeral of Margaret Thatcher in London
> in 2013

- Tom Hiley, a grade cricketer in Brisbane, was a member of the Queensland parliament assuming the office of Treasurer in the conservative government of Frank Nicklin in 1957. A wicketkeeper, Hiley was president of the Queensland Cricket Association in the late 1960s.

 The Country Party's Jack Pizzey, who succeeded Mr Nicklin as Premier in 1968, played for the state's Colts side. A slow left-arm bowler, Pizzey had been selected to make his first-class debut for Queensland in the early 1930s, but the match was washed out.

PETER BEATTIE'S DREAM TEAM

Matthew Hayden (A)	*Peter Beattie*
Bill Brown (A)	*– Queensland*
Greg Chappell (A)	*Premier from*
Viv Richards (WI)	*1998 to 2007*
Allan Border * (A)	*– and his all-*
Ian Botham (E)	*Queensland*
Tom Veivers (A)	*team*
Ian Healy † (A)	
Ray Lindwall (A)	
Wes Hall (WI)	
Jeff Thomson (A)	

- Former Indian batsman-turned-MP Navjot Singh Sidhu threatened to go on a hunger strike in 2013 over the stalling of funds for his constituency of Amritsar. Sidhu, who appeared in 51 Tests and began his political career in 2004, listed a string of developments which had been delayed, including bus services, bridges and waste management: **"I will sit on a fast unto death."**

- A school cricket match was abandoned in 2009/10 due to a lengthy interruption caused by a helicopter carrying a politician. The game between St Sylvester's College and Kalutara Vidyalaya in Kandy was called off when the chopper transporting a former Tourism Promotions Minister landed on the ground and stayed there all day.

- A Test famously attended by a US President contains the only instance of both captains taking five wickets in an innings in the same match. After Richie Benaud had taken 5-93 in the first innings of the third Test against Pakistan at Karachi in 1959/60, his counterpart Fazal Mahmood responded with 5-74. Dwight D. Eisenhower – the 34th US President – attended proceedings on day four.

- South African all-rounder Clive van Ryneveld, who appeared in 19 Tests during the 1950s, later played a major role in politics. In 1959, the year that followed his final Test, van Ryneveld was one of 12 MPs who quit the United Party to form the Progressive Party: **"The Nats had got in and they brought in a lot of legislation that was repugnant … the Group Areas Act; they expanded the Immorality Act to stop any sort of contact between white and black. You had separate education systems for blacks, which was very inferior. There were a lot of things that worried a lot of us. Our views were uncommon at the time for white South Africans. They just couldn't see all the Africans and the coloureds being able to take part in a democratic process. Whites were, frankly, quite afraid of what would happen if all the blacks got the vote. It was unusual and although there was a Liberal Party, it had no representation in politics at all."**

  In the general election that followed, 11 of the 12 MPs who defected, including van Ryneveld, lost their seats. In his 19 Tests, van Ryneveld scored 724 runs at 26.81 and took 17 wickets at 39.47. He scored four centuries in first-class cricket, with a highest of 150, and picked up 206 wickets, with a best return of 8-48.

- Irish politician Martin McGuinness lent his services to a fundraising campaign in 2015 by dressing up as W.G. Grace. The Sinn Féin minister was one of a number of prominent people from Northern

Ireland who took part to help raise funds for a children's hospice on the outskirts of Belfast: **"When I arrived for the photoshoot and saw the false beard and the cricket gear along with a make-up artist I wondered what in heaven's name I was getting into. But it's a fantastic idea."**

> **"I always admired the ability of a man to stand at a crease and take on all-comers."**
>
> Martin McGuinness

- Gloucestershire batsman Derrick Bailey, who appeared in 60 first-class matches in the 1940s and 50s, had impressive family and personal connections with leading political figures. One of his godfathers was Louis Botha, South Africa's first Prime Minister, while his half-brother was married to Winston Churchill's daughter Diana.

- Australian Labor Prime Minister John Curtin was a player and administrator who also umpired the occasional game in Perth. The country's 14th Prime Minister, Mr Curtin was a long-serving vice-president of the Cottesloe Cricket Club.

> **"He loved to read about cricket and it certainly inspired some of his speeches. I do think he was a *Wisden* addict. His knowledge of cricket was amazing."**
>
> John Curtin jr

> **"People who have met Mr Curtin in London speak with respect of his knowledge of cricket. He knows all the statistics. If you can persuade him to do it, he will join, I am told, with the precision of an expert in one of those discussions so dear to cricket zealots about 'The Greatest Eleven of All Time'."**
>
> *The Evening News*, 1944

- Sachin Tendulkar copped a barrage of criticism from Indian MPs in 2014 over his lack of attendance in parliament. In 2012, and while still a Test cricketer, Tendulkar was nominated to join the 250-member upper house of the Indian parliament, saying, at the time, that representing India would remain his focus, not politics. But two years after he accepted the nomination, and a number of months after retiring, Tendulkar had only attended parliament three times.

> **"This is an insult to the Indian Parliament and such people should not be nominated to this house."**
>
> Nationalist Congress Party MP D.P. Tripathi

> **"These MPs were selected so that they can be present and make a difference in the society. But I have never seen him in the house."**
>
> Samajwadi Party MP Naresh Agarwal

SHASHI THAROOR'S DREAM TEAM

Virender Sehwag (I)
Sunil Gavaskar (I)
Rahul Dravid (I)
Sachin Tendulkar (I)
Nawab of Pataudi jr * (I)
Gundappa Viswanath (I)
Kapil Dev (I)
Budhi Kunderan † (I)
Anil Kumble (I)
Bishan Bedi (I)
Zaheer Zhan (I)

Prominent Indian MP and minister Shashi Tharoor

- After Yorkshire had reached their highest first-class home total against Essex, they went on to achieve an innings victory on the day that Britons went to the polls in 2010. Their 516 included two centuries, with Yorkshire becoming the only First Division team to gain a positive result on election day.

- When the then-leader of the Federal Opposition was ejected from a session of the Australian parliament in 2012, one of his front-bench colleagues described the incident in cricketing terms as a "soft dismissal". In condemning the Prime Minister over the government's carbon pricing legislation, Tony Abbott became the first Opposition Leader to get the boot in 26 years.

Victorian Liberal MP Greg Hunt – who had once dated the granddaughter of former Australian captain Bill Woodfull – leapt to Mr Abbott's defence: "**If there was an action replay, I would think that most people would say the ball pitched well outside off stump … it wasn't going to even hit the stumps. It was a very soft dismissal.**"

"I can confirm that the carbon price was not responsible for the 2005 Ashes loss."

Australian Finance Minister Penny Wong
in the Senate in 2012, prior to the start-up of the Labor Government's
carbon pricing legislation

RICHARD MARLES'S DREAM TEAM

Herbert Sutcliffe (E)
Len Hutton (E)
Don Bradman * (A)
Sachin Tendulkar (I)
Graeme Pollock (SA)
Garry Sobers (WI)
Adam Gilchrist † (A)
Shane Warne (A)
Dennis Lillee (A)
Curtly Ambrose (WI)
Jeff Thomson (A)

The Australian Labor Party's Richard Marles, who became a federal minister in 2013

PHILIP RUDDOCK'S DREAM TEAM

Gordon Greenidge (WI)
Barry Richards (SA)
Sachin Tendulkar (I)
Don Bradman (A)
Viv Richards (WI)
Garry Sobers (WI)
Richie Benaud * (A)
Rod Marsh † (A)
Michael Holding (WI)
Shane Warne (A)
Wasim Akram (P)

The Liberal Party's Philip Ruddock, a former Australian Attorney-General

- A group of British activists sent out a letter to 600 politicians in 2005 seeking a game of cricket outside the Houses of Parliament on May Day. The group accused MPs of acting dishonourably over a number of issues, including the war in Iraq and identity cards: "**We the Space Hijackers, hereby challenge you and your fellow members of Parliament to a game of cricket. We challenge you to show us that your morals and behaviour are fit to govern this country. Prove to us that your support of the Olympic bid was not just more hot air. Prove to us and the rest of the country that you are what you claim to be. Prove it to us on the batting crease. We look forward to receiving your acceptance or decline of the challenge in the very near future. A decline of our challenge will be seen by us and the entire British public as acceptance that you are the morally and honourably corrupt government that we suspect. We shall see you at the pitch.**"

- Upon his triumphant return from England in 1921, Australia's winning captain Warwick Armstrong was feted by the Prime Minister of the day. Australia won the series 3-0, with Labor PM Billy Hughes presenting Armstrong with a £2,500 cheque: "**If ever there was a man singled out as a king of sport it was Mr Armstrong, who had gone out to give the people of England a chance to regain the Ashes and who had returned, like Imperial Caesar, who came, saw and conquered.**"

- Ian Botham copped a bouncer from Australia's Prime Minister in 1992 after the England all-rounder had walked out of a World Cup function when a comedian had lampooned the Queen. Paul Keating – Prime Minister between 1991 and 1996 – said Botham had over-reacted: **"These things happen. I'm not real dead keen on impersonators myself, but you've got to take all this in your stride."**

Australian Prime Minister Paul Keating with Mike Atherton and Mark Taylor during England's 1994/95 tour of Australia

- Former fast bowler Nathan Bracken stood as an independent candidate for a seat in New South Wales at the 2013 Australian federal election. Bracken, who appeared in five Tests and 116 one-day internationals, stood for the seat of Dobell, gaining over 6,000 votes and coming third behind the Liberal and Labor candidates.

    In 2010, one of Bracken's former fast-bowling team-mates was approached by the New South Wales Nationals to consider a career in politics. The leader of the Nationals party spoke to Glenn McGrath during the Sydney Test match in 2009/10: **"You never know what the future holds, but it's not something I'm seriously considering."**

- On the same day that the Kevin Rudd government lost power at the 2013 federal election, a former Labor leader tweeted news of a cricket win in Washington. Kim Beazley – who led the Labor Party to two election losses and later became Australia's top diplomat in the United States – proudly boasted that Australia had made the final of the Ambassadors Cricket Cup.

> **Kim Beazley** ✔
> @AusAmbUSA
> 🔵 Follow
>
> #Australia into the final of DC Embassy #cricket cup after semi-final win over @IndianEmbassyUS. Go, team!

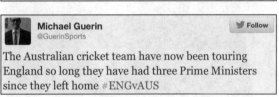

> **Michael Guerin**
> @GuerinSports
> 🔵 Follow
>
> The Australian cricket team have now been touring England so long they have had three Prime Ministers since they left home #ENGvAUS

- During an official trip to India in 2014, Australia's Tony Abbott met Sachin Tendulkar in Mumbai with the Prime Minister made a life member of the Cricket Club of India. Two months later, India's PM Narendra Modi travelled to Australia for the G20 summit, later paying a visit to the MCG. After the summit, held in Brisbane, Mr Modi attended a function hosted by the Queensland Premier and officiated by former Australian fast bowler Michael Kasprowicz.

> **Narendra Modi** @narendramodi   9h
> With @BrettLee_58. His love for India is truly admirable.

"Neither Australia nor India can live without cricket. Cricket has joined us."

Narendra Modi

One of the firmest and fastest bonds that Indians form with Australians comes from our love of cricket. Prime Minister Modi, in Australia we sometimes say that being captain of our Test team is the second toughest job in the country behind Prime Minister.

Some would say that we should never compare cricket with politics. After all, one is the cause of great national debates, intense passion, endless media commentary on controversial decisions and leadership speculation. And the other is just about deciding who governs Australia.

But in his 2011 Bradman oration, the "Wall of India", Rahul Dravid reminded Australians that on the 28th of June, 1930 when your illustrious predecessor Jawaharlal Nehru was arrested by the British, Sir Donald Bradman was busy decimating the English bowling attack, scoring 254 at Lord's. For Dravid and India's legendary cricket writer K.N. Prabhu, this was the motif of the 1930s. As Nehru went in and out of jail, Bradman just stayed in – and the Australian went after the English like "an avenging angel".

Dravid also quoted Bradman's advice to a young Richie Benaud, every cricketer is only a "temporary trustee" of the game. Indeed all of us, leaders, parliamentarians and citizens are the temporary trustees of our international relationship.

> – from an address to Australia's parliament in 2014
> by ALP leader Bill Shorten welcoming
> India's Prime Minister Narendra Modi

- Henry Mulholland was Speaker of the Northern Ireland House of Commons between 1929 and 1945 and played first-class cricket for Ireland and Cambridge University. In all first-class cricket he scored 1,642 runs with a best of 153 opening the batting for Cambridge against the touring Indians at Fenner's in 1911. Two years later, he returned the outstanding figures of 5-9 against Middlesex at the same venue.

  After the First World War, Mulholland entered politics, becoming a member of the House of Commons of Northern Ireland for the seat of County Down, and married Sheelah Brooke, sister of Basil Brooke, Northern Ireland's Prime Minister between 1943 and 1963.

- When Kevin Rudd became Australia's Prime Minister for the first time, in 2007, he revealed his childhood cricketing hero had been England's Colin Cowdrey. Mr Rudd also nominated as one of his fondest sporting moments the time Garry Sobers hit 254 for a World XI against Australia at the MCG in 1970/71: **"Just a stupendous batsman. I thought this guy has got the gift, the gift of the gods about him."**

Australian Prime Minister Kevin Rudd (right) with former Australian wicketkeeper Adam Gilchrist in 2013

"While I exhibited great enthusiasm for the game, I rarely troubled the scorers. The Peking Cricket Club wasn't exactly like the Gabba – instead of bowling from the Stanley Street end or the Vulture Street end, we'd be bowling from either the Temple of Heaven end, or the Long Live Marxism Leninism Mao Zedong Thought end.

My preference was the latter – but I say that by way of self-disclosure in case a journalist from *The Australian* happens upon it in a further exposé of my Chinese communist connections. I was, however, made wicketkeeper on the robust assumption that there was a limit to the amount of damage I could cause there. Alas, this assumption was again misplaced, as I soon became, affectionately, I hope, known as 'iron gloves'."

Kevin Rudd
on his cricket-playing days while a diplomat in Beijing

- Upon his retirement from cricket in 2012, rumours swept through Westminster in London that former England captain Andrew Strauss would switch from Lord's to the Commons. A staunch Conservative Party supporter, the South African-born Strauss had raised £25,000 at a Tory fundraiser in 2011.

> **"Many have been wondering why England captain Andrew Strauss has quit international cricket. While it's probably more to do with his bad couple of years at the crease, it's well known that Andrew is a Tory and rumoured that he has an interest in moving into politics."**
>
> UK political blogger Paul Staines

- Launching the Labor Party's campaign for the 2015 New South Wales election, Opposition Leader Luke Foley compared winning government to a famous Australian cricket victory. Mr Foley spoke about The Oval Test of 1882 in which England needed just 85 runs to win: **"Our greatest fast bowler – Fred Spofforth, 'The Demon' – told his team-mates at the final change of innings: 'This thing can be done'. And they did it. At this election, this can be done. Anyone who has lived through the last ten years of Australian politics and says an election is un-winnable is a fool."**

  In the match that gave birth to the Ashes, Spofforth took 7-44 opening the bowling with Tom Garrett, whose great-grandson Peter Garrett went on to become a prominent politician. Elected to the Australian parliament as a Labor Party member in 2004, he was appointed federal Environment Minister in 2007 and later School Education Minister.

- Braima Isaacs, a wicketkeeper who appeared in 53 first-class matches in South Africa, later turned to politics. Isaacs scored a century while opening for Western Province against Natal in Durban in 1979/80, later becoming an ICC match referee and then a member of the Western Cape parliament representing the New National Party.

- A day's play in a Habib Bank-Karachi Blues match in 2010/11 was lost due to the burial of a Pakistani politician who'd been assassinated in London. Another first-class match was similarly disrupted in the same season when a day was lost in the State Bank-KRL game in Rawalpindi following the murder of the Punjab governor.

Cricket and Crime

- Leeward Islands all-rounder Warrington Phillip, who appeared in 43 first-class matches, was sentenced to life in prison in 2009 for the murder of his wife. A few months on from his last match – for Dominica in the 2006 Stanford Twenty20 tournament – Phillip was arrested after his wife's body was found in a car with her throat cut.

- A 53-year-old who'd claimed thousands of pounds in disability payments ended up in court in 2013 after he was seen playing cricket. Stewart Lorains, a member of the Boosbeck club, had claimed the allowance from 2008, saying he was in constant pain and needed help washing, dressing and eating. Investigators from the Work and Pensions Department looked into his claims and found Lorains was active enough to be playing competitive cricket. Lorains's barrister admitted that her client had "exaggerated the extent of his condition". He was given a four-month suspended jail sentence.

- Bangladesh bowler Shafiuddin Ahmed, who appeared in 11 one-day internationals, was the subject of a major police hunt in 2003 after his girlfriend ended up in hospital with burns to 75 per cent of her body. The victim's family had alleged the cricketer threw petrol over Monika Afroze Mimi and set her alight.

- Pakistan fast bowler Mohammad Sami and his family were the victims of a violent home invasion in 2005. It was reported to police that four masked bandits had burst through the doors of their home in a daylight robbery during which members of Sami's family were held hostage: **"The robbers took away bonds, defence saving certificates, American dollars and jewellery. They tied our hands behind and threatened to kill us if we made any noise. We are all shell-shocked."**

- A few days after being named in Bangladesh's 2015 World Cup squad, Rubel Hossain was sent to jail pending a court appearance in relation to a complaint of a "false promise of marriage". A 19-year-old woman had lodged the grievance with police claiming the fast bowler had reneged on a pledge to marry her, an offence under Bangladeshi law.

  Released on bail so he could appear in the tournament, Hossain became a national hero when he took 4-53 at Adelaide to eliminate England from the World Cup in a match described as Bangladesh's greatest international victory. A few hours after the win, the woman's lawyer withdrew his services whereupon she announced she was dropping the charge.

- On the same night that Victorian coach David Hookes was fatally assaulted by a bouncer outside a Melbourne nightspot in 2004, Matt Gourlay, a bouncer himself, was hit with an autographed Bushrangers cricket bat. Gourlay and Hookes were both taken to the same hospital and spent time together in neighbouring cubicles in the emergency department. The bat used in the attack against Gourlay had been signed by all of the Victorian players who had triumphed over South Australia that fateful day in a limited-over match at the MCG.

- In 2005, a 32-year-old cricketer was charged with assaulting an opposition bowler half his age following his dismissal in a village cricket match in England. Michael Butt, who was playing for the Elsworth club, was punishing the bowling of the much younger Joshua Fay before he was clean-bowled. According to Butt, the youngster had called him a "tosser" upon his dismissal, whereupon he knocked him to the ground with his bat, punching him repeatedly. In court, Butt admitted his guilt to a charge of assault and was sentenced to 175 hours of community service.

- Despite his property having electric fencing and security gates, former South African bowler Pat Symcox was threatened by an armed intruder inside his house in 2011. Symcox said a number of items, including his laptop, had been stolen: **"I got up to go to the toilet and as I came back into the room, I came face to face with the intruder, who was holding my gun. There must have been at least two robbers in the house, as it appears they were passing stuff out through the window."**

- A British police officer had to interrupt his innings in a club match in 1991 to make an arrest. During his knock for the Gateshead Fell XI, PC Brian Arkle noticed an intruder in the club pavilion and ran from the field to investigate. After arresting the man, Arkle returned to the crease, going on to score a match-winning maiden century.

- A Sri Lankan male escort was handed a one-month suspended jail sentence in 2012 after breaking into the hotel rooms of Australian cricketers during the World Twenty20 tournament. The 21-year-old had entered the rooms of two players, offering sexual services.

- Two players from the Western Province Cricket Club were kidnapped at gunpoint after a match in Cape Town in 2003/04 and forced to fund a shopping spree. The pair was held captive for two days. Three men received jail sentences of between 16 and 20 years.

- A former Victorian batsman was sentenced to 18 months' jail in 2007 following a hit-and-run incident involving a cyclist. David Plumpton, who appeared in two limited-over matches in 2002/03, pleaded guilty to the offence that resulted in the death of a 32-year-old in Melbourne in 2005. The Victorian County Court was told that Plumpton had fallen asleep at the wheel of his vehicle when the accident occurred, fleeing the scene at high speed and dumping his car.

- A streaker who invaded the Gabba cricket ground in 2008 scoffed at suggestions that he might sue all-rounder Andrew Symonds who'd flattened him with a shoulder charge. Robert Ogilvie's indiscretion cost him $1,500 in the Brisbane Magistrates Court, but said he wasn't too fussed about the bone-crunching hit: **"It was great actually, it was just like playing football. You only live once, don't you?"**

- Two West Indian cricketers were arrested midway through a first-class match at Port-of-Spain in 2010/11 and locked up at a local police station. The Leeward Islands' Tonito Willett, who had scored 25 and taken 2-23, and Runako Morton, who had made seven for Trinidad at Queen's Park Oval, were arrested on drugs charges and took no further part in the match.

- While driving through the outskirts of Islamabad in 2004, former Pakistan captain Imran Khan was robbed by a group of men carrying semi-automatic weapons. Imran handed over an amount of cash, credit cards and mobile phone.

- Gunmen abducted the father of Afghanistan's cricket captain in 2013. Mohammad Nabi, who took to the game at the age of 28 while living in a refugee camp in Pakistan, had become his country's captain just a few months before the kidnapping.

- Former Indian captain Mansur Ali Khan was arrested in 2005 on suspicion of poaching an endangered species. He was one of eight people detained by police in Haryana after the carcass of an antelope, along with two guns and ammunition, was allegedly found in the boot of his car.

- Jacob Martin, who appeared in ten one-day internationals for India, was arrested in 2011 on charges of running an illegal immigration racket. Police had alleged that Martin had taken a number of men to England in 2004 as part of a bogus cricket team. In the same year – 2004 – Martin was arrested on a charge of breaking Gujarat's prohibition laws. The captain of the Baroda Ranji Trophy team, Martin was released on bail shortly after his arrest: "**I am innocent. I had gone to a friend's funeral. I was sitting in a small room with three other friends. We were waiting for the funeral procession to start, when the police raided the room, found a liquor bottle and we were arrested. I told the police that I don't drink, but to no avail.**"

- In 1996, police in the Indian state of Punjab claimed to have foiled an attempted kidnapping of a former national Test captain. Authorities said that Kashmiri militants had planned to abduct Kapil Dev in a trade-off for one of their own in prison.

- A teenage boy was sentenced to 15 years' prison in 2006 after he was found guilty of murdering a young girl following a game of cricket. Ten-year-old Lauren Pilkington-Smith had been playing cricket with a friend close to her home in a town near Manchester, when 18-year-old Kieron Smith joined in. The girl's battered body was found later the same night.

- An England cricket supporter was ordered by a judge to make a public apology during a Test match in South Africa in 2005 after being charged with scrawling racist graffiti on seats at the Newlands ground in Cape Town. The cricket ground authorities resisted the judge's order, saying it could "sour the game". Matthew Weller, from Wolverhampton, wrote an apology instead, after he was caught using a pen to make racist slogans and swastikas on a number of seats at the ground: "**I am extremely sorry for any offence caused to the staff and patrons of the ground who may have witnessed the act, or those involved in the cleaning operation. I wholly regret my actions, which were totally out of character and promise that I shall never again act in this manner.**"

- A club cricket match in England was interrupted in 2002 when a man began firing an air gun at the players, hitting one in the leg. Taplow bowler Mike Bradley was celebrating the taking of a wicket in the Chiltern League match against Amersham when he was struck: "**There was a whistling noise and it was like a real hard smack on the leg. It was quite a shock.**" The offender was later arrested and charged with intent to endanger life.

- While on bail on charges of arson in 2007, Zimbabwe batsman Mark Vermeulen was allowed to play club cricket, scoring a century in a match for Old Hararians. Charged with setting fire to the Zimbabwe Cricket Academy and the Harare Sports Club, Vermeulen hit 118 off 107 balls in a match against Uprising.

  Vermeulen was later cleared of the charges after pleading not guilty on the grounds of diminished responsibility: "[The trial] **was a long process and I learned a lot and I think I'm now a better person. I've been taking my medication. What happened was very unfortunate but I wasn't aware just how much I wasn't in control.**"

  He made his way back into the national team in 2009, and in his first one-day international in five years hit 92 opening the batting against Bangladesh at Bulawayo.

- An assault case mounted against former Zimbabwe captain Tatenda Taibu was thrown out of court in 2009 with the judge describing the prosecution's case as unreliable. Taibu had been charged with attacking a Zimbabwe Cricket employee in Harare after claiming he was owed money by the board. The magistrate ruled the court was unable to determine how the alleged assault could have occurred: "**Either this case was fabricated or the testimony of the witnesses is grossly exaggerated to the extent of making it unbelievable. The accused is accordingly found not guilty and acquitted.**"

- The father of an England wicketkeeper was jailed for 18 months in 2009 after being found guilty of a charge of dangerous driving causing death. In 2007, Ken Foster, the father of Essex's James Foster, had ploughed head-on into a motorcyclist on a road in Buckhurst Hill.

- A former Queensland cricketer jailed for sex offences against children was the victim of a bashing in Canberra's prison in 2013. Ian King, who appeared in eight first-class matches as a fast bowler, was admitted to hospital where he underwent emergency surgery losing an eye.

- A club cricketer who played in the English Ribblesdale League competition was sent to jail by a former first-class cricketer in 2007 on a charge of raping a 14-year-old girl. The judge, Edward Slinger – who made one appearance in first-class cricket for MCC against Oxford University in 1967 – imposed a non-parole period of five and a half years on the 40-year-old Ajmal Mohammad. While out on bail, it was reported that Ajmal had played for Blackburn Northerns in the Ribblesdale League while wearing an electronic tag attached to his ankle.

- Two teenage brothers on their way to play cricket in the Pakistan province of Punjab in 2010 were beaten to death by an angry mob after mistaking them for criminals. The two boys were then hung from a pole in an incident that sparked worldwide condemnation.

- A one-day international cricketer was hospitalised in 2010 after being attacked with a machete. Bermuda fast bowler George O'Brien – who made his ODI debut in 2006 – sustained an injury to his arm that required minor surgery.

- One of the most aggressive fast bowlers produced by South Africa in its isolation years was later sentenced to four years in jail. Garth Le Roux, who collected 838 first-class wickets, and his accountant were imprisoned on tax fraud charges.

- A former Victorian batsman ended up in hospital in Melbourne in 2005 after he fell over while in pursuit of a group of would-be car thieves. Russell Sincock, who played in two first-class matches in 1968/69, received cuts and bruises to various parts of his body after falling to the ground while chasing four teenagers near his home: **"My mates think it's a great joke, especially that I was starkers through the entire episode. There had been a couple of car break-ins in the street and the moment I heard a thud on the car, I knew someone was trying to get into mine. Heaven knows what they thought of a 200lb gorilla suddenly appearing at the front door, but they took off at a million miles an hour and with me after them, but all to no avail."**

- A former England batsman attracted a criminal record and a hefty fine in 2013 after appearing in court charged with harassing his former wife. Defending Kim Barnett – who appeared in four Tests in the 1980s – David Green said his client had found his marriage break-up difficult: **"We have two incidents on two separate days which are in my submission quite bizarre, but also in some ways quite childish."** The court heard Barnett had stuck a picture of his ex-wife next to a picture of a witch in his car window, with the words "Which is Witch?"

- A 91-year-old former wicketkeeper came to the defence of a traffic warden in 2013 who'd been attacked by a motorist. Rupert Webb, who appeared in 256 first-class matches between 1948 and 1960, confronted the 60-year-old driver who had punched the warden in a street in Worthing: **"I had a firm grip on my walking stick and I was about to give the attacker a jolly good clout. Fortunately, at that moment, a police car came round the corner and the man was arrested and taken away."**

- After captaining Derbyshire in the 1870s, Samuel Richardson moved to Spain having stolen £1,000 of the club's money. He absconded with the loot when he was in the trusted position of assistant secretary, and lived in Spain under a different name until his death, at the age of 93, in 1938.

- An arrest warrant was issued for the Indian Test captain M.S. Dhoni in 2014 after failing to appear in court following three summonses. A member of a right-wing political group filed a case against the then-captain accusing him of hurting religious sentiments after a picture of Dhoni as the Hindu god Vishnu appeared on the front cover of an Indian business magazine (pictured).

- During the Leicestershire-Nottinghamshire County Championship match in 1988, Kevin Lyons turned up one day to umpire in pinstriped trousers. His car containing his umpiring clothes had been stolen the night before.

- The son of a former Australian Test cricketer was placed on Interpol's watch list in 2014 accused of fraud and forgery in Afghanistan. Peter McCosker – whose father Rick appeared in 25 Tests – was the operator of Compass Integrated Security Solutions, a company named by a US Senate committee inquiry in 2010 as undermining the international war effort in Afghanistan.

Speed and Spin

- Balwinder Sandhu celebrated his first-class debut in 2011/12 by taking 5-66 in the first innings he bowled in. Playing for Mumbai against Punjab at the Wankhede Stadium, his five-wicket haul came 31 years after another player named Balwinder Sandhu had also taken a five-wicket haul (5-95) on his first-class debut at the same ground.

- When Gloucestershire put 646 on the scoreboard at Bristol in 2014, it became the highest total in all first-class cricket to include a hat-trick. Atif Sheikh – in his second County Championship match for Leicestershire and in just his third first-class match since his debut for Derbyshire in 2010 – took his first hat-trick in any class of cricket.

- Zimbabwe spinner Graeme Cremer began his one-day international career in record-breaking fashion by taking a wicket in his first five matches. Cremer dismissed Kenya batsman Collins Obuya in every match of a series of five ODIs in 2008/09, the first bowler to achieve such a feat. In 1995/96, England's Dominic Cork had taken the wicket of Gary Kirsten in five successive innings during a seven-match ODI series in South Africa.

- Sri Lanka won the 2014 Asia Cup one-day tournament after Lasith Malinga had become the first bowler to take all five wickets that fell in a one-day international innings. His 5-56 came in Pakistan's 260/5 in the tournament final at Mirpur.

- On his Test debut in 1980/81, India's Ravi Shastri picked up six wickets with four batsmen falling for a duck. The then-No. 10 – he would later open the Indian batting – took 3-54 and 3-9 in the match against New Zealand at Wellington. Shastri ended up with 151 wickets in his 80 Test appearances at an average of 40.96 and a strike rate of 104.3.

- Dharmendra Mishra enjoyed a spectacular first-class debut in 1990/91 by taking wickets with the first ball he bowled in both innings. Representing the Indian team Railways against Madhya Pradesh in Delhi, the fast-bowling Mishra emulated the West Indian-born Rudi Webster (7-56 and 4-44), who became the first debutant bowler to achieve the feat, for Scotland against MCC at Greenock in 1961.

- Bangladesh's Hasibul Hossain, a right-arm fast bowler, had a unique Test career playing five matches, all against a different country. In his time at the top – that lasted a little over a year in the early 2000s – Hossain took six wickets over six innings in five different countries. While his average in first-class cricket came in at 27.43, in Test cricket it was 95.16.

- South Australia's George Giffen marked the birth of the Sheffield Shield in 1892/93 by taking a wicket with the third ball of the competition's inaugural match. Representing South Australia against New South Wales at Adelaide, Giffen removed Sammy Jones for a duck, en route to the competition's first five-wicket (6-133) and ten-wicket hauls (12-191). Michael Pierce bettered Giffen by taking 13 wickets (8-111 and 5-145) in the match, the best return by a New South Wales bowler on his first-class debut.

- In an effort to raise money for his local cricket club in England in 2010, former Salesbury XI captain Jason Rawson sent down a ball in a Twenty20 match with a 1.6-mile run-up. He began the delivery at an Indian restaurant and ran down a major highway before letting go of the ball to the batsman who'd been waiting for 20 minutes.

- On the same day during the summer of 2009, two bowlers broke their club's record for most wickets in an innings. After Brad Klosterman took 9-15 for Hertfordshire club Leverstock Green's first XI, Imran Iqbal then grabbed 9-13 for the club's second XI.

- In a Ranji Trophy match in 1999/2000, Madhya Pradesh bowler Manish Majithia sent down 20 overs in an innings, all of which were maidens. His world-record figures of 20-20-0-1 came against his old team Railways at Indore. Following-on, Railways (86/5) batted out for a draw, scoring 83 runs off 104 overs, the fewest number of runs in a full day's play in first-class history.

- Fronting up for his final first-class match, Pakistani slow bowler Iqbal Qasim required just two wickets to reach the coveted milestone of 1,000 career wickets. Playing for National Bank against Habib Bank at Peshawar in the 1992/93 BCCP Patron's Trophy, Iqbal took 1-64 and 0-2, thus ending his 246-match first-class career with 999 wickets.

- After taking a record 15 wickets on his debut, Lahore's Nadeem Malik only played in another two first-class matches. Representing Lahore Reds, the right-arm quick took 8-58 and 7-44 against Sargodha in Lahore in 1973/74, for a match haul of 15-102, the best figures by a debutant since the Second World War.

- India's A.G. Kripal Singh, who scored 100 not out in his maiden Test innings, bowled a record number of balls before claiming his first wicket. Bowling in his tenth innings, he took his first wicket – that of England's Geoff Pullar at Delhi in 1961/62 – with his 652nd delivery.

- In a brief career of 11 one-day internationals, England's James Kirtley achieved his best bowling figures on his debut, taking 2-33 against Zimbabwe at Harare in 2001/02. He later matched his best in his penultimate appearance – against Bangladesh at Dhaka two seasons later – with the identical figures in both matches of 9.1-1-33-2.

- A teenage fast bowler made a dramatic entrance into the ranks of first-class cricket in 2011, coming into a County Championship match on the third day and taking five wickets in an innings. Nineteen-year-old Matthew Dunn was drafted into the Surrey side midway through the match with Derbyshire at Derby when Jade Dernbach was called up for England to replace an injured James Anderson. Dunn made an immediate impact by taking a match-winning 5-56, becoming the first Surrey bowler in 56 years to achieve a five-wicket haul on his County Championship debut.

- After a ten-year absence from first-class cricket, West Australian off-spinner Brett Mulder burst back with a ten-wicket haul and the record-breaking figures of 5-2 in a Sheffield Shield match in Perth. He followed up his 6-4-2-5 with career-best figures of 6-65 in the second innings of the match against New South Wales at the WACA in 1996/97.
  In the 2010/11 Sheffield Shield, Tasmania's James Faulkner took 5-5 off seven overs against South Australia in Hobart. The Redbacks went for just 55 in 137 balls, their third-lowest total in the Sheffield Shield, with Faulkner's 7-4-5-5 the second-cheapest five-wicket haul in the Sheffield Shield after Mulder. Despite the embarrassment of their 55-run total, South Australia came back with 416 following-on and a record-breaking win. Requiring 221 for victory, Tasmania fell apart for 177, with five wickets going the way of Peter George (5-28).

- In his penultimate one-day international, UAE's Arshad Ali was the eighth bowler used in a match against Bangladesh in the 2008 Asia Cup conceding a record 74 runs. His team-mate Khurram Khan – also appearing in his second-last ODI – was the seventh bowler used in the innings and he went for 78 runs.

- Sri Lanka's Chaminda Vaas achieved his maiden ten-wicket haul in his fifth Test match but had to wait another 50 Tests before his next. His maiden lot of 10-90 was against New Zealand at Napier in 1994/95, with his second (14-191) coming nearly seven years later against the West Indies in Colombo in 2001/02.

- In the 1913 County Championship, Yorkshire's Alonzo Drake returned the remarkable match statistics of seven for seven against Somerset at the Recreation Ground in Bath. In the first innings, he had figures of 4.3-1-4-4 and 6.1-4-3-3 in the second. In his penultimate first-class match, at Weston-super-Mare the following summer, he took 15 wickets for 51 against the same opposition, including 10-35 in the second innings.

- The only Test match played at Sheffield in northern England included five instances of five wickets in an innings. A record number for a single Test, the match, played in 1902, saw Sydney Barnes (6-49) and Wilfred Rhodes (5-63) take five-fors for England, while Monty Noble (5-51 and 6-52) and Jack Saunders (5-50) did so for Australia.

W. Rhodes

The Wrench Series. No. 1344

- On the first morning of the 77th Ranji Trophy in 2010/11, Hyderabad was reduced to rubble in just 78 minutes, thanks to an 18-year-old Rajasthan debutant who took 8-10. Deepak Chahar's eight wickets, off 7.3 overs, saw Hyderabad all out for a record tournament low of 21.

Chahar's first-up effort fell just short of the overall Indian record for a debutant held by Maharashtra's Vasant Ranjane, who took 9-35 – and a hat-trick – against Saurashtra (83) in the 1956/57 Ranji Trophy.

Chahar then picked up another four wickets in Hyderabad's second innings of 126, for a match haul of 12-64: "**I didn't feel any great pressure. I just felt positive and more confident because of the wickets I had taken in the first innings. All of India has supported me after that performance and that motivated me even more.**"

- Fast bowler Jayde Herrick caused a sensation in his first first-class match for Victoria with the umpires barring him from the attack. The paceman was removed after sending down a number of high full tosses during the Victoria-England XI match in 2010/11, finishing the innings with figures of 2-74 on his first-class debut at the MCG.

  Herrick was appearing in just his second first-class match, having made his debut in highly unusual circumstances the month before. The 25-year-old had received a call from fellow Victorian Damien Wright indicating the New Zealand club Wellington was in desperate need of a fast bowler: "**I flew in on Monday and was opening the bowling, first ball of the game, on Tuesday morning.**" He claimed six wickets in the Plunket Shield match against Otago, including, coincidentally, 2-74 in his first innings.

- In a first-class career of five matches, John Piton collected 13 wickets, all of which came in his second appearance. The first bowler to achieve a dozen wickets in his second match having not bowled in his first, Piton took 7-82 and 6-122 for Transvaal against Griqualand West at Johannesburg in the 1890/91 Currie Cup.

  The second bowler to do so was also South African. In 1965/66, Western Province's Michael Bowditch (12-120) took 9-52 and 3-68 in his second first-class match, against Natal in Cape Town.

- During a schools cricket match in England in the 1870s, H. Highley took all ten wickets in an innings in which no other bowler was used. After picking up two wickets in his first over, his captain thought so highly of him, he asked him to bowl the second over – taking four wickets – and the next over as well, in which he claimed the remaining four wickets.

- With figures of 5-16 against Kenya in the 2011 World Cup, Pakistan's Shahid Afridi became the first player to claim a five-wicket haul on his captaincy debut in the tournament. The only other captain to take four wickets in his first match as captain was Zimbabwe's Duncan Fletcher, who claimed 4-42 against Australia in 1983. Prior to Afridi's history-making performance, India's Kapil Dev had been the only other skipper with a five-for in the World Cup. Coincidentally, his haul of 5-43 was also against Australia in the 1983 competition.

  Three matches into the tournament, Afridi had become the first captain to obtain four or more wickets in three consecutive one-day internationals. After his 5-16 against the Kenyans, he picked up 4-34 against Sri Lanka and then claimed a man-of-the-match 5-23 against Canada, on each occasion leading Pakistan to victory. With 4-30 against the West Indies at Mirpur, Afridi became the first bowler to collect four four-fors in a single World Cup.

- For the first time in one-day international cricket, hat-tricks were achieved in consecutive matches during the 2011 World Cup. In the 13th match, the West Indies' Kemar Roach took 6-27 and a hat-trick against the Netherlands at Delhi, while Sri Lanka's Lasith Malinga replicated the feat the following day in Colombo. Opening the bowling against Kenya, Malinga also achieved a six-wicket haul (6-38) including three-in-three, becoming the first player to take two hat-tricks in World Cup cricket.

- Appearing in his first match in England's County Championship, Indian spinner Harbhajan Singh suffered the embarrassment of being no-balled for throwing. An attempted bouncer flew over the batsman and the wicketkeeper in the match between Surrey and Warwickshire in Croydon in 2005. Harbhajan took just three wickets in the match, while team-mate, the Pakistan fast bowler Mohammad Akram (5-51) achieved his first five-wicket haul for the county. Warwickshire's opening batsman Ian Westwood claimed his first wicket in first-class cricket, dismissing Jimmy Ormond who later reached the milestone of 400 first-class wickets by dismissing Westwood.

- The leading wicket-taker in South Africa's first-class competition in 2012/13, Dolphins fast bowler Kyle Abbott became the first bowler to take seven wickets in an innings against Pakistan on his Test debut. Abbott picked up 7-29 off 11.4 overs in the second Test at Centurion, the best-ever debut figures by a South African bowling in his first innings. The only Proteas bowler to do better on his Test debut was Abbott's coach at the Dolphins, Lance Klusener, who took 8-64 in the second innings against India at Kolkata in 1996/97.

- Australian left-arm quick Bruce Reid had a fondness for Test cricket in Melbourne, securing his best four innings returns at the MCG. His next best three in Tests also came at a particular venue, the Gabba in Brisbane, two of which were identical – 4-53. Reid – who was once described as "all arms and legs like a porn movie without the sex" – claimed yet another 4-53 in a Test, at the Adelaide Oval.

- During 2011, debutant bowlers combined to exceed 100 wickets in a calendar year for the first time in Test history. The previous best in a year had been 83 wickets by 48 players in 1948, and by 58 players in 1992. As many as eight bowlers picked up a five-wicket haul on their Test debuts in 2011, all in the last four months of the year with four in November. In all, 114 wickets were achieved by first-time bowlers throughout the year.

    The South Africa-Australia series featured two rising stars, with Vernon Philander and Pat Cummins starring in consecutive Tests. Philander took eight wickets against the Australians at Cape Town, with a second-innings haul of 5-15, while a teenage Cummins hogged the headlines in the following Test at Johannesburg.

It had been a meteoric rise for the right-arm Cummins in all forms of the game – already Australia's youngest Twenty20 international and one-day international player, he then became one of his country's youngest Test cricketers.

With just three first-class matches and nine wickets at a 46-run average, Cummins got the call-up for his Test debut against the Proteas and, at the age of 18 years and 193 days, became the second-youngest Australian Test cricketer and the country's youngest bowler. When he took the wicket of Hashim Amla, he became the youngest Australian bowler to take a Test wicket, replacing Tom Garrett who had set the record during the first Test of all – against England at Melbourne in 1876/77. With a haul of 6-79 in the Proteas' second innings, Cummins became the youngest Australian to achieve a five-wicket haul on his Test debut, and the second-youngest from any country to gain a six-for.

With an injury interrupting the charge of Philander, who'd collected four five-wicket hauls in his first three Tests, South Africa found an admirable replacement in a big quick bowler named Marchant de Lange. Debuting in the second Test against Sri Lanka at Durban, the 21-year-old struck gold, picking up 7-81, becoming only the seventh bowler in the world to take seven or more wickets in the first innings of their first match.

Australia's James Pattinson also produced a ripper on his Test debut in 2011, taking a man-of-the-match 5-27 in the second innings against New Zealand at Brisbane. At one stage, his figures were 5-7, after a three-wicket maiden over en route to his first-ever five-wicket haul in first-class cricket.

2011 FIRST-TIMER FIVE-FORS

Bowler	Figures	Match	Venue	Test #
Nathan Lyon	5-34 and 1-73	Australia v Sri Lanka	Galle	2005
Elias Sunny	6-94 and 1-34	Bangladesh v West Indies	Chittagong	2010
Doug Bracewell	1-51 and 5-85	New Zealand v Zimbabwe	Bulawayo	2013
Ravichandran Ashwin	3-81 and 6-47	India v West Indies	Delhi	2015
Vernon Philander	3-63 and 5-15	South Africa v Australia	Cape Town	2016
Pat Cummins	1-38 and 6-79	Australia v South Africa	Johannesburg	2018
James Pattinson	1-64 and 5-27	Australia v New Zealand	Brisbane	2020
Marchant de Lange	7-81 and 1-45	South Africa v Sri Lanka	Durban	2026

• In a Ranji Trophy match against Vidarbha at Amravati in 1976/77, Rajasthan's Kailash Gattani took 7-42 and 7-33. He became the first, and to date only, bowler to achieve the feat of two seven-wicket hauls in his first match as captain in the competition.

- During the 1985/86 Test series against England, two West Indies bowlers claimed 25 wickets, but neither managed five in an innings. Malcolm Marshall and Joel Garner both claimed 27 wickets in the five-match series, with a best return of 4-38 for Marshall and 4-43 for Garner. While England was flogged 5-0, as many as three of its squad – John Emburey (5-78), Richard Ellison (5-78) and Ian Botham (5-71) – managed a five-for, but only two – Emburey (14) and Botham (11) took more than ten wickets in the series.

- Despite Bangladesh scoring just 262 in their second innings against New Zealand at Chittagong in 2004/05, two of the Kiwi bowlers went for more than 100 runs. Paul Wiseman conceded 106 runs off 24 overs, while fellow spinner Daniel Vettori leaked 100 runs off 28.2. New Zealand won the match by an innings and 101.

- Two bowlers claimed a hat-trick in the Leeward Islands-Barbados match at North Sound in 2010/11, with one for each side. Leewards slumped to 17/3 in both innings, the second occasion after Pedro Collins had taken a hat-trick, a feat matched by slow bowler Justin Arthanaze on his way to a maiden five-wicket haul in first-class cricket.

- Together with his 6,912 runs in 232 one-day internationals, Australia's Michael Bevan also picked up 36 wickets with his slow left-arm chinaman deliveries. With an average of 45.97, all of his victims were different batsmen and most were from the top order.
  From New Zealand he dismissed seven batsmen – Roger Twose, Daniel Vettori, Gavin Larsen, Craig McMillan, Dion Nash, Chris Harris and Chris Cairns. He got an equal number from Pakistan, accounting for Aamer Sohail, Mohammad Wasim, Inzamam-ul-Haq, Shahid Afridi, Mushtaq Ahmed, Wasim Akram and Azhar Mahmood. He picked up five West Indians – Shivnarine Chanderpaul, Carl Hooper, Junior Murray, Sherwin Campbell and Nixon McLean – and five from England – Graham Thorpe, Darren Gough, Alan Mullally, Adam Hollioake and Andy Caddick. His Sri Lankan victims were Asanka Gurusinha, Roshan Mahanama and Aravinda de Silva. From South Africa he got Jonty Rhodes and Shaun Pollock, and Sourav Ganguly, Sunil Joshi and Vinod Kambli from India.
  Bevan also dismissed Zimbabwe's Murray Goodwin and Andy Flower and Kenya's Maurice Odumbe and Hitesh Modi.

- Ronit More, a medium-pacer from Karnataka, impressed on his 50-over debut, picking up a match-winning 6-18. The 20-year-old, who'd previously played for the Australian Institute of Sport in Queensland in 2011, took his six off 6.3 overs against Goa (54) in a 2011/12 Vijay Hazare Trophy match at Bangalore.

- A 20-year-old fast bowler lit up the 2009/10 Ranji Trophy by taking ten wickets and a hat-trick on his first-class debut. Playing for Karnataka, Abhimanyu Mithun took 6-86 and 5-95, with a hat-trick, in the match against Uttar Pradesh at Meerut.

- Australia's Shane Watson and Marcus North made history at Lord's in 2010 by both claiming a maiden five-wicket haul in a Test match. Watson, bowling medium-pace, took 5-40 in the first innings of the first Test against Pakistan, while spinner Marcus North took a record 6-55 in the second. In doing so, they became the first bowlers to capture five wickets in an innings of a neutral Test at the home of cricket.

- Appearing in his first match of the season, a teenage Gloucestershire paceman rocked his opposition with 7-29 in the 2010 CB 40-over competition. Essex went on to clinch victory in the match, at Chelmsford, despite 19-year-old David Payne taking five wickets in six balls, including four in four in the final over.

  At the same venue three seasons later, Essex's Graham Napier became just the sixth bowler to achieve four wickets in four balls in one-day cricket, taking 7-32 against Surrey.

- On his one-day international debut, Bermuda's Dwayne Leverock became the first bowler to send down as many as five maidens in his allotted ten overs. He finished the match against Canada at Port-of-Spain in 2006 with the figures of 10-5-14-1. Previously, the West Indies' Andy Roberts (2-16) had begun his ODI career with five maidens in a 12-over spell against Sri Lanka at Manchester in the 1975 World Cup, while England's Devon Malcolm (2-19) sent down five in 11 overs on his debut against New Zealand at The Oval in 1990.

- South Africa's Jackie McGlew claimed a hat-trick in first-class cricket yet never took more than two wickets in an innings in his career. Captaining Natal against Transvaal at Durban in 1963/64, McGlew took a hat-trick spread over both innings – his 2-4 in the second innings ended up being the best figures of his 190-match career.

- In the same match that he scored a career-high 96, fast bowler Andre Nel was suspended and fined £5,000. Playing for Surrey in the 2010 County Championship at Northampton, Nel took part in a last-wicket stand of 118 with fellow South African-born fast bowler Jade Dernbach (56*), with the pair going on to share seven second-innings wickets. After some sloppy fielding which cost him a wicket, Nel (4-68) flung the ball in frustration at the stumps, hitting Northamptonshire's Niall O'Brien.

- When Queensland's Michael Kasprowicz took 7-103 against Western Australia at the Gabba in 2005/06, he became the second-highest taker of five-fors in Sheffield Shield cricket. The fast bowler ended his career with 26 five-wicket hauls in the competition, a long way off the leader of the pack, Clarrie Grimmett, who achieved 48. Of the five bowlers with at least 20 Shield five-fors, three played for Queensland – Michael Kasprowicz, Craig McDermott and Andy Bichel.

MOST FIVE-WICKET HAULS
IN THE SHEFFIELD SHIELD

#	Bowler	Teams	Seasons
48	Clarrie Grimmett	Victoria, South Australia	1923/24 to 1939/40
26	Michael Kasprowicz	Queensland	1989/90 to 2007/08
25	Chuck Fleetwood-Smith	Victoria	1931/32 to 1939/40
22	Craig McDermott	Queensland	1983/84 to 1995/96
22	Andy Bichel	Queensland	1992/93 to 2007/08

- In a first-class career of 31 matches, which included a Test, Baqa Jilani took 12 wickets on his debut and the first hat-trick in the Ranji Trophy. In the first innings of the match against Sind at Karachi in 1934/35, Jilani – opening the bowling for Northern India – took 7-37 and 5-50. He later made history in his first Ranji Trophy match, with another five-for, this time against Southern Punjab at Amritsar. His second-innings figures of 4.1-1-7-5 contained the first-ever hat-trick in the competition.

- Within the space of two overs and ten minutes in a Test match at Kolkata in 2011/12, West Indies speedster Kemar Roach twice claimed the wicket of India's M.S. Dhoni off no-balls. Roach eventually got his man, third time lucky for 144, and finished the innings with figures of 2-106.

- When India's Javagal Srinath destroyed South Africa in a Test at Ahmedabad in 1996/97, the opening fast bowler took 6-21 with three sets of two consecutive wickets. Chasing a modest 170 for victory, Srinath got opener Andrew Hudson and their No. 3 Daryll Cullinan for ducks to leave South Africa reeling at two wickets down for none. He later removed middle-order batsmen Dave Richardson and Jonty Rhodes with consecutive balls and in his next spell shot out numbers ten and 11 with consecutive deliveries to finish the match, handing India a sensational 64-run win.

- In a first-class match against the touring Australians at Hastings in 1964, Glamorgan's Jim Pressdee passed the 100-wicket milestone for the season with two of his victims stumped off different wicketkeepers in the same innings. Playing for the A.E.R. Gilligan's XI, Pressdee had Bill Lawry stumped by Jim Parks and Graham McKenzie stumped by Ken Suttle. The match has a special place in history, with all 22 players bowling.

- India's Sunil Gavaskar had a Test bowling average of over 200.00, taking just one wicket in his 125-match career. He also claimed just one wicket in 108 one-day internationals, with both victims being the same batsman – Pakistan's Zaheer Abbas.

- In 2012, a schoolboy picked up six wickets with his first six deliveries in an under-13s match played at a ground by the River Thames. With figures of 1-1-0-6 for Maidenhead and Bray against Taplow, 11-year-old Kieran Gray was removed from the attack to give others a go.

- Having not played top-class cricket in a decade, and nearing the age of 40, former Australian slow bowler Brad Young made a comeback in 2012/13 appearing in the Twenty20 Big Bash League. Young appeared in six one-day internationals for Australia in the late 1990s, taking one wicket at the record-high average of 251.00. His main claim to fame is a hat-trick and figures of 4-4 off four overs against New Zealand (58) in a semi-final of the Commonwealth Games cricket tournament at Kuala Lumpur in 1998/99.

- With a haul of 5-179 against India at Mumbai in 2013/14, Shane Shillingford became just the fourth bowler to take a five-wicket haul in five consecutive Test innings. The previous bowler to achieve five five-fors in a row was England's Alec Bedser in 1953, while Australia's Charlie Turner holds the world record with six, against England in 1888.

  A month later, Shillingford's world came crashing down with the tall off-spinner banned from bowling in all international cricket after his action was deemed to be illegal.

• Playing in his first Test in three months since suffering a side strain in 2012/13, James Pattinson became the first Australian in nearly 90 years to bowl out the first three in the batting order. In the first Test against India at Chennai, Pattinson bowled Murali Vijay (10), Virender Sehwag (2) and Cheteshwar Pujara (44) in the space of 28 balls. Only the fourth Australian to bowl the first three batsmen in a Test innings, he became the first to do so since spinner Arthur Mailey at The Oval in 1926.

Pattinson finished with 5-96 and four bowled dismissals, while team-mate Nathan Lyon leaked 215 runs for three wickets, equalling fellow spinner Jason Krejza, who took 8-215 at Nagpur in 2008/09, the most runs conceded by an Australian in an innings against India. Ravichandran Ashwin (12-198) became the first Indian bowler to achieve a ten-wicket haul in a Test at his home ground, with all 20 Australian wickets falling to spinners.

TESTS IN WHICH ALL 20 WICKETS OF ONE SIDE FELL TO SPINNERS

Bowlers	Test	Venue	Season
Jim Laker (19), Tony Lock (1)			
	England v Australia	Manchester	1956
Bhagwath Chandrasekhar (7), Bishan Bedi (6), Erapalli Prasanna (6), Salim Durani (1)			
	India v England	Chennai	1972/73
Erapalli Prasanna (11), Bhagwath Chandrasekhar (8), Srinivas Venkataraghavan (1)			
	India v New Zealand	Auckland	1975/76
Iqbal Qasim (8), Mohammad Nazir (8), Abdul Qadir (4)			
	Pakistan v West Indies	Faisalabad	1980/81
Abdul Qadir (13), Tauseef Ahmed (4), Iqbal Qasim (3)			
	Pakistan v England	Lahore	1987/88
Ravichandran Ashwin (12), Ravindra Jadeja (5), Harbhajan Singh (3)			
	India v Australia	Chennai	2012/13

• When India's Bhuvneshwar Kumar dismissed David Warner at Hyderabad in 2012/13, he became the first bowler to obtain his first wicket in all three forms of international cricket by bowling his victim. On his Twenty20 international debut, he bowled Pakistan opener Nasir Jamshed for two at Bangalore in 2012/13; in his first ODI, against the same opposition at Chennai, he bowled Mohammad Hafeez for a duck, and got Warner (6) for his first Test wicket, in his second match.

In the same Test, Kumar's team-mate Ravindra Jadeja took two lots of 3-33. He became the first bowler in Test history to return identical figures in both innings of a match with all numbers being the same.

• During a four-day game at Providence in 2009/10, two Jamaican slow bowlers both achieved a career-best eight wickets in an innings and ten wickets in the match. Leg-spinner Odean Brown (10-133) took 8-54 in the first innings of the match against Combined Campuses and Colleges, while off-spinner Tamar Lambert (10-63) took 8-42 in the second.

Not two weeks later, Lionel Baker became the third bowler to achieve eight wickets in an innings and ten in a match. In the game against Campuses and Colleges at Gros Islet, the Leeward Islands fast bowler posted first-innings figures of 8-31 and match figures of 13-83.

- Curtis Reid, one of the umpires in the first-ever Test match, appeared in three first-class matches, taking 12 wickets in his second. After taking no wickets on his first-class debut, he collected a dozen (6-64 and 6-5) in a ten-wicket win by Victoria over Tasmania at the MCG in 1870/71.

- During the 1977/78 Test series against the West Indies, four Australians topped the wicket-taking list yet ended up on the losing side. Jeff Thomson took 20 wickets, while Wayne Clark, Jim Higgs and Bruce Yardley took 15 each. The best for the winners was 13 by Joel Garner.

- A late inclusion for a charity cricket match in 2014, an 11-year-old schoolboy took a hat-trick with one of the victims a former Test player. Dee Jarvis, who went along to watch the match at the Wormsley Cricket Cub but ended up playing, dismissed former England fast bowler Gladstone Small, ex-England A wicketkeeper Keith Piper and bowler Michael Ball.

- Shankar Saini achieved an unusual feat with the ball against Himachal Pradesh at Delhi in 1988/89, securing four wickets in four balls spread over two innings. When completing his maiden six-wicket haul in first-class cricket, he claimed two wickets with consecutive balls to end the first innings. He then took two wickets first up in the second innings, during which he claimed the wicket of Shakti Singh twice in his hat-trick. It's believed to be only the second occasion in all first-class cricket of a batsman out twice in the same hat-trick – the previous known instance was Kent's John Fagge in a William Clarke hat-trick at Canterbury in 1844.

- After dismissing Shane Warne with the final delivery in Australia's first innings at Sydney in 2006/07, England's Monty Panesar took a wicket with his next ball, but against a different country. With his next ball in a Test, against the West Indies at Lord's in 2007, Panesar bowled Devon Smith, joining compatriot Geoff Miller who also achieved the feat, against Pakistan and Australia in 1982.

- The first and second wickets of Australia's Ray Bright in one-day internationals came nearly three years apart, nabbing the same batsman each time. After dismissing England's Derek Randall at The Oval in 1977, Bright had to wait 909 days for his next wicket, again accounting for Randall, at the MCG in 1978/79.

  Back in the New Zealand one-day international side after a two-year absence, Daniel Vettori dismissed Sri Lanka's Mahela Jayawardene leg before wicket at Cardiff in the 2013 Champions Trophy. His previous ODI wicket was also that of Jayawardene – again lbw – 27 months previously in the 2011 World Cup. The biggest gap for a bowler taking two consecutive wickets in ODIs in which the batsman was the same is 1,293 days. The fifth victim for Sri Lanka's Hasantha Fernando was Bangladesh's Mohammad Ashraful in Colombo in 2002. His next, and final, wicket was also that of Ashraful, at Bogra in 2005/06.

- Called on to complete a Chris Cairns over at Harare in 2000/01, Craig McMillan collected two wickets. The first to achieve such a feat in Tests, McMillan had Andy Flower out lbw for 48 and got Mluleki Nkala for a duck.

- A month and a half after his 13th birthday, Mushtaq Mohammad achieved a five-wicket haul in the first innings of his first-class debut. Aged 13 years and 44 days, Mushtaq took 5-28 for Karachi Whites versus Sind at Hyderabad in 1956/57. In 1984/85, another 13-year-old took a five-for on debut with Zulfiqar Butt picking up 5-110 for Lahore City Whites against Karachi Blues at Sahiwal.

- When Abdur Razzak took 5-62 against Sri Lanka at Pallekele in 2012/13, he became the first Bangladesh bowler to reach the milestone of 200 wickets in one-day internationals. Along the way, he took an eye-popping three-wicket haul against all of the 17 different teams he'd played against. Apart from striking against all the Test-playing nations, the left-arm spinner also claimed a three-wicket haul in ODIs against Hong Kong, Bermuda, the United Arab Emirates, Ireland, the Netherlands, Kenya, Canada and Scotland: **"It is hard to make a distinction on which has been my best moment. There have been so many good moments. But I think I have enjoyed the fact that the 200 wickets have not taken too long. I have done it in 141 innings, which gives me a lot of pride."**

- In a one-day international at Dublin in 2013, England's Boyd Rankin dismissed Ireland's Ed Joyce for a score of one. In a one-day international at Providence in 2007, Rankin, then playing for Ireland, had dismissed Joyce, who was then playing for England, also for a score of one.

- In the 2013 County Championship, Lancashire duo Kyle Hogg and Glen Chapple bowled unchanged in consecutive innings twice while dismissing an opposition for less than 100. At Chelmsford, Hogg – grandson of the legendary West Indies spinner Sonny Ramadhin – took 4-11, while Chapple achieved 5-9 and a run out with Essex dismissed for a record-low 20. The following week, Hogg, with a career-best 7-27, and Chapple 3-34, combined to demolish Northamptonshire for 62 at Old Trafford.

- In his first 12 months of representing New Zealand, fast bowler Mitchell McClenaghan achieved a four-wicket haul on debut against a record six opponents in one-day internationals. After taking 4-20 in his initial ODI, against South Africa at Paarl in 2012/13, he took 4-56 on debut against England at Hamilton, 4-43 against Sri Lanka and 4-65 against Australia in consecutive matches in the Champions Trophy, 5-58 against the West Indies at Auckland and 4-68 against India, at Napier.

  Another fast-bowling Mitchell also claimed a four-wicket haul in his first ODI against six countries. Australia's Mitchell Starc took 4-27 against Sri Lanka at Brisbane in 2010/11, 4-47 against Afghanistan and 5-42 against Pakistan at Sharjah in 2012, 5-20 against the West Indies at Perth in 2012/13 and 6-28 against New Zealand at Auckland and 4-14 against Scotland at Hobart in the 2015 World Cup.

- Appearing in just his seventh first-class match, Barbados off-spinner Ashley Nurse took two lots of seven wickets in an innings. Playing against Windward Islands at Roseau in 2012/13, Nurse broke the regional record with a match haul of 14-40. The Windwards was decimated in its first innings, all out for 44, after Nurse achieved the record-breaking figures of 7-10, assisted by fellow spinner Sulieman Benn, who took 3-15. Following-on, they were then dismissed for 67, after Nurse (7-30) and Benn (3-35) had bowled unchanged.

  With six wickets in the Barbados innings of 212, Windward spinner Shane Shillingford passed the milestone of 70 wickets for the season, while Nurse finished his first season with 44 in the regional championship at 13.63. Jamaica spin bowler Nikita Miller also passed the 50-wicket milestone with 53 at a record-low average of 8.05.

FIFTY WICKETS AT AN AVERAGE UNDER TEN IN A FIRST-CLASS SEASON SINCE 1900

Bowler	Location	M	W	Avge	BBI	5WI	Season
Sydney Callaway (Canterbury)	New Zealand	5	54	8.77	8-33	8	1903/04
Ron Oxenham (Australians)	India	11	75	7.40	7-13	8	1935/36
Vintcent van der Bijl (Natal)	South Africa	8	54	9.50	6-30	3	1980/81
Nikita Miller (Jamaica)	West Indies	7	52	8.05	7-13	6	2012/13

- After once being belted for the most runs in a Test over, South African spinner Robin Peterson was hit for 35 in a one-day international in 2013. In the match at Pallekele, Sri Lanka's Thisara Perera (65) hit Peterson for the second-costliest over in a ODI to date, with five sixes and a four (6, W1, 6, 6, 6, 6, 4, 6). In 2003/04, Peterson had gone for 28 runs (4, 6, 6, 4, 4, 4) off the bat of Brian Lara in the first South Africa-West Indies Test at Johannesburg.

- When Chris Gayle took 5-91 against Pakistan at Bridgetown in 2005, he became the first bowler to twice take five wickets in the second innings of a Test having not bowled in the first. The year before, Gayle picked up a second-innings haul of 5-34 against England at Birmingham, becoming just the 12th player to achieve the feat in Test match cricket.

- In a special first-class match staged in Sydney in 1937/38 as part of Australia's 150th anniversary celebrations, a 79-year-old bowler sent down the first over. Although unrecorded on the scorecard, Tom Garrett – the sole survivor of the first Test in 1877 – delivered the first over of the match, billed as the Rigg's XI versus McCabe's XI. Twenty-two wickets fell on the second day, with Chuck Fleetwood-Smith taking 11 in the match.

- When Australia disposed of South Africa for 144 at Port Elizabeth in 1957/58, three bowlers were used with two taking a five-for. Alan Davidson took 5-38 and Richie Benaud 5-82, while Davidson's opening partner Ian Meckiff went wicketless, returning figures of 0-20 off 16 overs. Benaud reached three significant bowling milestones during his haul – 100 first-class wickets for the tour, 100 wickets in Tests and 500 in first-class cricket.

- With Griqualand West out for 74 on the opening day of a Currie Cup match in 1946/47, Raymond Beesly claimed a hat-trick, with all three wickets caught by the same fielder. Beesly took 4-11 for Border at Queenstown, with Cyril White completing three successive catches off his bowling.

- England slow bowler Ashley Giles had identical best-bowling figures in both Test and one-day international cricket. His best in a Test was 5-57 against the West Indies at Birmingham in 2004, while his best in ODIs was 5-57 against India in 2001/02. Indian batsman Sandeep Patil (2-28) also recorded identical best-bowling figures in both Tests and ODIs.

- In the same first-class match that Carl Rackemann claimed career-best bowling figures, two players took a hat-trick. Playing against South Africa at Johannesburg in 1985/86, Rackemann took 8-84 and 12 wickets in the match, while Garth Le Roux (3-11) and Clive Rice (3-8) both took hat-tricks in the Australian XI's second-innings total of 61.

- Queensland-born medium-pace bowler Steve Magoffin etched his name in the record books in 2013, taking one of the cheapest 12-wicket hauls in the history of first-class cricket. On his way to the milestone of 100 wickets in the County Championship, Magoffin took a match-winning 8-20 and 4-11 for Sussex against Somerset at Horsham.

- On his Ranji Trophy debut in 1985/86, Vidarbha opening batsman Manohar Agasti took a wicket with the only ball he delivered in first-class cricket. In the match against Railways at Yavatmal, the first-class debutant finished with figures of 0.1-0-0-1. Fellow Indian Basheshkar Khanna also ended his career with the same unusual feat, taking a wicket with the only ball he sent down in first-class cricket at Lahore in 1927/28. In his final first-class appearance, the Northern India captain picked up a wicket with the only delivery of his seven-match career in the game against a Punjab Governor's XI.

- After a nine-wicket haul in the opening Test at Brisbane in 2013/14, Mitchell Johnson ripped through England at Adelaide recording the best-ever Ashes return by a left-arm fast bowler. His 7-40 matched the 7-40 by England medium-pacer Dick Barlow at Sydney in 1882/83.

- Australia's Greg Matthews bowled a total of two balls to Sri Lankan batsman Marvan Atapattu in Tests and bowled him both times. In the first Test of the 1992 series at the SSC ground in Colombo, Matthews got the No. 6 for a first-ball duck in the first innings, and had him for one in the second.

- After taking nine wickets, and a second-innings haul of 7-6, on his first-class debut in 2012/13, Marcello Piedt became the first South African bowler to take more than 50 wickets in his first season. Representing South Western Districts, Piedt took 59 at 16.93 in 13 matches.

  In 2014, the unrelated Dane Piedt became just the second South African bowler to take a wicket with his first delivery on his Test debut. Piedt had Zimbabwe's Mark Vermeulen lbw with his first ball at Harare, finishing with match with 8-152 (4-90 and 4-62), the best return by a South African spinner on Test debut. The first South African bowler to take a wicket with his first ball in a Test was Bert Vogler, against England, at Johannesburg in 1905/06.

- Picked for his only Test at the age of 16, Pakistan leg-spinner Khalid Hassan took two wickets, both of which were centurions. After bowling Reg Simpson for 101 and Denis Compton for 278 at Nottingham in 1954, he became the youngest cricketer to play in his final Test, aged 16 years and 356 days.

- During a first-class match at Johannesburg in 1992/93, a bowler took a hat-trick which were the only wickets to fall in the innings. In Western Province's second-innings total of 46/3, Transvaal's Richard Snell took 3-25, dismissing Michael Voss, Lance Bleekers and Allan Lamb in a hat-trick.

- Appearing in his first Test against South Africa, India's Suresh Raina was given a bowl at Centurion in 2010/11, conceding a record number of runs. As the South Africans advanced to a first-innings total of 620/4 declared, Raina went for 11 runs per over, finishing with figures of 7-0-77-0.

- A 50-over match in Bangladesh in 2013/14 saw Alauddin Babu make the history books after conceding 93 runs off his ten overs. Bowling the last over to Elton Chigumbura in the Abahani Limited-Sheik Jamal match at Mirpur, Alauddin went for a world-record 39 runs (NB5, W1, 6, 4, 6, 4, 6, W1, 6).

- The West Indies' Pedro Collins played in four Tests against Bangladesh and in three of them took wickets with the first and last balls of an innings. When he first achieved the feat – at Dhaka in 2002/03 – only six bowlers before him had done so. He became the first bowler to pull it off twice, and it made three, during two consecutive Tests, at Gros Islet and Kingston in 2004. In each of the three Tests, Collins accounted for Hannan Sarkar with his first ball of the match.

- Twenty bowlers dismissed Sachin Tendulkar on their Test debuts. Zimbabwe's Neil Johnson is the only debutant bowler to dismiss him twice, for 34 and seven at Harare in 1998/99.

- Following a world-record caning in his previous Test, South Africa leg-spinner Imran Tahir came up with a match-winning maiden five-wicket haul, against the country of his birth. In the second Test against Australia at Adelaide in 2012/13, the Lahore-born Imran had figures of 0-180 off 23 overs and 0-80 off 14; in his next Test, at Dubai nearly a year later, he was instrumental in bowling out Pakistan for 99, taking 5-32.

- During a six-wicket haul at Brisbane in 1962/63, Richie Benaud became the first, and only, captain to reach the milestone of 50 wickets in the Ashes. At the end of the series – his last Ashes campaign – Benaud had extended his haul to 63 wickets against England, twice as many as the next most successful captain with the ball, Monty Noble, who took 31 wickets in 15 Ashes Tests, one more match than Benaud.

25 ASHES WICKETS BY A BOWLER AS CAPTAIN

#	Player	M	Inns	Balls	Runs	BBI	BBM	Avge	5WI	10WM	Span
63	Richie Benaud (A)	14	28	5017	1760	6-70	9-173	27.93	4	0	1958-63
31	Monty Noble (A)	15	24	2055	745	7-100	8-140	24.03	1	0	1903-09
27	Johnny Douglas (E)	12	20	1733	885	5-46	5-46	32.77	1	0	1911-21
26	George Giffen (A)	4	7	1418	581	6-155	8-40	22.34	3	0	1894-95

- Australia's Peter Siddle joined immortals Fred Spofforth and Charlie Turner in 2013 when he claimed a five-wicket haul on the opening day of the Ashes at Nottingham. Siddle (5-50) became the first bowler since 1893 to take five wickets on the first day of an Ashes series twice, having picked up 6-54 at Brisbane in 2010/11.

  Turner, who played all of his 17 Tests against England, achieved the feat thrice – 6-15 on his debut at Sydney in 1886/87, 5-44 at Sydney in 1887/88 and 6-67 at Lord's in 1893.

Australian fast-bowling legends Charlie Turner and Fred Spofforth

- Guyana fast bowler Brandon Bess made an unscheduled Test debut in 2010 arriving at the ground with the match already underway. He received a last-minute call-up for the third Test against South Africa at Bridgetown after Nelon Pascal had injured himself just before the start of play. In his only Test, Bess took one wicket.

- Zahid Shah only appeared in two one-day internationals, taking 3-49 in each. Opening the bowling on his debut for the United Arab Emirates against Bangladesh at Lahore in the 2008 Asia Cup, Zahid took 3-49 off ten, and two days later did the same against Sri Lanka at the same ground in what ended up being his final match.

- On his way to his fourth lot of ten wickets in a Test, Sri Lanka's Rangana Herath became the first left-arm bowler to take nine wickets in an innings. With first-innings figures of 9-127 against Pakistan in Colombo in 2014, Herath finished with 14-184 in a match that contained a record 29 wickets by left-arm bowlers. The previous best was 28 during the second South Africa-England Test at Cape Town in 1888/89 in which Lancashire spinner Johnny Briggs picked up 7-17 and 8-11. Herath took a record 22 wickets in the two-Test series against the Pakistanis after 9-164 at Galle.

- Mohammad Sharif, a medium-pacer who appeared in ten Tests for Bangladesh, conceded over 85 runs in all, bar one, of the 11 innings in which he bowled. Making his Test debut in 2000/01, he went for over 100 in the first innings of his first six matches.

- Appearing in his final match in top-class cricket, Adam Gilchrist took his only wicket with the last ball he bowled. With his first ball in Twenty20 cricket – and the 13th of his career – Punjab's wicketkeeping opening-batsman captain dismissed Harbhajan Singh for a duck to end the Mumbai innings at Dharamsala in the 2013 IPL.

ADAM GILCHRIST AT THE BOWLING CREASE

Figures	Format	Match	Venue	Season
2-0-10-0	List A	Young Australia v Leicestershire	Leicester	1995
0.1-0-0-1	Twenty20	Kings XI Punjab v Mumbai Indians	Dharamsala	2013

- Bowling for only the second time in his first-class career, Victoria's wicketkeeping captain Matthew Wade claimed a wicket with his second ball in Sheffield Shield cricket. In the second innings of the match against Queensland at the Gabba, Wade caught the first two Bulls batsmen, the first as a keeper, the second as a bowler.

- The Johannesburg Test against India in 2013/14 marked the first occasion that the opposing wicketkeepers had both bowled in the same Test. South Africa's A.B. de Villiers (1-0-5-0) sent down a single over on the third day, with India captain Mahendra Singh Dhoni (2-0-4-0) stepping up the crease on the fourth.

- Kerala's Subramaniam Santhosh made history in a first-class match in 1985/86 with five wickets in an innings, all of which were caught and bowled. His only five-wicket haul in a first-class career of 30 matches, Santhosh took 5-43 against Goa at Vasco da Gama with eight of their batsmen in the innings dismissed caught and bowled.

- Stepping up for his debut first-class appearance for Bangladesh, slow left-armer Saqlain Sajib recorded the best bowling figures in A-class Test match cricket. Representing Bangladesh A against Zimbabwe A in a four-day match at Cox's Bazar in 2014/15, Sajib took 9-82 and 6-50, the best innings and match figures to date for Bangladesh in first-class cricket.

- After a five-wicket haul on his Test debut, Bangladesh spinner Taijul Islam became the first bowler to claim a hat-trick in his first one-day international. Taijul took a man-of-the-match 4-11 against Zimbabwe at Mirpur in 2014/15.

HAT-TRICK ON INTERNATIONAL DEBUT

Bowler	Format	Match	Venue	Season
Maurice Allom	Test	England v New Zealand	Christchurch	1929/30
Peter Petherick	Test	New Zealand v Pakistan	Lahore	1976/77
Damien Fleming	Test	Australia v Pakistan	Rawalpindi	1994/95
Taijul Islam	ODI	Bangladesh v Zimbabwe	Mirpur	2014/15

- In a match against London County at Crystal Palace in 1902, two bowlers on their first-class debuts achieved a five-wicket haul in the same innings with both conceding the same number of runs. In their first first-class match for Ireland, Bill Harrington and Tom Ross took 5-26 in London County's first innings, with both taking three wickets each in the second.

- A former call-centre operator made history in 2014 when he took 15 wickets in a day in a County Championship match for Durham. Chris Rushworth brought up the season's best figures with 9-52 against Northamptonshire at Chester-le-Street, becoming the first bowler to achieve 15 wickets (15-95) for Durham, eclipsing Alan Walker who took 14-177 against Essex at Chelmsford in 1995. Rushworth achieved his haul with just 120 deliveries, the equal-fourth fewest number of balls in first-class history in taking 15 wickets in a match.

FEWEST BALLS FOR 15 WICKETS IN A FIRST CLASS MATCH

Balls	Bowler	Figures	Match	Venue	Season
92	William Brown	23-1-73-15 ‡	Tasmania v Victoria	Hobart	1857/58
95	Alonzo Drake	15.5-1-51-15	Yorkshire v Somerset	Weston-super-Mare	1914
117	Hedley Verity	19.3-8-38-15	Yorkshire v Kent	Sheffield	1936
120	Colin Blythe	20-6-45-15	Kent v Leicestershire	Leicester	1912
120	Chris Rushworth	20-3-95-15	Durham v Northants	Chester-le-Street	2014

‡ 4-ball overs and in Brown's only first-class match

- After a fruitless one-day international debut in 2010, Indian medium-pacer Pankaj Singh recorded the worst-ever figures by a bowler on his Test debut. With a return of 0-45 off seven overs against Sri Lanka at Harare in his first ODI, Pankaj conceded 146 runs without a wicket in the first innings of his Test debut, against England at Southampton in 2014. With 0-33 in the second innings, his match figures of 0-179 beat the previous worst in a Test of 0-164 (0-131 and 0-33) by Pakistan's Sohail Khan against Sri Lanka at Karachi in 2008/09.

  Later in the year, Indian leg-spinner Karn Sharma also made the record books in his first Test match by conceding the greatest number of runs in an over by a bowler on debut. In the 2014/15 Adelaide Test match, Mitchell Marsh hit him for 24 runs (6, 4, 0, 6, 2, 6) in the 64th over of Australia's second innings. The previous record was 21 runs, shared by three bowlers – South Africa's Lance Klusener at Kolkata in 1996/97, the West Indies' Colin Stuart at Melbourne in 2000/01 and Pankaj Singh at Southampton in 2014.

- A surprise hit in the 2013 Champions League, slow bowler Pravin Tambe made his first-class debut at the age of 42. The leading bowler in the Twenty20 tournament with 12 wickets at 6.50 for the Rajasthan Royals, Tambe was handed a first-class cap for Mumbai in the 2013/14 Ranji Trophy.

  In the 2014 IPL, Tambe (3-26) took a hat-trick for Rajasthan against Kolkata in Ahmedabad. His hat-trick – a wide and two legal deliveries – completed the worst collapse for the first six wickets (121/1 to 123/6) in Twenty20 history to date.

- When Stuart Broad took 7-72 against the West Indies at Lord's in 2012, each batsman was caught by a different fielder. A first in a Test in England, Broad equalled the feat of spinner Jack White during his 8-126 against Australia at Adelaide in the 1928/29 Ashes.

- David Hookes claimed two wickets for Australia, both of which came with the last ball he bowled in a Test and a one-day international. He claimed the wicket of New Zealand's

Martin Snedden in a World Series Cup ODI at the MCG in 1982/83 and got India's Shivlav Yadav with his final delivery in a Test, at Adelaide in 1985/86. Pakistan's Sarfraz Nawaz also claimed a wicket with his final balls in both Test and one-day international cricket.

• Neil Wagner, a South African-born pace bowler, established a world first in 2010/11 by taking five wickets in a single over during a first-class match in New Zealand. Representing Otago in the Plunket Shield, Wagner ripped through Wellington to set up an innings victory inside three days at Queenstown. He had opener Stewart Rhodes caught for 77, then clean bowled Justin Austin-Smellie, Jeetan Patel and Ili Tugaga for first-ball ducks. And although the No.10 Mark Gillespie survived the next delivery, he succumbed to the last ball of the over, with Wagner collecting 6-36.

FIVE WICKETS IN SIX BALLS IN A FIRST-CLASS MATCH

Bowler	Match	Venue	Season
Bill Copson	Derbyshire v Warwickshire	Derby	1937
William Henderson	NE Transvaal v Orange Free State	Bloemfontein	1937/38
Pat Pocock	Surrey v Sussex	Eastbourne	1972
Yasir Arafat	Rawalpindi v Faisalabad	Rawalpindi	2004/05
Neil Wagner	Otago v Wellington	Queenstown	2010/11

• To mark the opening day of the 2015 World Cup, Steven Finn became the first England bowler to take a hat-trick in the competition since it began in 1975. Finn took his trio with the last three balls of Australia's innings at the MCG on Valentine's Day. On the same day in the 2003 tournament, Chaminda Vaas had become the first Sri Lankan to grab a World Cup hat-trick, doing so with the first three balls of the match against Bangladesh at Pietermaritzburg. Australia's Mitchell Marsh matched Finn with a five-wicket haul of his own, taking 5-33 on his World Cup debut.

After figures of 5-71 – the most runs conceded while taking a hat-trick in a ODI – Finn was set upon by an in-form Brendon McCullum in England's following match at Wellington. On his way to a record-breaking 77 off 25 balls, McCullum took 20 runs off his first over and whacked him for four consecutive sixes off his second – and final – over. Finn finished with 0-49, the most expensive two-over stint in one-day international cricket, surpassing Shahadat Hossain's 0-38 for Bangladesh against New Zealand at Queenstown in 2007/08. For the hosts, Tim Southee took 7-33 in the Wellington match, the first New Zealander to achieve seven wickets in a one-day international.

Women in Uniform

- When an Indian cricket fan moved to New York in 2003 she "Googled" the USA Women's Cricket Association, a move that saw her later representing the United States. After clicking on to the association's website, Anahita Arora replied to a plea for female cricketers to turn up for selection trials. She went along, made the cut and ended up opening the bowling for the United States in the ICC Women's World Cup Qualifier 50-over tournament in Bangladesh.

- In a one-day international at the MCG in 2013/14, numbers four and five from both sides all scored an unbeaten half-century. A first in all international cricket, Australia's Alex Blackwell made 82 not out and Ellyse Perry 65 in an unbeaten fourth-wicket stand of 141 after the pair had come together at 68/3. For England, Lydia Greenway (69*) and Arran Brindle (64*) also joined forces at 68/3, going one run better with an unbeaten fourth-wicket partnership of 142.

- Mandy Kornet appeared in 15 one-day internationals for the Netherlands during the 2000s, making a duck in her final seven matches. After scoring 15 runs in her first five ODIs, she then had scores of 0, 0, 1, 0, 0, 0, 0, 0, 0 and 0.

- In a World Cup match at Sittingbourne in 1973, opposing bowlers took four wickets for less than ten on their debuts. England's Glynis Hullah snapped up 4-8, while Jamaica's Madge Stewart took 4-9.

- After being run out for 88 at the top of the order in a World Cup match at Wanganui in 1981/82, India's Fowzieh Khalili picked up five dismissals with three stumpings. She became the first, and to date only, wicketkeeper to achieve the double of a fifty and five dismissals in the same women's one-day international.

- Australia's Jill Kennare made the record books in 1984/85 when she scored one-day international centuries on consecutive days. She struck a match-winning 122 against England at the Aberfeldie Park ground in Melbourne and then made an unbeaten 100 against the same opposition at the same ground the following day.

  The next player to achieve the feat of consecutive ODI hundreds was New Zealand's Debbie Hockley who made two scores of 100 – 100 not out against Sri Lanka and 100 against the West Indies, both times at Chandigarh, over three days in the 1997/98 World Cup.

- The youngest female to appear in a one-day international destroyed a Japan XI at Amsterdam in 2003 with career-best figures of 7-4. Pakistan's Sajjida Shah – who made her ODI debut at the age of 12 in the year 2000 – was one of five bowlers used to extinguish Japan for 28 in 34 overs, a total bloated by 20 extras. Her team-mate Khursheed Jabeen returned the extraordinary figures of 10-8-2-3 with an economy rate of 0.20.

- On their way to a massive 233-run loss to South Africa at Savar in Bangladesh in 2011/12, the Netherlands fell apart for 36 with the only instance of a pair of bowlers bowling unchanged in a completed women's one-day international. Shabnim Ismail took 6-10 off 8.3 overs, while Moseline Daniels took 4-25 off eight.

- The New Zealand women's cricket team copped a hiding in their maiden Test match, sustaining the biggest-ever innings loss on record. After falling for 44 at the hands of England at Lancaster Park in Christchurch in 1934/35, the tourists responded with 503/5 declared, with centuries from wicketkeeper Betty Snowball (189) and Molly Hide (110). New Zealand managed 122 in their second innings, going down by an innings and 337 runs.

- In a 2005 Women's World Cup match in Pretoria, Sri Lanka suffered a 214-run defeat after a total of 70 in which no batter reached double figures. Chasing England's 284, more than half of the Sri Lankan total was made up of extras, with a whopping 38 wides and one leg bye.

- West Indies all-rounder Stefanie Taylor made history in 2013 when she was ranked the No. 1 batter and bowler in one-day international cricket. The then-22-year-old became the first-ever player – man or woman – to head both the batting and bowling rankings at the same time.

- Australia's numbers ten and 11 staged a rescue mission against England at Hove in 2005, raising the first last-wicket century stand in women's Test cricket. Debutants Shelly Nitschke (81*) and Clea Smith (42) shared a record 119-run partnership that took Australia to 355. The opening pair of Lisa Keightley (11 and 0) and Belinda Clark (0 and 0) had stands of nought and nought.

- While playing league cricket in England in 2008, Australia's Alex Blackwell was called on to assist in the aid of an 80-year-old man who'd collapsed in the stands. An appeal was sent out at the ground for anyone with medical experience and the former medical student was eager to help: **"Myself and another player, Louise, rushed over and immediately knew this man was in a great deal of trouble. With no breathing and absent pulse, we had to commence CPR. Louise was on compressions while I was delivering mouth-to-mouth. We continued CPR for nine minutes, and to be honest, I thought we had lost him, but we just kept going until paramedics arrived and were ready with the defibrillator."**

- Australia's youngest-ever Test cricketer went where no woman had ever been before in 2010 by playing with the men. Ellyse Perry became the first female to play grade cricket in Sydney, opening the bowling on her debut against Blacktown in an under-21s match in 2010/11. The then-20-year-old played a winning role for the Sydney club, taking 2-14 and scoring five not out: **"It was pretty much the same as every Sunday. The only difference was there were ten big, brute boys out there."**

  Her first victim was an English import, Joe Robbins: **"I'm happy to go down in history. You've got to give her respect – she's playing here on merit. When she's running in, you don't think to yourself it's a girl bowling. She was the best out of the four seamers. She was hard to face."**

- Ireland tasted immediate success at its first outing in Test cricket, attaining a crushing innings victory over Pakistan. The match, played in Dublin in 2000, was all over in two days, with Ireland (193/3d) blowing away the tourists for totals of 53 and 86. Isobel Joyce was named player of the match with second-innings bowling figures of 6-21.

- In a one-day international against Pakistan in Colombo in 2001/02, Sri Lanka's captain Suthershini Sivanantham led her country to a 104-run victory with the best batting and bowling figures in the match. She top-scored with 36 batting at No. 7 and then bowled her side to glory with the record-breaking figures of 5-2 with seven maidens.

- During the Netherlands-South Africa Test match at Rotterdam in 2007, two debutants were dismissed for a pair. The Dutch pair of Annemarie Tanke and Jolet Hartenhof both made two ducks in their only Test match appearance, with the former run out in each innings.

- All tickets for women's cricket matches at the 2010 Asian Games in the Chinese city of Guangzhou sold out within two days. With cricket included for the first time at the Games, a 12,000-seat stadium was purpose-built for the event. Hosts China (116/6) won the opening match of the Twenty20-style format, downing Malaysia (61/8) thanks to a 47-run effort from their No. 10 Sun Haun and a haul of 3-8 from Mei Chunhau.

  Pakistan went on to win the gold medal by defeating Bangladesh in the final, with its captain Sana Mir full of praise for the exposure the tournament gave to women's cricket: **"We never get this kind of media coverage back at home. I am just so glad the sport made it to the Asian Games. There is always TV coverage when the men's cricket team plays in Pakistan because it is huge, but you never see us playing on big screens or TVs."**

- Warwickshire captain Ian Westwood was moved to issue an apology in 2009 after bagging women's cricket during a club function. He labelled it "pointless and a waste of time", adding he would only attend a women's match if the players wore short skirts.

> **"I just hope that the thousands of women who follow Ian Westwood and Warwickshire don't withdraw their support, as the attendances at Edgbaston will be severely dented."**
>
> former England captain Rachael Heyhoe-Flint

- Appearing in her first match as England captain, Arran Thompson put Scotland to the sword with the newcomers falling for 24 and sustaining a 238-run defeat. None of the batters reached double figures in the match at Reading in 2001, with Laura Harper snaring 4-5. Aged 19 years and 260 days, Thompson became the first teenager – male or female – to captain a one-day international.

- After a history-making double-century on her Test debut, Australia's Michelle Goszko was unable to reach double figures in her remaining three matches. With 204 in her first Test, against England at Shenley, in 2001, Goszko made two consecutive ducks, then innings of four and nine for a career average of 43.40.

  As a 17-year-old in 1994/95, Goszko, a right-arm medium-pace bowler, had taken 6-9 on her debut for the New South Wales Under-21s.

- New South Wales kick-started the 2010/11 national 50-over competition in record-breaking style, falling five runs short of 400. Batting against Tasmania (160) at North Sydney Oval, the NSW Breakers raced to 395/5, with a record 157 from opener Alex Blackwell: **"As a team, never once have we ever spoken about making 400 runs before, but by the end, we were aiming for 400. All the way through our innings we had our goals … in the end we fell just short."**

- Australian Test players Alex Blackwell and Rachael Haynes got the 2013/14 season off to a flying start with a triple-century opening stand in a Sydney club match. The two put on 387 for Universities against Northern Districts, with Blackwell hitting 223 and Haynes 168.

- In the third match of the 1973 Women's World Cup, two of the debutants blossomed with centuries. England's Enid Bakewell (101*) and Lynn Thomas (134*) began their careers with a 246-run opening partnership in the match, against an International XI at Brighton.

  In 1999, an Indian pair reproduced the feat in a ODI against Ireland at Milton Keynes. Opening up for the Indians, debutants Reshma Gandhi (104*) and Mithali Raj (114*) put on a match-winning stand of 258, the highest unbroken partnership in a women's one-day international.

- The West Indies extracted a memorable Twenty20 win over South Africa at Paarl in 2009/10 after just one of their batters reached double figures. Brought undone for 97 in the final over, opener Deandra Dottin was the only one to pass ten, going on to 52 off 36 balls, with South Africa then making 95/6.

- England downed South Africa in a women's one-day international in 2011/12 on the back of two maiden centuries and a record double-century partnership. Lydia Greenway, with an unbeaten 125, and Arran Brindle, with 107 not out, shared an unbroken fourth-wicket stand of 218 in the match at Potchefstroom.

- After Nance Clements had made her Victorian debut against the visiting English team in 1934/35, she requested, as a souvenir, the MCG scoreboard banner that displayed her name. Clements was granted her request and later discovered the name of a famous England bowler – Harold Larwood – painted on the reverse side. Ground authorities had re-used banners from an MCG match during the 1932/33 Bodyline series.

- When New Zealand hosted England in the third Test at Auckland in 1968/69, a record number of players were stumped. Both wicketkeepers – NZ's Bev Bretnall and England's Shirley Hodges – achieved five dismissals in an innings, with a match total of seven stumpings overtaking the previous mark of six, established in the previous Test at Christchurch.

- New Zealand's Emily Drumm made history in 1996 by scoring centuries in her final two Tests. In her last match, Drumm hit 62 and an unbeaten 112 against England at Guildford, having scored 161 and 62 – both times unbeaten – in her final Test at home, against Australia at Christchurch in 1994/95. In her five Tests, Drumm scored 433 runs at an average of 144.33.

- After a pair of single-digit scores in her previous Test, New Zealand's Vera Robinson was brought back 20 years later for one more go at the highest level. With innings of two and four against England at Auckland in 1948/49, Robinson was resurrected for the first Test against England in 1968/69, a record break of 19 years and 323 days.

- Despite becoming the first Australian, man or woman, to take a five-wicket haul in a Twenty20 international, Julie Hunter was unable to win the player-of-the-match award. The Victorian medium-pacer took a match-winning 5-22 in a semi-final against the West Indies at the 2012 World Twenty20, with the gong going to Ellyse Perry for her 2-19, a run out and a catch.

- During the ICC Women's Twenty20 Qualifier tournament in 2013, Sri Lanka beat Japan inside two overs. After dismissing Japan in the match in Dublin for 21, the Sri Lankan openers hit the required 22 runs in 1.4 overs.

- In 2010, Rachael Heyhoe-Flint became the first female cricketer to be inducted into the International Cricket Council's Hall of Fame. She appeared in 22 Test matches, captaining England to victory in the 1973 Women's World Cup.

- A 13-year-old girl called up at the last minute to play for a men's team in Australia in 2010/11 took a hat-trick with the first three balls she bowled. Playing for Kingaroy Services, Holly Ferling (4-8) – a member of the under-15 Queensland women's side – also took a wicket with her fifth ball in the match, against South Burnett Warriors.

  The first female named Queensland Junior Cricketer of the Year, Ferling made her debut for Australia in 2012/13 at the age of 17, and took 2-10 against India in a Women's World Cup match at Cuttack.

- The South African side Kei had a tough time during the country's 50-over Provincial League in 2010/11, failing to reach 40 in their six innings. In a match against Eastern Province, Kei were dismissed for 30 chasing 494-4, and suffered a 533-run loss in their next match, against Boland.

  Throughout the competition, Kei's highest total was 36 – in their last match – which featured a score of ten by Nandi Maya, the only batter to reach double figures in any of the games. A total of 28 ducks was recorded by the team in the series, with seven in a match against Western Province.

- In her final Test match for Australia, Margaret Jennings uniquely captained the side as well as opening the batting and keeping wicket. With scores of 15 and 57 and two dismissals against India in Perth in 1976/77, Jennings led her side to a 147-run victory.

  Coincidentally, Jennings also captained, kept and opened in her final one-day international. In her farewell innings, she repeated her final Test match score with an unbeaten 57, and achieved three dismissals in an eight-wicket victory over England at Hyderabad in 1977/78.

- The fashion designer regarded as the creator of the miniskirt and hotpants is a major cricket fan who regards being out first ball one of the worst things in life. Britain's Woman of the Year in 1963, Mary Quant played the game while at school in Kent: **"Our games mistress was a horror. She made us go and pull up nettles in the long grass as punishment when we were out."**

- A British women's cricket team racked up one of the highest totals of all time in the 50-over game in 2011 with three of its batters scoring centuries. The Loughton Ladies XI hit 521/3 against Leeds & Broomfield (86), with rapid unbeaten hundreds from Lauren Onojaife, Beth Wild and Laura Owen.

  Onojaife (101*), who had just returned from a stint playing club cricket in Australia, reached her ton off just 42 balls, which included 16 fours and two sixes. She retired on 101, as did Wild.

- The two highest innings in women's one-day international cricket were both scored on the same day. On 16 December 1997, Australia's Belinda Clark pre-empted Sachin Tendulkar by hitting a ODI double-century – 229 not out – against Denmark at Mumbai in the World Cup, while England's Charlotte Edwards smashed an unbeaten 173 against Ireland at Poona. On both occasions, each player outscored the opposition on their own, with Denmark dismissed for 49 and Ireland for 116.

- Appearing in her first Test match on home soil, Rene Farrell took four wickets in five balls, including a hat-trick, in the 2010/11 Ashes Test in Sydney. With figures of 5-23 in just her second Test, Farrell became only the third player – after Australia's Betty Wilson in 1957/58 and Pakistan's Shaiza Khan in 2003/04 – to take a hat-trick in a women's Test match.

- India's Neetu David marked the 100th women's Test match by returning her best-ever figures of 8-53. It was a bittersweet moment for David, who supplied the first instance of a female bowler taking eight wickets in a Test innings only to end up on the losing side. England won the historic match at Jamshedpur in 1995/96 by the slender margin of two runs.

- In 1997/98, Sri Lanka's Chamani Seneviratna became the first female to score a century and claim a five-wicket haul on her Test debut. After taking 5-31 against Pakistan at Colombo, the 19-year-old then struck an unbeaten 105 batting at No. 8. Seneviratna became only the fourth female to achieve the all-round feat, and the first since England's Enid Bakewell in 1979.

- After losing its first six wickets for single-figure scores in a one-day international at Taunton in 2012, the Indian women's team ended up winning the match. Seemingly down-and-out at 34/6 batting first, India rallied to 129 off their 50 overs and then bowled out England for 115. In the fourth match of the series at Truro, India didn't score their first run until the fourth ball of the fourth over then lost their first wicket off the next ball.

- England medium-pacer Anya Shrubsole starred in her country's opening match of their 2011/12 tour of New Zealand by taking 5-5 in a 50-over match. Opening the bowling against a New Zealand Emerging Players XI (111) at Lincoln, she took her 5-5 off 5.1 overs with all of her victims dismissed for scores under ten. A few days later at Wellington, she picked up 5-11, her country's first five-for in women's Twenty20 internationals.

- West Indies off-spinner Anisa Mohammed dominated Pakistan in 2011, taking four five-fours in one-day internationals during a three-month period. After sensational figures of 10-6-5-5 at Kingstown in St Vincent, she then returned 10-5-7-5 in game two of the series at the same ground two days later. In the ICC Women's World Cup Qualifier tournament, Mohammed took 5-26 at Savar and a West Indies-record 7-14 at Dhaka.

  Mohammed had made her one-day international debut at the age of 14, in a match against Japan in 2003. She sent down ten overs, with six maidens, taking 1-4.

- Australian slow bowler Marie Lutschini appeared in nine Tests, with her first three wickets all coming via stumpings in the first innings of her debut. In the first Test against the West Indies at Montego Bay in 1975/76, the first three batters to fall were all stumped by Margaret Jennings off Lutschini, who finished her first innings with 4-48. Vivalyn Latty-Scott, who made her debut for the West Indies in the same match, took 5-48 with 17 maidens off 41 overs, in Australia's only innings.

- The opening match of the 2010 Women's World Twenty20 kicked off in record-breaking fashion with one player scoring the fastest century of all time and another taking a wicket with her first ball in international cricket. Deandra Dottin made history by becoming the first female to score a Twenty20 international century, smashing a 45-ball unbeaten 112 in the match against South Africa at Basseterre. She reached her 50 off 25 balls in 25 minutes, and blasted her way to the hundred-mark off 38 balls in 37 minutes. South Africa's only debutant in the match, 16-year-old left-arm medium-pace bowler Chloe Tryon, took a wicket with her first delivery and finished up with 2-28 off three overs.

- England introduced one of their youngest-ever debutants in 2001, a player with one of the longest, and most colourful, of names. Ebony-Jewel Cora-Lee Camellia Rosamond Rainford-Brent was 17 when she made her one-day international debut against the Netherlands at Reading, taking 1-8 in four overs: **"I was a bit concerned my name wasn't going to fit on the shirt."**

- In her final one-day international, against Denmark at Delhi in 1997/98, the West Indies' Carol-Ann James was left stranded one run shy of what would been a maiden century. In her only other ODI against Denmark – at Beckenham in the 1993 World Cup – James sent down a competition-record 11 maidens in her 12-over spell. Chasing 121 for victory, Denmark fell for 76, with James returning figures of 12-11-4-1.

- Australia smothered the West Indies in a one-day international series in 2014/15 with Ellyse Perry scoring a fifty in each of the four matches. Her scores of 53, 72, 64 not out and 74 not out followed an unbeaten 90 against England at Hobart in 2013/14. West Indies opener Hayley Matthews also scored half-centuries (55, 89, 60) in the first three matches. After a 4-0 win in the Twenty20 international series, Australia then wrapped up the ODI series 4-0.

- England's Arran Brindle, who made her Test debut in 2001, made history by scoring a century in a men's premier league match in 2011. Brindle struck 128 for Louth versus Market Deeping in the Lincolnshire League: **"I have played for Louth men's first XI for several years now, and I captained the side in 2007, 2009 and 2010. It's a totally natural environment for me."**

- Sri Lanka opened their 2013 World Cup campaign with a bang, securing a nail-biting win over England at Mumbai. They won by one wicket off the last ball of the match, both firsts in women's World Cup cricket. Their total of 244 was also the highest batting second in the competition, while their five sixes, including one off the final ball of the match, was a first in any World Cup game against England.

- When Ireland's Gaby Lewis took to the field in a Twenty20 match against South Africa in 2014, she became the first cricketer born in the 21st century to appear in an international cricket match. The daughter of Alan Lewis, who appeared in eight first-class matches for Ireland, and granddaughter of Ian, who played in five, Gaby made her debut at the age of 13 years and 166 days.

- After scoring a half-century in a one-day international in 2003/04, Anju Jain made four stumpings. Jain scored 67 and figured in a 152-run opening stand in the match, against the West Indies in Dhanbad. In 2005/06, her namesake Karu Jain achieved a record-equalling five stumpings in a ODI – and also opened the batting – against New Zealand in Lincoln. Compatriot Venkatacher Kalpana was the first to obtain five stumpings in a one-day international, against Denmark at Slough in the 1993 World Cup. She, too, opened the batting.

- When the West Indies women played their inaugural Test match, half of the line-up was aged over 35. The Test, against Pakistan at Karachi in 2003/04, featured a near-47-year-old Stephanie Power, a 41-year-old Envis Williams, Verena Felicien, aged 39, Jacqueline Robinson, 38, Felicia Cummings, 36, and Nadine George, 35. For each player, this was their only Test appearance.

- A 20-year-old member of the Lancashire women's cricket team made history in 2013 when she became the first female in over 100 years to appear in a league competition. On her debut in the Bolton Association, Chloe Wallwork starred with 4-11 in a win for Walshaw against Golborne: **"I didn't even know I was the first girl to play first-team cricket in the league for 125 years until I read about it."**

   In 2015, England Test bowler Kate Cross became the first woman to appear in the Central Lancashire League tournament. She marked the occasion with 3-19 on her debut for Heywood versus Clifton, and later took 8-47 against Unsworth. On her Test debut – against Australia at Perth in 2013/14 – Cross picked up identical hauls of 3-35 in each innings.

- While scoring her maiden Test century in 2013, Australia's Sarah Elliott breastfed her nine-month-old baby during the lunch and tea breaks. Elliott scored 95 before stumps on the opening day of the Ashes Test at Wormsley after getting up four times to feed her son the night before. She went on to score 104 in just her second Test as did England's Heather Knight, both of whom had made their debuts in the same match, at Bankstown in Sydney in 2010/11.

   Opening the batting, Knight hit 157 off 338 balls, sharing an England-record seventh-wicket stand of 156 with Laura Marsh who brought up her maiden half-century five years after making her Test debut. Batting at No. 8, Marsh reached her fifty off 291 balls and made it to 55 off 304 in 343 minutes.

- To celebrate the 100th women's one-day international, Australia's Ruth Buckstein scored a maiden century of exactly 100. Her opening partner Lindsay Reeler (143*) also scored a maiden ton and shared an Australian-record first-wicket stand of 220 in the match against the Netherlands at the Willetton Sports Ground in Perth in 1988/89. With a total of 284/1 off 60 overs, scored in exactly 200 minutes, the Netherlands were blown away for 29, with both openers out for ducks and seven in all failing to get off the mark. Karen Brown, a medium-pacer from Victoria, took career-best figures of 4-4.

   The Buckstein-Reeler stand beat by just one the previous best Australian partnership for the first wicket in a women's ODI. In

1996/97, Belinda Clark (131) and Lisa Keightley (156*) put on 219 against Pakistan at a suburban ground in Melbourne, with Australia surging to 397/4 off 50 overs, which also contained a 94 from Zoe Goss, batting at No. 3. Australia gained a massive 374-run victory, after disposing of Pakistan for 23, with no batters reaching double figures.

- In its first Test in eight years, and with as many as eight debutants in its ranks, India beat England at Wormsley in 2014 in a game that featured a record number of lbw dismissals in a women's Test match. Eight of the Indian line-up and 12 of England's were out lbw, with a record seven in the host's first-innings total of 92.

    Although she ended up on the losing side, Jenny Gunn was named player of the match after becoming the first England woman to achieve the all-round double of a fifty and a five-wicket haul in the same Test. Gunn scored an unbeaten 62 in the second innings and also claimed 5-19, becoming only the second to do so, after Australia's Ellyse Perry (71 and 5-38) against England at Perth earlier in the year.

- Described as one of the finest innings played by a female cricketer, England captain Charlotte Edwards saved her team from humiliation in the 2010/11 Ashes with an unbeaten century. After the first day of the Test at Sydney's Bankstown Oval, Edwards had reached 103 not out in a team score of 181/8. She remained undefeated with 114 out of 207, scored off 310 balls in 389 minutes.

- Appearing in just her second one-day international, an 18-year-old Meg Lanning became the youngest player to score a century for Australia. Lanning, who was born in Singapore, hit an unbeaten 104 against England at the WACA in 2010/11.

    After posting consecutive fifties against New Zealand two seasons later, Lanning hit the fastest ton by an Australian in a one-day international. In the third ODI at North Sydney, Lanning made 103, reaching the three figures off just 45 balls. Her knock included 18 fours and three sixes.

    In 2013/14, she then became the first Australian woman to score a hundred in a Twenty20 international. Batting at three against Ireland in the Women's World Twenty20 tournament at Sylhet, Lanning made 126 off 65 balls, hitting 18 fours and four sixes. Aged 21 years and 300 days, Lanning also became Australia's youngest-ever captain, when she led Australia in a ODI against England at the MCG in the same season.

- Rowan Milburn appeared in a total of 15 one-day internationals, playing her first seven for the Netherlands in the calendar year of

2000 and the remaining eight for New Zealand in 2007. The Otago-born wicketkeeper made one ODI half-century, an innings of 71 for the Netherlands against Ireland in the Women's World Cup at Christchurch in 2000/01. Her father Barry Milburn appeared in three Tests for New Zealand, also as wicketkeeper, against the West Indies in 1968/69.

- With a double-century to her credit in a 40-over match as a 12-year-old, Mignon du Preez became the first South African woman to score a century on her Test debut. Eight years after her ODI debut, a 25-year-old du Preez scored 102 in her first Test, against India at Mysore in 2014/15. Earlier in the match, Indian opener Thirush Kamini scored her maiden Test fifty in just her second appearance, reaching 192 and sharing a record second-wicket stand of 275 with Poonam Raut (130).

  Kamini and Raut, who also scored her first fifty in her second appearance, provided the first instance of two Indian women hitting a Test century in the same innings.

Births and Deaths

- When Steve O'Keefe made his Test debut against Pakistan at Dubai in 2014/15, he became the first Australian Test cricketer born in Malaysia. The only other Malaysian-born Test cricketer was India's Lall Singh, who appeared in a single match, against England at Lord's in 1932. With figures of 2-107 and 2-112, O'Keefe became just the seventh bowler to concede at least 100 runs in both innings of their debut Test match.

  During the same tour, his New South Wales team-mate Sean Abbott also made his debut, in a Twenty20 international, also at Dubai. He became just the third international cricketer to be born on 29 February. The other Leap Year Day players are England's Alf Gover and Australia's Gavin Stevens.

- A 33-year-old fast bowler collapsed on the pitch and died in 2012 having just taken a five-wicket haul in a club match in the UK. The match was abandoned after Richard Beaumont was airlifted to a nearby hospital in Birmingham.

- A number of cricket players were killed as a result of a mortar attack in Pakistan in 2012. A volley of shells hit a residential area of a tribal region that borders Afghanistan, including a cricket ground where a game was underway at the time.

- A former Ranji Trophy cricketer lost his life on a street in the Indian city of Bhopal in 2012 after suffering a heart attack. The Indian media reported that no one went to the rescue of Raja Ali who'd collapsed to the pavement until police rushed him off to hospital. The 36-year-old appeared in 87 first-class matches, scoring nine centuries after making his debut in 1996/97.

- Three of the greatest players to represent the West Indies share the same birthday of 21 September. Learie Constantine was born on this day, in 1902, as was Curtly Ambrose, in 1963, and Chris Gayle in 1979.

- Two Test cricketers who shared the same nickname of "Plum" also shared the same date of birth and death. Plum Warner, who appeared in 15 Tests for England, was born on 2 October in 1873 at Port-of-Spain and died on 30 January in 1963. Plum Lewis was born on the same date in 1884 and appeared in a single Test for South Africa. He also died on 30 January, in 1976.

- Rajesh Peter, an Indian fast bowler, was found dead in his flat in New Delhi in 1995 in what were described as suspicious circumstances. He appeared in 13 first-class matches for Delhi, scoring 67 not out in a ninth-wicket partnership of 118 with Rakesh Shukla (69*) in the 1981/82 Ranji Trophy Final against Karnataka.

- Sri Lankan-born batsman Sujeewa Kamalasuriya, who appeared in three first-class matches in 1988/89, lost his life in a devastating tsunami that struck southern Asia in 2004. He had moved to Australia and was back in his home country showing the sights to a friend when the giant wave hit.

- Two first-class cricketers died on the same day in 2012 in road accidents when returning home from a game. The West Indies' Runako Morton was killed after his car slammed into a pole, while Ranji Trophy cricketer Kishore Bhikane died after a truck hit his bike, which he had just won for the best bowling performance in a state-level cricket tournament.

  Morton, who made his West Indies debut in 2001/02, became the first Twenty20 international cricketer to die. East Africa's Don Pringle – who was also killed in a car crash, in 1975 – was the first one-day international cricketer to die, while the first Test cricketer to die was England's James Southerton, in 1880.

  At the age of 33 years and 226 days, Morton also became the shortest-lived West Indies ODI player after Jamaican all-rounder Laurie Williams. Aged 33 years and 270 days, Williams – who appeared in 15 one-day internationals – died in 2002 after his car collided with a bus.

- A former first-class cricketer lost his life during the crash of an Indian Airlines plane in the western city of Aurangabad in 1993. An airline employee, the 31-year-old Vivek Agarwal had appeared in a single first-class match, opening the batting for Haryana against Bengal at Faridabad in 1982/83.

- In 2008, former Victorian and Australian batsman Paul Hibbert was discovered dead in his Melbourne home by local police. The 56-year-old former opening batsman was found in his lounge room after a relative became concerned at not having heard from him for more than a week. Hibbert was called up for a Test match against India in 1977/78 following a maiden century (100) against the tourists, an innings without a single boundary, only the second such instance of the feat in first-class cricket.

- Pakistan's Aftab Baloch, who was born on April Fool's Day, made his Test debut at the age of 16, and later scored a mammoth 428 for Sind against Baluchistan at Karachi in 1973/74. A few months later, he toured England and was given room number 428 in one of the hotels that the Pakistan team stayed in.

- Wisdom Siziba, a Zimbabwean wicketkeeping opening batsman, died of heart failure in 2009 while doing his laundry. The 28-year-old, who suffered from epilepsy, made history in 1999/2000 when he became just the tenth batsman to carry his bat on his first-class debut.

- Nine British children died in 1943 when a plane careered into a cricket field while a match was in progress near the city of Bath. The pilot was also killed in the crash.

- When Auckland batsman Billy Hendy passed away in 1992 at the age of 92, he'd been New Zealand's oldest first-class cricketer. Appearing in two first-class matches in 1927/28, he famously hit an unbeaten 300 in a club game after reaching 200 by lunch.

- Wellington batsman Syd Ward died on New Year's Eve in 2010 at the age of 103, the second-oldest first-class cricketer of all time. Born in Sydney, Ward appeared in ten first-class matches in the early 1930s. The longest-lived cricketer is Derbyshire's Jim Hutchinson who died in 2000, aged 103 years and 344 days.

- On the opening day of the England-South Africa Test at The Oval in 2012, all of the dismissals that took place involved players born in the same country. Andrew Strauss was dismissed lbw by Morne Morkel, while numbers three and four, Jonathan Trott and Kevin Pietersen, were caught behind by A.B. de Villiers, off Morkel and Jacques Kallis, respectively. All six players were born in South Africa.

- A wicketkeeper-batsman who appeared in 15 first-class matches died in a freak accident in 2014 while helping to prepare a local sports ground. The 25-year-old Sandeep Singh, who made his first-class debut as an opening batsman for the Indian team Haryana in 2005/06, was killed when a tractor rolled over him.

- A 36-year-old woman who died after the collapse of her garage in Melbourne in 2006 was the sister of former South and West Australian batsman James Brayshaw. The daughter of Ian Brayshaw – the last bowler to claim all ten wickets in a first-class innings in Australia – Sally Weir was killed instantly when the façade of her brick garage in suburban Melbourne collapsed on top of her.

- When Jehan Mubarak made his debut for Sri Lanka in 2002, he became only the second American-born Test cricketer. Mubarak, born in Washington DC, followed Kenneth "Bam Bam" Weekes, who was born in Boston in 1912 and played in two Tests for the West Indies, making his debut at Lord's in 1939.

- A month after the death of the first Portuguese-born Test cricketer, Australia's Moises Henriques became the second. The Lisbon-born Dick Westcott, who appeared in five Tests for South Africa in the 1950s, passed away at the age of 85 in January 2013. In February, Henriques made his debut at Chennai, scoring a half-century in each innings. Henriques and the football champion Cristiano Ronaldo share a February birthday and the same place of birth – Funchal on the island of Madeira.

TEST CRICKETERS BORN IN CONTINENTAL EUROPE

Player	Team	Birthplace	Debut
Buster Nupen	South Africa	Norway	1921/22
Donald Carr	England	Germany	1951/52
Dick Westcott	South Africa	Portugal	1953/54
Ted Dexter	England	Italy	1958
Paul Terry	England	Germany	1984
Amjad Khan	England	Denmark	2008/09
Moises Henriques	Australia	Portugal	2012/13

- Two cricketers competing in seniors tournaments in Pakistan died during matches in 2009. A 53-year-old passed away after complaining of chest pains when bowling in a game in Karachi, while a 60-year-old doctor died when batting.

- The opposing captains for the England-West Indies Test series of 1976 were both born in Queenstown. Tony Greig was born in Queenstown in Cape Province in South Africa, while Clive Lloyd was born at Queenstown in the Guyana capital Georgetown.

- Ashwath Aiyappa, who appeared in three first-class matches for Karnataka, drowned in a river in 2014 while trying to rescue his brother. The 30-year-old made his highest score of 62 on his first-class debut in 2001/02.

- South African fast bowler Tertius Bosch met an untimely death in 2000, an event shrouded in mystery. The right-arm fast bowler, who took three wickets in his only Test – against the West Indies at Bridgetown in 1991/92 – reportedly died of a rare viral infection at the age of 33. In the midst of allegations of money laundering and extra-marital affairs, his body was exhumed with claims he might have been poisoned.

> "The body had been embalmed and was beautifully preserved, so I got really good organs, hair and fingernail specimens. The clinical presentation was one which supported poisoning ... his skin was dark with white spots, he had lost his hair and there were signs of kidney dysfunction. I was testing for various forms of heavy metal poisoning. Why someone would want to delay the natural decaying process, I can't say, but some people believe that the chemicals in embalming fluid remove traces of poison."
>
> South African forensic pathologist Reggie Perumal

- Frances King, who played one-day international cricket for New Zealand, died of meningitis at the age of 22 in 2003. She made her debut against Australia, taking 21 wickets at 19.23 in 15 ODIs.

- A week after being a part of cricket history, Abdul Aziz died after being struck on the body by a cricket ball during a first-class match in Karachi. In his previous match – for Karachi against Bahawalpur in 1958/59 – Aziz was at the crease when team-mate Hanif Mohammad scored a then-world-record 499. A few days later, at the same ground, Aziz was hit in the chest by Combined Services bowler Dildar Awan before he had scored in the first innings of the final of the Quaid-e-Azam Trophy. The 18-year-old died on his way to hospital.

- Just months before his death in 2014, Phillip Hughes had made the highest score of his first-class career and became the first Australian batsman to score a double-century in List A cricket. Opening the batting for the Australia A side against South Africa A, Hughes made 243 not out in a first-class match at Townsville having struck an unbeaten 202, with 18 fours and six sixes, in a 50-over match in Darwin.

  On the verge of a recall for the 2014/15 Test series against India, Hughes – playing for South Australia – was struck in the neck by a ball from New South Wales pace bowler Sean Abbott during a Sheffield

Shield match at the SCG. Batting in front of his mother and sister, he succumbed to his injuries two days later, becoming the second-youngest Australian Test cricketer to die.

Having made his Twenty20 debut for Australia alongside Abbott only a few weeks previously, Hughes became the youngest Twenty20 international cricketer – and the youngest Australian ODI cricketer – to lose his life. Hughes died 46 days after his last match for Australia, the second-shortest period between a player's last international match and his death. Fred Grace had passed away at the age of 29

Thank You

FROM THE HUGHES FAMILY

Words cannot express our sorrow at Phillip's passing, but your love and support has given us great strength at this very difficult time

Gregory, Virginia, Jason and Megan Hughes wish to express our sincere appreciation to the people of Australia following the passing of our dearly beloved son and brother, Phillip.

In particular we wish to thank:
Our family and friends for being here for us
The community of Macksville including Fr Michael Alcock, the management and staff of the Macksville Ex-Services Club and Macksville High School
Michael Clarke, past and present Australian and State cricketers and the extended Australian cricket family
Cricket Australia, South Australian Cricket Association and Cricket NSW
St Vincent's Hospital and the wonderful medical staff who cared for Phillip

from pneumonia two weeks after making his Test debut for England in 1880. W.G.'s younger brother died 14 days after playing against Australia at The Oval, a Test in which he made a pair.

Three days shy of turning 26, Hughes appeared in 26 Tests and scored 26 centuries in first-class cricket.

CRICKETERS TO DIE AFTER BEING HIT BY A CRICKET BALL IN A FIRST-CLASS MATCH

Player	Match	Venue	Season
George Summers	Nottinghamshire v MCC	Lord's	1870
Abdul Aziz	Karachi v Combined Services	Karachi	1958/59
Phillip Hughes	South Australia v New South Wales	Sydney	2014/15

First-class cricketers to die after being hit during club matches: Ian Folley, who played for Derbyshire and Lancashire, died after being struck while batting for Whitehaven in 1993; former Indian Test batsman Raman Lamba died after being hit while fielding in a game in Dhaka in 1998; former Border wicketkeeper Darryn Randall died after being hit in the head while batting in a match in the Eastern Cape town of Alice in 2013

- Two days after the death of Phillip Hughes, a former Israel cricket captain was killed after being struck by a ball while umpiring a match in the country's national cricket league. Standing at the bowler's end, Hillel Awasker was hit after a ball ricocheted off the stumps from a shot hit straight down the pitch. The incident occurred shortly after a minute's silence had been held for Hughes. The 55-year-old Awasker – who captained Israel at the ICC Trophy in 1982 and 1997 – suffered a heart attack after being hit and died in hospital.

- A player from Kolkata died in 2015 after an on-field collision with an East Bengal team-mate in a match against Bhowanipore. While fielding as 12th man, Ankit Keshri – a former Bengal Under-21 captain – was hit in the back of the neck by the other player's knee after attempting to take a catch. Shibsagar Singh, who appeared in 28 first-class matches for Bengal, attempted to revive him with mouth-to-mouth resucscitation before medics arrived at the ground. Keshri succumbed to a heart attack on his hospital bed several days after the accident.

- Two of Australia's opening batsmen during the 1926 Ashes series bore names of the towns in which they were born. Warren Bardsley was born in the New South Wales town of Warren; Bill Woodfull's middle name was Maldon, his birthplace, a town near Melbourne.

- Pakistan's openers for the under-19 World Cup in 2014 were both born on the same day in the same city. Sami Aslam and Imam-ul-Haq were both born on 12 December in 1995 in Lahore and began the tournament with a century opening stand in their first two matches.

- One of the 298 casualties of the shooting down of a Malaysian Airlines jet over Ukraine in 2014 was a cricketer from the St Mary Redcliffe club in Bristol. The 20-year-old Ben Pocock had been on his way to Australia to attend a university placement in Perth.

Team Triumphs and Tribulations

- In a first-class match at the SCG in 1956/57, both teams passed 400 in the first innings, yet no batsman from either side scored a century. Playing for the R.R. Lindwall XI against the R.N. Harvey XI, Ken "Slasher" Mackay hit 99. The match – a testimonial – contained 12 scores between 40 and 49, a record number in a first-class match.

- During the Matabeleland Tuskers first innings against Mid West Rhinos at Kweke in 2014/15, three of its batsmen fell in the nineties. For the first time in first-class cricket, three batsmen – Bornaparte Mujuru (96), Sean Williams (96) and Brian Chari (99) – had scores of between 95 and 99 in the same innings.

- Coming into a match at Multan in 2014/15, two bowlers with a combined total of ten first-class appearances between them demolished Islamabad with one taking eight wickets on the opening day. In his seventh match, Multan spinner Mohammad Asif (8-19) claimed a maiden five-for, while pace bowler Sadaif Mehdi chipped in with 2-24 to send Islamabad crashing to an all-out total of 54, with just one batsman reaching double figures. After dismissing Multan for 121, they then bounced back in spectacular fashion with the bat following the 54 with 575 which contained a 323-run sixth-wicket stand between Faizan Riaz (158) and Imad Wasim (207).

  While both of the Multan opening bowlers conceded less than 25 runs in the first innings, both went for more than 150 in the second, with Mohammad taking 4-151 and Sadaif 5-158. Islamabad's Zohaib Ahmed claimed ten wickets in the match with six in the second innings en route to a famous 303-run victory.

- After piling up 756/5 declared in a first-class match at Savar in Bangladesh in 2013/14, Dhaka Division gained a first-innings lead of 578 over Rajshahi, but decided against enforcing the follow-on. A new record high in first-class cricket for a team not imposing the follow-on, Dhaka's innings contained four centuries with its first three in the order all posting three figures.

  Two matches later, Rajshahi made 675/9 declared against Chittagong in the same competition after being 77/6. Batting first, Rajshahi lost its first three batsmen for single-digit scores, while numbers seven to nine all passed 150, a first in first-class cricket. Farhad Reza scored 259, Sanjamul Islam made 172 while Mukhtar Ali hit 168, an innings that contained 16 sixes. Farhad took part in two double-century partnerships for consecutive wickets – 347 with Sanjamul for the seventh and 224 with Mukhtar for the eighth.

  It was only the second time in first-class cricket that numbers seven to nine had passed 100 after Lee Germon (114), Mark Priest (102) and Gary Stead (113*) did so for Canterbury against Central Districts at Christchurch in a semi-final of the 1993/94 Shell Trophy. The 598 runs scored by Rajshahi after the fall of its sixth wicket beat the all-time first-class record of 535 by the Australians against Canterbury at Christchurch 100 years previously.

- Scotland attained a world-record win in a one-day international in 2014/15 with Afghanistan losing all ten wickets within 25 runs. Chasing 214 for victory at Abu Dhabi, the openers reached 38 inside seven overs but both lost their wicket in the space of five deliveries, with the rest falling in quick succession. All out for 63 in 18.3 overs, Josh Davey was named man of the match after a double of 53 not out and 6/28. The previous biggest collapse in ODI cricket had been by Zimbabwe which lost its ten in 30 runs (5/0 to 35) against Sri Lanka at Harare in 2004.

- When Australia knocked over England at Perth in 2002/03, the best bowling figures came from Brett Lee with a first-innings haul of 3-78. Australia needed just 16 wickets to wrap up the match, with Lee's contribution the most modest best-bowling performance for the country in Test history.

  During the summer of 1967/68, England (404 and 215-3) defeated the West Indies (526/7d and 92/2d) by seven wickets at Port-of-Spain with the best bowling figures being 3-107 from David Brown.

- On their way to a near-600-run total at Kochi in 2013/14, two North Zone batsmen scored centuries after both had retired hurt on 95. Ian Dev Singh went on to 145 in the match against East Zone, while Rajat Paliwal progressed to 106 not out.

177

- One of the biggest floggings of all time took place in Sri Lanka in 2010 with the Bandarawela Central under-13s scoring 553/3 and their opponents three. Damitha Prabatha scored 222 and Themiya Patabendi 103, while Isuru Dhananjaya took 7-2. The Pussellakanda Vidyalaya XI fared slightly better second time around, falling for 31 to lose the match by an innings and 519.

- In the wake of a players' boycott in 2009, a West Indies Test XI containing seven debutants, and led by a captain who hadn't surfaced for a decade, took to the field against Bangladesh. Floyd Reifer, who had played four Tests in the late 1990s, earned a reprieve replacing Chris Gayle, with the entire West Indies squad withdrawing their services in a dispute over contracts. The seven new faces who made their Test debuts against the Bangladeshis at Kingstown were Ryan Austin, Travis Dowlin, Nikita Miller, Omar Phillips, Dale Richards, Kemar Roach and Chadwick Walton.

  The Tigers went on to defeat the hosts by 95 runs, recording just their second Test victory – in 60 attempts – and their first overseas. With a 2-0 win in the Test series, Bangladesh then wrapped up the one-day international series 3-0.

- Australia beat Sri Lanka at Darwin in 2004 with none of its batsmen scoring a century. Adam Gilchrist's 80 was the highest individual score in the 149-run victory, signalling an end to a run of 17 consecutive Tests by Australia that contained a century. The record run began in 2002/03, with the first ten of the 17 matches establishing a record for most Tests that contained at least two batsmen scoring a century.

- Faced with just 11 runs for a ten-wicket Test win against Bangladesh in 2001/02, Zimbabwe lost two of its number for a duck. While Mashrafe Mortaza removed Dion Ebrahim and Stuart Carlisle for nought at Chittagong, opener Trevor Gripper remained calm, making all 11 runs needed on his own.

- The West Indies began the 2011/12 Frank Worrell Trophy series with a 400-run total which included all 11 batsmen reaching double figures for the first time in their history. Australia used as many as eight bowlers as they ran up 449/9 declared, with the best return of 2-45 coming from opening batsman David Warner, his first two wickets at Test level.

  In reply, Australia also declared its first innings after passing 400, with nine of its batsmen reaching double figures, including an unbeaten 68 from their No. 9 Ryan Harris and 40 not out from the No. 11, Nathan Lyon. It represented only the second occasion in history of at least 20 double-figure scores coming from the first innings of both teams in a Test, after Australia (10) and South Africa (10) at Melbourne in 1952/53.

Setting aside a Test in South Africa in 1999/2000 which saw a 0/0 declaration, and a forfeiture, Australia (406/9d and 192/7) became just the second country to win a Test after declaring with a first-innings deficit. In 1934/35, England had declared at 81/7 in Bridgetown, 21 runs behind the West Indies' first-innings total, and went on to win the match by four wickets.

- Bangladesh overcame the worst start to the fourth innings in the history of Test cricket in 2014/15 to beat Zimbabwe at Mirpur. Chasing a relatively small target for victory, Bangladesh lost their first three batsmen without a run on the board, and surrendered another four to finish at 101/7, securing a three-wicket win. With the third-best figures by a left-arm spinner in Test history, Taijul Islam (8-39) became just the second player – after Harbhajan Singh (8-84) against Australia at Chennai in 2000/01 – to take eight wickets in an innings and hit the winning run in the same Test.

- When Tim McIntosh and Brendon McCullum put on a first-wicket stand of 125 at Hyderabad in 2010/11, it gave New Zealand their first hundred-run opening partnership in six years. Forty-seven Tests, 87 innings and 19 different opening combinations had gone by since Mark Richardson and Stephen Fleming put on 163 against England at Trent Bridge in 2004.

India's openers also established a century partnership for the first wicket at Hyderabad, with another 100 runs added for the tenth. Two such stands – one at the top and one at the bottom of the same innings – had only occurred once previously in Test match cricket, by New Zealand against Pakistan at Auckland in 1972/73.

CENTURY STANDS BY OPENING AND LAST-WICKET PAIRS IN SAME TEST INNINGS

Wkt	Stand	Batsmen/Match	Venue	Season
1st	159	Rodney Redmond and Glenn Turner		
10th	151	Brian Hastings and Richard Collinge		
		New Zealand v Pakistan	Auckland	1972/73
1st	160	Gautam Gambhir and Virender Sehwag		
10th	105	Harbhajan Singh and Shanthakumaran Sreesanth		
		India v New Zealand	Hyderabad	2010/11

- Of the ten players who made their Test debuts at Melbourne in 1881/82, three would also end their careers in the same match five seasons later. The England trio of Dick Barlow, Billy Bates and William Scotton appeared in 17, 15 and 15 Tests respectively with each ending their careers in the second Ashes Test at Sydney in 1886/87.

- When India and New Zealand met at Dambulla on 10 August in 2010 it meant that a one-day international had been played on every day in the calendar year since the first ODI in 1970/71. The Kiwis (288) dispensed with India for just 88, which, at the time, was India's fifth-lowest score in a one-day international.

- Despite plummeting to a score of 32/8 against the Warriors at Bloemfontein in 2014/15, the Knights fought back to gain a first-innings lead and a win. After five ducks, numbers nine and ten – Corné Dry and Quinton Friend – each scored 51 to take the final score to 140, with the Warriors then dismissed for 137. In all first-class cricket, it was the second-lowest total at the fall of the eighth wicket by a side batting first that went on to a secure a first-innings lead – 28/8 by Otago versus Auckland at Dunedin 1889/90 and 32/8 by the same team against Canterbury, also in Dunedin, in 1863/64, New Zealand's inaugural first-class match.

- During Pakistan's first innings against Australia at Dubai in 2014/15, their wicketkeeper Sarfraz Ahmed fell to the last ball before tea, while the not-out batsman retired hurt. Zulfiqar Babar failed to resume his innings after the break, which resulted in the presence of two new batsmen – Rahat Ali and debutant Imran Khan – at the crease.

  This had happened just once before in the history of Test cricket, at Hamilton in 1995/96. Marking his 21st birthday on his Test debut, New Zealand's Greg Loveridge suffered a season-ending injury while batting against Zimbabwe, but stuck around until his batting partner Dipak Patel was dismissed. The match then saw debutants Robert Kennedy and Geoff Allott making their entry on to the Test match arena together, while Loveridge never got to bowl, or play for New Zealand again.

- Sri Lanka and India combined for a record-breaking one-day international in Hobart in 2011/12, with India reaching 321 with more than 13 overs to spare. Needing to reach its target by the 40th over to gain a bonus point and stay alive in the tri-series, India mauled Sri Lanka with Virat Kohli scoring an unbeaten 133 off 86 balls. India became only the second country – after Sri Lanka at Headingley in 2006 – to hunt down a 300-run total in under 40 overs, hitting 33 fours, equalling the highest number in a ODI innings in Australia. Lasith Malinga was a target, conceding a record 15 fours and 12.52 runs off his 7.4 overs.

  Earlier, Sri Lanka's Tillakaratne Dilshan scored an unbeaten 160 – then the highest one-day score by a visiting batsman in Australia – sharing the first double-century stand in a ODI at Hobart with Kumar Sangakkara, who made 105.

- When England trounced Australia 3-1 in 2010/11, they became the first country in 75 years to achieve three innings victories in an away Test series. The previous example had been by Australia in five matches against South Africa in 1935/36. The England tourists had warmed up for the Ashes by beating Western Australia in a three-day match in Perth. It was the first time England had won their opening first-class tour match in Australia since 1965/66, when they also beat Western Australia.

A fan all dressed up for the MCG Boxing Day Test in 2010/11, which England (513) won by an innings and 157 runs

- Appearing on his Test debut for Zimbabwe in 2003/04, Stuart Matsikenyeri scored a half-century in a team total that traversed the 500-run mark. Batting at No. 6 against the West Indies at Harare, Matsikenyeri's 57 was followed by another three consecutive fifties, only the second occasion numbers six to nine had done so in the same Test innings. The first such instance was also achieved by Zimbabwe, against Bangladesh at Dhaka in 2001/02.

HALF-CENTURIES BY NUMBERS SIX TO NINE IN A TEST INNINGS

Batsmen	Match	Venue	Season
Craig Wishart (94), Douglas Marillier (73), Heath Streak (65), Travis Friend (81)	Zimbabwe v Bangladesh	Dhaka	2001/02
Stuart Matsikenyeri (57), Tatenda Taibu (83), Heath Streak (127*), Andy Blignaut (91)	Zimbabwe v West Indies	Harare	2003/04

- When England played India at Lord's at 2007, a Test first took place with as many as nine different bowlers claiming a wicket lbw. Ryan Sidebottom (4), James Anderson (1), Monty Panesar (1) and Chris Tremlett (1) took at least one lbw for the home side, while Shanthakumaran Sreesanth (3), Zaheer Khan (1) Sourav Ganguly (1), Anil Kumble (1) and Robin Singh (1) did so for India. Previously, four Tests had featured eight bowlers taking a wicket lbw.

- Papua New Guinea made history in 2014/15 by becoming the first country to win its first two one-day internationals. The 26th nation to appear in ODI cricket, PNG defeated Hong Kong 2-0 in a two-match series played in Townsville, with Lega Siaka (109) scoring their maiden one-day international century in the second game.

   Prior to PNG's first win, the only others countries to have won their maiden ODI had been Australia, New Zealand, Zimbabwe, Bermuda and Afghanistan.

- Despite not enforcing the follow-on in a first-class match in Hyderabad in 1977/78, the Muslim Commercial Bank XI pulled off a stunning 609-run victory. In reply to MCB's first-innings total of 575, the Water and Power Development Authority was dismissed for just 98, with Anjum Nasir taking 6-22. MCB decided not to enforce the follow-on and piled on another 282 runs without loss, thanks to 105 from Qasim Umar and 161 from Azmat Rana. Set 760 to win, the WPDA fell for 150, with Anjum taking another five-for and 11 wickets in the match.

- During 1921, England used as many as 11 openers in 16 Test innings, a record they matched in 1935. They also used 11 in 26 innings throughout 1930. The greatest number of openers employed in a year by a country other than England is nine by Australia, in 25 innings in 1977, and across 28 innings in 1979.

MOST OPENERS USED BY ONE COUNTRY IN A SINGLE YEAR

#	Year	Country	M	Inns
11	1921	England	8	16
George Brown, Alfred Dipper, Charlie Hallows, Wally Hardinge, Jack Hobbs, Percy Holmes, Donald Knight, Ciss Parkin, Wilfred Rhodes, Jack Russell, Frank Woolley				
11	1930	England	14	26
Ted Bowley, Tich Cornford, Eddie Dawson, Harold Gilligan, George Gunn, Jack Hobbs, Maurice Leyland, Andy Sandham, Herbert Sutcliffe, Frank Woolley, Bob Wyatt				
11	1935	England	9	16
Fred Bakewell, Ken Farnes, Bill Farrimond, Jack Iddon, Maurice Leyland, Arthur Mitchell, Jim Smith, Denis Smith, Herbert Sutcliffe, David Townsend, Bob Wyatt				

- When Tasmania staged their inaugural first-class match in Hobart, none of their batsmen reached double figures in either innings, a unique occurrence in Australian first-class cricket. Taking on Victoria (78 and 67) in 1857/58, Tasmania (51 and 25) were bowled out for a record-low aggregate of 76, with Gideon Elliott (3-19 and 3-6) and Tom Wills (6-25 and 6-10) bowling unchanged throughout both innings.

  In the only first-class match played at the Lower Domain Ground in Hobart, Tasmania's captain William Brown took a record 15 wickets in his only first-class match.

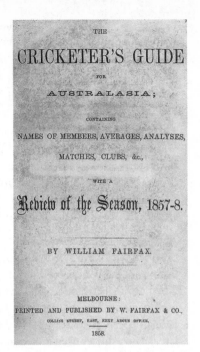

THE

CRICKETER'S GUIDE

FOR

AUSTRALASIA;

CONTAINING

NAMES OF MEMBERS, AVERAGES, ANALYSES,

MATCHES, CLUBS, &c.,

WITH A

Review of the Season, 1857-8.

BY WILLIAM FAIRFAX.

MELBOURNE:

PRINTED AND PUBLISHED BY W. FAIRFAX & CO.,

COLLINS STREET, EAST, NEXT ARGUS OFFICE,

1858.

SCOREBOARD
TASMANIA v VICTORIA – HOBART 1857/58

TASMANIA	1st innings		2nd innings	
T.F. Patterson	b Wills	6	(4) b Elliott	3
J.L.B. Tabart	b Wills	8	(6) b Wills	5
G. Marshall †	b Elliott	1	(8) b Elliott	0
W.A.B. Jamieson	b Wills	5	(2) b Wills	5
T. Westbrook	b Wills	0	(11) not out	0
G.W. Briant	c Box b Elliott	2	(7) b Wills	1
J.C. Mace	run out	2	(3) run out	0
J.B. Dixon	b Wills	7	(5) c Butterworth b Wills	1
W. Brown *	c Burchett b Elliott	7	lbw b Wills	0
T. Whitesides	not out	0	(1) c Box b Wills	0
G. Matson	b Wills	6	(10) lbw b Elliott	1
Extras	(5 b, 1 lb, 1 w)	7	(6 b, 1 b, 2w)	9
Total	(all out – 32 overs)	**51**	(all out – 30 overs)	**25**

- When India lined up against New Zealand at Nagpur in 2010/11, they became the first country to go into a Test match with a combined 50,000 runs. Leading the 11 with most runs was the redoubtable Sachin Tendulkar with 14,366.

- Between 1931 and 1948, England played a record 75 Tests in a row without fielding the same XI in consecutive matches. They won 24 of the matches, lost 14 and drew 37. England later equalled their own record with another sequence of 75 between 1966 and 1974. The results were remarkably similar with another 24 wins, plus 13 losses and 38 draws.

- The Bloomfield Cricket and Athletic Club exacted a memorable two-run win over Badureliya Sports in Sri Lanka in 2014/15 with both teams almost matching each other's runs in both innings. After Bloomfield were bowled out for excactly 100 in the first innings, Badureliya fell for 98. Batting a second time, Bloomfield made 175 with their opponents also out for 175 to lose by two runs.

- The Indian side Saurashtra passed the 600-run total for the third time in their history in 2008/09, with all three coming in consecutive innings in Rajkot during the Ranji Trophy. They beat Orissa (302 and 234), after declaring at 620/4, which included a world-record fifth-wicket stand of 520 between Cheteshwar Pujara (302*) and Ravi Jadeja (232*), who also claimed bowling figures of 5-44. A few days later, Saurashtra raised its second 600-run total with 679/8 in a drawn match against Punjab with 189 from Pujara. They made it a hat-trick in their next outing with 643/4 declared against Mumbai, with yet another big hundred from Pujara, his 176 being his third score of 150-plus in consecutive innings. A 21-year-old Chirag Pathak scored 170 on his first-class debut, sharing an opening stand of 275 with Bhushan Chauhan (104).

- A first-class match in Sri Lanka in 1999/2000 saw Kurunegala Youth make a total of 41 off 40.1 overs. Only one batsman – Darshike Jayakody (10) – reached double figures, while Sebastianites spinner Dinesh Perera took 5-5.

- In 2009/10, the North Sydney third-graders were bowled out for a record-low total of eight by Parramatta at suburban Merrylands, with eight of their number out for a duck. Anthony Karam was the destroyer with figures of 9.4-7-3-7, including two hat-tricks. His second hat-trick consisted of the last three balls of North's first innings, and with his first ball in the second innings took another wicket, making it four in four.

  It was a history-making summer for Karam, who followed his pair of hat-tricks with an unbeaten double-century in a semi-final against Manly. Karam and Madushanka Vithanage shared an unbroken tenth-wicket stand of 200 – the highest last-wicket partnership in any grade since the competition began in 1893.

PARRAMATTA v NORTH SYDNEY – MERRYLANDS 2009/10

NORTH SYDNEY	1st innings	R
J. Jenkins	run out	0
L. Smith	c S. Karam b A. Karam	0
J. Clarke	lbw b A. Karam	3
R. Rosenberg	lbw b A. Rizwan	0
M. Lloyd	not out	3
M. Jayawickreme	c Vithanage b A. Karam	0
P. Skerman	lbw b A. Karam	0
G. De Carvalho †	b A. Rizwan	0
P. Lindsay	lbw b A. Karam	1
F. Atshan	lbw b A. Karam	0
J. Keane *	b A. Karam	0
Extras	(1 nb)	1
Total	(all out – 19.4 overs)	**8**

Anthony Karam (at front, right) leads the charge after his record-breaking second hat-trick for Parramatta against North Sydney in 2009/10

- Vying for a well-earned spot in the West Indies first-class domestic final in 2012/13, Jamaica were beaten by Trinidad and Tobago in a semi, ending a 15-match winning streak. Jamaica had not lost since 2009/10, going 25 consecutive first-class matches without defeat.

- After Trevor Barsby and Matthew Hayden had put on a double-century stand against an England XI at Toowoomba in 1994/95, Queensland were quickly dismissed for 314. It became the lowest total in a first-class match in Australia in which both openers had scored a century, Barsby hitting 101 and Hayden 119. The lowest total in all first-class cricket to include centuries by their openers is 284 by Yorkshire against Surrey at The Oval in 1869.

- In consecutive Tests against England in 2002, Sri Lanka ended three consecutive centuries on the same score. In the first innings of the second Test at Edgbaston, Graham Thorpe was last man out for 123. In the first innings of the following Test, at Old Trafford, Mark Butcher and Alec Stewart were also dismissed for 123.

- To celebrate the opening of a brand new cricket ground in the Indian city of Hubli in 2012/13, Haryana passed 500 in the first innings with one of the biggest partnerships of all time. Surviving a shaky start of 168/7, they made it to 587/9 declared with an eighth-wicket stand of 392. On a ground that previously housed a toilet block, Amit Mishra (202*) and Jayant Yadav (211) both scored maiden first-class centuries, going on to doubles, while Kunal Kapoor (106 and 100*) scored the first two first-class hundreds of his career for Karnataka.

- Chasing a one-day international target of 360 at Jaipur in 2013/14, India smashed their way into the record books by passing the total with nine wickets and six overs to spare. After Australia posted a total which contained the first instance of the first five batsmen all scoring half-centuries, India responded with the first example of the first three in the order all passing 90.

  Rohit Sharma, with 141 not out, and Shikhar Dhawan, 95, raised an opening stand of 176, while Virat Kohli scored an unbeaten 100. India's 362/1 contained the first instance of two partnerships in excess of 175 in the same ODI innings, with Rohit and Kohli adding 186 – unbroken – for the second wicket. Their 362 became the first 350-plus total for the loss of just one wicket in a ODI, beating Sri Lanka's 348 at Kingston earlier in the year.

  Four days later, India became the first team to chase down a 350-run total twice when they thumped the Australians in game six of the seven-match series at Nagpur. Shane Watson (102) and George Bailey (156) scored tons for Australia (350/6) – the first instance of an Australian number three and four posting centuries in the same one-day international – while Dhawan (100) and Kohli (115*) did so for India (351/4).

  With two matches ruined due to rain, both teams, with two wins each, went to Bangalore for the decider which turned out to be another record-buster. Batting first, India rampaged its way to 383/6, with Sharma hitting the third double-century in one-day internationals. With 209, he became the first batsman to exceed 15 sixes in an innings (16) completing the series with 491 runs, a new record for the most runs in a bilateral series. The next best at the time also came in this series – 478 by Bailey.

Australia responded with 326, the ninth time 300 had been topped in the series, the most in a bilateral series, beating the previous record of six by Sri Lanka and India in 2009/10. With 60 at No. 6, Glenn Maxwell's half-century came off 18 balls, the equal-fastest 50 by an Australian in a ODI, while James Faulkner (116) hit a maiden century at No. 7, reaching three figures in 57 balls, then the fastest hundred by an Australian.

Nine centuries were scored in the series – the most in a bilateral contest – while 38 sixes were struck at Bangalore – 19 by each side – beating 31 by India and New Zealand at Christchurch in 2008/09. A total of 107 sixes was seen over the six matches played, obliterating the previous mark of 62 in a series between two countries.

- As many as 423 sixes were struck in Test matches in 2014, the first time 400 had been reached in a calendar year. The previous best was 375 in 2004.

- Having begun with the calendar year of 2013 by blowing away New Zealand for 45 in a Test match, South Africa then dismissed Pakistan for under 50, both instances coming within a month. Celebrating his 100th Test as captain, Graeme Smith scored 52 in the second innings of the first Test at Johannesburg, after Pakistan had been dismissed for 49, their lowest-ever Test score. Dale Steyn was the wrecker, with figures of 8.1-6-8-6, and 11-60 for the match.

  After pouching half-a-dozen catches in the innings, A.B. de Villiers took another five in the second to equal the world record of 11, established by England's Jack Russell, achieved at the same ground in 1995/96. With a score of 103 not out, de Villiers became the first wicketkeeper to achieve the double of a century and ten dismissals in the same Test.

- During the three-match Test series against the West Indies in 2009/10, Australia scored a record 15 fifties without a century. While Australia took out the series 2-0, the West Indies registered four hundreds, with two coming off the bat of skipper Chris Gayle. Australia made 520/7 declared in the third Test at Perth, only the fourth time that any team had reached 500 in a Test innings without the aid of an individual century. Five batsmen passed 50, with the top score, a 99, from opener Simon Katich.

- Jamaica began a first-class match against Barbados in 2012/13 in disarray, losing their first three batsmen for ducks. Barbados also lost both of their openers for nought, the first time all four openers had been dismissed for a duck in the first innings of a first-class match in the West Indies.

- A Queensland club team staged a monumental record-breaking comeback in a match in 2007/08 with its last pair putting on a triple-century partnership. After slumping to 136/9 against Maleny, Tewantin's last pair – that included debutant Dean Carlyle – took the score to 471 with the partnership unbroken at 335. Carlyle scored an unbeaten 132, while his partner, the No. 11 Tony Morgan, contributed 169.

- Despite posting two individual centuries and a record double-century partnership in Nairobi in 2006/07, Ireland went down to Kenya with one wicket and one over to spare. Ireland reached 284/4 off its 50 overs, with hundreds from William Porterfield (104*) and Kevin O'Brien (142) and a record-breaking fourth-wicket partnership of 227. Such feats proved not enough for victory though, with Kenya squeaking home after fifties from Nehemiah Odhiambo (66) and Thomas Odoyo (61*).

- The Australia-South Africa clash at Perth in 2012/13 featured the first-ever instance of fielders, other than wicketkeepers, from each side taking four catches in a Test innings. Mitchell Johnson took four for Australia – with two caught and bowled – while Graeme Smith took five in Australia's second-innings 322.

- After wobbling at two down for 12 on the first day of their match against Goa at Panaji in 1988/89, Tamil Nadu clocked up a record 912/6 declared. The unprecedented fightback included the first example of two triple-centuries in the same first-class innings – 313 from Venkat Raman and 302 not out from Arjan Kripal Singh, who posted the first 300 from a No. 7 in first-class cricket in just his third first-class match. Tamil Nadu added 652 runs after the fall of the fifth wicket, a record in first-class cricket that stood until 2014/15 when Karnataka played them in the Ranji Trophy Final at Mumbai. After being 84/5, Karnataka added 678 runs to finish at 762, including 328 by Karun Nair, the first first-class triple-century by a No. 6 batsman.

- In a first-class match against Kenya at Dubai in 2013/14, one of the six Afghanistan debutants took a wicket with his first ball while another hit his first ball for six. Opening the bowling, Sayed Shirzad bowled Dominic Wesonga for a duck, finishing with figures of 2-28. Opening the batting, Fazal Niazai struck the first ball of his first-class career for six, finishing with a score of 15.

- In a first-class tour match in the lead-up to the 2013 Ashes, Somerset reached 320 in the first innings after losing their last eight wickets for 16. With five batsmen out for a duck, six wickets fell with the score on 310. As many as seven wickets have fallen on the same score in first-class cricket, a record shared by MCC and Gauteng. After being nine down for eight against Surrey at Lord's in 1872, MCC's last wicket doubled their total, with their first seven wickets falling on nought. At Johannesburg in 1997/98, Gauteng lost their first seven wickets on 12 in the second innings against Northerns.

- New Zealand celebrated a rainy New Year's Day in 2014 with a remarkable record-breaking one-day international total against the West Indies in Queenstown. Played at a cricket ground nestled below the Remarkables mountain range, the Kiwis blasted their way to a massive 283/4 in a match reduced to 21 overs per side.

  Corey Anderson and Jesse Ryder shared a 191-run stand off 75 deliveries, with both scoring centuries off fewer than 50 balls, a first in one-day international cricket. Anderson, with a maiden ODI century, hit 131 not out reaching his hundred off 36 balls, breaking Shahid Afridi's long-standing world record of a ton off 37. Ryder scored 104, getting to the three-figure mark off 46 balls, which, at the time, was the sixth-fastest century in one-day international cricket.

  The Kiwis hit 22 sixes, the first time 20 had been seen in a ODI innings, with the West Indies providing the first instance of five or more bowlers having an economy rate of ten or more in a ODI innings.

- Despite being dismissed for just 65 in a first-class match at Centurion in 2000/01, the Northerns innings contained a half-century partnership. In the Super Sport Series game against Western Province, the only two batsmen in the innings to reach double figures combined for a fourth-wicket stand of 52. Finley Brooker scored 28 and Dirk de Vos 17, while Western Province's Claude Henderson took 5-6.

- When Saurashtra and Mumbai met at Rajkot in the 1996/97 Ranji Trophy limited-over tournament, four individual centuries were scored in a List A match for the first time anywhere in the world. Opener Shitanshu Kotak (122*) and No. 3 Bimal Jadeja (104) shared a double-century partnership for Saurashtra, while openers Sanjay Manjrekar (127*) and Rajesh Sutar (108) opened the Mumbai innings with a match-winning 154-run stand.

- In India's second innings against the West Indies at Ahmedabad in 1983/84, more than half of the team was dismissed for the same single-digit score. Six of them went for a score of one, a record number of identical non-zero dismissals in a Test innings.

- Despite a history-making middle-order slump at Lord's in 2010, England bounced back with Test cricket's biggest-ever eighth-wicket partnership. Batting first against Pakistan, England suffered a Test first when numbers four, five and six – Kevin Pietersen, Paul Collingwood and Eoin Morgan – were each dismissed for a duck, but recovered with a match-winning stand of 332 between Jonathan Trott (184) and Stuart Broad (169). Their partnership

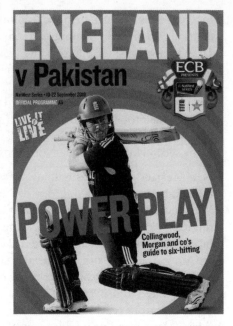

accounted for 49.78 per cent of England's runs (446), beating a 429-run stand between South Africa's Jacques Rudolph (222*) and Boeta Dippenaar (177*) at Chittagong in 2002/03 (48.75 per cent).

In a match tarnished by allegations of a form of match-fixing – claims that were later proven in court – Pakistan (74 and 147) were consigned to their biggest-ever Test defeat, going down by an innings and 225 runs.

- When South Africa A hosted Australia A in a four-day match at Pretoria in 2013, two batsmen from each side passed 150 in the first innings. David Warner hit 193 and Glenn Maxwell 155 not out for the Australians, while opener Dean Elgar made 268 and wicketkeeper Thami Tsolekile 159 for the hosts. Elgar's knock was a record-equalling high in unofficial Tests, while Tsolekile's was the best to date by a No. 7.

- The opening Test of the Bangladesh-New Zealand series at Chittagong in 2013/14 included the first instance of at least ten batsmen from one side hitting a six in the same match. Improving on, at least, six previous instances of seven, the Kiwis' No. 11 Trent Boult and opener Peter Fulton led the way with three each, while Hamish Rutherford (2), Ross Taylor (1), B.J. Watling (2), Ish Sodhi (2), Kane Williamson (1), Brendon McCullum (1), Corey Anderson (1) and Doug Bracewell (1) were the others. Only Bruce Martin missed out, while five Bangladeshi batsmen also hit at least one six.

- Trailing by 234 runs in a 2013/14 Sheffield Shield match at the SCG, Victoria went to stumps on day two with three wickets down and not a single run on the board. In a calamitous half hour before stumps, both openers went for ducks as did the No. 4. With the No. 3 out for nought the following morning, Victoria provided the first instance of the first four batsmen out for a duck in a first-class innings in Australia.

None of the first seven batsmen in the order reached double figures, with their wicketkeeping captain Matthew Wade also out for a duck at six wickets down for nine. Glenn Maxwell then came out blazing with 127 at No. 8 in Victoria's all-out total of 186. With 14 fours and seven sixes off 102 balls, Maxwell set a new record for dominance in a Sheffield Shield innings with 68.27 per cent of the total. Only ten runs were scored by the first seven in Victoria's innings, a record low number in all first-class cricket in which the No. 8 went on to a century.

SCOREBOARD
NEW SOUTH WALES v VICTORIA – SYDNEY 2013/14

VICTORIA	2nd innings	R	4s	6s	SR
P.S.P. Hanscomb	c Abbott b Bollinger	0	0	0	0.00
A.J. Finch	b Copeland	0	0	0	0.00
S.M. Boland	not out	0	0	0	0.00
M.P. Stoinis	c Rohrer b Copeland	0	0	0	0.00
J.M. Muirhead	not out	0	0	0	0.00
Extras		0			
Total	(3 wkts – 6 overs)	**0**			
Stumps day 2					

LOWEST TOTAL AT THE FALL OF THE SIXTH WICKET IN A FIRST-CLASS INNINGS IN AUSTRALIA

Runs	Total	Match	Venue	Season
5	18	Tasmania v Victoria	Melbourne	1868/69
7	75	Victoria v A. Shaw's England XI	Melbourne	1881/82
8	42	New South Wales v Victoria	Melbourne	1859/60
9	186	Victoria v New South Wales	Sydney	2013/14

- The second one-day international between Australia and the West Indies at Perth in 2012/13 was history-making with the top four in the visitors' batting order all dismissed leg before wicket. Mitchell Starc claimed all four of the dismissals, and finished the match with 5-32, his second five-wicket haul (5-20) in three days, against the same opposition, at the same ground.

Australia smashed the West Indies 5-0 in the series, becoming the first country to win 500 one-day internationals, reaching the milestone in game five at the MCG. Filling in for an injured Michael Clarke, Shane Watson became the first Australian captain to lose his wicket to the first ball of a one-day international, while West Indies opener Johnson Charles (100) scored his maiden century in any form of first-class, domestic or international cricket. Charles then quickly made it two in a row, pumping out 130 in his next ODI innings, against Zimbabwe at St George's.

- With a total of just 167, the West Indies side Combined Campuses and Colleges pulled off a major innings victory over the Leeward Islands in 2011/12 with off-spinner Ryan Austin claiming the second ten-wicket haul of his first-class career. Leeward collapsed in both innings for totals of 39 and 113, with Austin taking 5-19 and 5-52.

- On their way to a finals berth in the 2013 Champions Trophy, India won three consecutive matches by the same margin of eight wickets. In 2003, England won four one-day internationals in a row by seven wickets.

- When Pakistan fell for 170 against the West Indies in a 2013 Champions Trophy match, their innings, including extras, was composed entirely of even-numbered scores. After 3,363 one-day internationals, Pakistan's innings at The Oval became the first in which all 12 scores (2, 50, 4, 0, 96*, 0, 2, 6, 2, 0, 2, 6) were even numbers.

- A first-class match in Sri Lanka in 2013/14 featured three batsmen from the same side who each made the same score of 103. Representing Sri Lanka A against New Zealand A at Pallekele, Kaushal Silva hit 103 in the first innings, while Ashan Priyanjan made 103 and Chaturanga de Silva 103 not out in their second. New Zealand opener Carl Cachopa spoilt the party with a score of 104.

- When Australia beat Sri Lanka at Brisbane in 2007/08, five bowlers were used with each taking the same number of wickets in each innings. The first time as many as five had done so in a Test, Brett Lee took 4-26 and 4-86, Mitchell Johnson 2-49 and 2-47, Stuart MacGill 1-79 and 1-64, Stuart Clark 2-46 and 2-75 and Andrew Symonds 1-10 and 1-21.

- A cricket club in north-west England sent out an SOS to a number of former Test cricketers in 2014 after being bowled out for a total of three in the Cheshire League. Chasing a victory total of 109 set by Haslington, Wirral managed just one run off the bat – from their No. 11. Describing it as a "bad day at the office", the club sought some coaching from the likes of Andrew Flintoff and Michael Vaughan.

A few weeks later, the Pak Pakhtoon cricket club also fell for a total of three, by the Pioneers A's in the Birmingham Cricket League. A record-low total since the competition began in 1893, the match was over in 40 minutes and 13 overs. A 45-year-old Khalid Sadiq, nursing a calf injury, was the destroyer, taking 7-2 in seven overs.

SCOREBOARD
WIRRAL v HASLINGTON – 2014

WIRRAL

		R
R. Peel	b Istead	0
P. Clewes *	lbw b Gledhill	0
N. Jones †	b Istead	0
R. Johnson	b Gledhill	0
Dominic Develing	b Istead	0
Danny Develing	b Istead	0
S. Bowman	b Istead	0
R. Gambles	c Goodier b Gledhill	0
M. Garrett	lbw b Gledhill	0
D. Fletcher	c Goodier b Istead	0
C. Hobson	not out	1
Extras	(2 lb)	2
Total	(all out – 9.2 overs)	**3**

Haslington bowling	O	M	R	W	Econ
B. Istead	5	4	1	6	0.20
T. Gledhill	4.2	4	0	4	0.00

- India controversially conceded a one-day international in 1978/79 when 23 runs away from victory and two wickets down. Bishan Bedi pulled out of the match at Sahiwal after a barrage of short-pitched bowling from Pakistan's Sarfraz Nawaz.

- Australia were humbled at Cape Town in 2008/09 when the South Africans did them in by an innings, their first such defeat in more than a decade. Australia had played a world-record 127 Tests devoid of an innings defeat since going down by an innings and 219 runs at the hands of India in Kolkata in 1997/98.

- The Adelaide Test of the 2013/14 Ashes contained 12 half-centuries, all of which were scored by a different batsman. A record number in a Test match, seven Australians scored a fifty – Chris Rogers (72), Shane Watson (51), Michael Clarke (148), George Bailey (53), Brad Haddin (118), Ryan Harris (55*) and David Warner (83*) – while five England batsmen did so – Michael Carberry (60), Ian Bell (72*), Joe Root (87), Kevin Pietersen (53) and Matthew Prior (69).

   The Australians' first-innings total of 570/9 declared contained an Ashes-record 12 sixes, including five from Haddin and one from the No. 11, Nathan Lyon. In all, 20 sixes were seen for the first time in an Ashes Test with a total of 21 – 13 by Australia (12/1) and eight by England (4/4).

Australia made history again in the following Test at Perth, becoming the first team to set a victory target of more than 500 runs in three successive Tests against the same opposition – 561 at Brisbane, 531 at Adelaide and 504 at the WACA.

- During their match-winning total of 600 against Pakistan at Rawalpindi in 2003/04, India put on two consecutive identical century partnerships. A first in Test match cricket, Rahul Dravid featured in both during his Test-record high of 270 – 131 for the fourth wicket with V.V.S. Laxman (71) and 131 for the fifth with Sourav Ganguly (77). Dravid also added 129 for the second wicket with the wicketkeeping opener Parthiv Patel (69) and 98 for the sixth with Yuvraj Singh (47).

- Despite four ducks, the West Indies went past 500 in a Test at Georgetown in 2002. Carl Hooper (233) and Shivnarine Chanderpaul (140) scored most of the runs, with ducks from Brian Lara, Junior Murray, Mervyn Dillon and Cameron Cuffy in its first-innings 501 against India.

- Karnataka began a quarter-final match in the Ranji Trophy in 2013/14 with consecutive individual scores of 100, 0, 0, 0, 100 and 100. The three noughts and three exact scores of 100 formed part of a first-innings 349 against Uttar Pradesh at Bangalore, the lowest all-out total in first-class cricket to contain three individual centuries. With a 92-run victory, Karnataka became the first Ranji Trophy team to achieve six consecutive outright wins in the same season.

SCOREBOARD
KARNATAKA v UTTAR PRADESH – BANGALORE 2013/14

KARNATAKA	1st innings	R
R.V. Uthappa	st † Dwivedi b Murtaza	100
K.L. Rahul	c † Dwivedi b Rajpoot	0
R. Samarth	c & b Amit Mishra	0
M.K. Pandey	c Kaif b Amit Mishra	0
K.K. Nair	lbw b Murtaza	100
C.M. Gautam †	b Amit Mishra	100

- When Oxford University hosted a first-class match at The Parks in 1984 only three Somerset batsmen made it to the crease in the first innings and all scored a century. At the time, Somerset's 365/1 declared was the lowest first-class total to include three centuries – 152 not out by Peter Roebuck, 103 by Julian Wyatt and 100 not out from Martin Crowe.

- When Bangladesh hosted India at Dhaka in 2014, all 20 wickets fell for less than 200 runs, a first in one-day international cricket. Chasing India's 105, Bangladesh was routed for 58, with the aggregate of 163 beating the previous record of 203 by Kenya (134) and Zimbabwe (69) in Harare in 2005/06.

  One bowler from each side took five wickets in an innings in the Dhaka match. With 5-28, Taskin Ahmed became the first Bangladesh bowler to claim a five-for on his ODI debut, and, at 19, the first teenager to do so, while Stuart Binny's 6-4 represented the cheapest six-wicket haul in a one-day international to date. Both claimed their first five-wicket haul in List A cricket, with Binny, in just his third one-day international, taking his first three wickets against the Bangladeshis without conceding a run.

BOWLERS TAKING MORE WICKETS THAN RUNS CONCEDED IN A HAUL OF FOUR OR MORE WICKETS IN A ONE-DAY INTERNATIONAL

Bowler	Figures	Match	Venue	Season
Courtney Walsh	4.3-3-1-5	West Indies v Sri Lanka	Sharjah	1986/87
Phil Simmons	10-8-3-4	West Indies v Pakistan	Sydney	1992/93
Stuart Binny	4.4-2-4-6	India v Bangladesh	Dhaka	2014

TWO BOWLERS SHARING ALL TEN WICKETS IN A ODI INNINGS

Bowlers	Match	Venue	Season
Gary Cosier (5/18) and Greg Chappell (5/20)	Australia v England	Birmingham	1977
Chaminda Vaas (8/19) and Muttiah Muralitharan (2/1)	Sri Lanka v Zimbabwe	Colombo	2001/02
Paul Collingwood (6/31) and Chris Tremlett (4/32)	England v Bangladesh	Nottingham	2005
Stuart Binny (6/4) and Mohit Sharma (4/22)	India v Bangladesh	Dhaka	2014
Josh Davey (6/28) and Iain Wardlaw (4/22)	Scotland v Afghanistan	Abu Dhabi	2014/15

- After following-on at Georgetown in 2014/15, Barbados successfully defended a total of 69 to win the match by two runs. Guyana were dismissed for 66 in 29.1 overs, with three middle-order batsmen going for a duck and Dwayne Smith (5-17) achieving a maiden five-wicket haul after 13 years of first-class cricket.

  Earlier, Guyana spinner Veerasammy Permaul had taken a career-best 8-26, dismissing three consecutive batsmen lbw for nought. The previous lowest-defended first-class total in the West Indies was 73 by Demerara against Trinidad at Port-of-Spain in 1868/69.

- When Australia compiled 435 in the fifth Ashes Test at Sydney in 1932/33, the first six in the order made progressively higher scores, while the remaining five made progressively lower ones. In the first innings, Australia's individual scores in batting order were 0, 14, 48, 61, 73, 85, 52, 42, 19, 17 (not out) and 1.

- In the ninth match of the 2011 World Cup, both of the first wickets to fall in each innings was a stumping. A first in one-day international cricket, Bangladesh's Imrul Kayes was stumped for 12, while Ireland's Paul Stirling went the same way for nine in the match at Mirpur.

- Two New Zealand batsmen crafted one of Test cricket's masterpieces in 2014/15 with a world-record stand of 365 against Sri Lanka. In the second Test at Wellington, Kane Williamson (242*) – with a maiden Test match double-century – and B.J. Watling (142*) posted the highest-ever stand for the sixth wicket, which beat the previous best set just a year before which also involved the South African-born Watling. In doing so, Watling became the first player to feature in the top two stands for any wicket in the history of Test match cricket.

  At the same ground in 2013/14, Brendon McCullum – a wicketkeeper turned batsman – and Watling – a batsman turned wicketkeeper – had put on 352 for the sixth wicket, with the former producing the first Test match triple-century by a New Zealander. After a double-century in the first Test, McCullum scored 302 over 775 minutes and 559 deliveries, both records for a New Zealand batsman.

  New Zealand's sixth and seventh wickets added a record 531 runs in the second innings, beating 414 runs by Australia against England at the MCG in 1936/37. After a duck in the first innings, Watling achieved the double of a century (124) and five dismissals in an innings, while Jimmy Neesham scored 33 and 137 not out, batting at No. 8, on his Test debut. New Zealand declared at 680/8, the highest total in the second innings of a Test, overtaking its own 671/4 against Sri Lanka, at the same venue, in 1990/91.

- Of a total of ten ducks in the second Ashes Test at the MCG in 1901/02, eight came on the opening day. Victor Trumper, Monty Noble and Syd Gregory each made nought in Australia's first-innings total of 112; Tom Hayward, Willie Quaife, John Gunn and Arthur Jones then made ducks in England's 61, and by the time Australia stumbled to 48/5 in their second innings by stumps, Bill Howell had become the eighth duck of the day. The second, and final, day's play at Manchester in 1888 featured ten batsmen who failed to score, with eight dismissed for a duck.

- A day after copping a bruising defeat in the Clydesdale Bank 40-over competition in 2011, the Netherlands regrouped to thrash Yorkshire. In matches played at the Dutch venue of Amstelveen, centuries from the Sussex pair of Chris Nash (116*) and Lou Vincent (102) dashed any hopes for the home side which was bundled out for just 123 in a 148-run defeat. But the next day, it was Yorkshire dismissed for the same score of 123, as the Netherlands romped home with 75 balls remaining. The Pakistan-born Mudassar Bukhari took 3-28, while his opening new-ball partner Shane Mott, a grade cricketer from Sydney, took 2-18.

- After defeating England by 281 runs in the fifth Test at Sydney in 2013/14, Australia won their following Test by exactly the same margin. South Africa lost the first Test at Centurion by 281 runs, during which Mitchell Johnson took 12 wickets, and Alex Doolan became the first batsman to score 89 on his Test debut.

  The tables were turned for the following Test at Port Elizabeth with South Africa winning by 231 runs after a spectacular batting collapse by the Australians. Following a century opening stand in the second innings from Chris Rogers and David Warner, the nine batsmen to follow scored a total of 22 runs, the second-lowest for Australia in a Test innings, following 13 against England at Edgbaston in 1902. Australia's Nos. 3-7 scored a total of seven runs, with Doolan making five, Michael Clarke and Brad Haddin one each and Shaun Marsh and Steve Smith first-ball ducks. It represented the second-lowest aggregate for numbers three to seven for any team in a Test, with the lowest (5) also by Australia against South Africa, at Cape Town in 2011/12.

  When A.B. de Villiers (116) passed fifty in the first innings, he became the first batsman to score a half-century in 12 consecutive Tests, beating 11 by the West Indies' Viv Richards and the Indian pair of Gautam Gambhir and Virender Sehwag.

- When Victoria hosted Tasmania at Melbourne in 1951/52, their mammoth first-innings total of 647 was devoid of any extras. Jeff Hallebone scored 202 on his first-class debut, while Richard Maddocks achieved his maiden first-class century, going on to 271. Both Hallebone and Maddocks were late replacements for the match, and neither was selected for Victoria's following game.

  There was no play on the final day of the drawn match at the MCG to mark the death of King George VI. The second day of the fifth Test between England and India at Madras was also called off to note his passing.

- After losing the toss and being asked to bat in two consecutive Tests against New Zealand in 2001/02, Australia responded both times with a double-century opening partnership. Unique in Test match cricket, Justin Langer and Matthew Hayden added 224 at Brisbane and then 223 at Hobart, with both games drawn.

  In 2014, the West Indies celebrated their 500th Test with only the second instance of a team putting on a century stand after being sent in in two consecutive matches of a series. At Kingstown, Chris Gayle and Kraigg Brathwaite added 116 runs in a ten-wicket win against Bangladesh, while Brathwaite and debutant Leon Johnson put on a 143-run stand in a 296-run win in the second game at Gros Islet.

- In 2014, Ian Bell appeared in his 100th Test match with England going down by a margin of 100 runs. The Sri Lanka win at Leeds was just the third instance of a team winning a Test by exactly 100 runs, after England beat South Africa at Birmingham in 1960 and India's defeat of the West Indies at Chennai in 1974/75.

  As many as 11 ducks were seen in the Headingley match, including one by Stuart Broad who became just the ninth player to collect one on his birthday. With a hat-trick earlier in the match, two of Broad's team-mates hit maiden centuries after both had made their debuts in the previous Test of the series. Sporting the biggest beard by an England batsman since W.G. Grace, Moeen Ali batted for nigh on 385 minutes in scoring an unbeaten 108, the longest time spent at the crease by a batsman at No. 7 or lower in the fourth innings of a Test. Sam Robson was the other to raise his bat, hitting a first-innings 127.

  After a 55-ball duck in England's second innings, James Anderson then made the highest score by an England No. 11 in his next outing in the following Test – against India – at Trent Bridge. Anderson scored his maiden first-class fifty, going on to 81, sharing a world-record last-wicket partnership of 198 with Joe Root (154*). The two soaked up 320 deliveries – the most by a last-wicket pair – with the match providing the first instance of two tenth-wicket 100-run partnerships in the same Test, after Bhuvneshwar Kumar (58) and the No. 11 Mohammed Shami (51*) put on 111 in India's first-innings total of 457. It was also the first Test in which a No. 11 batsman hit a fifty for each side. Anderson slogged it out for 130 balls over 230 minutes, the longest-known innings by a No. 11 in Tests.

While Anderson broke the world record for most innings – 130 – before a maiden Test 50, Alastair Cook broke the record for playing most Tests – 105 – before claiming his first Test wicket.

- When Leicestershire gained a 101-run first-innings lead over North-amptonshire at Grace Road in 1977, they did so with nine single-figure scores, a century from the No. 8 and a 98 from their No. 11. Leicestershire's captain Ray Illingworth made an unbeaten 119, while Ken Higgs was run out two runs shy of a century in their all-out total of 273.

- There was chaos in a club match in New Zealand in 2011 when four batsmen were dismissed in two balls. Representing Napier Old Boys Marist, Indika Senarathne dismissed the Technical Old Boys' No. 7 batsman, stumped off a wide, and then bowled the next batsman. He followed it up with a wicket off his next ball to claim a hat-trick, his three wickets coming off two legal deliveries. The next batsman – who was also the scorer for the innings – got caught up in the excitement, and failed to make it to the wicket and was dismissed timed out.

- Coming in at 26/5 against the West Indies at Napier in the 2015 World Cup, UAE pace bowler Amjad Javed struck a maiden half-century and took part in their first hundred-run partnership against a Test nation. With their first six batsmen back in the shed with single-figure scores, Amjad (56), at No. 7, and Nasir Aziz (60), at eight, both peeled off a fifty and a 107-run seventh-wicket stand, equalling the World Cup record UAE had set at Brisbane just three weeks before. At the Gabba, Amjad (42) and Shaiman Anwar (106) had made the first-ever century stand for the seventh wicket in World Cup cricket, adding 107 against Ireland.

- When the West Indies beat Pakistan in a 2015 World Cup match at Christchurch, their numbers three to eight all scored 30 or more, a first in ODI cricket. Chasing 311 for victory, Pakistan fell to 4/1, the fewest number of runs accumulated by a top four in any one-day international. The match also contained the first instance of both number five batsmen being dismissed for exactly 50.

- After losing its first two batsmen for single-figure scores by Australia at Dubai in 2014/15, Pakistan's next five all scored half-centuries. Spluttering at 7/2, Azhar Ali then hit 53, Younis Khan 106, Misbah-ul-Haq 69, Asad Shafiq 89 and Sarfraz Ahmed 109, lifting Pakistan to a match-winning total of 454.

Opener David Warner also scored a century (133) at Dubai, his sixth consecutive 50-plus score in Tests. After a pair of centuries in his previous Test – at Cape Town – Warner became the first Australian batsman to score over 130 in three consecutive innings. For the seventh consecutive Test, one of Australia's openers scored a century, a world-record sequence, beating a run of six by India between 2008/09 and 2009/10.

- Pakistan scored nine centuries against Australia in the UAE in 2014/15, a record number by one team in a two-Test series. Younis Khan scored three, Misbah-ul-Haq and Azhar Ali two each, with one from Sarfraz Ahmed and Ahmed Shehzad. Australia scored just one. After a 221-run win in the first Test at Dubai, Pakistan flogged the Australians by 356 in the second Test at Abu Dhabi, their biggest victory by a runs margin to date.

Pakistan's appetite for big runs continued a week later against New Zealand posting a first-innings total of 566/3 declared at Abu Dhabi, with the first instance in Test cricket of the first five batsmen passing 80. Three passed the hundred mark, with Misbah (102*) becoming the first player in Test history to hit three consecutive tons when over the age of 40 and the first to do so at the same ground. Younis (100*) hit his fourth century in five innings, while Ahmed Shehzad (176), at the age of 22, became the youngest Pakistan opener to score 150-plus in a Test overtaking a 23-year-old Hanif Mohammad and his famous knock of 337 against the West Indies at Bridgetown in 1957/58.

SCOREBOARD
PAKISTAN v NEW ZEALAND – ABU DHABI 2014/15

PAKISTAN	1st innings	R	B	4s	6s	SR
Mohammad Hafeez	c & b Anderson	96	137	10	0	70.07
Ahmed Shehzad	hit wkt b Anderson	176	371	17	1	47.43
Azhar Ali	b Sodhi	87	215	4	0	40.46
Younis Khan	not out	100	141	10	0	70.92
Misbah-ul-Haq *	not out	102	162	9	1	62.96
Extras	(2 b, 2 lb, 1 nb)	5				
Total	(3 wkts dec)	**566**				

New Zealand ended day two at 15/0 with Tom Latham and Brendon McCullum leaving the field with scores of five not out and nine not out respectively. The following day, Pakistan also went to stumps at 15/0, with both batsmen – Mohammad Hafeez (5*) and Azhar Ali (9*) – scoring the same number of runs as the two New Zealanders, the first time this had happened in a Test match. With a 248-run victory,

Pakistan became the first country to achieve three consecutive Test wins by a margin of more than 200 runs.

After a drawn second Test, the third match of the series at Sharjah saw New Zealand take control with a first-innings 690, their highest total to date that surpassed 680/8 declared against India at Wellington earlier in the year. McCullum (202) led the charge, reaching 100 in 78 balls and then 200 off 186, the fastest double-century by a Test captain.

The first New Zealander to score four Test match double-centuries, McCullum also became just the fourth batsman to attain three in a calendar year, after Michael Clarke (4) in 2012, Don Bradman in 1930 and Ricky Ponting in 2003. Batting with Kane Williamson, who made 192, the pair produced a 297-run stand for the second wicket, New Zealand's first double-century partnership against Pakistan. Three batsmen – Ross Taylor, Corey Anderson and Tim Southee – were dismissed for exactly 50 in the innings, a first in Test match cricket.

The match began with Mohammad Hafeez dismissed for 197, signalling just the second time two batsmen had been dismissed in the 190s in the same Test. The first instance also involved Mohammad (196), and Sri Lanka's Kumar Sangakkara (192) at the SSC ground in Colombo in 2012.

A total of 35 sixes – 22 by New Zealand and 13 by Pakistan – was struck in the match, another record that busted the previous best of 27 by Pakistan and India at Faisalabad in 2005/06 and by Bangladesh and New Zealand at Chittagong in 2013/14. The 22 struck by New Zealand in its only innings beat Australia's 17 against Zimbabwe at Perth in 2003/04, while 59 in the series bettered by ten the previous best in a three-Test rubber by Pakistan and India in 2005/06.

- Led by a former South African one-day international captain, South Australia lost a Sheffield Shield match by an innings in 2014/15 after scoring 431. Johan Botha declared the first innings at eight wickets down and watched as Victoria piled on 607. The Redbacks then fell for 130, sustaining a loss of an innings and 46.

  It was only the second occasion in Sheffield Shield history that a team had lost by an innings after scoring 400-plus, but the first following a declaration. At the MCG in 1924/25, Victoria were dismissed for 413, whereupon New South Wales responded with 705 and then bowled out the Vics for 130 gaining an innings-and-162-run win.

- When Namibia played the Netherlands at Bloemfontein at the 2003 World Cup, their openers were both caught by the same substitute fielder for the same score of 41. Their numbers three and four both scored 52 while two Dutch bowlers returned the same figures of 4-24.

- Despite a 500-run total in a match during the 1995 County Championship, Nottinghamshire went on to lose by an innings. Batting first at Northampton, Notts piled on 527 with a double-century from Tim Robinson (209) and a century from Graeme Archer (158), the pair combining for a 294-run second-wicket partnership. But it wasn't enough, as Northamptonshire raced to 781, then declaring with seven wickets down after centuries from Alan Fordham (130), Allan Lamb (115), Russell Warren (154) and David Capel (114*).

  After taking 4-118 in the first innings, Anil Kumble took 5-43 in the second as Nottinghamshire crashed to an all-out total of 157 and an innings-and-97-run defeat. It represented the first occasion that a team had passed 500 in a first-class match and gone down by an innings.

- When Michael Clarke closed Australia's first innings against India at Adelaide in 2014/15, it was the 300th instance of a declaration of 500 or more in a Test. The hosts' 517/7 included three centuries – all by New South Wales batsmen – with each dedicating their innings to former Blues team-mate Phillip Hughes who had died two weeks before.

  David Warner scored 145 – the first of two centuries he made in the match – while Steve Smith (162*) passed 150 for the first time in a Test. After retiring hurt with a sore back, Clarke became the first Australian to resume his innings and go on to score a hundred. During his 128 – his 28th Test-match hundred – he also became the first batsman to take part in a century stand before and after leaving the field with an injury.

  With a century in his 40th Test as captain, his opposite number, Virat Kohli (115 and 141), scored two in his first, becoming only the second to do so after Australia's Greg Chappell (123 and 109*) against the West Indies at Brisbane in 1975/76.

  Australia went into Adelaide having nominated Phillip Hughes as their honourary 13th man and on the final day when they won the match, Hughes's brother Jason scored 63 in a grade match for Sydney club Mosman, the same score Phillip had made for South Australia in his final appearance at the crease. In the second Test at Brisbane, India was dismissed in its first innings for 408 – Hughes was Australia's 408th Test cricketer.

With Clarke out of the Gabba match with a hamstring injury, a 25-year-old Smith became Australia's 45th Test captain, and in his 45th Test innings marked his elevation with a century (133). With Kohli having done so at Adelaide, this became the first-ever Test series in which two players made a century in their first match as captain. Chris Rogers celebrated his 500th innings in first-class cricket with 55 – and backed it up with another score of 55 – while both teams bowled exactly the same number of overs – 109.4 – in the first innings.

The third Test at the MCG saw Smith become the first Australian captain – and the fifth overall – to score a century in his first two matches in charge, clubbing 192 the day after New Zealand captain Brendon McCullum was dismissed for 195 against Sri Lanka in Christchurch. With 117 at Sydney, Smith then became the first player to score a hundred in his first three Tests as captain and the first batsman to score a century in the first innings of each match of a four-Test series.

Kohli and Smith also provided the first instance of two batsmen making four centuries in a single Test series. With four hundreds and a further two fifties, Smith scored a total of 769 runs at 128.16 overtaking Don Bradman's long-standing record against India of 715 in five Tests in 1947/48. Kohli established a new benchmark for an Indian batsman in Australia with 692 runs at 86.50.

The series contained a total of 16 half-centuries by openers, the most for a four-match series, beating 13 by England and New Zealand in 1949, with Rogers hitting six in a row. Total runs in the series numbered 5,870, the most in a four-Test series overtaking an aggregate of 5,651 by the same two sides in 2003/04. On the bowling side, 25 instances of 100 runs in an innings were seen in the series, beating the previous record of 23 in five Tests between Australia and England in 1924/25. Nathan Lyon topped the list with six, a world record that equalled India's Subhash Gupte who conceded over 100 runs in an innings six times in a five-Test series against the West Indies in 1958/59.

For the first time in Test cricket, both teams passed 400 in the first innings of all four matches of a series, with Australia exceeding 500 on each occasion, another first in their history.

- A score of 101 not out by South Africa's Stiaan van Zyl in 2014/15 became the 100th century by anyone on his Test debut. It formed part of a formidable 552/5 declared against the West Indies at Centurion, which contained their first instance of numbers four through six all scoring centuries in the same innings. Hashim Amla, with 208, became the first South African captain to score a double-century in a Test on home soil, while A.B. de Villiers struck 152.

South Africa became the first team to reach 500 in a Test innings after losing their first three wickets on the same score (57), while the West Indies first innings of 201 saw the top four batsmen in the order dismissed between 30 and 35, another first in Test match cricket. When Marlon Samuels (33) hit a single off Kyle Abbott, he brought up the two-millionth run off the bat in Test match cricket.

In the ensuing one-day international series between the two sides, South Africa mauled the tourists in game two at Johannesburg with three batsmen scoring centuries in the innings, a first in ODI cricket. Amla scored 153 not out, Rilee Rossouw 128 and de Villiers 149 in a total of 439/2. De Villiers scored his runs off just 44 balls, with nine fours and 16 sixes, reaching his 50 off 16 balls, and his hundred off 31, both records in one-day international cricket.

With the 200th century by a captain in ODIs, de Villiers became the first batsman to score a hundred with a 300-plus strike rate (338.63), while the West Indies provided the first instance of opening bowlers – Jerome Taylor (95) and Jason Holder (91) – conceding 90-plus runs in an innings.

- After losing a wicket to the first ball of a one-day international against Sri Lanka at Dunedin in 2014/15, New Zealand went on to compile a match-winning 360/5. The highest ODI total after a team had lost a wicket to the opening ball, it featured a record-breaking innings from Luke Ronchi, who made 170 not out off 99 balls, the highest undefeated score by a wicketkeeper in one-day internationals and the highest innings by a No. 7 batsman in List A cricket. A 35-year-old Grant Elliott scored 104 not out with the pair becoming the first to reach 200 for the sixth wicket in a one-day international between Test-playing countries, finishing unconquered on 267. Their record sixth-wicket stand came in the same month as team-mates Kane Williamson and B.J. Watling made the highest sixth-wicket partnership in Tests – 365* – against the same team in Wellington.

  With 116, Tillakaratne Dilshan scored his 20th ODI ton for Sri Lanka, while a one-day international on the same day between Australia and England at Hobart contained a century from Ian Bell (141) and one from Steve Smith (102*), who became the first batsman to score a hundred on his debut as captain in both Tests and ODIs.

- After batting first and falling for 31 in a first-class match at Panagoda in 2014/15, the Galle Cricket Club went on to achieve a headline-making victory. With as many as eight debutants in their ranks, Galle regrouped to dismiss the Sri Lanka Air Force Sports Club for 107 after being set a victory target of 112. While no batsman reached double figures in their first innings, Galle made 295 in their second which contained a century from 17-year-old Charith Asalanka (114) on his first-class debut. Asalanka (4-34) then combined with fellow debutant Malith de Silva (6-46), sharing all ten wickets in the demolition of their opponents.

LOWEST FIRST-INNINGS TOTALS
TO WIN A FIRST-CLASS MATCH

Total	Match	Venue	Season
27	England v Sussex	Brighton	1827
31	Gentlemen v Players	Lord's	1848
31	Gloucestershire v Middlesex	Bristol	1924
31	Galle Cricket Club v Sri Lanka Air Force Sports Club	Panagoda	2014/15
32	South of the Thames v North of the Thames	Lord's	1867
34	Surrey & Sussex v England	Lord's	1852
37	Oldfield v MCC	Bray	1793
37	Kent v Sussex	Sevenoaks	1828
38	Surrey v Kent & Sussex	Hove	1858
39	R.N. Newman's XI v R. Leigh's XI	Navestock Side	1793

• In the first Test between Bangladesh and Pakistan at Khulna in 2015, two of the opening batsmen scored a double-century. A first in Test match cricket, Mohammad Hafeez made 224 – the highest innings by a Pakistan opener who had faced the first ball of his team's first innings – while Tamim Iqbal scored 206, Bangladesh's second double-century at the highest level. The top seven for both sides all went past 20 in the first innings – another first in Test match cricket – while Pakistan's batsmen made a 50-run partnership for the first six wickets, only the second this had happened, after Australia had done so in the tied Test against the West Indies at Brisbane in 1960/61.

Tamim and Imrul Kayes (150) then stunned the Pakistanis in the second innings with a match-changing world-record opening partnership. Their monster stand of 312 beat the previous second-innings best of 290 between England's Colin Cowdrey and Geoff Pullar against South Africa at The Oval in 1960. While Imrul (51 and 150) became the first Bangladesh batsman to score a 150 and a fifty in the same Test, Tamim became the first from his country to score a century in three consecutive Tests. In his previous two, Tamim had produced identical innings of 109, both against Zimbabwe, at Khulna and Chittagong, in 2014/15.

For only the second time in history – after Australia (533) versus the West Indies (616) at Adelaide in 1968/69 – the Khulna Test saw totals of over 500 (628 and 555/6) in the match's second and third innings.

Media Moments

- Of the 15 sixes struck by Australia in a ODI against Zimbabwe at Harare in 2014, one smashed into a broadcast box window with glass fragments hitting one of the commentators. Sporting a few minor cuts, former fast bowler-turned-broadcaster Pommie Mbangwa continued his stint after a beaming Mitchell Johnson had raised a hand in apology.

The result of a Mitchell Johnson six in a one-day international at Harare in 2014

- A BBC cricket broadcaster achieved an unusual hat-trick in 2011 when a six smashed through the commentary box during a match at Taunton. During a 59-ball century from Peter Trego, BBC commentator Edward Bevan was on air when the Somerset batsman smashed one of his six sixes: "**It's coming towards us ... is it going to hit us?**" It did, with Bevan forced to cut short his duties: "**It hit me on the back and I was quite shaken for a while. There's a bruise there – in fact I couldn't carry on.**"

   It was the third time in his career that Bevan's commentary duties had been interrupted by a cricket ball: "**Apparently when the ball went through the window, he [Trego] stood down and put his fist through the air as if to say 'I've been trying to do that for years and I've done it at last!'**"

- The BBC issued an apology in 2015 after being duped by an imposter who pretended to be a former Pakistan Test batsman and was paid to appear on a number of its cricket programmes. Nadeem Alam, a club cricketer who had only ever played for his home town Huddersfield, posed as Nadeem Abbasi, who appeared in three Tests in 1989: "**If I ever find Nadeem Alam, I will punch him in the face. The BBC is a big institution … surely they must check.**"

- A former Australian batsman was hired by ABC TV in 2010 to comment on the top stories of the country's daily newspapers. A contributor to the breakfast show on the News 24 network until 2013, Paul Sheahan appeared in 31 Tests and three one-day internationals.

- Tasmanian batsman George Davies was the son of the founder of the Hobart *Mercury* newspaper. A state captain, he appeared in seven first-class matches in the 1870s and 80s, scoring 149 runs and taking three wickets.

- The Trinidad-born Trevor McDonald, one of Britain's best-known TV newsreaders, cites cricket as providing one of his fondest childhood memories. Sir Trevor, who penned biographies on West Indies legends Clive Lloyd and Viv Richards, remembers "**… making cricket bats out of coconut branches and begging for tennis balls.**"

> **"In Jamaica I stayed in a hotel with the England team and I got to know a lot of the boys closely. I have no association any more with the West Indian players. So I'm afraid I love to see England win. I'm much more on the phone to Mr Kevin Pietersen these days than anybody else I know."**
>
> Trevor McDonald

- Former Australian wicketkeeper Adam Gilchrist threatened legal action in 2013 after a Twitter account bearing his name bobbed up during the Ashes series. During the Nottingham Test, England fast bowler Stuart Broad had gained worldwide media attention after edging a ball into the hands of Michael Clarke but, with the umpire ruling in his favour, stayed put. The ensuing free-for-all saw an Adam Gilchrist impersonator take to Twitter for some fun at the wicketkeeper's expense. A noted "walker", Gilchrist was unimpressed: "**AdamCGilchrist this is Adam Gilchrist here. Stop pretending to be me. I know you say 'parody' on your profile but now it's gone too far.**"

In the aftermath of the incident, the Brisbane *Courier Mail* newspaper refused to mention Broad in its copy during the Gabba Test in the follow-up series, while Australia's coach Darren Lehmann labelled Broad a cheat on a Sydney radio station. He was fined $3,000, a tab picked up the Triple M network which was later banned from interviewing

Gabba fans' silent weapon against smug Pommie cheat

BROAD BAN

anyone from the England squad after banners having a dig at Kevin Pietersen were flown over the Gabba.

- Rajdeep Sardesai played in seven first-class matches for Oxford in 1987, later becoming a senior editor at the CNN television news channel. A journalist and news presenter in India, Sardesai had a highest score of 63 not out, made on his first-class debut, against Kent at Oxford.

- A South African-born journalist who worked for CNN and the *Jerusalem Post* is credited with making cricket popular in Israel. A well-known face on TV screens around the globe for a decade or more, Jerrold Kessel played in 16 matches for Israel in the 1979, 1983 and 1990 ICC Trophies as a captain, wicketkeeper and middle-order batsman.

> "Jerrold worked for CNN for 13 years from 1990 to 2003 during some of the most spectacular highs and lows of the Middle East and was one of the network's regular reporting faces from the region. He was a passionate journalist and a guiding force for many he worked with."
>
> CNN Jerusalem bureau chief Kevin Flower

- When a high-profile Australian radio announcer was given the flick in 2012, the move drew plaudits from Shane Warne. The former Australian bowler gave the thumbs-up to the sacking after 3AW's Derryn Hinch had mocked Warne on his show: **"Well done 3AW on sacking Hinch. I used to think he was entertaining and clever, but in recent times he has just spoken rubbish and lost the plot."**

- For the opening Test of the Australian summer in 2011/12, a first took place with the man of the match award chosen by viewers of Channel Nine. James Pattinson was nominated by viewers as the best player in the first Test against New Zealand after viewers voted with their fingers through an app called Cricket Live. But the system was dumped after just two Tests when viewers got it wrong in Hobart, voting century-maker David Warner the best player of the second Test over New Zealand's Doug Bracewell who took a match-winning haul of nine wickets, including 6-40 in the final innings.

- In the same year that ABC cricket commentator Jim Maxwell was recognised for his services to broadcasting with an Australia Day honour, he was denied media accreditation to cover an Australia-India Test series. After the ABC had rejected a fee quoted by the Indian cricket board to broadcast all Tests of the 2012/13 Border-Gavaskar Trophy, the national broadcaster had decided on the next best thing – sending Maxwell to phone in reports from the grounds, a proposal rejected by the BCCI.

  Maxwell, who tried three times to gain an ABC cadetship before he was finally successful in 1973, was awarded an Order of Australia medal in 2013 for "significant service to sport, particularly cricket, as a commentator, and to the community".

- Freddie Grisewood, who appeared in one first-class cricket match, forged a successful career in television broadcasting. He played for Worcestershire in 1908, and was the voice for the BBC's first-ever live outside televised broadcast, the coronation of King George VI in 1937. He was also behind the microphone for the first TV broadcast of tennis from Wimbledon.

- An Australian TV sports presenter became a news item herself in 2013 when she was shown on live television while attending a Ryobi Cup match as a spectator. During play in the Queensland-Victoria match in Sydney, Channel Nine presenter Yvonne Sampson began to simulate a sex act while talking to two friends, all caught live on national TV: **"This is embarrassing. I was telling the story of how we were throwing mini Christmas trees in the studio one time when a cameraman was caught thrusting away on one."**

- A BBC commentator went undercover in 2011, turning out in disguise for a second-grade club in Yorkshire. In 2006, the Goldsborough XI put up a shameful batting display against Disforth, in which no batsman got off the mark. A rematch took place five years later, with the Goldsborough XI bolstered by the inclusion of former England captain Michael Vaughan, who played under the name of Gary Watson, sporting a tattoo, beer belly and mullet: **"The other side had no idea it was me. It was great fun getting dressed up, except for the original prosthetic fitting. I had to have this blue seaweed goo all over my face to make the cast, which made it difficult to breathe, let alone talk. Batting in the suit was pretty tough as I was sweating so much in the prosthetic mask. The pillow stuffed down my shirt to give me a beer belly made it hard to run. I was worried I might get run out. I had a decent knock of 28, the team played well and we won."**

A beaming Michael Vaughan gets a massage before going on air in his role as a BBC commentator during the 2010/11 Ashes series in Australia

- A British newspaper poll conducted in 2009 found that the laws of cricket were among the most confusing subjects in modern life. Topping the *Daily Telegraph* study of 5,000 respondents was foreign call centres, followed by algebra. The laws of cricket came in at No. 9.

- After making his first-class debut for Boland B in 1993/94, a future cricket commentator had to delay his debut for the first XI to attend his tribal circumcision ceremony. After a first-class career of 38 matches, Lulama Masikazana landed a gig in TV as a commentator thanks to leading South African journalist Neil Manthorp: **"He wasn't very good, but we had a lot of fun."**

- Notwithstanding his cult-like status as a cricket commentator, former Australian slow bowler Kerry O'Keeffe generated a Facebook page calling for his sacking from the ABC. Formed by a so-called "group of concerned cricket citizens", the page – replete with O'Keeffe's name misspelt – attracted next to no support.

Kerry O'Keeffe receives a special ABC cricket cap to mark his final stint in the commentary box, at the SCG in 2014

"'Peerless'. It was such a seamless style and there was never any chunkiness about anything he ever did on air. It was always measured, balanced and he was respected and admired by his broadcasting colleagues and the players – that's a unique reputation to have. Richie Benaud will be 2 for 222 forever. Whenever the scoreline gets to that, I'm sure his name will come up."

Kerry O'Keeffe
on the passing of TV commentator Richie Benaud in 2015

"If cricket had ever anointed a pope it would be Richie Benaud. He has been the most influential, revered and respected person in the game for fifty years. As a commentator he was precise, authoritative and deliciously understated. Richie was the master of the pause. Silence marked him as the best exponent of television's essential craft; let the picture tell the story, then utter appropriate gravitas, a memorably droll bon mot. If you ran a poll today on the most popular cricket commentator in Australia, Richie would still be number one."

Jim Maxwell

CHANNEL NINE COMMENTATORS: AN ANNOYANCE

Ben Pobjie – Australian writer and comedian

The Australian sporting public is, I submit, a generally forgiving bunch. We forgave Shane Warne. We even seem to have forgiven Margaret Court, in as much as we have not yet placed her in an institution. But even the most happy-go-lucky, laid-back of sporting publics has its breaking point. And I fear that breaking point may be approaching if drastic changes are not made to the Channel Nine commentary team.

Now, please bear in mind, I do realise that Nine's commentators are some of the greats of the game, with magnificent playing records that command respect. So don't think for moment that the vicious character assassination in which I am about to engage reflects on their sporting achievements in any way.

I'm not saying the Nine team is beyond hope. The situation is not irreparable. There is nothing wrong with Channel Nine's cricket coverage that could not be fixed by sacking the entire commentary team and replacing them with a CD of soothing ocean noises. Because I'm not sure I can take much more.

Of the banter – the match situation assessments which veer between the blindingly obvious and the bewilderingly inaccurate. Of the cringe-worthy plugs for other shows on Nine. It's beyond a joke.

All of the commentators are culpable, with Mark Taylor's rapid-fire babbling which spills haphazardly out over the game like tomato sauce out of a bottle that's been struck too hard on the bottom. I don't even know what he's saying when he starts talking: my brain just sends the signal that someone in the background has turned on a Fujitsu air-conditioner, and I adjust accordingly.

Meanwhile, beside "Tubby" sit his erstwhile team-mates, Michael Slater and Ian Healy, the latter of whom is mostly occupied with describing events in the fantasy game being played inside his own skull rather than the one actually happening, and the former of whom's main job is to engage in lively banter about which member of the commentary team the viewers would most like to see French-kiss a mongoose, as measured by the Vodafone Viewers' Verdict, a brilliant new innovation for the telecast, inspired by Nine producers' belief that the last thing any cricket fan wants to do with his time is watch the cricket. And then of course there are the old reliables. Bill Lawry still keeps plugging away, desperately trying to convince everyone that life is much, much more exciting than it really is.

And then there's Ian Chappell, who pops into the commentary box every now and then to continue a thought he started to have in 1987 but hasn't quite fully teased out yet about David Boon's wrists.

212

Ah, but what of Mark Nicholas, you say? Well, when he first arrived, I liked Mark. He was British, which meant he was classy-sounding, and he seemed to have something of a handle on the game. But it turns out he's just like all the rest – he will happily fake enthusiasm at ten consecutive overs of batsmen tapping singles to deep fielders in the middle overs of a one-day game.

And even worse, at every opportunity he'll grovel to the cricketing greats in the box, meekly asking them "what's it like, playing Test cricket?" Which frankly makes me lose all respect for him, and irritates me because the fact he's asking the questions suggests he thinks any of us care what these senile fools think about anything.

And yet despite all this, cricket commentary on Nine does not actually hit rock-bottom, until James Brayshaw steps up to the microphone. And with a mix of pig-ignorance, faux-blokey anti-comedy, dementedly facile analysis, and an all-round on-air personality that will soon be banned by the UN as a chemical weapon, "JB" plumbs depths of commentary undreamed of since Geoff Boycott ate some funny mushrooms and asked Jonathan Agnew to marry him.

Listening to James Brayshaw commentate on cricket is the sports-viewing equivalent of having your kidneys forcibly removed by chimpanzees. So what are we to do, to improve this situation.

Well, here is my theory: Nine's woes stem from the fact that it has always been obsessed with employing ex-cricketers. Feeling the achievements of its team lent gravitas to the coverage, they recruited yesteryear's greats to provide comment and analysis.

Admittedly, Nicholas and Brayshaw break this rule somewhat, but they are at least both former first-class cricketers, and in Brayshaw's case, in possession of some compromising photos of Nine directors.

The point is, it's time for something new. We've tried experience, we've tried deep knowledge, and it's been an unmitigated failure. It's time for a fresh approach: let's try ignorance. Let's put some complete noobs up in the commentary box and see how they go. And I don't just mean people with no broadcasting experience, or people who haven't played at the highest level.

I mean people who have never even watched a game of cricket. Possibly people who don't even WANT to watch a game of cricket. That way we'll get a refreshing new perspective on the game: through their virgin eyes, we too shall see the game anew, reinvigorating our enthusiasm for it. Just imagine how fun it will be watching cricket to the sounds of:

"Ah ... the ... tall one ... the bowlman I think he's called ... he's thrown the ball at the batman, and ... the batman ... has hit it maybe? It's gone ... somewhere, I dunno. One of these guys is running, not sure why. Oh actually a few of them are running. The ones with the sticks are running too, the batman and his friend. What do you think Sam?" "OH MY GOD THIS IS BORING."

I think with this sort of commentary we can make cricket come alive again, and win back all those fans who deserted Nine's commentary in favour of watching drug addicts ride up hills in France. A clean slate, a new era, a vibrant new start for the art of cricket commentary.

- In what was claimed to be a world first, a village cricket match in Lancashire was streamed live over the internet in 2011. Staged to promote the need for fast broadband in rural areas, the match was between the village of Wray and a team billed as the Rest of the World.

- Former Fleet Street editor-turned-CNN host Piers Morgan was a handy cricketer in his younger days, once taking all ten wickets in an innings in a schools match. In 1977, a 12-year-old Morgan took 10-9 off 11.2 overs for Cumnor House against Copthorne: "**I was a fast bowler in those days. One year I got picked for the England Prep School squad but never played. My best bowling tally was ten wickets for nine runs. Later, I became an off-spinner and focused more on my batting. I joined Newick cricket club at 13 and my best batting scores include 107 and three others in the 90s batting at No. 3. In 1983, I was a member of the side that toured Malta and my first-ever published article was actually a write-up of this event in a local paper.**"

"Cricket's all about having great teas, beers afterwards and it's the camaraderie that's unique. I always think that if you meet someone who likes cricket, it's a great camaraderie kind of sport cricket. It's a very civilised sport. I've never met anyone who plays and loves cricket who I didn't basically like."

Piers Morgan

- A motoring mishap in 2008 saw Australia's Michael Clarke make the pages of a Sydney newspaper after rescuing his then-off-field partner Lara Bingle whose car had run out of petrol on a busy thoroughfare. The Clark-Bingle bungle resulted in a Sydney radio station challenging its listeners to deliberately disrupt peak-hour traffic by running out of fuel. The competition earned the station a rebuke from police after the winner caused havoc on the Sydney Harbour Bridge at 7am.

- Nasser Hussain found himself in the centre of a media storm in 2011 when he compared some of India's players to donkeys. During a commentary stint on Sky for the England-India Twenty20 international at Manchester, the former England player noted: "**I would say the difference between the two sides is the fielding. England are all-round a good fielding side. I do believe that India have few ... three or four very good fielders and one or two donkeys in the field.**"

  The donkey comparison didn't go down well with Rajiv Shukla, vice-president of the Indian cricket board: "**One should adopt restraint while making observations about players. Commentators should not make such comments. We will definitely look into it. Every player has to be respected irrespective of his performance. I don't think this comment was appropriate.**"

> **"I don't want to say too much about this because I have found the reaction amazing. I just can't believe the fuss over what is a bit of cricket slang. It's a term I used all the time when I was a captain. Nothing personal was intended."**
>
> former England captain-turned commentator Nasser Hussain

- A grandfather of prominent Australian journalist Jennifer Byrne appeared in first-class cricket scoring two centuries with a best of 143. Dallas Brooks, who was Governor of Victoria for 14 years, appeared in 29 matches under the name of Reginald Brooks, once taking 8-90 in a first-class match at The Oval in 1927.

- David Warner was handed a maximum penalty of almost $6,000 by Cricket Australia in 2013 after opening up on Twitter. Upset at the placement of his photograph next to a story about gambling in the IPL, Warner took to Twitter to attack two News Limited journalists, Malcolm Conn and Robert Craddock: "**In hindsight, clearly I let my frustrations get the better of me and posted some inappropriate tweets. While I disagreed with the story and my** image being used alongside the story, I could have chosen my words better."

- Iconic UK broadcaster Henry Blofeld once appeared in an episode of the radio series *The Hitchhiker's Guide to the Galaxy*. Awarded an OBE for services to broadcasting in 2003, Blofeld appeared in 17 first-class matches for Cambridge University, scoring a century (138) opening the batting against the MCC at Lord's in 1959.

Henry Blofeld, who made a duck in his first first-class innings and a half-century in his only List A innings

THE FIRST-CLASS BATTING RECORD OF HENRY BLOFELD

M	Inns	NO	Runs	HS	Avge	100s	50s
17	32	1	758	138	24.45	1	2

"I hate listening to myself on the radio. I always think I sound like such an ungovernably pompous prat."

Henry Blofeld

- Australia's national broadcaster broke new ground during its cricket coverage in 2014/15 by introducing its first blind commentator. James Pittar – one of the world's premier marathon swimmers – joined Jim Maxwell behind the microphone on ABC radio, describing play for three overs on the second day of the fourth Test against India in Sydney: **"I've met James before so I knew he had the confidence to speak. But to sit there and feed off the sound and create the commentary was remarkable and inspirational. He was able to keep giving the score, which is easy enough for us because we can see it, but he obviously couldn't."**

- Former New Zealand cricketer Iain O'Brien issued an apology in 2012 after tweeting that he was making a comeback. O'Brien, who had twice retired from the game, said sorry after a number of journalists took up the story on April Fool's Day.

- India's Virat Kohli celebrated a groundbreaking milestone in 2015 by becoming the first cricketer to attract 5 million followers on Twitter. Kohli went past Sachin Tendulkar who'd commanded a following of some 4.9 million at the time.

- TV broadcasting history was made in England in 2010 with a one-day international shown in 3D for the first time. British TV network Sky Sports was the first channel to go three-dimensional, for the match between England and Bangladesh at Trent Bridge.

- The father of a New Zealand Test cricketer was once a voice on ABC Radio in Australia. Lou Vincent's father Mike has worked as a print, radio and television news journalist in a number of cities in Australia as well as for Radio New Zealand in Auckland and at a community radio station as a night-time DJ.

- A BBC commentator had to leave the box during an on-air stint in 2012 after feeling sick. While Kevin Pietersen was batting, Mark Church stepped outside, vomited, and returned to his seat without missing a ball.

  Church had another memorable moment behind the microphone during the year when he and a fellow commentator got the giggles during a match at The Oval. While on air with Johnny Barran, the latter referred to modern-day batsmen as "slappers", a derogatory term used mostly to describe women who enjoy frequent sex: **"I think most, a large proportion of players are natural slappers ... slappers of the ball I should say** [laughter] **... I can't believe what I just said. I do apologise."**

- An Indian father-and-son combination graced the airwaves for the first time in 2014 with Sunil and Rohan Gavaskar sitting side by side in a

TV commentary box. The two came together for coverage of the Ranji Trophy semi-final between Maharashtra and Sunil's old team Mumbai. Sunil appeared in 348 first-class matches – for India, Mumbai and Somerset – while Rohan played in 117, mostly for Bengal.

- Three British journalists were kicked out of Australia in 2014 after covering the Ashes and the ensuing one-day series. *The Sun*'s John Etheridge, Dean Wilson from *The Mirror* and *The Daily Mail*'s Paul Newman had been travelling around the country on 90-day working visas which expired.

> **"We had hoped to stay long enough to see England win a match."**
>
> John Etheridge

- An Australian radio producer was stood down as a ground announcer during England's tour of Australia in 2013/14 after allegedly introducing Monty Panesar to the crowd at Alice Springs in an Indian accent. The ABC's David Nixon was reportedly sacked from his role on advice from Cricket Australia: "**It comes as a complete surprise to me to be at the centre of a controversy about racial slurring, and I absolutely refute any allegation that I feigned an Indian accent. 'There's a change of bowler at the Traeger Avenue end ... it's Montyyy!' That was it.**"

- The Zimbabwe and Ireland teams at the 2015 World Cup joined forces in condemning a newspaper article that attacked Irish all-rounder John Mooney and his battle with depression and alcohol. Mooney had taken a disputed boundary catch in a match at Hobart which ultimately saw Zimbabwe eliminated from the competition.

Writing for the *Zimbabwe Herald*, journalist Robson Sharuko accused Mooney of dishonesty in claiming the catch that resulted in the exit of Sean Williams on 96: "**A recovering alcoholic, who was so depressed last year he even contemplated killing himself, was the Irishman who sealed Zimbabwe's fate at this World Cup in Hobart with a shameless piece of fielding dishonesty that has soiled this global cricket showcase.**"

Cricket Ireland chief executive Warren Deutrom described the article as "crass" and "childish diatribe": "**We understand, as does John, that public figures may occasionally be subject to negative comment, but in mocking John in such a contemptuous fashion, and using his personal difficulties as a mere punchline, the *Zimbabwe Herald* has demonstrated breath-taking crassness and a gross error of editorial judgement.**"

Cricket and Combat

- The highly-decorated British army officer Bernard Montgomery demonstrated his fighting spirit early in life by gaining selection for the cricket team at St Paul's School in London. *Wisden Cricketers' Almanack* mentioned one match the future Field Marshal played in, in 1905, in which he scored an unbeaten 60 against Merton College: **"... they gave a good account of themselves, and showed their ability to play an uphill game, Cooper and Montgomery putting on over 100 for the last wicket when a severe defeat seemed impending."**

"I once saw a bowler in Australia thunder to the wicket and bowl a flat-out under-arm to the batsman. No warning given. Quite rightly too. In my profession you have to mystify the enemy."

Field Marshal Bernard Montgomery

- The son of Australian spinner Arthur Mailey was awarded a Distinguished Flying Medal in 1942. Walter Mailey was recognised for his leadership of fighter planes in a battle in the Middle East during the Second World War.

- The only medal recognised for bravery during a cricket match was awarded to a major of the Indian Army in 1934. Douglas Brett saved a number of fellow players and spectators from possible injury when Hindu protestors attacked a match at Chittagong. Major Brett was awarded the Empire Gallantry Medal, which was later exchanged for the George Cross.

- William Davidson, a former first-class cricketer, lost his life at the age of 65 during the First World War. Thought to be the oldest British casualty of war at the time, Davidson had appeared in a first-class match, for MCC in 1877.

- Don Denton appeared in seven first-class matches for Northamptonshire, including three after he'd lost part of his leg in the First World War. He had to bat using one of his brothers as a runner and fielded exclusively at point during his three post-war appearances.

- While serving his country in the Middle East during the Second World War, New South Wales all-rounder Cec Pepper scored a blazing century in a game of cricket against a team of British soldiers. In recognition of his innings, Pepper's unit was given a bat by future England captain Len Hutton, a sergeant in the Green Howards regiment of the British Army.

  Pepper was a member of the Australian Services XI that played five goodwill matches against England in 1945, known as the Victory Tests. The first match began less than two weeks after the end of the Second World War.

- New Zealander Bill Carson, who once shared the world record for the highest third-wicket partnership in first-class cricket, died of wounds sustained during the Second World War. Carson was wounded in battle in Italy in 1944 while serving with the 5th Field Regiment of the New Zealand Artillery. In 1936/37, Carson (290*) – appearing in just his second first-class match – and Paul Whitelaw (195) had put on 445 for Auckland against Otago at Dunedin.

- During the First World War, soldiers were trained in the throwing of hand grenades by using an action similar to bowling. A bomb called the "cricket ball grenade" was used for a brief period during the war, including in the Gallipoli campaign.

- England suffered two defeats against the Australians on the same day in 2007, one in South Africa, the other in war-ravaged Iraq. Paul Collingwood's England XI suffered an eight-wicket flogging in a World Twenty20 Championship match at Cape Town, while a team of British soldiers went down by exactly the same margin to an Australian contingent in the southern Iraqi city of Tallil.

- Adolf Hitler apparently considered using cricket in the training of German troops. According to a book published in 2010, Hitler thought that cricket would be the ideal preparation for war, but after taking part in a match, said it was "insufficiently violent". He also thought that pads were "unmanly and un-German".

- R. Cook was a club cricketer who lost both of his feet during the Second World War. In the late 1940s, Cook, playing with artificial feet, was one of Braintree Cricket Club's leading bowlers.

- One-Test wonder Harry Lee was shot in the leg during the First World War, lying wounded for three days. Presumed dead, a memorial service was held in his honour, with attendees unaware he was being held by the Germans. He was later released and, despite his injury, went on to appear in hundreds of matches for Middlesex, making a single Test appearance, against South Africa at Johannesburg, in 1930/31.

- British army commander Miles Dempsey, who led the Second Army during the D-Day landings in the Second World War, played first-class cricket. In 1919, he appeared in two matches for Sussex.

- A direct descendant of Oliver Cromwell had a promising cricketing career expunged in 1915 when he was killed in action during the First World War. In 1893, Oliver Field had scored an unbeaten 100 for Trinity College against Malvern College.

- On the eve of a tour of duty in Afghanistan, a British soldier was drafted into the Gloucestershire cricket team in 2010. David Wade, a Lance Corporal with the Royal Signal Corps, is a right-arm fast bowler who was part of Hampshire's youth set-up until he was 17: **"My fellow soldiers are right behind me in the decision I have made and wish me well. It's a last roll of the dice for me as far as playing professional sport is concerned and I will be giving it all I've got."**

- The name of Don Bradman was invoked during a major battle in Italy in the Second World War. "Bradman will be batting tomorrow" was used as code by Allied forces to begin an attack on a monastery at Monte Cassino in 1944.

Don Bradman, who joined the Royal Australian Air Force in 1940 and then the Army in 1941

- Gary Bricknell, who appeared in 14 first-class matches, lost his life on his way to serve in the South African Border War, a conflict that took place from 1966 to 1989. A left-arm spinner, Bricknell was 22 and travelling on a train with his South African army regiment when it crashed in 1977.

- A 33-year-old air force pilot and former team-mate of New Zealand batsman Ross Taylor was killed on Anzac Day in 2010 when a helicopter he was flying crashed near Wellington. Flight Lieutenant Hayden Madsen, a captain of the NZ Defence Force cricket team, had played as an all-rounder alongside Taylor and Jamie How in the Hawke Cup in the early 2000s.

- Moments before he was shot dead in battle in the Middle East during the First World War, New South Wales fast bowler Tibby Cotter was said to have tossed up a ball of mud, saying **"That's my last bowl. Something's going to happen."** Described in official war history as "a man without fear", Cotter served with the Australian Light Horse regiment and appeared in 21 Test matches.

- John Evans, an all-rounder of some note, appeared in a Test match for England in 1921 having escaped from a POW camp during the First World War. A member of the Royal Flying Corps, Evans wrote *The Escaping Club*, an account of his escape from Fort 9 in Germany: **"We passed our time, like all prisoners-of-war, working, reading (for there was a good library), carpentering, writing and acting plays, and towards the end, when we had matters more our own way, playing hockey or cricket."** Evans later appeared in a single Test match, against Australia at Lord's in 1921.

- A few weeks after taking a record six wickets in a one-day international, Sri Lanka's army-serving Ajantha Mendis was promoted to the rank of Second Lieutenant. A gunner in the Sri Lankan Army artillery unit, the then-23-year-old spinner took 6-13 against India in the final of the Asia Cup at Karachi in 2008, finishing the tournament with 17 victims at an average of just 8.52: **"I joined the army to play cricket."**

- Three years after fighting in the Vietnam War, Queensland fast bowler Tony Dell was playing in an Ashes Test match. Forty years later, Dell recalled few memories of his Test debut – when he shared the new ball with Dennis Lillee at the SCG in 1970/71 – due to the effects of post-traumatic stress disorder. Dell was serving with the Australian army in Nui Dat in 1968 when the North Vietnamese and Viet Cong launched the so-called Tet Offensive, a series of attacks which caught the US military and its allies by surprise: **"I came back to a very foreign world of psychedelia, Jimi Hendrix, miniskirts and** anti-Vietnam fever. Had I wasted the last year of my life? In the space of a few weeks I went from a botched-up night ambush outside of Nui Dat to being paid up at Enoggera [army barracks in Brisbane] and then back to my civilian job. They teach you to kill, but they don't unteach you.

"Not for one minute do I paint myself as any sort of gung-ho soldier. I was just an ordinary Digger who ended up experiencing and seeing extraordinary things and, on a few occasions, fearing for my life. These were the seeds for the PTS, which wasn't diagnosed for another 40 years. I have outbursts ... the thrill of playing a Test match with Ian and Greg Chappell, Rod Marsh, Dennis Lillee was out of this world and there's a bit I remember. I remember a few wickets I took but by and large it's a mystery."

- A 28-year-old former member of Afghanistan's national cricket team was killed in a raid by international forces in 2008 in the war-torn province of Khost. The death of Rahmat Wali – on the 100th anniversary of Don Bradman's birth – was confirmed by the country's then-captain Nowroz Mangal: "**Foreign troops attacked Rahmat Wali's home. They locked him up in a room and used poison gas and then a hand grenade. He had no links to Taliban or any other opposition. He was a great player. His death is a big loss.**"

A game of cricket between Australian and British forces at Kandahar in Afghanistan

- The beloved BBC radio commentator Brian Johnston won the Military Cross for his services during the Second World War. He fought in Normandy, where he was recognised for his bravery and leadership.

> **"Could you send a parcel sometime containing wicket-keeping gloves, three cricket shirts, three pairs white socks ... etc."**
>
> Brian Johnston
> in a letter to his mother posted from Germany, 1945

- In 2008, former Test all-rounder Kapil Dev was commissioned as an honourary Lieutenant Colonel in India's Territorial Army, a part-time citizen force. Kapil was inducted into a battalion of the Punjab Regiment: **"This is my second innings. Earlier, I fought for the country in my white uniform. Now I will do the same in my olive-green army uniform."** Two years later, Sachin Tendulkar was made an honourary captain in the Indian Air Force, while M.S. Dhoni received a similar honour from the Army in 2011.

- The only batsman to score a double-century in his only first-class innings lost his life two years later in France in the First World War. Batting against Queensland at Sydney in 1914/15, an 18-year-old Norman Callaway became the youngest batsman to score a century on his first-class debut for New South Wales, a record he held until 2010/11. Batting at No. 5, Callaway reached his century with a six and became the first Australian batsman to score a double-century in his first first-class match. He went on to 207 in 214 minutes, sharing a fifth-wicket stand of 256 with Charlie Macartney in a total of 468.

  His untimely death on the battlefields of Bullecourt in 1917 left Callaway with the highest average – 207.00 – of any batsman in first-class cricket.

- A cricket match left unfinished due to the outbreak of the First World War in 1914 was replayed and concluded a century later. The game between the Lee cricket club and Manor House was affected by rain and then by the announcement that Britain had declared war on Germany. With the match abandoned, all players had vowed to come back and complete the fixture, but it never happened with three of them killed in action and a number of others wounded.

  In their memory, the game was replayed in 2014 at the Chiltern Manor Park ground in front of Liz Stewart-Liberty, whose father-in-law Ivor had been captain of the orginal Manor House XI.

- Graham Williams, a former South Australian fast bowler and prisoner-of-war, played in the 1945 Victory Tests, claiming the wicket of former army sergeant and England batsman Len Hutton four times. Williams spent nearly four years in a German prison camp after being shot down during the Libyan campaign in the Second World War.

The Low and the Slow

- New Zealand's Chris Martin played his 100th innings at Test level in 2012, by which time he had gathered just 123 runs at 2.51. Martin's average was helped by 51 not outs with a highest score of 12 not out. The previous record-holder had been Australia's Glenn McGrath, who made 423 runs by his 100th innings, exactly 300 more than Martin.

  At the time of his retirement in 2013, Martin was the only one of the 62 bowlers who had taken 200 wickets whose batting average (2.36) was lower than his economy rate (3.37).

CHRIS MARTIN AT THE BATTING CREASE

Format	M	Inns	NO	Runs	HS	Avge	0s	Pairs	4s	6s
Tests	71	104	52	123	12*	2.36	36	7	15	0
ODIs	20	7	2	8	3	1.60	2	-	0	0
Twenty20Is	6	1	1	5	5*	-	0	-	0	0
First-class	192	244	115	479	25	3.71				
List A	142	57	27	86	13	2.86		-		
Twenty20	60	7	6	16	5*	16.00		-	0	0

> "The batting average was around four for a while, which was not completely ridiculous."
>
> Chris Martin

- After scoring a maiden Test century, Australia's George Bonnor failed to reach double figures again in the final ten innings of his career. In his 12th Test – against England at Sydney in 1884/85 – Bonnor hit 128, but fell away with scores of 4, 2, 0, 3, 6, 8, 0, 5, 5 and 0.

- Matthew Hayden, who scored close to 15,000 runs for his country, was dropped after his very first Test match and then dumped from Australia's one-day international squad after 13 appearances. Following scores of 15 and 5 on his Test debut – against South Africa at Johannesburg in 1993/94 – he was forced to wait nearly three years for a second chance, losing his place in one-day internationals a month later. Getting back in the one-day squad took a little longer – he had to wait nearly six years, missing 142 matches in between, then a record break for an Australian batsman.

- Appearing in his debut Test match on home soil, Australian fast bowler Ryan Harris suffered the ignominy of bagging a king pair. His double failure in the second Test against England at Adelaide in 2010/11 was only the second instance of a player out first ball in both innings of an Ashes Test, after Nottinghamshire's Dick Attewell, at Sydney in 1891/92.

> "[Ryan Harris] **completed the surely unique experience of being given out four times in two deliveries.**"
> Australian cricket writer Gideon Haigh
> after Ryan Harris had unsuccessfully called for a review of his two
> dismissals at Adelaide in 2010/11

- In his first six matches at first-class level, Mashonaland's Tatenda Manatsa was unable to score a single run. After three consecutive nought not outs from his debut in 2008/09, Manatsa then scored a pair in 2011/12, followed by a duck, nought not out, a duck and another nought not out. He finally got off the mark with an unbeaten three – and then a duck – against Matabeleland in Harare during the 2011/12 Logan Cup.

- India's Sourav Ganguly made a century on his Test debut and finished his career with a duck. He made a first-ball duck in his final Test innings, becoming the first, and to date only, batsman to do so having scored a hundred in his first innings.

- Glenn McGrath was out for a first-ball duck in his first Test and in his first one-day international. And although he wasn't required to bat on his first-class debut, in 1992/93, McGrath was out for a duck on the first occasion he went to the crease in a Sheffield Shield match, against Queensland at Brisbane. West Indies wicketkeeper Chadwick Walton joined McGrath in 2009/10, by becoming only the second player to be dismissed first ball on both their ODI and Test debuts.

- West Indies opener Desmond Haynes made three ducks in the second innings of Test matches, all of which came against Pakistan. He remained on nought not out two times in Tests, both against India.

  When Haynes fell for his first duck in a Test match on home soil, his partner-in-crime Gordon Greenidge also went for nought. In the first innings of the second Test against India at Port-of-Spain in 1982/83, the Haynes-Greenidge ducks were followed by a score of one from No. 3 Viv Richards. Larry Gomes (123) and Clive Lloyd (143) then came to the rescue with a 237-run partnership, the biggest fourth-wicket fightback in Test history from three wickets down for one.

- After scoring a double-century on his Test debut in 1999/2000, Mathew Sinclair then failed to reach double figures in his next four innings. Only the fourth double-centurion on debut, the Australian-born New Zealander followed his 214 – against the West Indies at Wellington – with 8, 6, 4 and 0 in two Tests against Australia later in the same season.

- During the 2011 World Cup, Kenya's Shem Ngoche faced just three balls in the entire tournament and was dismissed for a duck each time. Ngoche's noughts gave him a World Cup record, beating Zimbabwe's Adam Huckle who was out to the only two balls he faced in the 1999 tournament.

- In the wake of scoring five and 16 on his Test debut in 2005, Zimbabwean opening batsman Neil Ferreira was dropped after New Zealand claimed victory on the second day of the match in Harare. He joined a list of 20 other players whose Test careers ended after two days, and the first since 1945/46.

- During the three-match Test series against the West Indies in 1990/91, Pakistan managed just 20 runs from their opening batsmen over six innings. Up against a fast-bowling attack of Curtly Ambrose, Courtney Walsh, Ian Bishop and Malcolm Marshall, Pakistan tried four different opening combinations that contributed partnerships of 2, 15, 1, 0, 2 and 0 for an average of 3.33, the lowest for any Test series with a minimum of five innings.

- Indian opener Kris Srikkanth, who finished his career with an identical highest score (123) in both Tests and one-day internationals, began his journey with a duck in both forms of the game. During the 1981/82 tour of India by England, debutant Srikkanth and his opening partner Sunil Gavaskar were both dismissed for a duck in the first one-day international at Ahmedabad. Srikkanth then made a duck on his Test debut, at Mumbai, that followed two days later.

- Uttar Pradesh opener Shivakant Shukla was hailed a hero in 2008/09 when he almost single-handedly batted his team into the final of the Ranji Trophy. The 22-year-old scored an unbeaten 178 against Tamil Nadu at Nagpur, occupying the crease for 821 minutes, which, at the time, was the fourth-longest innings in all first-class cricket.

- After two match-winning unbeaten ODI fifties in England in 2004, Andrew Symonds then put together a sequence of five ducks in six innings. The Queenslander marked his first match at Lord's with a century (104*) against Pakistan and in the next game in which he batted, made 71 not out, off 74 balls, against New Zealand in the ICC Champions Trophy at The Oval. He then made three consecutive ducks, a 20, and another two ducks in his next six one-day internationals.

  Despite his run of outs, Symonds went on to claim the award for the Best One-Day International Player for 2004, while South Australia batsman Mark Cosgrove was named Young Cricketer having just incurred three consecutive ducks in the Pura Cup. Cosgrove was then dropped from the Redbacks XI after a succession of six single-figure scores (0, 0, 0, 1, 8, 0).

- Appearing in his 150th Test match, Australian captain Ricky Ponting marked the milestone with a golden duck in the first innings against England at Adelaide in 2010/11. His predecessor Steve Waugh had also made a first-ball duck in his 150th Test, against Pakistan at Sharjah in 2002/03.

- After suffering the humiliation of being dismissed without facing a ball on his Test debut, Pakistan's Umar Gul copped a first-ball duck in his next innings. His diamond duck came against Bangladesh at Karachi in 2003, with his first-baller in the following Test of the series at Peshawar.

  In 1984/85, New Zealand opener Ken Rutherford launched his Test career with a pair, after being run out in the second innings without facing a ball.

- Hoping to force his way into the Australian side as a specialist batsman for the 2013 Ashes, wicketkeeper Matthew Wade was dismissed for a first-innings duck in a tour match against Sussex. It was Wade's first duck in first-class cricket – coming in his 104th innings – having made his debut in 2007/08.

- After a series of five ducks and unbeaten zeroes, Indian fast bowler Commandur Rangachari scored his first run in Test match cricket in his final innings. His first run came in his fourth and final Test, scoring an unbeaten eight at No. 11 against the West Indies at Mumbai in 1948/49.

- Having made his debut in 1988/89, Sachin Tendulkar had never scored a first-class duck in Indian domestic cricket until he incurred a 15-ball nought on the first day of the 2008/09 Ranji Trophy Final in Hyderabad. Representing Mumbai, Tendulkar fell for nought in the first innings to 18-year-old Uttar Pradesh fast bowler Bhuvneshwar Kumar.

- When Perth staged a one-day international in 2010/11, both of England's openers were dismissed for a duck. Andrew Strauss and Steve Davies provided the 32nd instance of two openers from the same side making zero in the same ODI. They were later joined by West Indies pair Chris Gayle and Adrian Barath, who made ducks against Sri Lanka at Colombo, the first time that two sets of openers had been dismissed for ducks in two one-day internationals played on the same day in different parts of the world.

- South Africa's A.B. de Villiers came into the 2007 World Cup without a single duck beside his name in either one-day international or Test cricket. Having made his debut in both forms of the game in the summer of 2004/05, de Villiers played his first 30 one-day international innings without a duck, but then picked up four at the World Cup, two of which came against lower-rated contenders, the Netherlands and Ireland. His first duck at Test level came in 2008/09 in his 79th innings.

- Following a score of 11 on his debut for Zimbabwe, Pommie Mbangwa never again reached double figures in his 29 one-day internationals or 15 Tests. A genuine No. 11, the fast bowler had a highest Test score of eight in 25 innings, and finished his career with a record-low batting average of just 2.00 (0, 2, 0, 4, 0*, 0, 0, 0, 0, 2*, 3, 2, 0, 1*, 2, 0*, 0*, 1*, 3, 0, 0, 1*, 8, 0*, 5). In his first one-day international – against Pakistan at Lahore in 1996/97 – Mbangwa smashed 11 off just six balls with one six, ending up with a career average of 4.85 (11, 0*, 3, 2, 8, 0, 0*, 0, 0*, 5*, 4, 0*, 1*). Coincidentally, he made a total of 34 runs in both forms of the game.

- Ireland's William Porterfield began and ended the 2012 World Twenty20 with two ducks in two balls. Australia's Shane Watson and West Indian Fidel Edwards were the bowlers responsible, becoming the first two to claim first-ball wickets in the tournament's history.

  The only other batsman to cop two first-ballers in consecutive matches in the competition previously had been Scotland's Colin Smith in the 2009 edition. He'd also been dismissed first ball in the previous Twenty20 international in which he batted, against the Netherlands in 2008.

- After launching his Test career with scores of four, eight, one, three and a duck, New Zealand batsman Bill Playle finally produced a maiden double-figure innings, at Headingley in 1958. His 18 runs spanned an excruciating three and a quarter hours of play, at one stage going for 63 minutes without scoring.

  Playle's international career ended after eight appearances – all against England – in 1962/63 with scores of nought and three. He went past the half-century mark just once, scoring 65 at Wellington in his penultimate appearance, in which team-mate Bob Blair (64*) also scored his one and only Test match half-century. Both got to the milestone with a Test batting average under seven.

LOWEST AVERAGES BY TOP-ORDER BATSMEN WHO PLAYED THROUGHOUT A FIVE-MATCH TEST SERIES

Batsman	M	I	R	HS	Avge	Series	Season
Bill Playle (NZ)	5	9	56	18	6.22	England v New Zealand	1958
Learie Constantine (WI)	5	9	65	14	7.22	Australia v West Indies	1930/31
Tommy Andrews (A)	5	6	49	15	8.16	England v Australia	1926
Mike Atherton (E)	5	9	79	32	8.77	England v West Indies	1991
Plum Warner (E)	5	9	85	51	9.44	South Africa v England	1905/06
Peter Carlstein (SA)	5	8	77	19	9.62	England v South Africa	1960

- Bangladesh batsman Mohammad Ashraful was fined in 2008 following an altercation with two fans who said his batting was "rubbish". Ashraful, who had scored just 17 runs in a series of three one-day internationals against South Africa, reportedly slapped one of the men during a practice session in Dhaka.

- South African Test batsman Martin van Jaarsveld suffered golden ducks on consecutive days during his stint with Kent in 2007. The first came on Don Bradman's birthday in a NatWest Pro40 match against Somerset at Canterbury, while the second came in the first innings of the County Championship match against Lancashire the following day at the same ground.

- Sherwin Campbell was demoted as an opener during the West Indies' 1999/2000 tour of New Zealand after losing his wicket to the first ball in two consecutive one-day internationals. On both occasions – in the second ODI at Taupo and in the third match at Napier – Campbell was dismissed for a duck by Chris Cairns. Campbell became only the fifth batsman – after New Zealand's John Wright, Pakistan's Ramiz Raja, Sri Lanka's Roshan Mahanama and West Indian Philo Wallace – to be twice dismissed by the first ball in a one-day international, but the first to fail in consecutive matches.

- During England's 1953/54 tour of the West Indies, Tony Lock went for 115 consecutive balls in Tests without scoring a run. In the first Test at Kingston, he failed to score off the last 18 deliveries he faced and made nought not out off 45 balls and a duck off 22 in the second Test at Bridgetown. He then struck a run in the first innings at Georgetown, becoming the first only-known batsman to face 100 balls in Tests without scoring.

- Gogumal Kishenchand was a big scorer of runs in India's domestic Ranji Trophy, but made a duck in each of his five Tests. With 15 hundreds at first-class level, and an average nudging 48, he made nought in the second innings of his first four Tests – all against Australia in 1947/48 – and a duck in the first innings of his fifth, and final, match, against Pakistan at Lucknow in 1952/53.

- During the first Sri Lanka-Australia Test of 2011, one of the openers from each side was dismissed by the first ball of their innings. Shane Watson and Tharanga Paranavitana were both dismissed in the 20s in their first innings, with both then making a duck while facing the opening ball in the second.

- UK club cricketer Rob Pritchard was dismissed for an eighth consecutive duck in 2013. A middle-order batsman, Pritchard went two years without scoring for the Ingatestone and Fryerning cricket club before finally tasting success with an unbeaten five against Great Totham. He also copped a bleeding nose, after being struck facing his fifth ball.

- West Indies leg-spinner Dinanath Ramnarine began and ended his Test career with a duck, exiting with a pair in his final appearance. He failed to score a single run in his final eight Test innings (0*, 0, 0, 0*, 0, 0, 0, 0) in matches against Sri Lanka and Pakistan in 2001/02.

- While New Zealand's Northern Territory-born Mathew Sinclair scored a double-century on his Test debut, he flopped on his limited-overs debuts. He made a first-ball duck in his first one-day international – against Australia at Christchurch in 1999/2000 – and marked the first-ever Twenty20 international – also against Australia, at Auckland in 2004/05 – with another first-baller.

- During the second Test against Sri Lanka in Colombo in 2014, South Africa's J.P. Duminy played two of the top ten slowest 50-ball innings of all time. He scored a pair of threes – the first off 58 balls, the second off 65 – with strike rates of 5.17 and 4.61. Duminy scored off only six off the 123 deliveries he received in the entire match. No batsman had ever scored so few runs while facing so many balls in a Test before.

- Don Bradman's famous last-innings duck at The Oval in 1948 was nominated by the British *Observer* newspaper in 2002 as being the greatest "sporting shock" of all time. Bradman was clean-bowled by Eric Hollies, which denied the Australian the chance to leave the international stage with a Test batting average of 100.00: "**Some people said I got out because I had tears in my eyes. That's rubbish. Obviously I was very emotional, but I wasn't that bad … I think I used the expression, 'Well, fancy doing that'. That's all there was to it.**"

DON'S DUCKS

Inns	Dismissal	Bowler	Match	Venue	Season
2nd	bowled	Herman Griffith	5th Test v West Indies	Sydney	1930/31
1st	bowled	Bill Bowes	2nd Test v England	Melbourne	1932/33
2nd	caught	Gubby Allen	1st Test v England	Brisbane	1936/37
1st	caught	Bill Voce	2nd Test v England	Sydney	1936/37
1st	bowled	Alec Bedser	4th Test v England	Adelaide	1946/47
2nd	caught	Alec Bedser	1st Test v England	Nottingham	1948
1st	bowled	Eric Hollies	5th Test v England	The Oval	1948

- West Indian Phil Simmons had a wretched time with the bat in the early part of 1997, finishing a tour of Australia with two consecutive ducks against Pakistan in the finals of the one-day international series, and getting another in the fifth Test at Perth. Back home in the Caribbean, he made it five ducks in a row when he recorded a pair for Trinidad and Tobago in the Red Stripe Cup match against Jamaica at Pointe-à-Pierre.

- Battling to save the Auckland Test in 2012/13 which ended in a nail-biting draw, England's Stuart Broad established a new record for a batsman taking the longest time to get off the mark. He spent 102 minutes on nought and 137 in scoring six.

- During the 60-over 1975 World Cup, New Zealand's Glenn Turner played the two longest innings on record in one-day international cricket. The only batsman to soak up 200 deliveries in a ODI innings, his unbeaten 171 against East Africa at Birmingham came off 201 balls, and he faced 177 in an innings a week later, scoring 114 not out against India at Manchester. On the same day that Turner made his 201-ball 171 at Edgbaston, India's Sunil Gavaskar compiled an unbeaten 36 spread over 60 overs against England at Lord's.

- After posting a century in his first World Cup innings, New Zealand's Nathan Astle made a duck in his last. The opener struck 101 on his Cup debut, against England at Ahmedabad in 1995/96, which was followed by innings of 0, 1, 2, 6 and 1. In his final three innings of his last World Cup campaign, in 2003, Astle scored 102 not out, 0 and 0. Despite two hundreds in World Cup cricket, his tournament average was just 20.15.

- During a three-month period in 2013, West Indies batsman Darren Bravo was out for a duck in the last innings of all three international formats in which he batted. He made nought in a Twenty20 international against Zimbabwe at North Sound and nought in the second Test against the same opposition at Roseau in March, then made a duck in a one-day international against Pakistan at The Oval in June.

- With just a draw good enough to give it victory in the 2006/07 Mercantile Cricket Association B-grade grand final, Vic Tamils opener Damien Cleary set about an occupation of the crease that lasted well over nine hours and 500 balls. The wicketkeeping opening batsman reached stumps on the first day of the match against Reds at South Yarra in Melbourne with a score of 16 not out, and by lunch on the second day had progressed to 21.
  He reached his half-century in the 152nd over in 505 minutes, one of the slowest fifties on record at any level of the game. Cleary's match-winning effort eventually came to an end on 59 facing the third new ball of the innings, having seen off 168 overs.

- Opening the batting on the first day against Middlesex at Lord's in 2013, Derbyshire's Billy Godleman took 323 minutes and 244 balls to reach 50. Reportedly the slowest-ever half-century in a County Championship match, Godleman was out for 55 after 354 minutes at the crease and 265 deliveries against his old team, for whom he made his first-class debut as a 16-year-old in 2005: "**I just love batting. I don't necessarily see it as grinding, although the spectators might have a different view. It wouldn't surprise me if it was a record because it was pretty slow.**"

In the second innings, Derbyshire collapsed for an all-out total of 60, their lowest-ever score against Middlesex, incurring a nine-wicket defeat.

- Afghanistan made World Cup history in 2015 by dismissing both of Sri Lanka's openers for first-ball ducks at Dunedin. The only previous such instance in a ODI was in 2006 at Georgetown when Zimbabwe's openers were both dismissed for a golden duck by Fidel Edwards.

- Northamptonshire bowler Jim Griffiths took 444 wickets in first-class cricket, but managed just 290 runs in 177 matches at an average of 3.33. After scoring six on his first-class debut in 1974, Griffiths went for eight matches and ten innings over a three-year period without scoring a single run. So celebrated was his inability with the bat, the seam bowler's testimonial brochure labelled him the "Wally of the Willow".

MOST CONSECUTIVE FIRST-CLASS INNINGS WITHOUT A RUN

#	Batsman	Teams	Seasons
12	Mark Robinson	Northamptonshire	1990
10	Jim Griffiths	Northamptonshire	1974 to 1977
10	Peter Visser	Central Districts	1984/85 to 1985/86
10	Abdul Jabbar	Singha, Sebastianites, Galle	1997/98 to 2001/02

- In the same match that Michael Clarke made his first-ever Test duck, team-mate Mike Hussey became the first Australian batsman to generate 2,000 Test runs without one. After scoring 1,822 runs, Clarke's inaugural duck came first ball in the second innings of the second Test against India at his home ground, the SCG, in 2007/08. In the following Test, Hussey followed suit, incurring his maiden duck, also on his home ground, at the WACA in Perth.

- On his return to the national side in 2015 following a self-imposed exile due to depression, Jonathan Trott became the first England opener to record three ducks in a three-match Test series. Facing the West Indies in the Caribbean, Trott made a duck in each of the three Tests, reaching double figures just once. Upon his return home, he promptly retired from international cricket: "**I was honoured to be given the opportunity to come back and play international cricket again. I'm disappointed it didn't work out.**"

- Following a score of four against England at Nottingham in 2009, Shane Watson then fell for a duck in his next three one-day internationals. By failing to get off the mark against the same opposition at Chester-le-Street, and against the West Indies at Johannesburg and India at Centurion in the Champions Trophy – all within nine days – Watson became the first Australian opener to make three successive ducks in one-day internationals.

  Colin Ingram – the first South African to achieve a century on his ODI debut – also suffered three ducks in a row, in the calendar year of 2013. The first South African opener to suffer such misfortune, Ingram broke his drought with a score of four against Pakistan at Dubai in 2013/14.

- Given his chance in South African colours for the first time in 2014, Rilee Rossouw became the first specialist batsman to begin his one-day international career with two first-ball ducks. Opening the batting on his debut, against Zimbabwe at Bulawayo, Rossouw was run out for nought, and a week later batting at four, went without scoring at Harare. His two ducks saw him match New Zealand slow bowler Nathan McCullum, who also made golden ducks in his first two innings, against Sri Lanka and Pakistan, in 2009/10.

  Sachin Tendulkar was another to make ducks in his first two one-day internationals, not scoring his first century until his 78th match. His debut hundred – 110 against Australia in Colombo in 1994 – was then followed by three consecutive ducks. Coincidentally, both batsmen launched their ODI careers with the same three scores. Rossouw's numbers were 0 (off 1 ball), 0 (1) and 36 (39); Tendulkar's were 0 (2), 0 (2) and 36 (39).

  Rossouw's misery continued in his following ODI series, in New Zealand in 2014/15, completing a third first-ball duck in his fifth match, at Mount Maunganui. He then fell for a three-ball duck in the following game in Hamilton, joining Kenya's James Ngoche and Scotland's Navdeep Poonia who also made four ducks in their first six one-day international innings.

- After taking three catches in the first innings of the Oval Test in 2013, Brad Haddin was then dismissed for a golden duck, something his counterpart Matt Prior had done in the previous match at Chester-le-Street. Previously, only four other wicketkeepers had achieved the double of three or more catches in an innings and a first-ball duck in an Ashes Test – Affie Jarvis at Sydney in 1884/85, Les Ames at Adelaide in 1936/37, Wally Grout at Sydney in 1965/66 and Ian Healy at Birmingham in 1997.

- When India's Umesh Yadav was out for a duck at Kingston in 2013, it was the first time he'd been dismissed in a one-day international since making his debut three years earlier. In his first 23 matches, Yadav had batted just eight times (3*, 6*, 11*, 0*, 6*, 0*, 0*, 0*) without being dismissed.

- Plucked from the obscurity of club cricket in England in 1981, Mike Whitney made his Test debut in an Ashes series and made the record books with one of the longest pairs in Test history. Batting at No. 10 at Manchester, he faced seven balls before going for a duck in the first innings, and slotting in at No. 11 in the second, saw off 42 balls to complete his pair. With the number of balls faced not recorded for all Tests, Whitney's 49 balls soaked up in making a pair is classed as one of the longest in the game.

  Other recent instances of more than 40 balls faced include New Zealand's Iain O'Brien – 44 (6 and 38) against Australia at Adelaide in 2008/09 – and India's Suresh Raina, with 42 (29 and 13) balls faced versus England at The Oval in 2011.

Australia's Mike Whitney, who made a fighting pair on his Test debut, against England at Manchester in 1981

Writers and Painters

- A painting of Sachin Tendulkar by a British artist sold for a record-breaking $US750,000 in 2012. The frame of the artwork is made from 12 bats signed by the world's top-scoring batsmen, together with six balls autographed by the all-time top six wicket-takers sewn into the canvas. The painting by Sacha Jafri also features the handprints of 40 cricketers, including Tendulkar, Brian Lara, Ricky Ponting and Andrew Strauss.

- A former senior British civil servant once wrote a book about famous people from Yorkshire and although it mentioned Fred Trueman and Len Hutton, Geoff Boycott failed to make the cut. Bernard Ingham admitted *Yorkshire Greats: The County's Fifty Finest*, published in 2005, was **"the most dangerous book I'll ever write."**

- Essex batsman John Pawle, who appeared in a total of 34 first-class matches in the 1930s and 40s, later became a prominent artist. Having studied at the Westminster School of Art, Pawle had his paintings displayed at galleries in several cities, including London and Edinburgh.

View from Gassin, an oil painting by former Essex, Cambridge and MCC cricketer John Pawle

- *Figure in Movement*, a 1985 painting of a cricketer by British artist Francis Bacon, sold for $US14m when it went under the hammer at Sotheby's in New York in 2010. Bacon, an avid cricket fan, collected photographs of, and books by, cricketers, including one volume by David Gower that remained in his studio until his death in 1992.

- The creator of Sherlock Holmes had a great day on the cricket field during a match in 1893 by taking a hat-trick for the County Asylum club. Arthur Conan Doyle – who was good enough to appear in ten first-class matches – achieved an innings haul of 8-9, a feat noted by the *Eastern Daily Press*: **"County Asylum have recently been favoured with the assistance in the bowling department of no less a personage than Dr Arthur Conan Doyle, the well-known contributor to the *Strand Magazine*. Judging by the Doctor's analysis his bowling is obviously as thrilling as his stories."**

- The name of possibly the most famous figure in the English language can be found in the scorebooks of first-class cricket. William Shakespeare appeared in 26 first-class matches between 1919 and 1931 with a top score of 67 not out, on his debut for Worcestershire, against Warwickshire at Edgbaston.

  Charles Dickens penned some of literature's most famous novels including *Great Expectations, Bleak House, David Copperfield* and *A Tale of Two Cities*. Another Charles Dickens played first-class cricket, for the South African provincial side Griqualand West in the 1940s and 50s. In a match against Orange Free State at Kimberley in 1948/49, Dickens was dismissed by a player named Keats.

A SELECTION OF FIRST-CLASS CRICKETERS WHO SHARE THEIR NAMES WITH FAMOUS WRITERS

Player		Major Teams	First-class Debut
William Shakespeare	English playwright	Worcestershire	1919
Charles Dickens	English novelist	Griqualand West	1945/46
George Bernard Shaw	Irish playwright	Glamorgan	1951

- British artist Henry J. Ford, who gained fame as a book illustrator, comes from a large cricketing family with one of his brothers playing against Australia. Francis Ford appeared in the five Ashes Tests in Australia in 1894/95, scoring 168 runs, with a best of 48 on his debut in Sydney.

  Henry also played the occasional game of cricket, turning out for the Allahakbarries club, run by *Peter Pan* author J.M. Barrie. The amateur team functioned between the years 1877 and 1913, and included a number of famous writers, including Arthur Conan Doyle, Jerome K. Jerome and A.A. Milne.

- Former England captain, and part-time artist, Michael Vaughan created what was described as the world's biggest "artball" painting in 2010, when he splattered an image of a car with paint-covered cricket balls. It was estimated that Vaughan (pictured) hit the canvas some 5,000 times to complete the work.

- Best-selling British author Jeffrey Archer sent out a tweet in 2013 that promoted a new book while also noting an Indian Test win in Chennai. The long-time cricket fanatic tweeted that while Australia may not have won the cricket, they'd be able to get a copy of his new novel *Best Kept Secret* in India two weeks ahead of the rest of the world.

  Later in the year, Archer umpired a special cricket game in London that celebrated the 150th edition of *Wisden Cricketers' Almanack* and the publication of the book *The Authors XI*. A Wisden XI took on the

THE AUTHORS CRICKET CLUB

  Authors XI, whose innings was opened by Charlie Campbell – author of *Scapegoat: A History of Blaming Other People* – and Sam Carter, an editor with one of the UK's leading political publishers.

- Basil Foster, who appeared in 34 first-class matches, was caught by the creator of Winnie the Pooh off the bowling of the creator of Jeeves and Wooster for 100 in a one-day match at Lord's in 1907. Foster's wicket was one of two taken by P.G. Wodehouse, who opened the bowling with Arthur Conan Doyle for the Authors versus Actors match. Pooh Bear creator A.A. Milne scored five with the bat for a team that also included E.W. Hornung, famed for his Raffles novels.

SCOREBOARD
ACTORS v AUTHORS – LORD'S 1907

AUTHORS		R
A.I. Conan Doyle	c & b Egerton	4
F.G. Guggisberg	lbw Smith	56
A. Anderson	b Foster	22
C. Headlam	b Smith	29
A.H. Wood	b Smith	0
E.B. Noel	c Pearce b Smith	17
A.A. Milne	st Knox b Smith	5
P.C.W. Trevor	b Smith	25
P.G. Wodehouse	b Wilde	1
P. Graves	c & b Smith	19
E.W. Hornung	not out	7
Extras	(5 b, 2 lb, 1 nb)	8
Total	(all out)	**193**

Actors bowling	W
Egerton	1
Smith	7
Foster	1
Wilde	1

ACTORS		R
V.R. O'Connor	b Wodehouse	51
B.S. Foster	c Milne b Wodehouse	100
H.E. Pearce	c Anderson b Conan Doyle	39
T.S.H.O. Asche	run out	0
W. Wilde	not out	48
C.A. Smith	not out	15
D. Ferguson	did not bat	
A.S. Homewood	did not bat	
B. Egerton	did not bat	
P.F. Knox	did not bat	
H.H. Ainley	did not bat	
Extras		0
Total	(4 wkts)	**253**

Authors bowling	W
Wodehouse	2
Conan Doyle	1

Actors won by six wickets

- P.G. Wodehouse appeared in six matches at Lord's with his penultimate appearance producing the all-round double of a half-century and four wickets. Playing for the Authors against the Publishers in 1911, Wodehouse took 4-75 and scored 60. Team-mate Arthur Conan Doyle removed both openers for ducks, finishing with 2-38.

- Hampshire all-rounder Reginald Hargreaves, who appeared in 25 first-class matches, married Alice Liddell, the inspiration for Lewis Carroll's *Alice's Adventures in Wonderland*. Hargreaves, an underarm bowler, played his first-class cricket between 1875 and 1885.

- When cricket writer Neville Cardus died in 1975 his obituary in *The Guardian* was written by three fellow writers, including novelist J.B. Priestley. A keen player, Priestley mentions cricket in a number of his works, including the 1939 novel *Let the People Sing* and *Bright Day* published in 1946. He also wrote the foreword to *The Golden Age of Cricket 1890-1914* by David Frith, released in 1978.

> **"In spite of recent jazzed-up one-day matches, cricket to be fully appreciated demands leisure, some sunny warm days and an understanding of its finer points."**
>
> J.B. Priestley

- Jack Russell, the former England wicketkeeper-turned-artist, unveiled an unusual item in 2011 that was painted on cricket bats. Commissioned by the Chance to Shine charity, Russell painted a quintessentially English village cricket scene on a canvas of 36 full-size bats, joined together in two rows of 18. Russell spent some 100 hours on the painting, using a dozen tubes of paint: **"Painting on a canvas of cricket bats was certainly different, but I enjoyed the challenge."**

Jack Russell, with England fast bowler Chris Tremlett, and his so-called "cric-art" painting at Lord's in 2011

- Former England spinner Phil Tufnell, who made his Test debut in a team that included artist and wicketkeeper Jack Russell, unveiled his first major collection of paintings in 2014. His one-man exhibition in Birmingham featured ten paintings in a series of works based on his alter ego "The Cat": "**I love art. In fact, it's a close call between art and cricket. It's fantastic to get down to my studio, where I've got**

Rain Stops Play *by Phil Tufnell*

everything I need and I get tons of inspiration. I think people are sometimes surprised that art is my thing. I got an O-level in art at school and my dad was a silversmith, so there's a history of creativity in my family.

"**I'm not a landscape water-colourist or anything – you won't bump into me and my easel on a country walk. Instead, I love to work in abstract art and with different techniques.**"

- After a decade with Cricket Australia as its media spokesman, Peter Young pulled up stumps in 2014 to pursue his passion for painting. The first painting he sold was one of a country cricket match: "**I was named as one of Australia's 50 most influential corporate affairs practitioners, but I got a far bigger buzz doing a cricket painting and selling it through the Trentham Easter Art and Craft Show.**"

- When Joseph Wells took four wickets in four balls in a first-class match in 1862, one of his victims was a nephew of Jane Austen. Representing Kent in a county match against Sussex at Hove, Wells – whose son H.G. would later pen the science fiction classic *The War of the Worlds* – dismissed three batsmen for a duck, including Spencer Leigh, who'd changed his name from Spencer Austen in 1837.

- While a member of the Australian cricket team, Arthur Mailey was employed by the Sydney *Sun* newspaper as its sporting cartoonist. A talented painter, Mailey attended art classes conducted by J.S. Watkins, a leading British landscape artist.

- Henry Aubrey-Fletcher played minor counties cricket in the 1920s and was also a noted author of detective novels penned under the name of Henry Wade. His son, John Aubrey-Fletcher, appeared in two first-class matches for Oxford University in 1933.

- Steve Waugh set an Australian record in 2013 when he signed over 2,000 copies of a new book at a single sitting. His self-published book *The Meaning of Luck* became a No. 1 best-seller. Waugh's successor also topped the charts in the same year. Publishing house Harper Collins revealed that Ricky Ponting's autobiography *The Close of Play* would become its first Australian cricket book to be translated into Hindi.

- Welsh author Leslie Thomas, who penned the comic novel *The Virgin Soldiers* published in 1966, had previously worked for the London *Evening News* writing articles for England batsman Len Hutton. Thomas, later a book reviewer for *Wisden*, met his second wife on a train journey to Lord's: "**I love the game. I love playing it, watching it, reading about it. Everything about it.**"

- Mitchell Johnson's record-busting haul of wickets in the 2013/14 Ashes inspired an award-winning painting. New South Wales artist Judy Nadin, who drew inspiration from the Miley Cyrus music video 'Wrecking Ball', took out top prize at the 2014 Bald Archy, a competition that parodies the prestigious Archibald Prize for portraiture: "**I happened to get a couple of my friends to pose for me, so maybe that's why it's got a bit of a feminine element, but Mitchell is kind of a sexy guy. I did put hair on the legs though, so that butched him up a little bit.**"

- Murray Webb appeared in three Tests for New Zealand in the 1970s, later becoming a respected artist. A prolific caricaturist of famous faces from around the world, he provided the illustrations for the book *100 Great Rugby Characters* by Joseph Romanos and Grant Harding, published in 1991.

- A Yorkshire artist surprised his neighbours in 2012 when he painted a giant cricket ball on the side of his house. Barry Langroyd Hanson, a former cricket club groundsman, calls himself "Bradford's other artist", a reference to the internationally-acclaimed David Hockney: "**Hockney did a painting of trees called *Bigger Trees*. I've created *A Bigger Ball.***"

- British author Virginia Woolf, whose major works include the novels *Mrs Dalloway* and *To the Lighthouse*, played cricket when a child with her sister Vanessa, later a respected painter. Virginia was known to

Regarded as one of the greatest writers of the 20th century, Virginia Woolf (at front) playing cricket with her sister Vanessa in 1894

have had a liking for the game when as young as four: **"Vanessa and I were both what we call tomboys, that is, we played cricket, scrambled over rocks, climbed trees, were said not to care for clothes and so on."**

- The celebrated writer Oscar Wilde included a reference to cricket in his final work published in 1898. The second verse of his poem *The Ballad of Reading Gaol* contains the lines: "He walked amongst the Trial Men/In a suit of shabby grey/A cricket cap was on his head/And his step seemed light and gay."

    Never a lover of sport, Wilde once famously declared: **"I never play cricket. It requires one to assume such indecent postures."**

- British cricket artist Christina Pierce has a family cricketing connection with her son playing for the Surrey under-nines at the age of seven. Acclaimed for her portraits of leading Test cricketers, including Andrew Strauss, Stuart Broad and Sachin Tendulkar (pictured), her paintings have been exhibited at a number of major venues including Lord's and The Oval.

CHRISTINA PIERCE'S DREAM TEAM

David Gower (E)
Chris Gayle (WI)
Viv Richards (WI)
Kevin Pietersen (E)
Ian Botham (E)
Andrew Flintoff (E)
Mahendra Singh Dhoni *† (I)
Shane Warne (A)
Graeme Swann (E)
Shoaib Akhtar (P)
Monty Panesar (E)

Cricket artist Christina Pierce

"Her work is wonderfully commemorative. She can capture the moment, and life is all about moments."

former England bowler Ashley Giles

- Antony Kamm appeared in a number of first-class matches in the 1950s, later becoming a distinguished writer. The son of a publisher who founded Pan Books, Kamm produced the *Collins Biographical Dictionary of Literature* in 1993, having played nine first-class games for Oxford University and Middlesex.

- The father of Agatha Christie, one of the most popular crime fiction writers of all time, was a player and president of a cricket club in Torquay. A large oak tree at its ground is named in honour of the author, under which she spent many a day as a young girl watching her father play. When her grandson Mathew Prichard captained the Eton first XI at Lord's in 1962 she described it as one of the happiest days of her life.

> **"There is a delightful informality about staying at Greenway** [Agatha Christie's home]**. The gong goes for breakfast but guests go down whenever they want. After breakfast, Agatha said, 'We do exactly what we like in this house. Most of us play cricket in the morning.' It seemed a very odd pastime but it was for the benefit of her eight-year-old grandson. The house had a cricket net and we took turns in bowling at Mathew, excepting Agatha, who declared herself umpire. Every time he was out, Agatha called, 'No ball'."**
>
> British theatre impresario Peter Saunders

Cricket and the Classroom

- When South Africa lined up against England at Lord's in 1960, five of their players had attended the same school. Trevor Goddard, Colin Wesley, Jon Fellows-Smith, Hugh Tayfield and Geoff Griffin were all former students of Durban High School.

> **"We were very close at school, but also very competitive. I was laid back at school, just wanting to play games, and he was a bit of a hoofseun [headboy], wanting to study. I remember one particular night before our exams when we were in Standard 9. I bothered him the whole night and the next day in the test; I obviously had no clue. So, during the test, I was like, 'Hey, A.B., show me your work there, let me copy a few answers.' He took his suitcase, put it in the middle and turned himself the other way! So obviously I failed that test. Afterwards he said, 'You wanted to bother me last night, so there was no way I was going to help you.'"**
>
> Faf du Plessis
> on A.B. de Villiers, who attended the same school and later played together for the same provincial side and for South Africa

- British schoolgirl Holly Colvin, who made her England Test debut at the age of 15, became, in 2008/09, the first overseas player to represent the New South Wales women's team. A spinner, Colvin got straight A's at school in 2006, winning *The Daily Telegraph* Female Pupil of the Year award.

- Whenever Sri Lanka's Kumar Sangakkara made a Test match century, his mother would pay tribute to his former school principal. According to the batsman's mum, it was his headmaster at Trinity College in Kandy, Leonard De Alwis, who realised his potential: **"The boy showed talents in both cricket and tennis at school, and his mother was confused, but I advised her to encourage him to pursue cricket. I still follow his game and am proud of my pupil."**

- Pakistani opening batsman Nasir Jamshed was arrested in 2010 for cheating during a school examination. According to a senior police official, Nasir was caught "red-handed" while taking a secondary school English exam: **"The invigilator at the examination centre immediately informed the police who have registered a case against Nasir for cheating under sections three and 420."**

  Having scored 74 on his first-class debut as a 15-year schoolboy, the left-handed batsman made his one-day international debut in 2007/08.

- A call went out in India in 2011 for major cricket tournaments not to be scheduled when schools are conducting exams. On the eve of the World Cup, Rakesh Sachdeva from India's Board of Secondary Education rued the timing of the competition: **"Every year there is a cricket tournament, which is a huge distraction for the whole country. It really affects students' academic performance. There is no academic atmosphere. We feel the timing is very difficult. It is unfair on the students. We can only counsel … they should not be wasting their time with cricket."**

> **"I don't like cricket. I love it. But my mum's still upset I'm watching TV and not studying."**
>
> **"Most of the matches clash with our exams. My results are bound to be screwed."**
>
> **"God has not been kind to us. Or else why would the cricket coincide with exams?"**
>
> Indian schoolboys commenting on the 2011 World Cup

- While playing Test cricket for Australia, opening batsman Paul Sheahan also worked for the Victorian Education Department. With a Bachelor of Science and a Diploma of Education from the University of Melbourne, Sheahan later rose to the rank of headmaster at Geelong College and Melbourne Grammar School.

- When Indian fast bowler Ishant Sharma made his name in the national team in 2008, a former teacher revealed how she had to constantly remove him from the classroom. Babita Mann, a teacher at the Ganga International School, recalled how she frequently had to bring a young Ishant into line by throwing him out of class: **"I was sick of his low attendance. Even if Ishant came, I asked him to stand out. It was not fair on the students who attended regularly. I remember scolding him every day and he would always give me the excuse that he was out playing cricket."**

"I was very naughty. I'm still like that. Once, at school, I shot at a beehive, after which there was complete chaos. When they found I was the culprit, the teachers gave me a lot of stick."

Indian spinner Harbhajan Singh

- Reflecting on the 40th birthday of Sachin Tendulkar in 2013, another Indian legend reminisced on how a 17-year-old Tendulkar took along his school books on his first tour of England in 1990. Kapil Dev revealed he'd been advised to look after the young Tendulkar and roomed with him during the tour: **"On that first tour, he was carrying his school books to study in tenth grade. He was shy and was just a normal kid."**

A school photograph featuring Sachin Tendulkar (second row from top, seventh from left) from 1979/80

- In 2014, the Maharashtra government announced it was including a chapter on Sachin Tendulkar in the school syllabus. Sunil Gavaskar and Chandu Borde had previously been included in school textbooks in the state.

- After making a single first-class appearance for Cambridge in 1939, Christopher Newton-Thompson opened a school in Swaziland. One of its students was future British actor Richard E. Grant, who featured scenes of cricket in his 2005 film *Wah-Wah*.

- A special moment in the history of the Millfield School in Somerset took place on 12 May 2013 when four of its former pupils all scored first-class centuries. After both making ducks in the first innings in a match at Worcester, Surrey's Rory Hamilton-Brown then scored 115 and Tom Maynard 143 in a fifth-wicket stand of 225. Elsewhere, West Indian Kieran Powell made 108 against the England Lions at Northampton, while Wes Durston hit 121 for Derbyshire versus Hampshire at Southampton. Another former student just missed out on three figures on the same day, with Craig Kieswetter left unbeaten on 96 for Somerset against Durham at Chester-le-Street.

- Ryan Carters, who made his first-class debut for Victoria in 2010/11, was a model student at school, crowned dux of Radford College in Canberra. He finished his high school studies as one of the top students in the city gaining a university admissions score of 99.95, the equal second-best in the ACT. Studying English, maths, physics and chemistry at school, Carters went on to juggle a degree at Sydney University with first-class cricket for New South Wales.

> "Education is a gift that lasts a lifetime. It enables people to make their own choices in life – about where they find employment and how they raise their family – with an educated mind."
>
> Ryan Carters

- In 2008, the city of New York became the first US school district to introduce cricket as a sport in public high schools. The cricket commissioner of the Public Schools Athletic League conceded that cricket would never replace football or basketball but hoped that it might catch on.

- Two of the USA's most prestigious universities contested their first-ever cricket match in 2012. Played under floodlights, Harvard defeated Yale in a Twenty20 match by 175 runs.

With Bat and Ball

- After securing his 50th first-class wicket of the season in 2014, Worcestershire's Jack Shantry then brought up a maiden first-class century in the same match against Surrey at New Road. With bowling figures of 6-87 and 4-44 and an unbeaten 101 in the second innings, Shantry became the first player to take ten wickets and score a century at No. 9 or lower in the same first-class match.

- Yorkshire's George Macaulay celebrated the first day of 1923 and the first day of his Test career by dismissing South African opener George Hearne for a duck with his first ball in Test match cricket. Macaulay (1*) later made the winning run in England's one-wicket victory in the match at Cape Town.

- India's Irfan Pathan achieved a unique Test match double during 2005/06 by scoring a half-century as an opening batsman and taking a hat-trick as an opening bowler. After making a duck in the first innings of the Delhi Test match against Sri Lanka, Pathan was promoted to open the second with Gautam Gambhir and scored 93, hitting ten fours and two sixes. The following month, and playing against Pakistan at Karachi, Pathan then became the first bowler to take a hat-trick in the opening over of a Test match.

- After the humiliation of seven consecutive Test match ducks against Australia and nine scoreless efforts in 11 innings, India's Ajit Agarkar had the last laugh by topping the batting averages in the 2004/05 series. Agarkar came out on top with a 59.00-run average, after scores of 15 and 44 not out in his one appearance at Nagpur. He was not so lucky with the ball, however, languishing at the bottom of the list with an average of 169.00.

- After taking a career-best eight wickets at St Vincent in 2013/14, Campuses and Colleges off-spinner Ryan Austin became just the fifth batsman to be timed out in first-class cricket. Opening the bowling against Windward Islands, Austin took 8-64 – and 11 wickets for the match – but when it came his time to bat in the second innings, Ryan failed to make it to the crease in time and was given out.

- On top of scoring two fifties at Lord's in 1952, India's Vinoo Mankad also claimed five wickets in an innings. Despite ending up on the losing side, the Indian opener scored 72 and 184 and, with the ball, took 5-196 in England's first-innings total of 537. He remains the only player to achieve the all-round feat of a century, a fifty and five wickets in an innings in the same Test at the home of cricket.

- Bangladesh fast bowler Nazmul Hossain once took Test wickets with consecutive deliveries, but seven years apart. After dismissing India's No. 11 Harbhajan Singh with the final ball he bowled on his Test debut in 2004/05, he then claimed a wicket with his first ball in his comeback Test, against Pakistan in Dhaka in 2011/12. And following a first-ball duck in his first Test innings as a just-turned 17-year-old, Hossain copped another on his return. Batting at No. 11 against India at Chittagong in 2004/05, he was run out for a duck, repeating the feat in his second Test, in 2011/12: **"If I play my third Test after seven years then my career's over."**
  In the same innings of the Dhaka Test, Hossain's team-mate Shakib Al Hasan was run out for 144, and by taking 6-82 became the first Bangladeshi to achieve the all-round feat in the same Test.

FIVE-WICKET HAUL AND CENTURY BY SAME PLAYER IN A TEST DEFEAT

Player	Figures	Match	Venue	Season
Jimmy Sinclair	6-26 and 106	South Africa v England	Cape Town	1898/99
Vinoo Mankad	5-196 and 184	India v England	Lord's	1952
Polly Armiger	5-107 and 172*	India v West Indies	Port-of-Spain	1961/62
Shakib Al Hasan	6-82 and 144	Bangladesh v Pakistan	Dhaka	2011/12

- On the same day that he scooped up a handy haul of four wickets for 13, South Africa's Jacques Kallis also scored one of Test cricket's fastest fifties. His winning double came on the opening day of the first Test against Zimbabwe at Cape Town in 2004/05, which saw the tourists disintegrate for 54. Kallis scored as many runs as Zimbabwe did on his own, his 54 including three fours and five sixes, three coming successively off the bowling of Graeme Cremer. He reached his half-century in 36 minutes off just 24 balls on the way to becoming the first batsman to aggregate 1,000 Test runs at the Newlands ground.

- Pakistan's Abdul Razzaq played a blinder with both bat and ball in a Twenty20 international against New Zealand in 2010/11, hitting an unbeaten 34 off 11 balls with a strike rate of 309.09. After being dropped by Nathan McCullum in the penultimate over, his next two scoring shots were sixes, both of which were caught in the stands at the AMI Stadium in Christchurch. He then faced four balls of the final over, hitting another six and three fours.

  Back on the field, Razzaq then opened the bowling and had New Zealand in tatters at 11/5, the lowest score in a Twenty20 international at five wickets down. New Zealand's first four batsmen made ducks, with Razzaq in the thick of it, at one stage, brandishing figures of 3-3. The previous – and first – occasion that an international Twenty20 innings had begun with four ducks was at Durban in 2007/08 when New Zealand had the upper hand over Kenya.

- During the 1983/84 Christchurch Test against England, Richard Hadlee achieved a unique double of a fifty and a five-wicket haul. With 99 in New Zealand's first innings and 5-28 in England's follow-on, Hadlee became the first, and to date only, player to achieve the only 50 and the only five-for in a single Test.

- Appearing in his second List A cricket match, the Netherlands' Edgar Schiferli scored an unbeaten 89 and took four wickets for 35. In the ICC Six Nations Challenge match against Canada at Windhoek in 2001/02, Schiferli made history with the bat, making the highest-ever score by a No. 10 in List A cricket.

- In an under-19 Test against England in 2000/01, India's Vidyut Sivara-makrishnan became the first bowler to take eight wickets in an innings on his debut. The slow left-armer took 4-84 and a match-winning 8-38 in the first Youth Test at Mumbai, the first instance of 12 wickets by a debutant. Two months later, he entered the record books again, but this time with the bat – his innings of 115 for Tamil Nadu against Delhi at Chennai was the first century by a No. 11 in the Ranji Trophy.

- Pakistan's Rana Naved-ul-Hasan had a scorcher of a match for Sussex at Lord's in 2005, scoring a century in under a hundred balls and dismissing four Middlesex batsmen for a duck in a single over. In Sussex's innings of 522/9 – scored on the opening day – Naved hit 139 batting at No. 8 with 11 fours and four sixes, reaching his century off 94 balls in 125 minutes. Middlesex (128 and 162) then fell to pieces, losing by an innings and 232 runs, for its heaviest defeat at Lord's since 1946, Naved taking 3-42 and 4-54. The second innings featured six consecutive ducks, with Naved responsible for four in one over (W, W, 0, W, 0, W).

- After scoring a pair of centuries in a County Championship match for Yorkshire in 2007, Pakistan's Younis Khan then produced his best bowling figures in first-class cricket. With the bat, he scored 106 and 202 not out in the match against Hampshire at Southampton and then came perilously close to bowling his side to victory with a career-best 4-52.

- Gloucestershire's Will Gidman triumphed with both bat and ball in 2011, becoming the first England-born player to secure the double of 1,000 runs and 50 wickets in his debut season of County Championship cricket. The seventh overall to achieve the feat, he reached the milestone in a record 16 matches, ending the season with 1,006 runs and 51 wickets. Topping both the batting and bowling averages for his county, his highest score was 116 not out, while his best with the ball was 6-92.

1000 RUNS AND 50 WICKETS IN DEBUT COUNTY CHAMPIONSHIP SEASON

Player	County	Season	Runs	Wkts
Vic Jackson	Leicestershire	1946	1025	81
Ken Grieves	Lancashire	1949	1177	51
Bill Alley	Somerset	1957	1310	64
Tony Greig	Sussex	1967	1193	63
Garry Sobers	Nottinghamshire	1968	1570	83
Clive Rice	Nottinghamshire	1975	1128	53
Will Gidman	Gloucestershire	2011	1006	51

- In a Ryobi One-Day Cup match at Burnie in 2012/13, Tasmania's seven and eight both scored fifties in a century partnership and then took four wickets each. James Faulkner won the man-of-the-match award for his double of 66 and 4-32 while Evan Gulbis scored an unbeaten 57 and took 4-36 in an 85-run win over Western Australia.

- Just days after hitting the winning run in a one-day international, Mick Lewis found himself on the losing side with 100 runs beside his name. Batting against South Africa at Durban in 2005/06, Lewis scored four not out – the only runs of his seven–match career – becoming the first Australian No. 11 to hit the winning run in a one-day international. In his next match – his final one – he became the first Australian to concede 100 runs in a one-day international, going for 113 off his ten overs in a high-scoring match at Johannesburg which saw South Africa successfully chase a victory target of 435.

- After knocking up a score of 287 in a limited-over club match in India in 2013/14, Vivek Yadav then bowled his side to victory with figures of 7-1. Playing against Saint Angel, Yadav struck 49 fours and five sixes, as Aravali galloped to a 50-over total of 512/8.

• During Bangladesh's domination over Zimbabwe at Khulna in 2014/15, Shakib Al Hasan became the first spinner to score a century and take ten wickets in the same Test. With 137 in the first innings and two five-wicket hauls, Shakib became the third player to achieve the all-round double and the first since Imran Khan in 1982/83.

THE 100 RUN–TEN WICKET DOUBLE
IN THE SAME TEST

Player	Runs	Wickets	Match/Venue/Season
Alan Davidson	124 (44 and 80)	11 (5-135 and 6-87)	Australia v West Indies Brisbane 1960/61
Ian Botham	114 (114)	13 (6-58 and 7-48)	England v India Mumbai 1979/80
Imran Khan	117 (117)	11 (6-98 and 5-82)	Pakistan v India Faisalabad 1982/83
Shakib Al Hasan	143 (137 and 6)	10 (5-80 and 5-44)	Bangladesh v Zimbabwe Khulna 2014/15

Shakib then became just the second player to achieve the double of 250 runs and 15 wickets from three or fewer Tests of a series. With 251 runs and 18 wickets, he joined Mitchell Johnson, who had 255 runs and 16 wickets against South Africa in 2008/09.

In the one-day international series that followed the Tests, Shakib shone again with 101 and 4-41 in the first match at Chittagong. In doing so, he became the first player to achieve the double of a century and a five-for in a Test and a century and a four-for in a one-day international. In 2015, Shakib was crowned the top all-rounder in the ICC's Test, one-day international and Twenty20 ratings, the first player to be top of the pops across all three formats simultaneously.

• Foffie Williams celebrated the West Indies' return to Test match cricket after the Second World War by recording career-best figures with both bat and ball. In the second innings of the first Test against England at Bridgetown in 1947/48, Williams smacked a thunderous 72 with the bat, including six, six, four and four off the first four balls he faced from Jim Laker, and another two fours off the next deliveries from Jack Ikin, a record-breaking start to a Test innings. His fifty took just 30 minutes, one of the fastest on record in the game. A fast-medium bowler, Williams returned the figures of 11-8-3-1 in his first spell in the match, finishing the innings with 3-51 off 33 overs, including 15 maidens.

• India's Yuvraj Singh pulled off one of the great doubles in Twenty20 cricket on his 28th birthday. After taking three wickets against Sri Lanka at Mohali in 2009/10, he then hit an unbeaten 60 off 25 balls, clobbering five sixes: **"This is my best birthday till now."**

- New Zealand's John Reid, an all-rounder who appeared in 58 Tests between 1949 and 1965, is the only cricketer to attain the Test treble of 20 wickets, a century and a stumping. While captaining the Kiwis in the fourth Test against England at Manchester in 1958, Reid claimed a wicket and a stumping in the same innings.

  Reid finished his career with a batting average of 33.28 and a bowling average of 33.35, the smallest difference – 0.07 – by any player in Test match cricket.

- Mitchell Johnson achieved an unusual double at Hamilton in 2009/10, becoming the first Australian fast bowler to gain a ten-wicket haul and a pair in the same Test. With the ball, he took 4-59 and 6-73 and was dismissed for a duck in each innings, both times by New Zealand captain Daniel Vettori.

- The first Bangladeshi to take a hat-trick in a Test match set an unusual record with the bat during the 2003 World Cup. In a match against Sri Lanka at Pietermaritzburg, Chaminda Vaas had the Bangladeshis reeling at four wickets down for five with Alok Kapali facing the sixth ball of the first over. He remains the only No. 6 batsman to face a delivery in the opening over of a one-day international.

- Paul Collingwood celebrated his first-class debut by taking a wicket with his first delivery and scoring more than 100 runs. Representing Durham, Collingwood accounted for former Test player David Capel with his first ball, and with the bat, topped the 100-run mark (91 and 16) in the match against Northamptonshire at Chester-le-Street in 1996.

- After conceding a massive 300 runs with the ball in a Ranji Trophy semi-final in 1945/46, B.K. Garudachar came good with the bat, scoring a maiden first-class century. The Mysore captain took 4-301 at Indore when Holkar made a record 912/8 declared, an innings that contained six individual centuries. With 18 in his side's response of 190, Garudachar then hit 164 following-on, beating his previous best first-class score of 94.

- At Sharjah in 2013/14, Sri Lanka's Rangana Herath became the first player to collect a king pair and concede 100 runs in an innings in the same Test. Playing against Pakistan in the third Test of the series, Herath was out first ball twice and gave away 100 runs in *both* innings – 5-125 and 0-100. Two others had previously bagged a pair and leaked 100 runs in each innings of a Test – the West Indies' Alf Valentine (8-104 and 3-100) – on his Test debut – against England at Manchester in 1950 and England's Derek Underwood (7-113 and 4-102) at Adelaide in 1974/75.

- Appearing in his first match back home after the 1948 Invincibles tour, wicketkeeper Don Tallon starred with the bat and ball. Playing against a Queensland Country XI at Bundaberg in the summer of 1948/49, Tallon ditched his gloves and bowling leg-spin, picked up 10-30 and then scored a century (106*).

- Warwickshire all-rounder Chris Woakes put in one of the best match-performances of all time in English first-class cricket in 2011, but ended up on the losing side. Batting at No. 8 against Hampshire at Birmingham, Woakes top-scored in each innings with 64 and 23 not out and picked up ten wickets (7-20 and 3-103) only to see Hampshire triumph by 209 runs. Chasing 308 to win, Warwickshire were shot down for 98, with five of the top six making ducks within 33 balls.

- Picked as a replacement for an unfit Ray Lindwall in the summer of 1946/47, Victorian all-rounder Fred Freer marked his only Test match for Australia by taking a wicket in his first over and, batting at No. 9, scoring an unbeaten 28 in his only innings. Freer claimed the wicket of England opener Cyril Washbrook for one with his fourth delivery in the second Test at Sydney, and finished the game with 3-74 as Australia cruised to an innings-and-33-run victory. A pace bowler, Freer claimed a total of 104 wickets at first-class level and made three centuries, all of which were scored on a Commonwealth tour of India in 1949/50.

- After scoring a near run-a-ball fifty in a one-day international against Zimbabwe at Harare in 2004, Australia's Darren Lehmann then put on a show with the ball. The sixth bowler used, Lehmann returned figures of 4-7, the cheapest four-wicket bowling performance by an Australian in one-day international cricket.

- During the three-match Test series against India in 1992/93, Graeme Hick was the only England batsman to score 300 runs, topping both the batting and bowling averages. He also took the most wickets and most catches. Although he ended up on the losing side, Hick scored 315 runs at 52.50, took eight wickets at 25.25 and held on to five catches.

M. C. C.

TOUR IN AUSTRALIA

1924-25

- Australia's Arthur Richardson averaged 31.00 with both bat and ball in the 1924/25 Ashes. He also had a batting average of 31.00 in the follow-up series, in 1926, concluding his nine-match Test career with an average of 31.00.

- Appearing in just his fourth first-class match, E.M. Grace achieved both his maiden century and maiden haul of five wickets in an innings. Playing for the MCC, Grace carried his bat for 192 and with the ball claimed 15 wickets, including ten (10-69) in the second innings of the match, against the Gentlemen of Kent at Canterbury in 1862.

- England's David Steele only appeared in eight Tests, topping the batting and bowling averages in his first series. From three Tests against Australia in 1975, he scored 365 runs at 60.83 and took two wickets at 10.50. The next debutant to achieve the all-round feat was Michael Clarke in 2004/05. In four Tests against India, Clarke hit 400 runs at 57.14, and picked up six wickets at 2.16.

- On his Test debut for India, at the Adelaide Oval in 1967/68, all-rounder Abid Ali took 6-55 and, batting at No. 7, achieved identical scores of 33 in each innings. He was opening the batting two Tests later, scoring 78 and 81 in the final match at Sydney. His second-innings effort at the SCG and his six-wicket haul at Adelaide proved to be his best performances with both bat and ball in his 29-match Test career.

- The Pakistan-born Frasat Ali made history in 1975 by becoming the first player to open both the batting and bowling in a one-day international, doing so on his debut. Frasat appeared in three ODIs for East Africa in the 1975 World Cup.

- After scoring an unbeaten century against Bangladesh at Potchefstroom in 2002/03, South Africa's Jacques Kallis took five wickets in the space of just 12 balls to consign Bangladesh to an innings defeat. On a pitch described as "flatter than the highway running to Johannesburg", Kallis picked up 5-21 off 4.3 overs.

- South African Martin van Jaarsveld put on a one-man show during a County Championship match in 2008 with two unbeaten centuries and a five-wicket haul in the only innings he bowled. Representing Kent in a match against Surrey at The Oval, van Jaarsveld secured his first five-for (5-33) in a first-class innings and his third instance of twin hundreds (114* and 115*). Van Jaarsveld became the first Kent player to achieve the feat of two centuries and five wickets in an innings in the same match, and just the 12th in all first-class cricket: **"I'm completely humbled. Not in my wildest dreams did I think that I would have a match like this."**

  The only player to have secured two centuries (111 and 117*) and two lots of five wickets (6-70 and 5-45) in the same first-class match is Yorkshire's George Hirst, against Somerset at Bath in 1906.

- Nathan Lyon celebrated the return of the Ashes urn in 2013/14 after taking a wicket in every innings in which he bowled while remaining unbeaten in the six innings in which he batted. After reaching the milestone of 100 wickets during the MCG Test, the off-spinning Lyon finished the series with 19 wickets at 29.36 and 60 runs batting at No. 11.

MOST INNINGS BY A PLAYER NOT DISMISSED IN A TEST SERIES

#	Player	M	Runs	HS	Avge	Series
6	Bill Johnston (A)	3	22	9*	-	England v Australia 1953
6	Corey Collymore (WI)	4	15	6*	-	West Indies v England 2003/04
6	Nathan Lyon (A)	5	60	18*	-	Australia v England 2013/14

- Appearing in his fifth Test match, Australia's Mitchell Starc achieved his maiden five-wicket haul and maiden fifty in first-class cricket. Although Australia was thumped by South Africa in the match, at Perth in 2012/13, Starc took 6-154 and then top-scored for Australia in the fourth innings with an unbeaten 68 batting at No. 10.

- Of the four batsmen who struck a hundred in the West Indies-Australia Test at Bridgetown in 1955, two also went for 100 runs in an innings with the ball. A unique occurrence in Test match cricket, Australia's Keith Miller scored 137 in the first innings and then took 2-113, while Denis Atkinson returned a double of 219 and 2-108. Miller repeated the feat in the following Test at Kingston, with 109 and 6-107.

- Jack Massie, the son of Australian Test captain Hugh Massie, appeared in 16 first-class matches for New South Wales taking 99 wickets. With the bat, the fast bowler scored 199 runs.

- After his first three Tests for Sri Lanka, Nuwan Pradeep had a world-record bowling average of 345.00 and a batting average of 0.50. After making his Test debut at Abu Dhabi in 2011/12, the fast-bowling Pradeep put up bowling figures of 0-107, 0-3, 0-28, 1-56, 0-103 and 0-48. With the bat, he had scores of 1, 0, 0 and 1.

- In a comeback match for Pakistan in 2013, Shahid Afridi became the first player to score a 50 and take seven wickets in a one-day international. After smashing 76 against the West Indies at Providence, Afridi then took a match-winning haul of 7-12. He also became the first player to reach the ODI career double of 7,000 runs and 350 wickets.

The only other player to previously achieve the 70 run–seven wicket double in a List A match is Peter Sainsbury (76 and 7-30), for Hampshire against Norfolk at Southampton in 1965.

- Following his dumping from the Australian Test side in 2010, Nathan Hauritz posted his best figures with both bat and ball in first-class cricket. After bowling New South Wales to victory with 5-39 at Perth in the 2010/11 Sheffield Shield, he then scored his maiden hundred in the following match at the SCG. His 146 against South Australia was promptly followed with another ton in his next innings – an unbeaten 110 against Queensland at Blacktown.

- England's Jim Smith, who once famously scored a 14-minute fifty in a first-class match, opened the batting and bowling on his Test debut. He opened the bowling with Ken Farnes in both innings of the first Test against the West Indies at Bridgetown in 1934/35, with the pair opening the batting in their second innings. West Indies debutant Leslie Hylton – who, two decades later, became the only Test cricketer to be executed – also opened both the batting and bowling during the match.

- Before a record-breaking four-wicket haul at Harare in 2013, Zimbabwe's Graeme Cremer scored a pair of scores in the 40s. Cremer hit 42 and 43 batting at number eight against Bangladesh, then took 4-4, the cheapest four-wicket haul in the history of Test match cricket.

- In the same match that he scored a maiden first-class century, Bloomfield's Suraj Randiv took nine wickets in an innings. After scoring 112 at No. 3 against the Sri Lanka Army Sports Club at Colombo in 2009/10, Randiv then took a match-winning 9-109 and 13 wickets for the match and was at the crease with an unbeaten 48 in the second innings when Bloomfield claimed victory.

- In 2011/12, West Indies fast bowler Ravi Rampaul became the first No. 10 batsman to score a half-century in the first innings of a one-day international. With a knock of 86 not out against India at Visakhapatnam, Rampaul hit the highest score by a No. 10, overtaking Mohammad Amir's unbeaten 73 for Pakistan against New Zealand at Abu Dhabi in 2009/10. Batting with Kemar Roach (24*) at No. 11, Rampaul hit a record six sixes for a No. 10 and shared a 99-run last-wicket stand.

In the following match at Ahmedabad, Rampaul picked up the man of the match award for his bowling with 4-57. He collected the prized wickets of opener Virender Sehwag and No. 3 Gautam Gambhir, both for first-ball ducks. Coincidentally, Rampaul had inflicted similar damage upon Pakistan in a one-day international at Bridgetown earlier in the year. In the match at Kensington Oval, Pakistan's No. 2 Ahmed Shehzad and No. 3 Asad Shafiq were also dismissed for a first-ball duck by Rampaul.

- While captaining Lancashire against Gloucestershire in a County Championship match in Liverpool in 2013, Glen Chapple reached the first-class milestones of 9,000 wickets and 8,000 runs on the same day. The following month, Chapple was in the thick of it in a match at Chelmsford, scoring an unbeaten 50 at No. 10 and taking 5-9 with Essex all out for 20.

  Kyle Hogg took 4-11 in the demolition, and also scored a half-century (58) in the innings-and-105-run win. Slow bowler Simon Kerrigan also starred, securing a relatively rare feat with the bat. After taking 2-62 in Essex's first innings, he then made 31, outscoring his opposition's total, batting at No. 11.

NUMBER 11 BATSMEN OUTSCORING AN OPPOSITION'S TOTAL IN FIRST-CLASS CRICKET

Batsman	Score	Match	Venue	Season
Tom Emmett ‡	47*	Yorkshire v Gloucestershire (40 and 46)	Hunslet	1869
Wilfred Rhodes	38*	England v Australia (36)	Birmingham	1902
John Scott	50	New South Wales v Tasmania (49)	Sydney	1910/11
Bill Copson ‡	30*	Derbyshire v Warwickshire (28)	Derby	1927
David Brown	25*	Warwickshire v Sussex (23)	Worthing	1964
Simon Kerrigan	31	Lancashire v Essex (20)	Chelmsford	2013

‡ *Emmett also took 16-38 (7-15 and 9-23) in the match; Copson took 5 wickets in 6 balls*

- On top of taking a five-wicket haul in a Sheffield Shield match at the Adelaide Oval in 2012/13, Western Australia's Michael Hogan also took part in two half-century last-wicket partnerships. He shared a tenth-wicket stand of 69 with Mike Hussey (99*) in the first innings, and a last-gasp one of 68 with Ashton Agar in the second, which saw WA pinch a miraculous one-wicket victory.

- Alongside scoring a double-century against Sri Lanka at Cape Town in 2011/12, Jacques Kallis also took six catches and three wickets in an innings. An unprecedented all-round feat in a Test match, Kallis had also weaved his magic in the previous summer, scoring a double-hundred and taking two wickets and two catches against India at Pretoria.

- In the same match that Garry Sobers scored his maiden century in the Sheffield Shield, the great West Indies all-rounder also achieved his then-best figures in first-class cricket. Representing South Australia in

1961/62, Sobers hit 251 and backed it up with 6-72 in a 130-run win over New South Wales in Adelaide.

In 2005/06, fellow West Indian Marlon Samuels began a tour of Australia with a maiden double-century and a maiden five-wicket haul in the same first-class match. Playing against Queensland at the Allan Border Field in Brisbane, Samuels scored 257, with 34 fours and eight sixes, and then bowling some gentle off-spin, returned career-best first-class figures of 5-87.

INNINGS OF 250 AND A FIVE-FOR IN A FIRST-CLASS MATCH IN AUSTRALIA

Player	Runs	Wkts	Match	Venue	Season
George Giffen	271	9-96 and 7-70	South Australia v Victoria	Adelaide	1891/92
Garry Sobers	251	6-72	South Australia v NSW	Adelaide	1961/62
Doug Walters	253	7-63	NSW v South Australia	Adelaide	1964/65
Marlon Samuels	257	5-87	West Indians v Queensland	Brisbane	2005/06

- Afghanistan's Mohammad Nabi turned in one of the great all-round performances in 2013 with an unbeaten 80 and a five-for in a 50-over match against Namibia. In the ICC World Cricket League Championship match at Windhoek, Nabi scored 81 not out with four fours and five sixes – at a strike rate of 180.00 – and then took 5-12 with an economy rate of 1.46.

- To accompany a century in the opening match of the 2008/09 Logan Cup, two Easterns players also achieved career-best bowling figures. Hamilton Masakadza returned a match double of 107 and 5-1-11-4 in the match against Westerns at Harare, while his team-mate Steven Nyamuzinga hit 120 in the same innings and posted bowling figures of 4-3-2-3.

- Quintin McMillan was a South African leg-spinner who played in just nine first-class matches at home, five of which were Tests. He took nine wickets (3-24 and 6-48) on his first-class debut, for Transvaal against Eastern Province at Cape Town in 1928/29 and then scored an unbeaten 185 in his second match, against Orange Free State.

- Pakistan achieved a win at Newlands in 2013/14 after their two debutants starred with both bat and ball. In the opening match of the ODI series in South Africa, Pakistan reached 218/9 thanks to an entertaining eighth-wicket 74-run stand between new boys Bilawal Bhatti (39) and Anwar Ali (43*). The duo then ripped through South Africa (195) with Bhatti taking 3-37 and Ali 2-24.

- Opening the bowling and batting at No. 11 at Dubai in 2011/12, Pakistan's Aizaz Cheema achieved identical figures with both bat and ball in each innings. In the third Test of the series against England, Cheema scored 0 not out and 0 not out and had twin returns of 4-0-9-0.

- On his way to becoming the first New Zealander to take eight wickets on his debut, Mark Craig became the first player to hit a six off the first ball he faced in a Test. The Otago off-spinner snared 4-91 in the West Indies' first innings at Kingston in 2014, scored seven not out with a six, and then took 4-97: "**It was nice to go bang-bang there, bit of a dream start.**"

  West Indies spinner Shane Shillingford took five wickets in the match and coupled it with a maiden Test fifty. Batting at No. 11, he made the highest score in the second innings with an unbeaten 53 off 29 balls. He got to his half-century off just 25 deliveries – a West Indies record – becoming the first No. 11 to hit five sixes in an innings.

- In the Ashes opener of 2013/14, Mitchell Johnson took 9-103 and scored 103 runs. He became only the third player to score and concede the same number of runs in excess of 100 in the same Test, after Viv Richards and Tony Mann.

CONCEDING AND SCORING SAME NUMBER OF RUNS (100 PLUS) IN A TEST

#	Bowling	Batting	Player	Match	Venue	Season
137	0-73 and 1-64	69 and 68*	Viv Richards	WI v Australia	Adelaide	1988/89
112	0-63 and 0-49	7 and 105	Tony Mann	Australia v India	Perth	1977/78
103	4-61 and 5-42	64 and 39*	Mitchell Johnson	Australia v England	Brisbane	2013/14

- On the final day of the fourth Test against England at Birmingham in 2004, West Indies opener Chris Gayle achieved his first-ever five-wicket haul in first-class cricket and then brought up a fifty with ten fours and a six. Gayle scored 82, falling 18 runs short of becoming the first player in history to score a century and take five wickets (5-34) on the same day of a Test match.

- In the same match that he became the 2,000th player to bowl a ball in a Test, West Australian spinner Ashton Agar became the first No. 11 to score a half-century on his Test debut. After scoring a new high for a No. 11 with 98, he then became the first teenage Australian spinner to claim a Test wicket when he picked up the prized scalp of England captain Alastair Cook.

- After one of the worst possible starts to a player's first-class career, Tasmanian all-rounder Evan Gulbis later became the first Australian to score a double-century batting at No. 8 in a first-class match. In 2011/12, Gulbis made a pair on his first-class debut, and copped another in his second match. He became just the second specialist batsman in Sheffield Shield history – and the first in a century – to make ducks in his first four innings. William Carlton, who made his Sheffield Shield debut for Victoria in 1901/02, was the other to begin his career in similar circumstances. Only bowlers Albert Wright (6), Wayne Holdsworth (5) and Troy Cooley (5) had experienced longer scoreless stints to the starts of their Shield careers.

Facing South Australia at Hobart in 2013/14, Gulbis came to the crease with just 217 runs in 17 first-class innings and a highest score of 80. He went on to achieve his maiden first-class century, finishing on 229, the highest-ever score by a No. 8 batsman in Australian first-class cricket. To cap off a remarkable day, he then picked up a wicket with his second delivery in South Australia's second innings and mopped up the tail finishing with 4-7 in a massive innings victory: "**It was obviously my day wasn't it? Cricket can be like that. I've seen the other side of it as well so it is good to have a bit of a leveller in this game.**"

- Facing defeat at Delhi in 2012/13, the big-hitting Glenn Maxwell was promoted to open the second innings, becoming the first Australian in nearly 85 years to open both the batting and bowling in the same Test. Percy Hornibrook was the previous player to do so – on his Test debut – against England at the MCG in 1928/29. Just two Tests later – against England at Lord's in the 2013 Ashes – it happened again, with opening batsman Shane Watson sharing the new ball with Ryan Harris in the second innings.

- During his best score in a one-day international, fast bowler Brett Lee hit 50 runs in boundaries having just conceded 50 runs in boundaries with the ball. Batting at No. 8 in the fourth one-day international against the West Indies at Gros Islet in 2011/12, Lee hit 59, his first half-century in six years. The highest score for Australia in the match, Lee struck five fours and five sixes, having opened the bowling with 2-72, during which he was hit for 50 runs in fours (8) and sixes (3).

- After passing 150 with the bat for the first time, Northerns wicketkeeper Heinrich Klaasen took a wicket in the same match with his first delivery in first-class cricket. In the 2013/14 Provincial Three-Day Competition match against South Western Districts at Pretoria, Klaasen took five catches behind the stumps, scored 185 and took 1-12 in the second innings in which all 11 Northerns players bowled.

- Although he presided over a loss at Savar in the 2013/14 Bangladesh Cricket League, Mohammad Mahmudullah became the first captain to achieve the all-round feat of a century and four wickets in four balls in first-class history. Only the second player to secure such a double – after Hampshire's Kevan James against the Indians at Southampton in 1996 – Mahmudullah scored 105 not out and returned match figures of 5-144 for Central Zone against North Zone.

- In the same match that he shared a half-century tenth-wicket partnership, New Zealand's Trent Boult achieved his maiden ten-wicket haul in a Test. After Boult and wicketkeeper B.J. Watling had become the first pair to record three 50-run tenth-wicket stands in Test cricket, he took 10-80 in an innings victory against the West Indies at Wellington in 2013/14.

- Pakistani batting legend Javed Miandad began his Test career in 1976/77 with a century on debut and the wicket of New Zealand all-rounder Richard Hadlee. Miandad went on to capture as many as 13 wickets in his first six Tests, but managed just four more in his next 118. A leg-spinning all-rounder in his early days, he claimed 191 wickets in first-class cricket, with a best innings-return of 7-39.

- Captaining the West Indies against South Africa at Sydney in the 2015 World Cup, Jason Holder became the first bowler to concede over 100 runs and score a fifty in the same one-day international. Opening the bowling, Holder returned figures of 1-101 and with the bat scored 56 at No. 9, his maiden half-century in one-day international cricket.

  A.B. de Villiers took a particular liking to Holder, taking 76 runs off his bowling on his way to 162, reaching 150 off a record-breaking 64 balls. De Villiers struck seven fours and six sixes off the 21 deliveries he received from Holder, who also became the first bowler to give away 100 runs when captaining his side in a one-day international.

  In the West Indies' previous match – against Zimbabwe in Canberra – Chris Gayle had become the first player to score a double-century (215) and take two wickets (2-35) in the same one-day international.

This Sporting Life

- A future British Open golf champion and a future Australian rugby league Test captain both played C-grade cricket in Queensland in the early 1970s. The Sunshine Coast competition in 1972/73 featured Ian Baker-Finch, who played for Southern Districts, and Mal Meninga, who represented the Maroochydore club.

- West Indies batting legend Brian Lara took to another sporting field in 2010 playing football for a Rest of the World squad against a composite England team. Lara played alongside footballing giants Zinedine Zidane and Ryan Giggs in a UNICEF charity event staged in Manchester.

Brian Lara (right) and the Premier of Bermuda Ewart Brown enjoy a practice round of golf prior to a PGA tournament in 2010

- During a Sheffield Shield match at the SCG in 1950/51, a horse race that stops a nation enabled a brother of Neil Harvey to achieve his maiden century in first-class cricket. Mick Harvey was gifted a four by New South Wales to reach his hundred so Queensland might declare and allow the players to leave the field and listen to the running of the Melbourne Cup.

- An Australian NRL footballer, who made his competition debut in 2011, was named after an Ashes-winning Test captain. David Gower, the footballer, was named after David Gower, the cricketer when

England won the 1985 Ashes. He revealed had England not been victorious, he would have been named Neil. Gower played in his first NRL match for the Dragons, alongside another player who shares the name of an England Test cricketer, Matt Prior.

- Golfer Nick Cullen, who won his first major tournament in 2012, is the twin brother of an Australian Test cricketer. Nick's breakthrough first win came at the Indonesia Open, while his brother Dan appeared in a single Test, against Bangladesh at Chittagong, in 2005/06.

- The famous Gary Lineker, who appeared in 80 football matches for England, captained the Leicestershire Schools cricket team. Lineker (pictured) hit a century in a David Gower benefit match in 1987, and once scored an unbeaten 102 for the Bunbury Cricket Club before achieving a hat-trick for Tottenham Hotspur against West Ham on the same day: **"I was captain of the Leicestershire Schools cricket team from 11 to 16 and thought at the time I would probably have more chance afterwards in cricket than football."**

- World Formula 1 champion Lewis Hamilton faced up to the bowling of Shane Warne in 2009 and dispatched three of the seven balls he received for six. The friendly match-up took place on the eve of the Australian Grand Prix in Melbourne.

- Sachin Tendulkar followed in the footsteps of football legend Pele in 2011 when he waved the chequered flag at India's debut motor racing Grand Prix. Pele had done the same at the Brazilian Grand Prix in 2002.

> **"You can write on your grave, 'one of best cricketers that ever lived' and the pleasure you gave to people, you contributed to society. I'll see you in heaven one day, maybe we'll have a game of golf, and I'll fling a few off-spinners at you."**
>
> South African golf legend Gary Player
> on the retirement of Sachin Tendulkar in 2013

- John Hastings, who made his one-day international debut in 2010, played rugby union for the Australian schoolboys team. A second-rower, Hastings is also a qualified PE teacher.

- Fast bowler Alex Tait, who appeared in five one-day internationals for New Zealand, later became a professional golfer, achieving his first win in 2007. Representing Northern Districts ten years previously, Tait had rewritten the record books with a cricket ball, achieving a first-innings haul of 9-48, and 16 wickets for the match, against Auckland in Hamilton. He also won a bronze medal with his NZ cricketing team-mates at the 1998 Commonwealth Games in Kuala Lumpur.

- England football coach Gary Neville is a former team-mate of Australian batsman Matthew Hayden. In 1992, Neville, then an apprentice footballer at Manchester United, joined Hayden at the crease in a match for the Greenmount club. Both scored centuries, with Neville hitting a maiden hundred.

- Of the four England players who made their debuts in the third Ashes Test at Leeds in 1921, two became double internationals. Wally Hardinge and Andy Ducat had both played football for England and, coincidentally, both made their one and only Test cricket appearance at Leeds.

  Hardinge (pictured) passed 1,000 runs in a season on 18 occasions for Kent and was capped at centre-forward in a football Test against Scotland in 1910. Ducat scored 52 first-class centuries for Surrey over 25 years and appeared in six football internationals.

- The only New Zealander to win the Miss Universe beauty contest was married to a rugby union All Black and later a Test cricketer. Lorraine Downes took the title at St Louis in 1983, marrying Martin Crowe in 2008. Her previous husband was Murray Mexted, who played in 34 rugby Tests up until 1983, the year she won the coveted crown.

- In the same year that she married a former leading Australian Test cricketer, Kim Moore trained the winner of a major horse race. In 2005, she tied the knot with Mark Waugh, and trained *Mahtoum* which came in first in the Sydney Cup. When Mark's twin Steve attended the 2011 Melbourne Cup, he got his own fanfare upon his arrival with a band playing the Channel Nine cricket theme.

- In 2010, former Indian captain Sourav Ganguly made his debut on the soccer field. While still active in first-class cricket, Ganguly lasted 60 minutes before being substituted in his first game for the Mohammedan Sporting Club (0) against East Bengal (1) in the Platinum Jubilee Cup in Kolkata.

- Zimbabwe's Mark Vermeulen swapped his cricket bat for a golf club in 2011. Vermeulen appeared in eight Tests and 43 one-day internationals against a backdrop of a number of indiscretions both on and off the field: **"Everyone has been holding me back ... the administrators and the umpires, so I have decided I can do something better with my life. I dreamt of playing in the national team again and representing the country in Tests but I am quitting to pursue a career in golf."**

- Shane Warne dropped a few catches during his stint in the 2012/13 Big Bash tournament but made the news when he caught a ball off the racket of tennis superstar Roger Federer at the Australian Open. Warne was sitting courtside at Melbourne Park for the 2013 semi-final involving Andy Murray, and when Federer miscued a shot, the former Australian bowler was there to grab it much to the delight of the capacity crowd.

- A future international rugby union centre played against the likes of Courtney Walsh in 1983 in a series of junior 50-over matches. A team-mate of Graeme Hick's in the Young Zimbabwe side, David Curtis later played in four first-class matches for Oxford University and won 13 caps for Ireland's rugby side in the early 1990s.

- George Giffen, one of Australia's leading Test match all-rounders, is credited with kicking the first-ever goal for his club in the South Australian Football Association competition. The first Australian to reach the milestone of 10,000 runs and 500 wickets in first-class cricket, Giffen played Australian Rules football for the Norwood club in the 1870s and 80s.

- In the same year that Myrtle Craddock made her Test debut, she went on to become the first woman to represent Australia at two sports. A few months on from her first Test – against New Zealand at Wellington in 1948 – she then won the first of ten caps for the Australian netball team.

- Australia's Ellyse Perry made history in 2011 when she gained selection for her second World Cup tournament but in different sports. The teenager (pictured) got the call-up for the FIFA Women's World Cup in Germany, having appeared in the Twenty20 World Cup in the Caribbean the year before: **"Having had that experience with cricket and also winning a World Cup, I know how great that is and how enjoyable that is. I absolutely love playing football as much as I love playing cricket."**

- West Indies batter Deandra Dottin, who once scored a 38-ball century in a Twenty20 international, is a champion track and field competitor. She achieved a number of wins in shot put and the discus and javelin categories at the Caribbean Free Trade Association Games between 2006 and 2009. In the 2010 Women's Twenty20, Dottin had come in at No. 6 against South Africa in St Kitts and smashed a record unbeaten 112 off 45 balls with seven fours and nine sixes.

- In 1885, Aberdeen club Bon Accord suffered the biggest defeat in British football history, going down 36-0 to Arbroath in the Scottish Cup. It later transpired that Bon Accord were a cricket team mistakenly invited to the tournament instead of the Orion football club. Coincidentally, Aberdeen is the city that also hosted the biggest defeat in one-day international cricket history, when New Zealand flogged Ireland by 290 runs in 2008.

- In 2012, former batsman-turned-golfer Greg Blewett joined a select group to have represented South Australia at two sports. A noted big-hitter on the cricket field, Blewett gained selection in the state squad in the Australian Interstate Teams amateur championship. Three years previously, Blewett had claimed the title of Australia's best golfing athlete by winning the inaugural Golf Australia Champions Trophy, a contest designed for players from a range of other sports, including rugby league, rugby union, AFL and tennis.

Don Bradman, the golfer, who represented South Australia at cricket and squash

- The record holder for Test cricket's fastest double-century took his thirst for speed to another track in 2010, making his debut as a sprint car driver. In his debut season in the V8 category after two years racing a modified sprint, former New Zealand batsman Nathan Astle achieved his first top-three finish in 2013, coming in third in the South Island sprint car championship: **"When you're out there you forget what's around you and you kind of feel how fast you do go. You don't have time to think. You are down the straight and you're into the corner and same again. It's just having your wits around you."**

- The brother of a current Test cricketer won a national athletics title for the first time in 2013 with a personal best performance in the high jump. Brandon Starc – the younger brother of Australian fast bowler Mitchell Starc – also won a silver medal at the 2010 Summer Youth Olympics in Singapore.

  In 2009/10, Trent Copeland made his first-class debut, opening the bowling with Mitchell Starc for New South Wales in a Sheffield Shield match at Sydney. At the 2014 Commonwealth Games, Starc's brother came eighth in the high jump, while Copeland's wife Kimberlee Green won a gold medal as part of the Australian women's netball team that beat New Zealand 58-40 in the final.

- A former first-class cricketer swam the English Channel in 2013 to raise funds for a trust set up in memory of a batsman who died the year before. Tom Mees – who appeared in 11 first-class matches – joined two others, including former club cricketer Adam Shantry, in a relay swim, completing the 21-mile journey in a little under 14 hours.

- New Zealand athlete Stuart Farquhar gave up a promising cricket career to concentrate on the javelin. A fast bowler at school, Farquhar was selected for the Northern Districts side through junior grades: **"I won both the national junior and senior titles while still playing cricket and this gave me the impetus to give javelin my full attention."** He went on to represent New Zealand at the 2004, 2008 and 2012 Olympic Games.

- A galaxy of Australian sporting stars turned up at a suburban cricket ground in Sydney in 2010 to take part in a Twenty20 fundraiser. Some of the big names who picked up a bat included soccer international Mark Bosnich, boxer Daniel Geale, Olympic swimming medallist Eamon Sullivan and rugby league stars Mick Crocker, Jason Ryles and Robbie Farah, plus some blasts from the past, Ricky Stuart and Paul Osborne.

  Jason Stevens lasted just two balls in the match, slipping over while taking a quick single. The former Australian rugby league representative had to be taken off in an ambulance to hospital with a dislocated shoulder.

World record-breaking Australian swimmer Eamon Sullivan and boxer Daniel Geale at a celebrity Twenty20 match in Sydney in 2010

- South African opening batsman Mandy Yachad, who appeared in a single one-day international, also represented his country at hockey. He partnered Jimmy Cook at the top of the order in a one-dayer against India at Gwalior in 1991/92.

- Aub Carrigan, a batsman who appeared in 50 first-class matches for Queensland, later represented his state at lawn bowls and once took out a table tennis championship. Captain of Queensland in 1951/52,

Carrigan also played Australian Rules football, appearing at a number of national carnivals.

- The Christchurch-born Durham all-rounder Ben Stokes, who made his Test debut for England in 2013/14, is the son of a former New Zealand rugby league player. Gerard Stokes appeared in a single league Test for NZ and was named the country's coach of the year in 2000.

- The world-famous Grand National horse race of 1937 featured a runner named after a famous Test cricketer. A crowd estimated at some 300,000 saw *Don Bradman,* ridden by Alec Marsh, finish seventh.

- A British golfer who made his European Tour debut in 2010 is a former Surrey under-17 opening batsman. James Morrison also played in England's youth team that included Alastair Cook, Tim Bresnan and Ravi Bopara: **"I thought I'd be better at golf than cricket and I get more enjoyment out of golf. What's more enjoyable, standing in a field for four days or playing golf? I've got zero regrets."**

  His first tournament win on the tour came in the same year, when he triumphed in the Madeira Islands Open in Portugal by one stroke.

- A former head of the International Olympic Committee revealed an interest in cricket in 2011, expressing an admiration for players such as Shane Warne. Jacques Rogge, a former Belgian rugby union player, was introduced to the game as a youngster by relatives in the UK: **"Let's be very clear, I can't play cricket, but I know the rules. I love the game. I have watched Sachin Tendulkar, Kevin Pietersen, Shane Warne, Ian Botham. It's tactically very interesting, a game of patience, a game of great skills and the only sport where, after five days, you can have a draw!"**

ANNA MEARES'S DREAM TEAM

Don Bradman (A)
Steve Waugh * (A)
Sachin Tendulkar (I)
Mike Hussey (A)
Matt Prior † (E)
Brian Lara (WI)
Jacques Kallis (SA)
Shoaib Akhtar (P)
Glenn McGrath (A)
Shane Warne (A)
Muttiah Muralitharan (SL)

Australian Olympic track cyclist Anna Meares

STEVEN BRADBURY'S DREAM TEAM

Graham Yallop (A)
Brian Lara (WI)
Sachin Tendulkar (I)
Don Bradman (A)
Jacques Kallis (SA)
Steve Waugh * (A)
Adam Gilchrist † (A)
Wasim Akram (P)
Shane Warne (A)
Glenn McGrath (A)
Curtly Ambrose (WI)

Speed skater Steven Bradbury – Australia's first Winter Olympic gold medallist

- In the same year that he made his Test debut for Australia, Norman O'Neill married a gold medal-winning athlete. In 1958, O'Neill, who went on to score six centuries in 42 Tests, married Gwen Wallace, a member of the victorious Australian sprint relay team at the 1954 Empire Games in Vancouver.

- When Adam Ashley-Cooper celebrated his 100th Test match for the Australian rugby team, he surprised his team-mates by turning up for a celebratory photograph dressed in cricket gear. Just the sixth Wallaby to appear in a century of Tests, Ashley-Cooper walked out on to the Suncorp Stadium turf in Brisbane in 2014 in whites with a raised cricket bat.

- Although he lost the Melbourne Ashes Test in 2010/11, Ricky Ponting had a consolation win when one of his greyhounds came first in a race in Launceston. *Strapper's Boy* won his owner $1,195 on day two of the MCG Test which Australia went on to lose by an innings.

- The appropriately-named Welsh rugby football player Jake Ball played cricket for Western Australia. Ball, who made his Test debut for Wales in 2014, opened the bowling for WA in the 2008/09 Australian Under-19 Cricket Championship: **"I was a fast bowler and I played alongside the Marsh boys. I miss the competitive edge of bowling, but I hated standing in the field. I realised that cricket wasn't the path I wanted to go down. I missed my rugby."**

- Chris Green, a South African-born off-spinner who made his one-day debut for New South Wales in 2014/15, is the son of professional tennis players. His father Warren appeared at Wimbledon in 1989, while Chris himself was once rated one of the top ten players in New South Wales.

- Warwickshire batsman Laurie Evans, who made his first-class debut in 2007, is the nephew of a gold medal-winning Olympian. His uncle Greg Searle won Olympic gold in the coxed pairs rowing event at the 1992 Games in Barcelona.

- The world's No. 1 female tennis player of the day was presented with a promotional cricket bat in 2010 at the launch of the World Twenty20 tournament. Serena Williams, of the United States, showed off her batting skills decked out in tennis gear at the event staged in Barbados. She was back with a bat in 2014, appearing alongside her sister Venus at a promotion on the eve of the Australian Open in Melbourne. On the roof of a city hotel, the tennis legends received some tips from Melbourne Renegades stars Aaron Finch and Muttiah Muralitharan.

> "I just hit it as hard as I could. But the bat was heavy. We don't play cricket, it's not our sport, but we were excited to come out and try."
>
> Venus Williams

> "Viv Richards was the Rod Laver of cricket."
>
> American tennis legend John McEnroe

- Trinidad batsman Kenneth Trestrail, who made 85 as a 16-year-old on his first-class debut, was also his country's tennis champion. He appeared in 41 first-class matches, touring England with the West Indies in 1950 and with his adopted Canada in 1954.

- A Sri Lankan who carried his bat for a century on his first-class debut captained his country at both cricket and rugby union. Representing Ceylon, Mahesa Rodrigo scored an unbeaten 135 against the West Indians in Colombo in 1948/49.

- Alex Johnston, who scored the first try for South Sydney in their 30-6 victory against Canterbury in the 2014 NRL Grand Final, showed promise as a cricketer in his younger days, hitting a double-century in an under-14s match. The future football star, of Papua New Guinean descent, carried his bat for 229 in a limited-overs match for the La Perouse club at Moore Park in Sydney in 2009.

- Scotland rugby international Stuart Moffat has a first-class batting average of 169.00. In 2002 – the same year that he made his rugby

Test debut – Moffat scored 169 in his only innings in first-class cricket, for Cambridge University against Oxford.

- Swapping his cricket bat for a golf club in 2013, former England batsman Mark Butcher won a Mercedes-Benz after a hole-in-one. Appearing at a charity event at the Burhill Golf Club in Hersham, Butcher aced the par-three 178-yard fourth hole: "**I played a seven-iron, hoping to hit a soft fade into the front of the green. Unbelievably, the ball came off the club exactly as intended – a rarity. When it landed it looked close but none of us on the tee could be sure. When I got to the green I tiptoed up to the hole and there it was. I jumped into the arms of one of my playing companions and we proceeded to dance a jig around the green. I think it's the most excited I've been in my life.**"

- Doug Siggs was a hockey player and a wicketkeeper who appeared in two Sheffield Shield matches in the 1940s. He made his first-class debut for Queensland in 1948, the same year as his hockey debut for Australia, once captaining a team to New Zealand.

- When hockey international Liz Perry made her Twenty20 international debut at St Kitts in 2010, she joined two others in the New Zealand XI who had also represented the country at another sport. Suzie Bates was part of the NZ basketball team at the 2008 Beijing Olympics, while Sophie Devine is also a hockey international. Also in the team was Sarah McGlashan, a former member of New Zealand's under-19 soccer squad and netballer Nicola Browne.

- The tall Netherlands all-rounder Logan van Beek, who took 3-27 on his debut in the Under-19 World Cup for New Zealand, is a dual international. A few months before his NZ cricket debut, van Beek had appeared at the World Under-19 Basketball Championships in 2009: "**Sometimes the two sports clash and I've had to take time off from cricket to prepare for basketball, but most of the time I play cricket in the summer and basketball in the winter. I feel privileged to be playing both sports.**"

- Middlesex bowler Billy Williams is credited with developing a cabbage patch in London that turned into Twickenham, one of rugby union's most famous grounds. An honorary member of the Wimbledon Park Golf Club and a player for the Harlequins rugby club, Williams appeared in 38 first-class matches between 1885 and 1902.

- On-field football rivalries spilled over on to a cricket field in 2011 when two Australian rugby league teams played each other in a Twenty20 match in Sydney. The Manly Sea Eagles and Wests Tigers – two of the game's greatest rivals – staged a friendly cricket match to raise funds for charity, but things turned sour according to former rugby league legend Matthew Johns: **"Charity cricket games are all about goodwill, but these guys were competitors and there was a feeling that one side treated the game as 'win at all costs'. Manly won the game with a ball to spare, but the Tigers had their nose out of joint. There were a couple of things … there was a gentlemen's agreement that all batsmen would declare at 50.**

   "Two of the Manly batsmen got to about seventy-odd. The Tigers boys were going, 'Come on, you've gotta declare.' The Manly blokes were laughing. My competitive spirit was burnt out ten years ago, but the Tigers believe they were ambushed and on the end of unsportsman-like behaviour."

- Former Test captain Ricky Ponting caddied for Australian golfer Daniel Popovic at the 2014 Victorian Open. A week later, the pair played together in the pro-am section of the New Zealand Open at the Millbrook course near Queenstown. Ponting picked up six birdies in the opening round, producing a combined first-round seven-under-par score of 65.

> **"I gave him** [Ponting] **a bit of stick because he played off the ladies' tees. But, in reality, they were only a few metres up from where I was playing, so it was a great effort. He just hits the ball really well – doesn't do too many things wrong out there. He looks like a professional, to be honest. In fact, on the range, if you saw him hitting balls, you wouldn't be able to tell the difference from the pros."**
>
> former Australian PGA champion Daniel Popovic

> **"He** [Ricky Ponting] **hits it super long, he's a great putter and he just loves golf. He spends time with his mate Marc Leishman, he has dozens of sets of golf clubs … I've seen his garage. He lives and breathes golf."**
>
> former Australian batsman-turned-golfer Dean Jones

- The father of Australian wicketkeeper Matthew Wade played in the AFL. Scott Wade appeared in 12 matches for Hawthorn in the early 1980s, while Matthew's cousin Jeremy Howe made his AFL debut for the Melbourne club in 2011.

- England soccer legend Jimmy Armfield played cricket before finding his feet with football, captaining the Blackpool Schoolboys XI. Inducted into the Football Hall of Fame in 2008, Armfield played as a wicketkeeper and later as a medium-pace swing bowler.

- Sprint superstar Usain Bolt showed off his cricketing skills in 2014 playing alongside Indian greats Yuvraj Singh and Zaheer Zhan in an exhibition match in Bangalore. A hit-and-giggle affair, the four-over seven-a-side match saw the Olympic gold medallist hit the final two deliveries for six, finishing with a match-winning 45 not out.

> **"I think cricket is there in Usain Bolt's blood. Since I got to watch from close quarters, it was amazing to see him run up to bowl. The perfect delivery stride is understandable because he is a world champion athlete. But the manner, he loaded at the crease and then bowled the ball left me zapped. He looked like a natural cricketer. Probably, he would have been as successful playing cricket as he had been in athletics."**
>
> Harbhajan Singh

- During the lead up to the 2010 Melbourne Cup, the 12-times winning 83-year-old trainer Bart Cummings thought of cricket when asked if he'd consider retiring if his horse *So You Think* won the big race. A clear favourite heading into the 150th running of the Melbourne Cup, Cummings's four-year-old came in third: **"It's like cricket. You don't change the bowler when he's taking wickets and I'm getting wickets out on the track, so why would you change? The opposition might like to see me retire but I certainly won't. I've got a lot of nice young horses coming through. Who would train them if I left the crease?"**

- Australia's Josh Hazlewood, who picked up a five-wicket haul on his Test debut in 2014/15, is a junior champion at javelin. Ten years before his first Test, the tall quick had taken out the New South Wales state title and was winner of a gold medal at the National All-Schools Athletics championships. He also represented his state at discus and shot put when aged ten and 11.

- Stephen Coniglio was a talented up-and-coming batsman in Western Australia who later pursued a full-time career in Australian Rules football making his AFL debut for Greater Western Sydney in 2012. Two years later, another former junior WA batsman joined the ranks of the same football club, with Cam McCarthy debuting alongside Coniglio in a round 23 match against the Western Bulldogs.

  Hooking up with the same club that had former Test batsman Simon Katich as a runner, McCarthy took the leap from cricket to AFL after missing out on an under-17 cricket trip to Tasmania: **"It was a bit of a bummer for me, then the footy season came along and I thought I'd give it a red hot crack and here I am now."**

- Canterbury all-rounder Tony Wilding appeared in two first-class matches in the early 1900s, later winning the Australian Open tennis tournament. He took out the championship on two occasions, in 1906 and 1909, before winning Wimbledon four years in a row between 1910 and 1913. Wilding (pictured) had a first-class batting average of 20.00 and a bowling average of 17.33.

  In 1878, the Wimbledon championship was contested by two first-class cricketers. Middlesex's Frank Hadow beat Surrey's Spencer Gore – the first Wimbledon winner – 7-5, 6-1, 9-7.

> **"No, sir. It's a sissy's game played with a soft ball."**
>
> Frank Hadow,
> when asked if he would defend his 1878 Wimbledon title

- Australia captain Michael Clarke took to the high seas in 2014, joining a yachting crew on board *Loyal* for the Sydney-Gold Coast race. Clarke signed up for the event despite a fear of water: **"My old man used to own a fishing charter and I was hopeless. I'm so nervous around water I check the bath for sharks."**

  Former team-mate Matthew Hayden had preceded Clarke in 2010 as a crew member on the same yacht in the famous Sydney-Hobart race: **"It is a love of the ocean. I have always been intrigued by sailing and adventure but I have never had the time to do a race like this. It is all about the camaraderie of being at sea among** some skilled warriors and getting a bit of a taste for it. It's such a different sporting culture and rates up there with some of the best teamwork I have ever seen. In a way it surpasses the challenges on a still playing field."

- The first player to take a hat-trick for England in a Twenty20 international was born in Japan and played in Poland's women's football league at the age of 12. Born in Tokyo, Natalie Sciver – an aspiring tennis player – achieved a match-winning hat-trick against New Zealand in Barbados in 2013/14.

- Tennis champion Roger Federer inadvertently upset a legion of fans in Pakistan in 2015 when he appeared in a photo admiring an Indian World Cup cricket shirt. On the eve of the Dubai Open, Federer took part in a promotional photo-shoot (pictured), but it backfired with Federer forced to issue an apology: **"It was more of a Nike thing to be quite honest. It was a Nike campaign they had because I met some of the Indian players and I had just spent some time in India so they presented the shirt to me. I support South Africa and everybody knows that. The idea wasn't to spark any fire and I'm sorry if I did that."**

- Gil Merrick kept goal for England in the 1954 World Cup and played cricket for Warwickshire's second XI. Considered one of his country's best keepers during the 1950s, Merrick appeared in 23 matches for England.

Personal Matters

- At the age of 62, Imran Khan became the oldest Test cricketer to marry. Imran revealed in 2015 that he had secretly wed a former BBC weather presenter, Reham Khan. It was the former Pakistan captain's second marriage, following a nine-year union with Jemima Goldsmith.

Newlyweds Imran Khan and Reham Khan

- Sri Lankan batsman Sanath Jayasuriya married for the first time in 1998 with the partnership lasting six months. He married a further two times, with all three of his wives being flight attendants.

- Hot on the heels of being named a *Wisden* Cricketer of the Year in 2013, England's Nick Compton was linked romantically with a member of the country's royal family. The friendship between the opener and Kitty Spencer, a niece of the late Princess Diana, was made public when the couple attended a function at Lord's.

- A mass marriage ceremony was held in the Indian city of Udaipur in 2011 to mark the staging of the World Cup. Forty-five cricket-loving couples tied the knot in the town's municipal hall.

- The mother of Australian fast bowler Mitchell Johnson took a swipe at her estranged son in 2011 after being left off the invitation list for his wedding. Vikki Harber said she was "gutted" at being snubbed: **"He's really hurt me. To send me a Mother's Day message and never even mention he'd got married … I hadn't heard from him for months and I was so pleased to get his email. I wrote back at once telling him how much it meant to me. Two days later one of my daughters found out about the wedding on Facebook. I was devastated."**

  Johnson had a public falling out with his mother in 2009, a feud that boiled over during the Ashes tour of England. She claimed that his future bride Jessica Bratich had "stolen" him from her.

- Disgraced American-born cricket entrepreneur Allen Stanford was forced to issue an apology during the running of his multi-million dollar Twenty20 tournament in 2008 after he was seen flirting with a number of cricketers' wives and girlfriends. During a live telecast of the Stanford Super Series, he was filmed with his arm draped around two women, while bouncing the pregnant wife of England wicketkeeper Matt Prior on his knee.

> **"There were a few gobsmacked faces. I did not see it because I was bowling at the time but I think Matt Prior had a look of shock on his face."**
>
> Stuart Broad

A few days later, Stanford was forced to deny claims that his fiancée had been fired from her job on the board of the Stanford 20/20 company because of a liaison with West Indies batsman Chris Gayle: **"Those rumours are complete horse manure. We've been together seven years and we're happier than ever."**

- Former Australian batsman Dean Jones was stripped of his Victorian Father of the Year title in 2010 following revelations of a love child. Jones had begun an extra-marital affair with a Sydney model after meeting at a sporting event in the late 1990s: **"Following an on-and-off relationship, a child was conceived and subsequently delivered."**

- A week after he was sacked by Sussex in 2013, the former wife of Monty Panesar took out a restraining order against him. Her legal move followed an incident in which the slow bowler had been fined £90 by Brighton police after urinating on nightclub bouncers. Upon being asked to leave following complaints from female patrons, the left-arm spinner urinated on the club employees. Panesar then ran off but was chased by the bouncers and brought back to the club and held until the police arrived.

- The couple that holds the record for the biggest partnership in Test match cricket were best men at each other's weddings. During their union against South Africa at Colombo in 2006, the Sri Lankan pair of Kumar Sangakkara (287) and Mahela Jayawardene (374) put on a record-breaking 624 for the third wicket.

- Called up as a late starter for a County Championship match in 2012, Middlesex off-spinner Ollie Rayner had to cancel his plans to be best man at his cousin's wedding, but then went on to score a maiden first-class century on the same day. German-born Rayner hit an unbeaten 143 in the match at Nottingham, and later took 4-67.

- Eric Tindill played for New Zealand in a first-class match against MCC on his wedding day in 1937, scoring an unbeaten 24. Later in the day, he boarded a boat for the voyage to England alongside his NZ team-mates, with his new bride following behind in another vessel.

- The mother of an Indian cricketer claimed in 2013 that her son had threatened to kill her. The 70-year-old mum of Manpreet Gony, who appeared in two one-day internationals in 2008, alleged the threat was made in relation to a disputed property in Mohali: **"If something happens to me it will be Gony who will be responsible for it."**

- When Sachin Tendulkar appeared in his 200th and last Test, one of the throng who turned up on the first day at the Wankhede Stadium in 2013 was his mother who had never previously seen him play in an international match. The elderly wheelchair-bound Rajni had previously found it too nerve-racking to even watch her son live on television, preferring to watch highlights packages.

- Northamptonshire batsman Russell Warren was forced to leave the club in the early 2000s after dating the fiancée of team-mate Toby Bailey. Graeme Swann later revealed so thick was the tension within the team over the dalliance that another Northants player, Malachy Loye, refused to talk to Warren when the two batted together.

- A Sydney woman went online in 2014 seeking a man to take her to the cricket. Describing herself as "very good-looking, smart, funny and single", the 28-year-old offered a free corporate hospitality ticket to an Australia-England match at the SCG to the right man: "**Must be knowledgeable about sport, witty, know their difference between 'your' and 'you're', and enjoy a drink or two. Bogans, those taking steroids and lacking manners and education need not apply. Good banter and collared shirt essential.**"

- James Anderson broke new ground in 2010 by becoming the first England cricketer to pose for a gay magazine. Anderson was featured on a front cover of the popular British publication *Attitude*: "**I think I probably will get some stick for it, but I'm more than prepared for that. I'm quite happy to take it, because I'm delighted that I've had the chance to do it. I would never change it.**"

> "**I have got nothing to hide and I am ready to tell people ... I feel it is right to be out in the open about my sexuality. I'm comfortable with who I am and I'm happy to say who I am in public. To speak out is a massive relief for me personally. At the end of my career I want to be remembered as a good cricketer, not just as a gay cricketer.**"
>
> England wicketkeeper Steven Davies
> in 2011, after becoming his country's first capped cricketer
> to announce he is gay

Pitch Perfect

- A limited-edition picture disc version of the music used by the BBC as its cricket theme hit the record shelves in 1987. Part of a boxed set of ten iconic singles released by the Stax record label, Booker T and The MGs' 1968 classic 'Soul Limbo' features a picture of a cricket ball on one side and cricket cards and bails on the other. The B-side of the single is 'Heads or Tails'.

- The late British glam-rock star Alvin Stardust made an appearance in a cricket-inspired musical in 1986 that was commissioned to celebrate the Queen's 60th birthday. Stardust – who had top ten hits with 'My Coo-Ca-Choo' in 1973 and 'Jealous Mind' the following year – was a member of the cast in the Tim Rice and Andrew Lloyd Webber mini-musical *Cricket*.

- One of the sons of Caribbean reggae legend Bob Marley was named after West Indies batsman Rohan Kanhai. Bob Marley's uncle Robert Cecil Marley played first-class cricket, appearing in seven matches for Jamaica between 1928/29 and 1946. An opening batsman, his highest score was 40 against MCC in Kingston in 1929/30.

- During their tour of Australia in 2010, Irish rock band U2 made mention of the Ashes tour at their concert in Perth. Bono, the group's frontman, spoke of the Australia-England Test which was being played at the same time at the WACA.

- Chris Jordan, who made his Test debut for England in 2014, went to the same school in Barbados as pop star Rihanna. Jordan attended Combermere High School in Bridgetown where he studied alongside the soon-to-be global singing sensation: "**I remember Rihanna well. I guess she was always a good singer at school. I like her songs very much and they're on my iPod, but I don't think she has much interest in cricket.**

   When I go back to Barbados we see each other and stuff. She's a very humble girl and I'm just glad everything worked out well for her."

- After attending an American Major League baseball match at the SCG in 2014, Australian singer Marcia Hines fired off a tweet after meeting a former Test captain. Hines – an Australian Queen of Pop – tweeted a photo of herself and Ian Chappell, but with the caption: "**Look who I bumped into at the baseball – the one and only Tony Greig.**"

- Ageing rock star Ronnie Wood contemplated joining a Surrey cricket club in 2010 to help him stay fit and sober. The Rolling Stones guitarist came up with the idea after taking a walk in a local park: "**I went for a walk and the cricket team asked me to join. Now I'm getting notes through the door asking me to be the new batsman. I said I'd love to if I had the time. I've been practising my bowling too.**"

- Three club cricketers from the UK featured in a musically-themed dismissal in 1979 when Martin Mendelssohn lost his wicket in a game for the Northwood club. Mendelssohn was caught Wagner, bowled Haydn.

LETTER TO THE EDITOR
The Times – 17 June 2013

Watching the New Zealand fast bowler Neil Wagner during a quiet period of play at Lord's recently my friend and I put together the following XI made up of composer-cricketers: Adams, John and Jimmy; Arnold, Malcolm and Geoff; Barber, Samuel and Bob; Benjamin, Arthur and Winston; Bird, William and Dickie; Elgar, Sir Edward and Dean; Smyth, Dame Ethel and Richard; Sullivan, Sir Arthur and John; Wagner, Richard and Neil; Watkins, Huw and Allan; Weir, Judith and Lindsay.

- Tom Chaplin, the lead singer of the UK pop band Keane, was once described by former England captain Bob Willis as a "massive cricket nut". Chaplin was a handy junior cricketer, playing for Sussex until the age of 15.

- Australian cricketer Ellyse Perry was immortalised in song in 2014 with a recording by a four-piece band from Tasmania. Brandish initially released 'The Ellyse Perry Song' on YouTube, later receiving radio airplay across the nation.

- It was estimated that some 5,000 fans turned up on a rainy day in 1982 to watch the inaugural cricket match staged by the charity Bunbury Cricket Club. The brainchild of David English, a former manager of The Bee Gees, the match attracted rock music icons Bill Wyman, Eric Clapton, Ringo Starr and Phil Collins, who kept wicket.

Rock legend Eric Clapton

- One of the originators of Jamaican ska music recorded a famous song in celebration of cricket. 'West Indian Test Cricket' by Laurel Aitken was released as a single in 1964 and is included on a best-of album, *Anthology: Godfather of Ska*. The flip-side of his single is a tribute to West Indies legend Frank Worrell, '3 Cheers for Worrell'.

- Record-breakers Dennis Lillee, Rod Marsh and Doug Walters all share an unusual musical distinction. In 1972, the trio was part of the Australian cricket team that recorded a single, 'Here Comes the Aussies', to coincide with the Ashes series in England. A top-40 hit in Australia, all three players were later celebrated on vinyl, with a variety of commercial singles released in their honour – 'Lillee' by Steve Bailey, 'Dennis Lillee' by The Wozzers, 'The Hero of the West (A Tribute to Rodney Marsh)' by Australian country music legend Smoky Dawson and 'Dashing Dougie' by New Zealand Maori singer Nash Chase.

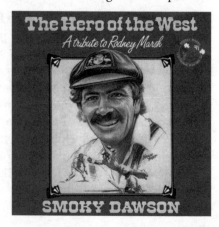

- Australian country-pop singer Mike McClellan honoured Mark Taylor's historic Test innings of 334 not out against Pakistan with a song called 'The Mark of the Man'. The 1998 CD single also includes 'An Enigmatic Man', a tribute to Don Bradman whose Australian Test-record innings Taylor equalled in the Peshawar Test of 1998/99.

- During the 1990s, an Australian jazz musician who bears the name of an Australian Test captain played with the resident band on Channel Nine's *Midday Show*. During an interview with Mark Taylor, the host turned to the band and brought saxophonist Mark Taylor into the conversation asking what it was like to have the same name as the former Test captain: **"I simply explained that I used it to my advantage as regularly as possible and with great results ... restaurant bookings, flight upgrades, first-class service ... amazing such a famous name can open doors! Later in the show, Tubby and I reversed roles. He grabbed my alto sax for a blow and me his cricket bat for a few practice drives."**

Saxophonist Mark Taylor and cricket player Mark Taylor swap their tools of trade on the set of Channel Nine's Midday Show *in 1996*

DAN FORSHAW'S DREAM TEAM

Graham Gooch (E)
Alastair Cook (E)
Mike Atherton (E)
Brian Lara (WI)
Mark Waugh * (A)
Andrew Flintoff (E)
Adam Gilchrist † (A)
Shane Warne (A)
Courtney Walsh (WI)
Allan Donald (SA)
Glenn McGrath (A)

British jazz saxophonist Dan Forshaw

- Famed British conductor John Barbiroli undertook his first tour of Australia in 1950, lured by the prospect of Test match cricket. Said to be unavailable previously for such a tour, Sir John agreed when told that his concerts would be arranged so he could attend two Tests of the 1950/51 Ashes series.

- A cricket-loving Indian dentist recorded an album in 2011 in honour of Sachin Tendulkar. Prior to its general release, C.V. Ranjith presented a copy of the album *Shan-e-Hindustan* to his hero: **"It was my dream to give the first copy to Sachin."** The video album features the dental surgeon singing in 20 different languages: **"The main reason to come out in 20 languages is to make it easy to understand among the public that Sachin has thousands of fans across India and abroad."**

  Indian artist Arnie B also paid tribute to Tendulkar in song in the same year penning a number to coincide with the World Cup. 'Master Blaster' followed Arnie B's 'King of Spin' that celebrated Shane Warne.

THE SHANE WARNE JUKEBOX

'Shane Warne'	Greg Champion	1995
'Bowlin' Shane'	Haskel Daniel vs Sideshow	2000
'Horny Warnie'	Horny Warnie & The Whites	2003
'The Shane Warne Song'	Kevin "Bloody" Wilson	2003
'Shane Warne'	Handsome Young Strangers	2007
'The Shane Warne Song'	Paul Kelly	2007
'The Tale of Warne', 'Shine Like Shane', 'What About That, Shane?' *Shane Warne: The Musical*		2008
'Jiggery Pokery'	The Duckworth Lewis Method	2009
'King of Spin'	Arnie B	2011

- Set to the tune of a Jennifer Lopez hit, a radio duo from Sydney came up with a song in 2011 lampooning Shane Warne. Breakfast show hosts Ryan Fitzgerald and Michael Wipfli wrote 'Get with Shane Warne' based on J-Lo's 'On the Floor': "Shane Warne/In your car/ Beep your horn for Shane Warne."

> **"We break every now and then for food and we spend a lot of time rubbing our balls on our trousers."**
>
> former England all-rounder Andrew Flintoff
> explaining cricket to US singer Jennifer Lopez

- Robert Nicholson was a baritone singer of some note who also played cricket, taking part in a legendary Australian match in which Don Bradman scored a century off three overs. Nicholson opened the batting for a Lithgow team against Blackheath in 1931, for which Bradman and a New South Wales team-mate Wendell Bill were guest players. On his way to a massive 256, Bradman savaged his opponents by hitting 33 runs off an over, followed by 40 off the next and 27 off the third, an effort lauded as a world record. Nicholson sang at a post-match concert, impressing the Don who invited him to perform at his wedding. He later sang with the Metropolitan Opera in New York.

- Campbell Burnap, an internationally-acclaimed jazz trombonist, was a big cricket fan who was once employed as a ball-by-ball commentator of County Championship matches. A member of MCC and the Derbyshire County Cricket Club, Burnap was a playing member of The Ravers, a cricket team originally made up mainly of jazz musicians. On stage, he was a long-time member of the Acker Bilk band and led a jazz group called Outswingers that performed at Lord's during the lunch interval of Test matches.

Music at lunchtime at Lord's

LETTER TO THE EDITOR
Sydney Morning Herald – 10 February 1888

At the recent inter-colonial match no music was provided, whilst at the match last Saturday a good band played through a programme, comprising items of a very pronounced funereal and doleful type, and this appeared to be a very general opinion judging from the remarks heard all-round. At the risk of being considered plebeian, allow me to suggest a programme that would be more in accord with the public taste on such occasions, viz., 'Tommy Dodd', 'Shoe Fly', 'Masher March', 'Old John Brown', 'The Girl I Left Behind Me' and, if the public would like something sentimental, let it be 'Home, Sweet Home', or some similar air, with which they are familiar.

- The grandson of an England Test legend released a debut record in 2014. Julius Cowdrey – whose grandfather Colin and father Chris both captained England – put down the album *Shoot Out To Me*, replete the lyrics written by his cricket-playing brother Fabian: **"I can be playing the piano in one room and he'll come in and say 'that sounds quite good'. Then ten or 15 minutes later he'll come back with the lyrics to go with the song. Usually they're bang on."**

> **"It's mainly cricket the family is known for on my dad's side but my mum sang jazz. I think that's really where I got my love for it. It's not from my dad, he's tone deaf."**
>
> Julius Cowdrey

- Indian spinner Harbhajan Singh turned singer in 2013. His debut recording was a Punjabi song, 'Ek Suneha'.

- Top-selling Australian singer Clare Bowditch has a lucky cricket ball. While overseas one year, and having what she described as "one of the worst days of her life", Bowditch bought herself a present from a second-hand shop in London: **"I needed a symbol of hope and there it was. She was just sitting there ... tucked away in a little corner ... she had the most beautiful seams and reminded me of home, so I bought it and have carried it with me ever since."**

- In the year of his retirement from Test match cricket, Australian fast bowler Brett Lee set off on his first overseas tour with his two-man outfit White Shoe Theory. With Mick Vawdon on lead vocals and Lee playing guitar, the duo undertook a mini tour of India in 2010.

> **"If you took cricket out of my life, I'd be sad. If you took music out of my life, I'd be devastated."**
>
> Brett Lee

- England spinner Graeme Swann lent his voice to an album of children's nursery rhymes in 2013, recording a version of 'Dingle Dangle Scarecrow'. Swann and his rock band Dr Comfort and the Lurid Revelations put down the track for a CD released to raise money for charity.

- Singer and comedian Harry Secombe played in a benefit match for Glamorgan stalwart Don Shepherd in 1960. Best known for his role in the BBC Radio series *The Goon Show*, and for a string of Top 40 hits, Secombe scored 15 batting at No. 5 in the one-day match for Glamorgan against North Wales at Colwyn Bay.

> "There was the cricket match that dad held every year in the ground opposite our house in Cheam, London. Tommy Cooper would turn out to play, as well as professionals such as Alec and Eric Bedser, Colin Cowdrey, Fred Trueman and Ted Dexter. And I remember Shirley Bassey turned up once, though not to play."
>
> Andy Secombe

- Australian and Chennai Super Kings fast bowler Doug Bollinger made an appearance at a concert in 2012 when he joined singer Katy Perry on stage during a performance in the Indian city of Chennai. In a show marking the opening of the Indian Premier League Twenty20 tournament, Bollinger taught the American pop sensation how to hold a cricket bat while using her microphone.

Former England opener Geoff Boycott meets US pop star Katy Perry in 2014

- England batsman Alastair Cook, a former choirboy at St Paul's Cathedral, once sang with the internationally-renowned opera star Kiri Te Kanawa. Proficient at the saxophone, clarinet and piano, Cook performed a sax solo that was included on the soundtrack for a BBC children's programme in 2008.

The Bedford School's grade seven clarinet group, featuring future England captain Alastair Cook (right)

- Thomas Beecham, who was associated with leading orchestras such as the London Philharmonic and the Seattle Symphony, said he only became a conductor because of cricket. An accomplished concert pianist, Sir Thomas decided to pick up the baton after playing a game of cricket: "**I kept taking wicket after wicket, in fact, I think I almost established a record. And that night, when I sat down to play at my concert, my fingers were so stiff. So I gave up the piano.**"

- UK pop singer David Essex and lyricist Tim Rice once played together in a charity cricket match for the Lord's Taverners XI in Los Angeles. Despite the songwriter boasting a career average of around seven, Essex – who enjoyed a string of top-40 hits in the 1970s – rated Sir Tim as quite a handy bat: "**He can play well, he bats very solidly.**"

- Australian rock legend Jim Keays, who fronted the top-selling band The Masters Apprentices, was a fast bowler at his school in Adelaide. The Scotland-born Keays once took 10-40 in a match for Norwood High.

JIM KEAYS'S DREAM TEAM

Don Bradman * (A)
Sachin Tendulkar (I)
Viv Richards (WI)
Greg Chappell (A)
Brian Lara (WI)
Adam Gilchrist † (A)
Ian Botham (E)
Shane Warne (A)
Dennis Lillee (A)
Jeff Thomson (A)
Wes Hall (WI)

Jim Keays, who fronted the legendary Australian rock band The Masters Apprentices

- An album released during the 2013 Ashes featured an iconic image of a streaker at Lord's on the front cover. In 1975, Michael Angelow – a 24-year-old seaman – got his gear off for a £20 bet with Australian fans attending the Ashes Test at the home of cricket. His antics received worldwide attention and nearly 40 years later, the image, of Angelow hurdling the stumps, was resurrected for the front cover of the *Sticky Wickets* album by the Duckworth Lewis Method.

The Irish band's second album, some of the songs included are 'Boom Boom Afridi', 'It's Just Not Cricket', 'The Umpire', 'Third Man', 'Chin Music', 'Out in the Middle' and 'Line and Length'.

- A song on the 1986 album *No.10, Upping Street* by the British group Big Audio Dynamite includes a reference to two England Test captains. 'Ticket' – the second track on side two – mentions W.G. Grace and Ian Botham: "Botham is cool/Selectors are spaced/England's losing again/W.G. Disgrace."

  The 1973 album *Vagabonds of the Western World* by the Irish rock band Thin Lizzy includes a line about cricket on the track 'Little Girl in Bloom': "Little girl in bloom/You watch the men play cricket from the window in your room/See the ball go from bat to wicket/Pass away the afternoon."

- One of the big new names to emerge on the UK music scene in the 2010s featured cricket in the video for his debut single under his stage name King Krule. Londoner Archy Marshall is seen holding a cricket bat in the official 'Easy Easy' video, a song taken from his debut album *6 Feet Beneath the Moon* released in 2013.

- Lancashire batsman David Hughes, who also played first-class cricket for Tasmania, was the subject of a song recorded in 1972. 'Ballad of David Hughes' by The Twelfth Man appears on the flip-side of 'Red Rose' sung by members of the Lancashire county cricket team.

- Iconic British DJ John Peel once made a deal with a producer that upon Peel's death he would arrange to play Roy Harper's classic cricket song 'When an Old Cricketer Leaves the Crease' at his funeral. Although John Walter's death preceded Peel's, the BBC announcer played the song in memory of Walters: **"I always expected that John, despite his illness, would outlive me because he was absolutely determined to be at my funeral in order to deliver the eulogy which would have been enormously long but very, very funny and I suspect would have reflected a great deal of credit on him and not nearly so much on me. But one of the things he was determined to do was to play at some stage of the ceremony Roy Harper's record 'When an Old Cricketer Leaves the Crease'. I'm sorry you didn't have the much longer innings you deserved."**

Roy Harper performs 'When an Old Cricketer Leaves the Crease' live on the BBC's Test Match Special

Australian singer-songwriter Greg Champion recorded an album in 1995 dedicated to cricket. His CD *Everybody Loves to Watch the Cricket* includes a number of tracks honouring top cricketers such as 'Big Merv', 'Take Me Home Jonty Rhodes', '(The Kiwis are not the Same Without) Ewen Chatfield' and 'Our Don Bradman'.

On the eve of the 2010/11 Ashes series, he teamed up with singer David Brooks for the CD *Cricket Chants: Songs for Singing at Cricket Matches*: **"These are songs to rival the Barmy Army. They constantly out-sing our supporters."** In 2008, Champion had recorded a tribute to Don Bradman – 'I Was a Mate of Don Bradman' – with Australian crooner Kamahl.

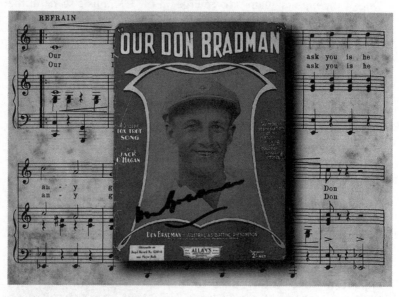

THE DON BRADMAN JUKEBOX

'Old Fashioned Locket'	Don Bradman	1930
'Our Don Bradman'	Art Leonard	1930
'Bradman'	Paul Kelly	1987
'The Tiger and The Don'	Ted Egan	1990
'Sir Don'	John Williamson	1996
'An Enigmatic Man'	Mike McClennan	1998
'I Was a Mate of Don Bradman'	Kamahl & Greg Champion	2008

Two singles recorded by British bands in the late 1970s had cricketing songs on the flip-side. The B-side of The Shadows' 1977 single 'Another Night' was 'Cricket Bat Boogie'; the B-side of the 1979 single 'Save Me' by Violinski was 'Cricket, Bloody Cricket'. Each track was also the opening track on albums by the two groups – *Tasty* by The Shadows and *No Cause for Alarm* by Violinski.

- When the British heavy metal band Iron Maiden performed at Bangalore in 2007, concert posters promoting the gig featured cricket. It was the group's first-ever concert appearance in India.

- Upon the death of American soul singer Percy Sledge in 2015, speculation was revived as to whether his name had given birth to the cricket term "sledging". The BBC's Pat Murphy believes it originated when players had sung his No. 1 hit 'When a Man Loves a Woman' during a Sheffield Shield match in the 1960s: **"My understanding is that it came from the mid-60s and a guy called Grahame Corling, who used to open the bowling for New South Wales and Australia. Apparently the suggestion was that this guy's wife was** [having an affair] **with another team-mate, and when he came into bat** [the fielding team] **started singing 'When a Man Loves a Woman'."**

- Two members of the US rock band Good Charlotte performed at the Australia Day Twenty20 international in Sydney in 2012/13 as part of a marketing campaign for the KFC food group. Twins Joel and Benji Madden also appeared in a number of cricket-themed ads for KFC over the summer, which also featured Australian captains Ricky Ponting, Michael Clarke and George Bailey.

Joel and Benji Madden from the US rock group Good Charlotte try their hand at cricket during a promotion for KFC in Australia in 2012/13

- Left-arm spinner Tom O'Dwyer, a member of Western Australia's Sheffield Shield-winning team in 1947/48, was known as the "bowling baritone". After making his first-class debut against MCC in 1946/47, he claimed nine wickets (7-79 and 2-47) in a match against Queensland at Brisbane in the season that WA lifted the Shield at their first attempt. O'Dwyer appeared in a number of musicals in Perth and sang in his church choir for seven decades.

ANDY KENT'S DREAM TEAM

Barry Richards (SA)
Lance Cairns (NZ)
Viv Richards (WI)
Neil Harvey (A)
Garry Sobers * (WI)
Kapil Dev (I)
David Gower (E)
Rod Marsh † (A)
Dennis Lillee (A)
Ewen Chatfield (NZ)
Ross Edwards (A)

*Bass player
Andy Kent
from the
Australian
alternative
rock band
You Am I*

- Fresh from a performance at the Glastonbury music festival in Somerset, the Dalai Lama's Gyuto Monks of Tibet visited Lord's ahead of the 2013 Ashes. Fresh with a new album – *Chants: the Spirit of Success* – the cricket-loving monks performed a special blessing at the famous ground.

- During the Rolling Stones tour of Australia in 2014, frontman Mick Jagger and drummer Charlie Watts met Don Bradman's son John, who gave the cricket-loving rockers a private tour of the Bradman Collection museum in Adelaide. The Stones later played at the Adelaide Oval in front of some 50,000 fans. Watts was able to fit in watching some cricket in between concerts, attending a Sheffield Shield match and a Twenty20 international between Australia and South Africa at the MCG.

Mick Jagger holding the World Cup trophy on the eve of the Rolling Stones concert at the Adelaide Oval in 2014 and at the 1972 Ashes Test at The Oval (right)

- When asked to name the best celebrity to have played for the Bunbury charity cricket club, founder David English plumped for McFly drummer Harry Judd. He said the worst was American pop singer Donny Osmond: **"Lovely bloke, completely uncoordinated ... when I was at Barry Gibbs's house in LA, I did persuade Michael Jackson to turn out the next season, even though he didn't have a clue what I was on about. Unfortunately, though, he died."**

  A talented cricketer at school, according to the 2005 *Wisden*, **"Harry Judd, who scored 252 runs last season, left Uppingham to become a full-time drummer in the pop group McFly. The summer ended well for the side, with four wins in the last five matches, but even better for Harry Judd: McFly topped the UK singles chart twice, with 'Five Colours in Her Hair' and 'Obviously'."**

- In 2001, England batsman Mark Butcher made a guest appearance on the BBC's *Jamie Theakston Cricket Show*. Armed with his guitar, Butcher played an acoustic version of The Stranglers song '(Get a) Grip (On Yourself)' with the band's former frontman, and cricket enthusiast, Hugh Cornwell.

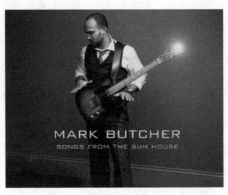

Mark Butcher's debut album – Songs from the Sun House – *released in 2009*

HUGH CORNWELL'S DREAM TEAM

W.G. Grace * (E)
Moeen Ali (E)
Hashim Amla (SA)
Mohammad Yousuf (P)
Viv Richards (WI)
Yusuf Pathan (I)
Jack Blackham † (A)
Daniel Vettori (NZ)
Kane Richardson (A)
Malcolm Marshall (WI)
Merv Hughes (A)

Hugh Cornwall, of the UK band The Stanglers, and his "facial-haired" XI

- Former Pakistan superstar Wasim Akram made an appearance on a pop music video in 2008. The "Sultan of Swing" is featured throughout the video for the song 'Soona Soona' by Pakistan rock group Fuzon: **"He loved the songs and wanted to be part of the album. When we were working on the song, which is a sad love song, we thought of him."**

- West Indies all-rounder Andre Russell turned pop star in 2014, releasing two hip-hop singles. Russell collaborated with Grammy Award-winning reggae star Beenie Man for 'Sweat Whine' and backed it up with a solo single called 'Sweetheart': **"The same way I put my all on the field is the**

same thing I will be doing to my music career because the sky is the limit."

With 'Go Gyal Go', national team-mate Dwayne Bravo also released a debut solo single in 2014. Bravo had also previously recorded a song with Beenie Man, in 2011: **"Music is a passion and a way of life for me. Had I not carved out a career as a cricketer, I would have ended up in the entertainment industry."**

- When the Texas-born singer-songwriter Stephen Stills based himself in the UK he embraced all things British including cricket. A member of the groups Buffalo Springfield and Crosby, Stills, Nash and Young, he appeared as a guest on the BBC's *Test Match Special* in 2010.

"I'd bought Ringo Starr's mansion for £100,000 – he bought it from Peter Sellers – and I had the most rock'n'roll fun ever living in Britain. I loved it all, the fresh mown grass and the spring air. I played cricket; I even know the rules. In fact I still watch the big matches on Sky."

Stephen Stills

ANDY SCOTT'S DREAM TEAM

Mike Atherton * (E)
Geoff Boycott (E)
Denis Compton (E)
David Gower (E)
Joe Root (E)
Alec Stewart † (E)
Ian Botham (E)
Andrew Flintoff (E)
Graeme Swann (E)
James Anderson (E)
Fred Trueman (E)

Andy Scott – guitarist and vocalist from the iconic 1970s glam-rock band The Sweet

JOEL QUARTERMAIN'S DREAM TEAM

Gordon Greenidge (WI)
Matthew Hayden (A)
Don Bradman (A)
Sachin Tendulkar (I)
Viv Richards * (WI)
Garry Sobers (WI)
Adam Gilchrist † (A)
Shane Warne (A)
Wasim Akram (P)
Dennis Lillee (A)
Malcolm Marshall (WI)

Joel Quartermain from the Australian rock group Eskimo Joe

- A tweet from a member of the British boy band One Direction noting the death of Australian batsman Phillip Hughes in 2014 generated some 95,000 retweets. Harry Styles was in Sydney for the ARIA Awards when Hughes was felled by a bouncer at the SCG: **"RIP Phillip Hughes. What an incredibly sad day. Thinking of him and his family."**

- An England cricketer revealed in 2013 that Elton John had saved his career after joining him on a four-week concert tour of Asia. The cricket-loving pop star (pictured) had contacted Surrey's Steven Davies after learning of his depressive state following the death of county team-mate Tom Maynard in 2012: **"It was crazy when he got in touch. He's a lovely guy, really kind**

301

and generous. He knew that I was struggling with stuff so he invited me over. It was exactly what I needed. If I'd gone on another [cricket] tour I felt like I would have given up the game."

> "I want to dedicate this song to the memory of Phil Hughes and to the Australian team and all the cricketers in Australia who knew him because he gave me so much pleasure. This is for you Phil."
>
> Elton John
> dedicating his song 'Don't Let the Sun Go Down on Me' to the late Phillip Hughes at a concert in Munich in 2014

- A leading exponent of calypso music released an album in 1976 that included a song about Viv Richards. The album *Ghetto Vibes* by King Short Shirt contains the track 'Vivian Richards', a song featured in the 2010 documentary *Fire in Babylon* that traces the rise of West Indies cricket in the 1970s and 80s. Four decades later, Sir Viv was the subject of another song with INXS drummer Jon Farriss recording a debut single called 'Smokin Joe'. Richards provided spoken-word vocals for the song released in 2015.

- Two of the fastest bowlers of all time received a musical salute in the mid-1970s with the West Indies' Michael Holding and Australia's Jeff Thomson both commemorated on vinyl. Jamaican DJ I-Roy's 'Tribute to Michael Holding' appears on his 1976 album *Musical Shark Attack*, while the 1975 single 'We Got Thommo' by Smith & Weston became a minor hit in Australia the following year.

- An Australian dancer with Britain's Royal Ballet was signed up by the England and Wales Cricket Board to give aspiring international coaches a pep talk. The cricket-loving Alexander Campbell trained with the Academy Ballet school in Sydney before being appointed as a soloist with the Royal Ballet in 2011: "**I can't remember a time when I didn't have a cricket bat or ball in my hand. I had to choose between ballet and cricket, and I struggled with the decision for a long time. But my love for ballet, and the opportunity to do something that seemed so unusual for a kid from Sydney, was enticing.**

  "**I'm not sure my ballet teachers would tell you that cricket improved my ballet training, but I certainly think it helped. I developed all sorts of skills – hand-eye coordination, timing, sharpness, explosiveness, agility – that perhaps wouldn't have developed in the same way had I just been trained as a dancer.**"

Sundries

- A Sri Lankan batsman caused a mid-air scare in 2013 when he tried to open a cabin door on a flight from St Lucia to Gatwick. Returning from the Sri Lankan A tour of the West Indies, Ramith Rambukwella said he mistook a cabin door for the toilet door. According to a passenger, **"Suddenly he came over and tried to open the cabin door several times. It went on for a few minutes. He was pulling quite heavily. The flight attendants came running down the aisle and tried to calm him down. He seemed quite disorientated."**

- International economist Mervyn King played cricket at school, once taking seven wickets before the lunch break in a match in 1965. His next five-wicket haul – 5-15 in a limited-over match – came 38 years later in 2003, the year he was appointed Governor of the Bank of England: **"I claim a record for the longest time between successive five-fors."**

- Afghanistan all-rounder Mohammad Nabi set a new benchmark in world cricket in 2015 when he became the first player to appear in each of a country's first 50 one-day internationals. He was there for Afghanistan's first ODI – against Scotland at Benoni in 2009 – and was captain in its 50th, against New Zealand at Napier in the 2015 World Cup.

- All-rounder Jimmy Allan had the unusual experience in 1966 of playing both for and against the same county in consecutive first-class matches. After turning out for Warwickshire in a County Championship match against Glamorgan at Swansea, he then played for Scotland – a team he had represented since 1954 – against Warwickshire at Edgbaston three days later.

- Coinciding with the West Indies' 500th Test match, senior batsman Shivnarine Chanderpaul became the first cricketer to witness 500 dismissals from the other end. In the first innings of the second Test against Bangladesh at Gros Islet in 2014, the removal of Jermaine Blackwood was the 500th time Chanderpaul had seen one of his team-mates dismissed while batting. For his part, Chanderpaul kept his own wicket intact both times, finishing the match with two unbeaten scores of 84 and 101.

- Umpiring history was made when England hosted India at The Oval in 2014 with the two men in the middle, the TV umpire, the reserve umpire and match referee all being former Test players. Sri Lanka's Kumar Dharmasena and Paul Reiffel were the umpires, England's Tim Robinson and Neil Mallender occupied the positions of TV umpire and reserve umpire respectively, while Sri Lanka's Ranjan Madugalle presided over his 150th Test as referee.

- A squabble over a cricket match on TV and smoking saw the arrival of the riot squad to a pub in Warwickshire in 2007. John Vaughan had been watching the last few minutes of a cricket match on the pub TV when someone changed the channel to football. When his pleas to staff to put the cricket back on failed, he decided to light up a cigarette in defiance of a smoking ban: **"The cricket only had ten minutes left, but the football wasn't even going to start for another 45 minutes. We complained but nothing happened. So I decided to light up out of protest. They pressed a panic button and the next thing I knew, there were six policemen in the pub and two outside."**

- A former Zimbabwe cricketer had a close encounter with a crocodile in 2013. Guy Whitall – who appeared in 46 Tests – lived to tell the tale of being asleep one night, not knowing that an eight-foot crocodile had been hiding under his bed: **"The really disconcerting thing about the whole episode is the fact that I was sitting on the edge of the bed that morning, barefoot and just centimetres away from the croc. Crocodiles are experts at hiding, that's why they have survived on Earth for so long and why they are the ultimate killers in water."**

- During a County Championship match at Huddersfield in 1919, Yorkshire's 12th man fielded for the opposition and caught four of his team-mates in the first innings. Billy Williams appeared on the field in the match for Leicestershire, taking five substitute catches in all.

- In 2007, Shane Warne became the first cricketer in philatelic history to be honoured with a series of stamps. The Caribbean nation of Grenada commissioned the set, a distinction which, at the time, had not even been bestowed upon one of its own citizens. Later in the same year, Sri Lanka's philatelic service released a stamp shaped like a cricket ball commemorating Muttiah Muralitharan's feat of breaking Warne's record of most Test match wickets.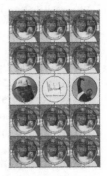

- Three players named S. Banerjee have played Test cricket for India, with each making just one appearance. S.A. Banerjee played in his one and only Test against the West Indies at Kolkata in 1948/49; S.N. Banerjee's only Test came against the same opposition, at Mumbai, in the same series, while S.T. Banerjee played against Australia at Sydney in 1991/92.

- The West Indies began its tour of New Zealand in 2013/14 with just five players. With the rest of the squad in India, the West Indians included six New Zealanders – Jeet Raval, Aaron Redmond, Sam Wells, Robert O'Donnell, Tim Johnston and Ili Tugaga – in its tour opener against a New Zealand XI at Lincoln.

- A large number of villages across northern India were banned from playing cricket in 2007, because it was deemed a "meaningless game". Village elders issued a decree stating that no one was permitted to play cricket or watch matches on television, adding that cricket led young people into gambling.

- In between two first-class matches for Scotland, Robert Clark was a crew member on board explorer Ernest Shackleton's *Endurance* that sank in the Antarctic in 1915. A biologist, Clark made his first-class debut against Ireland in Dublin in 1912, appearing in his final match 12 years later, against the South Africans, in Glasgow in 1924.

- English adventurer Bear Grylls, who was appointed Britain's Chief Scout in 2009, has a family connection with first-class cricket. His maternal grandfather was Neville Ford, who appeared in 75 first-class matches, for Derbyshire, Middlesex and Oxford University in the 1920s and 30s.

- Former New Zealand wicketkeeper Adam Parore was on top of the world in 2011 after successfully scaling the world's tallest mountain. Suffering altitude sickness and battling poor weather conditions, Parore made it to the top of Mount Everest in a climb that raised money for the Make-a-Wish Foundation.

- The famed British astronomer Patrick Moore listed cricket as his favourite sport. A bowler by trade, he regarded his "finest hour" on the cricketing field when he came in to bat at No.11 with his team floundering at 27/9 and scored a match-winning 63. He claimed nine wickets in an innings on three occasions in village cricket, but never quite took all ten: "**I was playing in a match where I had nine for 45. In came the No. 11 who was no batsman at all. The first ball shaved the stumps. He blocked the next, then called for a run and ran himself out! He bought me a large drink after the game.**" Sir Patrick's final game came at the age of 77, in which he took 6-41.

> "There are 100,000 million stars in our galaxy and 1,000 million galaxies. Many a world must be inhabited. I am sure cricket must be being played somewhere. They must be if they are civilised."
>
> Patrick Moore

- Play in a club match in Hampshire in 1982 included an unscheduled break to accommodate the landing of a hot-air balloon. After running out of fuel, it came to rest in between the stumps during the Curdridge-Medstead match near Southampton.

- In 2005, a Pakistani businessman offered the Pakistan Cricket Board £1m if it would pick him to play against India. The Karachi newspaper *The News* revealed that the London-based M. Jamshaid had made the same offer a number of times, all to no avail.

A hot-air balloon makes its way over a match between Oxford University and Middlesex

- Henry Edward Manning, the Archbishop of Westminster between 1865 and 1892, has a special place in cricket history. The future Cardinal Manning played for Harrow against Winchester at Lord's in 1825, the first game between the two schools.

- England batsman Geoff Pullar appeared in a record 16 Tests before taking a catch in his 17th, against Pakistan at Lahore in 1961/62. The Lancashire batsman – who made 75 on his Test debut and had a highest score of 175 – took only two catches in the field in his 28-Test-match career.

- When Kumar Sangakkara played in a Twenty20 fixture against Bangladesh at Pallekele in 2012/13, he became the first player to reach the milestone of 500 international matches without ever taking a wicket. In 117 Tests, 340 one-day internationals and 43 Twenty20 internationals, the Sri Lankan batsman had only delivered 78 balls in three innings since his debut in 2000. His only wicket in his entire career of 764 other matches – first-class, List A and Twenty20s – up to that point had been Zimbabwe A batsman Elton Chigumbura, at Harare in 2004.

- A computer cricket game smashed its way to the top of the charts in England just two weeks after its release in 2005. Labelled the "best cricket game on PS2" by the *PlayStation 2* magazine, *Brian Lara International Cricket* became the first cricket game to capture the No. 1 spot on the UK All-Formats chart since the best-seller list began in 1997.

- During Surrey's loss to Hampshire in a 2006 C&G Trophy one-day match at Croydon, a shot off the bat of Jonathan Batty hit the three-year-old son of his team-mate Ali Brown in the head. The Hampshire physiotherapist was on hand and administered first aid.

- After being banned for abusing a team-mate in a match in England in 1938, an 84-year-old retired doctor was allowed back in to the club 70 years later. Dennis Hibbert had been banned by the Kimberley Institute Cricket Club after calling a fielder a "big fat fool". When Hibbert turned up to a club function in 2008, it was pointed out by the club's secretary Jim Dymond that his ban had never been annulled: "**It must be the longest on record.**"

- The Mauritius-born Owen Cowley appeared for two states but never played a first-class match on Australian soil. Cowley played in 11 matches on two tours of New Zealand – seven matches for New South Wales in 1893/94 and four for Queensland in 1896/97.

- When Canterbury were playing Central Districts in a first-class match at New Plymouth in 2009/10, one player from each side was called up by New Zealand for international duty. After scoring an unbeaten 227 and sharing an unbroken stand of 379 for Canterbury, Shanan Stewart left the game at lunch on day four, while fast bowler Michael Mason was withdrawn on day two. Seventeen-year-old Adam Milne, making his first-class debut in place of Mason, hit the winning runs for Central Districts with two balls to spare.

- A cricket fan attending the England-New Zealand one-day international at Trent Bridge in 2013 went home £50,000 richer after pulling off a bowling challenge during a break in play. Set the task of hitting the stumps with his first ball, then two stumps with his second ball and a single stump with his third, 50-year-old Chris Newell managed the feat in front of a 16,000-strong crowd in Nottingham: **"I'm originally from Yorkshire, so I guess there's a bit of Fred Trueman in there somewhere."**

- During the Pakistan A tour of England in 1997, two future Test players made their first-class debuts at the age of 15. Shoaib Malik – who made his Test debut in 2001/02 – was 15 years and 151 days old on the first day of his first first-class match, against Nottinghamshire. A week later, Irfan Fazil – who later appeared in a single Test match in 1999/2000 – made his first-class debut against MCC at Shenley, aged 15 years and 249 days.

- G.H. Hardy, a prominent British mathematician, once described German counterpart David Hilbert as "the Don Bradman of mathematics". Found amongst Hardy's possessions after his death in 1947 were a number of cricket teams he'd jotted down on scraps of paper. One of the teams was, in batting order, Jack Hobbs, Archimedes, William Shakespeare, Michelangelo, Napoléon Bonaparte (captain), Henry Ford, Plato, Ludwig van Beethoven, boxer Jack Johnson, Jesus Christ and Cleopatra.

- When Fiji toured New Zealand in 1953/54, two of their players were just 5ft 1in tall. Fijian wicketkeeper Patrick Raddock and batsman Naitini Tuiyau are amongst the shortest players in first-class cricket history, with both appearing in their final first-class match together, against Auckland at Eden Park.

- An Indian-born businessman who assumed the top job at Microsoft in 2014 attributed his rise in the corporate world to cricket. Satya Nadella became the third CEO of the world's largest software maker: **"I think playing cricket taught me more about working in teams and leadership that has stayed with me throughout my career."**

- Google paid tribute to a cricketer on its homepage in 2013. On 5 September, the internet search engine noted the 187th birthday of John Wisden, who appeared in 187 first-class matches.

- During the 1990s, Sachin Tendulkar appeared in a record number of consecutive international matches. Between April 1990 and April 1998, he played in 239 matches in a row – 54 Tests and 185 one-day internationals.

MOST CONSECUTIVE INTERNATIONAL MATCHES FOR A TEAM

Player	Team	M	T	ODIs	T20Is	Period
Sachin Tendulkar	India	239	54	185	-	25-04-90 to 24-04-98
Andy Flower	Zimbabwe	224	52	172	-	23-02-92 to 15-06-01
Brendon McCullum	New Zealand	208	46	122	40	10-09-04 to 23-05-10

- A prominent trade union official who was struck down by an influenza pandemic in 1919 scored a century on his first-class debut. Frank Hyett, who played a major role in the formation of the Australian Railways Union, scored an unbeaten 108 at No. 10 for Victoria against Tasmania at the MCG in 1914/15.

- Wellington fast bowler Ili Tugaga was suspended for six weeks in 2010 after lying to his club to fulfil a modelling contract in the United States. He told his club coach he needed a leave of absence to visit a sick relative, but instead travelled to San Francisco to further his modelling career.

- A "fishy" dismissal took place in a junior match in England in 2011, when Toby Codd was caught by Alex Bass off the bowling of Robert Pike. The dismissal *Codd c Bass b Pike 2* can be found in the scorebook of the under-13s match between Devon and Hampshire in Taunton.

- A piece of cheese held up play in a Test match in England in 2014. After becoming the third victim of a Test match hat-trick by Stuart Broad at Leeds, Sri Lanka's No. 10 Shaminda Eranga was struck by a Mini Babybel thrown by a spectator. Play was halted for a few minutes with the perpetrator ejected from the ground.

> **"We were disappointed, but [umpire] Billy Bowden said it's cheese, it's not rock."**
>
> Sri Lanka's Dinesh Chadimal

- When asked to nominate the "three most beautiful things in England", Australian Test all-rounder Keith Miller came up with the hills of Derbyshire, the leg sweep of Denis Compton and Princess Margaret. Once romantically linked with Miller, according to previously secret documents published in 2013, Princess Margaret was known to be "happy watching cricket for a reasonable length of time".

A press clipping from 1953, and Princess Margaret meets members of the West Indies cricket squad in 1955

- The Duke of Cambridge and Prince Harry played in a charity cricket match at Windsor Castle in 2014 that also featured former Test cricketers such as Azhar Mahmood and Devon Malcolm. Staged to raise awareness of illegal wildlife trading, Prince Harry was among the wicket-takers with his side United for Wildlife dismissing The Royal Household for 145.

Prince Harry, the cricketer, in a Twenty20 match at Windsor Castle in 2014

- To mark a call by Pakistan's Chief Justice to end discrimination against the country's eunuch population in 2009, a special cricket match was played in the southern city of Sukkur. A team of eunuchs took on a team of so-called "normal men" and came out on top claiming victory. In the same year, a team of HIV-positive players from Pakistan also took to the field for the first time. Said to be the world's first such side, they attained a seven-wicket victory over a youth club from Hyderabad.

- Pakistan's blind cricketers were barred from entering Britain in 2009 to compete in the Blind World Cup after immigration authorities suggested they might do a runner. The Pakistan Blind Cricket Council chairman Syed Sultan Shah described the refusal of visas as ridiculous: **"It is insulting. How can a blind man run away when he can't go anywhere without help?"**

- In the Auckland Test match against India in 2013/14, Indian-born Ish Sodhi was dismissed by the same combination in each innings. Caught by Rohit Sharma off Ishant Sharma, Sodhi became the first player in Test history to be dismissed in both innings of a match by a pair of players with the same surname.

- For the 1965 Test series between England and South Africa, both of the captains, Mike Smith and Peter van der Merwe, wore glasses. A unique occurrence in Tests, other bespectacled captains include Walter Hadlee, Pankaj Roy, the Maharajkumar of Vizianagram, Zaheer Abbas, Clive Lloyd and Daniel Vettori. The 1965 series featured five players who wore glasses – Smith, van der Merwe, England's Geoff Boycott and Eddie Barlow and Harry Bromfield for South Africa.

- When Hunter Poon played for Queensland at the MCG in 1923/24, he became the first player of Chinese descent to appear in a first-class match in Australia. During England's tour of Australia in 1932/33, they played against a Queensland Country team at Toowoomba in which Poona took two good wickets, Herbert Sutcliffe for 19 and Gubby Allen for a duck.

- Warwickshire County Cricket Club and the local police joined forces in 2014 to improve pitches at Edgbaston. The club used hot lamps confiscated by West Midlands Police from cannabis growers in the region to promote grass growth on the ground's playing surface.

- Appearing in his final match, South Africa's Jacques Kallis became only the second fielder to take 200 catches in Test cricket. In his 166th Test, Kallis passed the milestone on 27 December during the second Test against India at Durban in 2013/14. In 2010/11, India's Rahul Dravid had become the first to achieve the feat, doing so on the same date and at the same ground.

- Australian umpire Bill Smyth received an appeal from the very first ball in the first Test in which he stood. A former fast bowler in Melbourne club cricket, Smyth made the first of his four appearances in the middle in an Ashes Test at the MCG in 1962/63: **"It has stuck in my mind I got an appeal first ball. The very first delivery was from Fred Trueman and he appealed for a leg before wicket against Bill Lawry and I was quite happy to say, 'Not out'. Bill Lawry was a left-handed batsman and the ball was pitched outside his leg stump. Freddy Trueman knew it because he came back and said, leaving the language out of it, 'Just making sure you're awake!'"**

  Coincidentally, Smyth's first and last first-class matches as an umpire coincided with those of Lawry as a player.

- During the 1894/95 Ashes series, Syd Gregory and Jack Blackham combined for a 154-run stand in the second Test at Sydney, the only 19th-century Australian partnership record that still stands. In 2004, Julian Blackham – the wicketkeeper's great-great nephew – and Bruce Chapman – Gregory's great-great nephew – combined to produce a discussion paper for the Australian National University titled *The Value of Don Bradman: Additional Revenue in Australian Ashes Tests*.

*A novelty $100 bank note featuring Don Bradman and
a $5 legal tender coin released by the Royal Australian Mint*

- Ratilal Parmar is a Sachin Tendulkar fan of some note. A resident of the Gujarat town of Morbi, Parmar has spent a small fortune over the years collecting banknotes with serial numbers that mark significant events and milestones in Tendulkar's life, including 160312, the date in 2012 that the Little Master scored his 100th international century: **"This isn't easy to do. I knew some people in banks and they would help me find notes matching a particular event. At times, I would have to plead with them."**

- Sri Lanka's Muttiah Muralitharan appeared in close to 500 international matches without captaining his side. A record number, he played in 495 matches – 133 Tests, 350 one-day internationals and 12 Twenty20 internationals.

- A former Australian captain had a flower named after him in the year he retired from Test match cricket. The Greg Chappell rose, a small apricot-coloured hybrid tea rose, was introduced to the Australian market in 1984. Another Australian captain was similarly honoured in 2002, with the release of the dark red Sir Donald Bradman Rose (pictured).

- On his first-class debut in 1949, Fred Titmus played in the same Middlesex XI as Horace Brearley who was making his final appearance. When Titmus played in *his* final first-class match 33 years later, he played under the captaincy of Horace's son, Mike Brearley.

- In the wake of a pub altercation with an England batsman ahead of the 2013 Ashes, American wrestling icon Hulk Hogan challenged Australia's David Warner to a rumble. In a video sponsored by a betting company, Hogan predicted England would thrash Australia 5-0, and challenged Warner to take him on: **"David Warner, if you're watching and I know you are brother, next time you wanna throw a punch, how about picking a fight with someone that's got 24-inch pythons** [his biceps].**"**

- Ed Cowan was called from the members' bar at the SCG in 2005 to act as a substitute fielder for Australia. On the field for an injured Michael Clarke during the third Test against Pakistan, Cowan later refused to accept the gear he'd been wearing. Cowan – who made his Test debut in 2011/12 – said at the time he hadn't yet deserved such an honour: **"They're sacred things in Australian cricket and you need to earn them. That culture of earning your place is deeply ingrained into you."**

From the Cowan family photo album – a young Ed Cowan obtaining the autograph of Pakistan legend Imran Khan

- Stephen Russell, a captain of Oxford University at first-class level, later became a captain of industry. In 1967 – his final year of first-class cricket – Russell made his debut for Surrey and also joined Boots, a UK pharmaceutical chain that he later headed.

- Following the death of Osama bin Laden in 2011, it emerged that children had lost many a cricket ball hit into the compound of the al-Qaeda leader who lived in the Pakistan town of Abbottabad. Instead of allowing the children to retrieve the balls, and possibly discover bin Laden, locals say they were given money: "**If a ball went into bin Laden's compound the children would not be allowed to get it.**"

  Bin Laden's compound was just a short distance from a village cricket ground, with Abbottabad a participant in Pakistan's first-class competition, the Quaid-e-Azam Trophy. The last first-class match in the town prior to the assassination of bin Laden produced a 500-run total by the opposition and the first instance of a 300-run partnership at the ground. The Karachi Whites scored 583/3 declared at the Abbottabad Cricket Stadium in 2010/11 with an unbeaten fourth-wicket stand of 332 between Khalid Latif (200*) and Asif Zakir (219*).

- History was made in the summer of 2013/14 when, for the first time, the opposing captains for a Test match both made their 100th appearance. Alastair Cook and Michael Clarke were the history-makers at Perth, with Cook becoming the first player to complete 100 Tests with a career not yet eight years in length, doing so in seven years and nine months. He also beat Sachin Tendulkar as the youngest to reach the milestone at 28 years and 353 days.

  When Clarke reached two in the second innings, he and Cook had 15,921 runs and 51 centuries between them in 200 Tests combined, exactly the same set of total of runs and hundreds attained by Tendulkar on his own in his 200 Tests.

  Chasing a 504-run victory target, captain Cook was out to the first ball of the innings – his first first-ball duck in a Test – becoming the first player to mark his 100th Test with a golden globe, while Clarke celebrated the occasion with two plum prizes – the ICC Cricketer of the Year award and the Ashes.

- In 2007, Zimbabwe's cricket authorities ordered a number of players to have a haircut or be dropped. At least three members of the national team – Keith Dabengwa, Tawanda Mupariwa and Christopher Mpofu – were ordered to turn up for duty in short back and sides or face the consequences. Mupariwa resisted initially, submitting an impassioned plea to keep his dreadlocks, but later relented.

- A London resident who had his home on the market in 2001 contacted the Wisden website seeking their assistance, believing that cricket fans might be interested in his somewhat unique piece of real estate. The four-bedroom Victorian terrace house, with a price tag in excess of £400,000, was located at 10 Dulka Road.

- A windfall payment came the way of charity organisation Oxfam in 2010 after acquiring the first four editions of *Wisden Cricketers' Almanack*. A donor had left a box of old books containing the antiquarian cricketing volumes for the charity in the English town of Hertford. The lot fetched £8,500 at auction, with the first edition, published in 1864, realising £3,120.

  At an auction in England in 2012, a cricketing-themed car number plate – W15 DEN – went under the hammer for £1,500, almost four times its reserve.

- When Derbyshire hosted Lancashire at the Park Road Ground in 1975, no play was possible on the second day due to snow. Although the summer of 75 was one of Britain's hottest on record, a freak storm hit the County Championship match in Buxton – England's highest town – bringing rain, hail and snow.

  The match itself was a one-sided affair with Lancashire declaring at 477/5 after 100 overs and disposing of Derbyshire for 42 and 87. The margin of an innings and 348 runs represented one of the biggest defeats in the history of the County Championship.

Lancashire's Peter Lever, Clive Lloyd, Frank Hayes and David Lloyd with umpire Dickie Bird (second from right) on a snow-covered pitch at Buxton in 1975

> "I pulled back the curtains. The old Railway Hotel, I recall, and there was snow everywhere ... in June. I was rubbing my eyes in disbelief."
>
> Lancashire batsman Clive Lloyd

> "When I went out to inspect the wicket, the snow was level with the top of my boots. I'd never seen anything like it."
>
> umpire Dickie Bird

- For the first time in history, a one-day international was washed out due to rain in the United Arab Emirates in 2014/15. After 30 years and 271 ODIs, the Ireland-Scotland match in the Dubai Triangular Series was abandoned without a ball bowled.

- A world first took place in Europe in 2006 when a cricket match was played in two countries at the same time. The game, organised by the Fellowship of Fairly Odd Places Cricket Club, took place on a piece of land which had the international border between the Netherlands and Belgium running straight across the wicket (pictured).

- A former Australian cricketer ended up in hospital in 2015 when a kangaroo knocked her off her bike while cycling in surburban Canberra. Bronwyn Calver – who appeared in three Tests against England in 1988 – received eight stitches as a result of the collision: **"While the roo did hop away it was subsequently hit by a car and killed. They don't call Canberra the Bush Capital for nothing."**

- A South Australian fast bowler received a suspension from the game in 2013/14 after an incident at a suburban cricket ground in Melbourne. Daniel Worrall, who made his first-class debut in 2012/13, was punished after scratching an image of a penis and testicles into the pitch at the Toorak Park ground.

- While touring Pakistan in 1998/99, two Australian players were reprimanded after being photographed holding AK-47 assault rifles during a trip to the Khyber Pass. The decision by Justin Langer and Gavin Robertson to be photographed by Pakistan guards at a location near the border with Afghanistan was described by ACB official Denis Rogers as **"... naïve and ill-considered and offensive to the wider Australian community."**

- David Hay, who appeared in four first-class matches for Oxford University, later became a career diplomat, rising to the position of Australia's ambassador to the United Nations in 1964. Hay, who had a highest score of 96 against Lancashire in 1938, was the grandson of William Moule, a judge, who played for Australia in their first Test in England, at The Oval in 1880.

- Kenya team-mates Steve Tikolo and Thomas Odoyo both appeared in 134 one-day internationals, starting and ending their careers in the same match. They both debuted in Kenya's first ODI – against India in the 1996 World Cup at Cuttack – and left the game in the same match, a 2011 World Cup fixture against Zimbabwe at Kolkata.

- India's Ghulam Ahmed appeared in 22 Tests over a period of exactly ten years, with his first and last played against the same opposition, at the same ground and at the same time of the year. Both his debut and final Tests came against the West Indies at Kolkata and were played between 31 December and 4 January in 1948/49 and 1958/59. The only other player to achieve such an unusual double is South African spinner Paul Harris – against India at Cape Town – between the second and sixth of January in 2006/07 and 2010/11.

- One of Australia's top-selling board games was recognised by the country's philatelic agency in 2009. A family favourite since the 1950s, the 'Test Match' cricket game was featured on a 55 cent stamp for Australia Post's 'Classic Toys' series. Australia Post released another cricket stamp in the same year, part of a six-stamp series, 'Let's Get Active'.

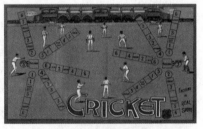

An Australian cricket board game, dated 1913

- Kevin Pietersen went global in 2015 when he revealed a massive tattoo of a map of the world with red stars indicating where he scored centuries in international cricket. The body art (pictured) was done by acclaimed Melbourne tattooist Mick Squires: **"If you can go and score as many centuries as he has and be able to put them on a world map then you've got something to say."**

- On the eve of the 2011/12 Border-Gavaskar Trophy an Australian university researcher declared than Sachin Tendulkar was statistically a better batsman than Don Bradman. Nicholas Rohde, from the University of Griffith, claimed that statistics proved Tendulkar is the greatest batsman of all time: **"It's an emotional issue and there will always be debate between followers of Test cricket about the relative career performances of various batsmen. But by using the principles of opportunity cost and supernormal profit, the ranking procedure is actually very simple.**

  "Essentially, each player is scored according to their career aggregate runs, minus the total number of runs that an average player of that era would accrue over the same number of innings. The rankings are designed to allow for meaningful comparisons of players with careers of different lengths."

  Dr Rohde's research, based on figures up to 2010, was published in the December 2011 issue of *Economic Papers*, which had Bradman at No. 1. He said, though, that based on performances since its publication, Tendulkar had dethroned Bradman to assume the top ranking. Jacques Kallis slotted in at No. 3, followed by Rahul Dravid, Brian Lara, Garry Sobers, Allan Border, Sunil Gavaskar, Steve Waugh and Javed Miandad.

Don Bradman and Sachin Tendulkar in 1988

- Afghanistan's Nasir Ahmadzai was dismissed in the most unusual of circumstances when he made his first-class debut in 2014. Batting in the second innings against Zimbabwe A in Harare, the non-striker Sharafuddin Ashraf let out a huge scream as the wicketkeeper attempted to take a catch off the bowling of Cuthbert Musoko. With the chance put down, the umpires decided to give Nasir out obstructing the field under law 37.

  Nasir became only the third player to be dismissed in such fashion on his first-class debut, after Dera Ismail Khan's Qaiser Khan – in his only match – against Railways at Lahore in 1964/65 and Sukkur's Arshad Ali against Quetta at the Racecourse Ground in 1983/84.

- After 338 matches and 125 years of Test cricket, South Africa introduced their first black batsman in 2014/15. Temba Bavuma made his Test debut against the West Indies at Port Elizabeth, scoring ten in his only innings. He opened his account with a boundary off the first ball he faced, but failed to score a run off his next 25.

- Shane Warne ended his Test career in 2007 with a record 12 consecutive victories. Next on the list is England's George Ulyett and the West Indies' Eldine Baptiste, who both finished their Test-playing days with ten wins in a row. For Baptiste, it represented his entire career.

- An animal rights group named and shamed former Australian fast bowler Glenn McGrath in 2015 by releasing photographs of him hunting wildlife in Africa. McGrath, who had previously indicated  a love of hunting, was pictured beside the dead carcasses of a number of animals, including a buffalo and hyenas: **"In 2008, I participated in a hunting safari in Zimbabwe that was licensed and legal, but in hindsight highly inappropriate. It was an extremely difficult time in my life and looking back I deeply regret being involved."**

Credits

Books
Wisden Cricketers' Almanack (John Wisden & Co, London – various years).

Websites
www.cricketarchive.co.uk, www.cricketcountry.com, www.espncricinfo.com, www.facebook.com/asksteven, www.guardian.co.uk/sport/cricket, www.howstat.com.au, www.sportstats.com.au, www.thecricketer.com, www.wikipedia.org.

Photographs
10 Downing Street, AUSPIC, Mike Ashton, Australian Broadcasting Corporation, Australian Government Department of Defence, Authors Cricket Club, Bedford School, Christopher Benson, Sarang Bhalerao, *Big Hitter*, Black Spyda Records, Brett Boardman, Channel Seven, Charles Leski Auctions, Hugh Cornwell, Cricket Foundation (chancetoshine.org), Crow Crow Productions, Keith Curtis, James Davies, Fellowship of Fairly Odd Places Cricket Club, Dan Forshaw, Fieldsports Channel, Peter Giafis, Nick Gill, Hampstead Cricket Club, David Harper, Jan Hopgood, International Cricket Council, Kent & Curwen, Burgan Kino, Robert Kottman, Keith Lawson, Lord's, Lord's Taverners, Dave Napper, National Archives of Australia, Peter Nicholson, Julian Pawle, Christina Pierce, Thomas Plant, Elliot Quince, Stephen Roberts, Royal Australian Mint, Imran Schah, George Serras (National Museum of Australia), John Shakespeare (Fairfax), Clare Skinner, Mark Taylor, *Test Match Special*, Phil Tufnell/Turner Fine Arts, Umbrella Entertainment Pty Ltd (www.umbrellaent.com.au), United for Wildlife.

Every effort has been made to identify owners of photographs. If any omissions have been made, acknowledgements will be made in any future editions.

Personal thanks
Terese Abbey, Julian Abbott, Keith Andrew, Charles Davis, Courtney Dawson, Michael Jones, Marcus Kelson, Tom Moody, Aslam Siddiqui.

Notes
All information and statistics in this book were correct at the time of printing.